Napoleon's Egypt

INVADING THE MIDDLE EAST

Napoleon's Egypt

INVADING THE MIDDLE EAST

Juan Cole

palgrave
macmillan

NAPOLEON'S EGYPT
Copyright © Juan Cole, 2007, 2008.
All rights reserved.

First published in hardcover in 2007 by PALGRAVE MACMILLAN™ 175 Fifth
Avenue, New York, N.Y. 10010 and Houndmills, Basingstoke, Hampshire, England
RG21 6XS. Companies and representatives throughout the world.

PALGRAVE MACMILLAN is the global academic imprint of the Palgrave
Macmillan division of St. Martin's Press, LLC and of Palgrave Macmillan Ltd.
Macmillan® is a registered trademark in the United States, United Kingdom and
other countries. Palgrave is a registered trademark in the European Union and
other countries.

ISBN-13: 978-0-230-60603-6
ISBN-10: 0-230-60603-2

Library of Congress Cataloging-in-Publication Data
Cole, Juan Ricardo.
   Napoleon's Egypt : invading the Middle East / by Juan Cole.
      p.   cm.
   Includes bibliographical references and index.
   ISBN 1-4039-6431-9 (alk. paper)
   ISBN 0-230-60603-2 (paperback)
   1. Egypt—History—French occupation, 1798–1801.   I. Title.
DT100.C65   2008
962'.03—dc22

                                                              2007024215

A catalogue record of the book is available from the British Library.

Design by Letra Libre

First PALGRAVE MACMILLAN paperback edition: June 2008
10 9 8 7 6 5 4 3 2 1
Printed in the United States of America.

Transferred to Digital Printing 2011

CONTENTS

Ten pages of illustrations appear between pages 122 and 123.

To Arman and Sheena

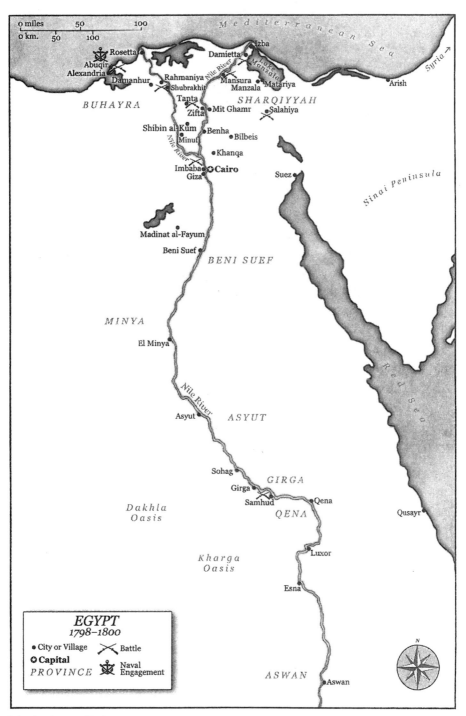

Map by Arman H. Cole

LIST OF ILLUSTRATIONS

ACKNOWLEDGMENTS

*N*apoleon's Egypt concerns the political, military, and cultural encounter of the French and Egyptians in the late eighteenth century, and is primarily based on a wide reading in eyewitness memoirs and letters, not least those of Napoleon Bonaparte himself. Although it has elements of a biography of Bonaparte in Egypt, its canvas is wider than that, and substantial attention is paid to his coterie of officers as well as his Ottoman and Egyptian enemies and collaborators. It is the first extended treatment in English by a Middle East specialist such that the French sources have been read through the lens of Egyptian realities. This book attends more closely than have others to French struggles in the Egyptian Delta region, to the Middle Eastern (Ottoman, Egyptian, and Muslim) cultural and institutional context of resistance to the occupation, and to the interplay of the ideas of the French revolutionary period with Ottoman and Egyptian ways of life. It aims at being an intimate history of what the French *Annales* school calls "*mentalités*," that is, a history of mindsets. Although many books have been written on Bonaparte in Egypt in French, the last extended account in English came out in 1962, and its author was not an Arabist. Even in the Francophone literature, few authors have treated at length these issues in cultural dialogue and debate—and some manage virtually to ignore the presence in Egypt of Egyptians! One of my central questions is how the French and the Egyptians constructed and remembered one another. This book is not, however, about a "clash of civilizations," but has as its premise that the Greater Mediterranean has been a single civilization for a very long time. Clashes are produced by struggles over power, not by cultures, which are themselves often shaped and altered by mutual interaction and conflict. I take the story to the eve of Bonaparte's departure for his Syria campaign because these first eight months raise all the key issues I want to address in military and cultural interplay in Egypt, and because Syria has a significantly different local context.

The title appears to contain two anachronisms: At the time of the invasion Bonaparte was not yet Napoleon I, and contemporaries would have spoken of the Orient rather than "the Middle East." The title is a recognition that the book concerns memories and constructions of Egypt, including those written by Napoleon long after he became emperor. As for the subtitle, the profound confusion produced for contemporary readers by a subtitle such as "invading the Orient" would have outweighed any gains in verisimilitude. I have used the phrase "Middle East" in the text, as well, inasmuch as I am writing twenty-first century English.

My late mentor, Marsden Jones, suggested this project to me many years ago. I was exceedingly fortunate that in 1993 Philippe de Meulenaere brought out his priceless critical bibliography of eyewitness accounts, and that in recent decades several rich French memoirs (e.g., those of François Bernoyer, Joseph-Marie Moiret, and Charles Antoine Morand) have been published. I was also fortunate in that some relevant Arabic materials have been published in recent decades, including the earliest chronicle by historian 'Abd al-Rahman al-Jabarti (perhaps co-authored with Hasan al-'Attar), the chronicles of Izzet Hasan Darendeli and 'Abdullah al-Sharqawi, and contemporary letters from Yemen. The translations into English of the works of al-Jabarti, by Shmuel Moreh and by a team of scholars under Thomas Philipp and Moshe Perlmann, have been very useful to this book. I have always consulted the Arabic text, however, and sometimes have preferred to paraphrase directly from it. I have also used al-Jabarti's untranslated *Muzhir al-Taqdis*, which contains material, and pregnant silences, not present in the other works.

I had the good fortune of studying modern Egyptian history at UCLA with Afaf Lutfi al-Sayyid Marsot. Everyone who works in this field is profoundly indebted to André Raymond, who has revolutionized our understanding of eighteenth-century Cairo. Henry Laurens has shed loads of illumination on the French in Egypt with his own books and articles and his editions of primary texts. My friends and colleagues Kenneth Cuno, Jane Hathaway, Gabriel Piterburg, Peter Gran, and Daniel Crecelius further taught me through their talks and writings about the Ottoman beylicate and its era in Egypt. Edward Said's work on Orientalism made possible many of the insights herein.

I am deeply indebted to Alessandra Bastagli, my editor at Palgrave Macmillan, for her gentle persistence in pulling this book out of me, for her canny suggestions about writing strategies, and for the way her sage blue pencil and suggestions for additions improved the book. My gratitude also to Alan Bradshaw, Jodie Hockensmith, and Erin Igoe at Palgrave Macmillan for their invaluable help. I also want to express warm thanks to David Pervin for recognizing the promise of this project. Even though they came late to this particular party,

Brettne Bloom and Steve Wasserman of Kneerim & Williams, now my literary agency, gave key encouragement and help, for which I am most grateful. The enthusiasm of my son, Arman, and the patience and warm encouragement of my wife, Shahin, sustained me in this project.

A trip to Paris to consult materials in the Bibliothèque Nationale was funded by the History Department and the College of Literature, Science, and the Arts, at the University of Michigan, as was a semester of research while I held the Hudson Professorship, for which I am grateful. I would like to thank kind colleagues who made it possible for me to try out some of my ideas in formal talks and conference papers, including the conference of the American Research Center in Egypt (spring 1996), the History Department at Oregon State University (Carson Lecture, fall 1996), the History Department and the von Grunebaum Center for Near and Middle East Studies at UCLA (1997, 2000), and the Middle East Studies Association conference (1999). I use in this book with the kind permission of Garnet Publishing material that appeared in a different form in my article, "Mad Sufis and Civic Courtesans," in Irene A. Bierman, ed., *Napoleon in Egypt* (London: Ithaca Press, 2003), which came out of the 1997 UCLA conference.

The circulation department and the interlibrary loan staff at the Hatcher Research Library of the University of Michigan in some key ways made this book possible, as did the generosity of the lending libraries. Late in the project, Google Books began to be available and was of help. Colleagues Joshua Cole and John Shy were kind enough to react to an early manuscript of this book. Lynn Hunt commented on some of the material here, presented in a different form at a conference. David Bien generously discussed the project with me and offered excellent advice. They are responsible for any improvements, not for any errors that may remain. My friends and colleagues in France (where I spent many years of my childhood and youth) and Egypt (where I lived for three years) have been generous with their time and gracious in their hospitality, and without those experiences this book would be much the poorer in insight.

Napoleon's Egypt

INVADING THE MIDDLE EAST

THE GENIUS OF LIBERTY

*T*he top-secret mission that brought 20,000 soldiers and thousands of sailors together in the southern French port of Toulon in May 1798 baffled even junior officers such as Captain Joseph-Marie Moiret. On the road down to the port, which lay at the foot of towering jade hills, the troops brought in from the north saw unfamiliar olive groves and occasional palm or orange trees. Toulon's cerise-tile roofs sloped gently down toward the harbor. Its narrow, winding, unkempt streets overflowed with soldiers in their revolutionary blue uniforms, knee-length black leggings, and white breeches, some sporting red pom-poms and cuffs or chartreuse epaulettes. The soldiers and sailors had suddenly doubled the city's normal population. Beneath a brindled sky, the spires of the Church of Saint Louis looked down on a coppice of white masts in the harbor. A vast naval force stretched for miles, composed of thirteen ships of the line, seventeen frigates, 30 brigs, and nearly 250 corvettes, gunboats, galleys, and merchant ships. They jostled on the choppy Mediterranean that spring, awaiting the complete assemblage of troops on shore.

Captain Moiret, a fastidious man from a small town north of Toulon, was descended through his maternal grandmother from a line of local nobles, making him faintly disreputable in revolutionary France. He had studied Latin and humanities with the curate of a neighboring parish, and attended the Dominican seminary in Lyons for a while, before dropping out and joining the army. Like many in his generation, he later gravitated from the Church to a rationalist view of the world rooted in the philosophy of the Enlightenment, promoted by thinkers such as François-Marie Arouet de Voltaire, Jean-Jacques Rousseau, and Thomas Paine—though Moiret did not give up his faith. For his forebears, the scientific ideas of the late eighteenth century, the dethroning of the Catholic Church in France, and the advent of popular sovereignty (in the place of monarchy) would have been unimaginable, but he and his contemporaries lived through and adapted to these developments.

Recruited into the Aquitaine Regiment, Moiret had risen to sergeant major. He had served as a subaltern at Savoy (the Alpine border region between what is now France and Italy) when the French Republic annexed it from the king of Sardinia in 1792. Such "officers of fortune" who rose through the ranks seldom went beyond captain, but in any case Moiret was said to be reluctant to leave the old friends in his corps for a chance at promotion. He led not an impersonal fighting machine but a portable village of dense social networks. The 75th Infantry Demi-Brigade in which he served had recently earned the nickname "Invincible" for having fought so well in Italy against the Austrians at Lodi and elsewhere. These units were created early in the Revolution to accommodate the influx of untrained volunteers, mixing one battalion of experienced soldiers with one of newcomers.[1] A demi-brigade formally comprised 3,000 men, though many at Toulon were only at half strength, in part because of desertions by troops who had not been paid in a long time or who were unwilling to set out on a mysterious adventure across the sea.

Gen. Napoleon Bonaparte, a Corsican who had come to France for his education at the Royal Military Academy and excelled in mathematics and the deployment of artillery, had been given command of the Army of England after his brilliant successes against the Austrians in northern Italy. He and the French executive closely guarded the secret destination of this expedition, even from the minister of war, Barthélemy Schérer![2] Moiret and his fellow junior officers, equally uninformed, speculated about the purpose of the expedition. Was it to resemble more the invasions of the Normans or those of Saint Louis during the Fifth Crusade? The Normans had invaded England from the French coast in 1066, whereas Saint Louis had set out to subdue the Near East. Everyone knew that preparations were being made for an eventual republican assault on royalist Britain, and the army being assembled had been drawn in part from the French Army of England. Although launching an attack on Britain from the Mediterranean did not make sense logistically, it could not be ruled out as a strategy for surprise, especially if coupled with preliminary operations in Spain.

The Revolution of 1789, which asserted the rule of the people, had set most of the crowned heads of Europe against the French, and some publics as well. In the wars that followed the 1793 beheading of the French monarchs Louis XVI and Marie Antoinette, revolutionary France had defeated most of its opponents. In response, the British had launched into action most aggressively at sea, and had attempted, with indifferent success, to blockade some French-held ports on the Continent. Captain Jean-Honoré Horace Say, an engineer from a prominent Huguenot family and the brother of the eminent economist Jean-Baptiste Say, also reported for duty during those days in Toulon. In an anonymous memoir historians have traced to him, he recalled, "The . . . French Republic wanted at last to revenge itself on London for the defeats and adversities that afflicted our nascent liberty and through which the British Cabinet has sought, for many years, to strangle the inexorable expansion of a new republic, which sooner or later must defeat them."[3] Some officers hoped the fleet would head west, pass the straits of Gibraltar, and make immediately for England. Many thought that dislodging King George III's navy from the Mediterranean, as Bonaparte's artillery had displaced the British from their brief occupation of Toulon itself in 1793, might be a preliminary to such an invasion. For this strategic purpose, the islands of Sardinia, Malta, and even Sicily would make sense as targets, as building blocks toward a French Mediterranean Empire.

Some speculated that the force would strike at British links with India by attacking Egypt. British goods and soldiers bound for Calcutta most commonly, at that time, sailed around Africa and the Cape of Good Hope. But when British officials wished to send emergency dispatches, they could cut thousands of miles off the journey by sending envoys via the Mediterranean to Alexandria, up the Nile to Cairo, and thence overland to the Red Sea. There they could board vessels that glided past coffee-rich Yemen into the Arabian Sea and across the glassy Indian Ocean. This shorter route would not become commercially viable until steamships began plying these waters decades later, but it had strategic importance for Britain's communications with the Jewel in the Crown of its empire. Few officers thought an Egyptian campaign likely, but Moiret found that the civilian intellectuals, scientists, and artists who had, somewhat mysteriously, been recruited to accompany the expedition put it forward with some certitude. The Commission of Science and Arts consisted of 151 persons, 84 of them having technical qualifications and another 10 being physicians, and they formed the largest such body of experts to have accompanied a French military expedition.[4]

The twenty-eight-year-old Bonaparte himself had secretly departed Paris early on the morning of 5 May, with his attractive wife, Josephine. Bonaparte, having determined to embark on a dangerous adventure, faced a painful personal dilemma. He was seriously thinking about taking Josephine with him on the expedition. The previous winter, he had confronted her with gossip that she was having an affair. She had denied it all. He believed her because he wanted to, but the rumors were true. It may be that he did not trust her to stay behind without him. He had no idea then that she had cut back to just one affair at a time. Having her accompany him to the port at least allowed him to put off the difficult decision whether to take her with him.

The young general—notorious for his opportunism and mercurial temperament—was experiencing a rare moment of genuine love and affection for his wife of two years. Josephine had grown up on the island of Martinique in the Caribbean, a daughter of down-on-their-luck minor nobles named Tascher de la Pagerie (her father had been reduced to performing manual labor on the estates of others). Originally known as Rose, she had come to France, married a wealthy officer, Alexandre de Beauharnais, and established a literary salon. But after the Revolution, she had seen her husband, an aristocrat and an officer who lost a major battle with the Prussians, executed as a counterrevolutionary. Then the Jacobins clapped her in prison, as well, and scheduled her date with the guillotine. A well-connected lover rescued her. She later had a number of affairs, one with a budding politician named Paul Barras, who went on to become a member of the French executive. Finding her a spendthrift, he introduced her to the romantically naïve young Bonaparte, who renamed her Josephine and pursued and married her. In one of his early letters to "Madame Beauharnais," full of Corsican misspellings, he wrote, "I wake up full of you. Your portrait, and the intoxicating memory of last night, left my senses altogether bereft of repose."[5] In 1796 Barras arranged for him to become supreme commander of the French army invading Austrian-ruled northern Italy, a campaign that separated him from his new bride for most of the following two years. He wrote frequently and passionately. She seldom replied. During the campaign, he remonstrated with her from Bologna, "You are sad, you are sick, you never write to me. . . . Don't you love your good friend any more? . . . Perhaps I will make peace with the Pope and will be with you soon." Rumors reached him of her affairs, but despite flying into a rage at first, he generally dismissed them.

Neither of them appears to have been eager for another long separation. In Toulon, Josephine expressed her confidence that, given her upbringing in Martinique, the rigors of his exotic destination held nothing new for her. They waited together in the port for a storm to blow over, touring his magnificent flagship, the *Orient*, and welcoming the generals and scientists who were to participate in the expedition. In private, they discussed earnestly the question of whether Josephine should accompany her husband abroad, and in between their deliberations they made passionate love. Gen. Alexandre Dumas at one point blundered in on one of their arguments, finding Josephine in bed in a state of undress and weeping at her husband's indecision. In the end, Bonaparte decided to postpone the decision, sending her to take the waters at a health spa, Plombières, in the mountains southeast of Paris. He said he might bring her to him once he had secured his new conquest, given the dangers of the expedition. But leaving the oversexed Josephine alone in France was attended with dangers of its own.

On 9 May 1798, the newly arrived Bonaparte passed in review of the Republican soldiers, and gave a speech that attempted to stir their sense of adventure and that also held out to them a promise of land on their return. In the latter pledge, published in the official *Moniteur* (The Monitor), he overstepped his authority, since as a general he was in no position to legislate on civilian land rights, and, facing the fury of his superiors, he had to brand the transcript inaccurate. In its stead, the military issued a further communiqué, represented in a subsequent number of the *Moniteur* as the actual text of the speech delivered.[6] Bonaparte ordered that this second communiqué be disseminated widely, and even made it up as a poster. Therein the general compared the French Army of England to the troops of the Roman Republic who had fought against despotic Carthage in North Africa. He thundered, "The genius of liberty, which has since its birth rendered the Republic the arbiter of Europe, is now headed toward the most distant lands."

Bonaparte's compliments bolstered the army's aplomb. Moiret asserted that the army maintained its cool, its sangfroid, confident of securing its goal, whatever that might be. Others shared Moiret's assessment of Bonaparte's charisma. A young officer at Toulon, Michel de Niello Sargy, later wrote, "I was far from having any idea of the nature of the armament that was prepared, and even less of its destination, when I threw myself—like so many other young persons—into that audacious expedition. I was seduced by the renown of the commander in chief and by the glory of our arms. It was a delirium, a nearly universal compulsion." Bonaparte's fervor and charisma, despite the Italian accent and grammatical errors, produced the most extraordinary effect. His incredible Italian campaign of 1796–1797 had induced hero worship among many of the officers and troops. Later, after he had become Napoleon I, he remarked, "The military are a freemasonry and I am its Grand Master."[7]

The enthusiasms of the French troops and officers were very much shaped by the Revolution and by the ideology of the early Republic. The French of this era employed keywords such as nation, fatherland (*patrie*), constitution, law, regeneration, and virtue to mark membership in the revolutionary community. A prominent historian of the period argued that "revolutionaries placed such emphasis on the ritual use of words because they were seeking a replacement for the charisma of kingship."[8] Republican rhetoric deployed "liberty" as its refrain. In response to Bonaparte's 9 May speech, which evoked many of the same central terms, the soldiers had shouted, "The Immortal Republic forever!" That night,

the authorities had the house of the Commune (the revolutionary municipal government of Toulon) illuminated and the troops planted at its door a tree of liberty with the inscription, "It grows each day."[9] Supporters of the Revolution
throughout France planted liberty trees each May, often decorated in the colors
of the French flag. The authorities designed the ritual planting at Toulon as a
means of reinforcing solidarity among the troops. Bonaparte in his communiqué
clearly conveyed the idea that the Republican army incarnated the virtue of liberty, and was now exporting it to an exotic locale, engaging in what was in effect
a vast tree-planting ceremony.

The weather was still not cooperating. Bonaparte wrote back to his political
superiors in Paris, "We have been here at anchor three days, Citizen Directors,
ready to depart. But the winds are extremely strong and contrary."[10] He issued
orders on how to punish the substantial number of soldiers and sailors who
jumped ship at the last moment, who declined to go off into the unknown and
so would be missing their chance to "reestablish the glory of the French navy."
Some may have left just for lack of nourishment. The merchant Grandjean later
grumbled that hunger gnawed at him during his two days of filling out paper-
work in Toulon, which thus seemed to him like two centuries, since the crush of
newcomers had made even a crust of bread hard to find, and then at astronomical prices. At last, on the eighteenth of May, the mistral died down.

A memoirist, who was a young sailor at the time, recalled,

> One of the last days of [that month], the commander in chief, Bonaparte, ac-
> companied by his numerous and brilliant general staff, boarded the *Orient* and
> afterwards visited all the ships of the line. During that day, the entire fleet cele-
> brated, and each ship fired a twenty-one gun salute, while the batteries
> throughout the city, the port and the harbors rang out, responding with all
> their artillery. What a magnificent spectacle! On arriving at our ship, the
> *Dubois*, I saw General Bonaparte for the first time, and I was struck by his se-
> vere and imposing features. Although short in stature, he was enveloped by a
> halo of glory that made him seem very great to me.

The troops boarded their vessels with a show of great élan, reminding more
than one observer of grooms going off enthusiastically to their weddings. The
cannoneer Louis Bricard, who left instead from Marseilles, spoke of a "supernatural joy" among them, though he said that their girlfriends in the port did
not share it, complaining tearfully about the flower of French young manhood
being sent far away from France "without knowing their destination," and worrying that "they might never return."[11]

The quartermaster François Bernoyer, a fierce republican and devotee of rationalist Enlightenment philosophy, also remarked on the festive mood of the troops. Born in Avignon in 1760, the civilian Bernoyer headed up the uniforms department. He wrote that, to the accompaniment of artillery salutes, the squadron set sail on 19 May, at first following a circuitous route and sometimes finding itself becalmed. Would it follow the coast? Speculation was rife. Then the order came to set out to sea, and some felt confirmed in their belief that Sicily was the object. First, there was a rendezvous with additional ships at Corsica. On 31 May the fleet was rallied, or reoriented, according to technology-loving Bernoyer: "This maneuver is a thing of beauty, since one moves about the great masses of these vessels, just as one maneuvers troops on the ground."[12] The squadron then passed Sicily with such speed that rumors about a landing there were quashed. The betting now focused on Malta, a tiny island not far from Tunis, which had been for centuries in the hands of the Knights of St. John of Jerusalem.

All obsessed anxiously about the possibility of encountering the British navy. Initially, French intelligence had indicated that no British fleets were patrolling the Mediterranean. Then sightings of Nelson's squadron were reported, though with no consistency or clarity. One day, French sailors spotted sails above the horizon, and alarm spread about a deadly encounter with the British; but the masts turned out to belong to a French convoy from Civitavecchia in Italy that General Bonaparte had ordered to join the convoy. Admiral Horatio Nelson was in fact at that very moment searching desperately for Bonaparte's convoy. In the early 1790s, after war broke out between Great Britain and France, British authorities had dispatched Nelson to Naples so that he could help bring reinforcements from there to Toulon. Local French aristocrats opposed to the Revolution had delivered Toulon, in August 1793, to a joint British and Spanish naval force. The revolutionary army marched south to push out the invaders. Bonaparte himself, the most energetic of the French officers commanding the artillery assault, pioneered new ways of exploiting increases in the power and range of the French guns, and had defeated the British fleet, ending their effort to hold French soil for counterrevolutionary purposes.[13] Nelson saw subsequent history as a world-straddling grudge match.

While Bonaparte was staging his army at Toulon for an even more powerful challenge to the British navy, Nelson, alerted by the British consul at Leghorn, had brought a squadron into the Mediterranean to hunt down his old nemesis. Late spring squalls in the Mediterranean had damaged some of his vessels' masts and forced him to put to shore for repairs just as Napoleon sailed from Toulon. His ships then headed back out to sea, and at one point, the two fleets passed one another in the foggy dark, unbeknownst to those aboard. Later, Nelson, afraid the French had eluded him, so pushed his ships that they far outran the French vessels.

Only thick fog could have made the huge French fleet invisible. Along with the men carried on French vessels that rendezvoused with the main squadron from Corsican ports, the number of troops under arms had swollen to about 36,000. They included 276 officers, 28,000 infantrymen, 2,800 cavalrymen, 2,000 artillery-men, 1,157 military engineers, and 900 physicians, pharmacists, nurses, scientists, artists, and writers.[14] If one counted, as well, all the bureaucrats, sailors, merchants, and hangers-on, some 54,000 men were now racing for parts unknown across the indigo Mediterranean—in all, the equal of a fair-sized city at the time.

The rough waters sent many troops abovedeck to feed their lunches to the fish. Even General Bonaparte himself had his bed mounted on casters in hopes of alleviating the symptoms of seasickness while he tried to sleep. Bernoyer once went over to visit the massive flagship *Orient*, which, he wrote, carried 120 cannon, 1,300 sailors, and hundreds of soldiers, and there he saw Bonaparte's quarters and his comportment. He said the general's rooms were furnished lavishly and in good taste, and that his opulent receiving room "was more made to accommodate a sovereign, born in flabbiness and ignorance, than a republican general, born for the glory of his country." The officers gambled on a gold table, "as though we were setting out to conquer Peru." Bernoyer disapproved of the ostentation, which reminded him more of royally chartered Conquistadors sent to the New World in search of precious metals than a Republican army fighting for liberty, equality, and fraternity. He added that there "reigns here a most severe discipline among the troops, and with the general they observe the strictest etiquette. They seek to copy the former usages of the court, which usages seem just as ridiculous to us as those of a great feudal lord would be in the middle of a camp of Spartans." The testy Bernoyer spoke for many in the Republican ranks who remained suspicious of Bonaparte's tendency to put on airs and create new hierarchies to replace those overthrown in 1789.

✤

On 9 June 1798, the squadron arrived at Malta. Bonaparte demanded from the Grand Master of the Order of St. John of the Hospitallers, who ruled the main island along with the smaller islands of Gozo and Cumino, that his ships be allowed to enter the port and to take on water and supplies. The Grand Master, Baron Ferdinand von Hompesch, replied that only two foreign ships could be allowed to enter the port at a time. Bonaparte, aware that such a procedure would take a very long time and would leave his forces vulnerable to Nelson, immediately ordered a cannon fusillade by way of rebuttal.

Bonaparte did not expect hospitality. He had opposed the German Hompesch's installation as Grand Master two years before, wanting that position in the hands of a national friendly to France. Captain Say wrote in his memoir that the islands had a population of about 150,000. Most of the men were sailors, and the women spun and wove cotton. The Maltese population spoke a dialect of Arabic, and was devoted to Roman Catholicism. The Knights could theoretically have fielded 16,000 soldiers, but at that time their actual troop strength was much reduced. Nevertheless, taking Malta could have been fraught with difficulties. "The whole of the inhabited part of the island was an effective fortification for all the purposes of annoyance and offensive warfare," the visiting British essayist Samuel Taylor Coleridge wrote a few years later. It was, he said, "subdivided . . . into small fields, scarcely larger than a cottage garden, and each of these little squares of land [was] inclosed with substantial stone walls."[15] He also reported that eighteenth-century naval officers had a saying that Egypt was the key to India, and Malta the key to Egypt.

The French had many grounds for grievance against the Knights, who had authorized the British to recruit sailors there. When Spain had joined the first Grand Coalition against revolutionary France, the Grand Master furnished arms to Madrid and allowed it also to hire Maltese sailors. Partisans of the Revolution on the island had been persecuted, and many of them arbitrarily exiled. In May 1797, a large number of the democratically minded on the island had been arrested and imprisoned as common criminals. At length, the Grand Master had sought the protection of reactionary Russian Tsar Paul I, a determined enemy of the Republican revolution.[16]

Bonaparte's troops disembarked in Malta at seven points on the morning of 11 June. Gen. Louis Baraguey d'Hilliers, who had barely survived the radicals' attempts to purge him during the Terror and later served as governor of Lombardy during the Italian campaign of 1796–1797, landed soldiers and fieldpieces in the western part of the main island of Malta. Throughout, he and his men took artillery fire from the Maltese battlements. French soldiers met some initial resistance but managed to push it back. The ill-prepared and somewhat dissolute Knights in that region, numbering only about 2,000, regrouped. The French pressed their attack. After a fierce gun battle lasting twenty-four hours, most of the Maltese in the west were forced to surrender. Gen. Claude-Henri Vaubois took possession of the old city situated in the center of the island, as well, which opened its gates without firing a shot. The Knights, originally founded in Jerusalem and a fixture of the short-lived Crusader kingdoms in the Levant before the Muslims forced them to the western islands, were a holdover from a feudal, chivalric, and religious past. Now they were on the verge of being finished as a military force, victims of the Enlightenment.

Bonaparte opened negotiations with the fortress capital of Valletta, offering to buy off the Knights. Faced with vastly superior French forces, the Grand Master negotiated for himself a comfortable retirement and then opened his doors to Bonaparte, who thus took one of the more impregnable fortresses in Europe without firing a shot at it. Bonaparte later remarked, "The place certainly possessed immense physical means of resistance, but no moral strength whatever. The Knights did nothing shameful; nobody is obliged to perform impossibilities."[17] Captain Moiret said that he and others in the advance guard entered Valetta on 12 June, and the next day the troops from the fleet followed them. He, too, felt that Valetta, the chief town and port of northeastern Malta, should have been able to hold out far longer. "We were a little surprised," Moiret admitted, "to find ourselves in possession of so fortified a city." Unlike his general, he branded the defenders poor soldiers, badly led.

What he did not say was that about half the Knights were French, and most of them had refused to fight. In addition, when the revolutionary government came to power after 1789, it gradually took property and wealth away from the old aristocracy and the Church. Since the Knights had received support from these sources, the French Revolution had fatally weakened their financial position. Bonaparte put Hompesch on a pension in Germany and offered many of the older French Knights the opportunity to return to France with a stipend. The Knights were not so much defeated as bargained down to surrender. The junior cavalry officer Nicolas Philibert Desvernois, from Lons-le-Saunier near Geneva, estimated the total cost to France at 3 million francs.

During the week before the French departed, Bonaparte set up a local administration and Republican constitution, declared Malta a French dependency, and arranged for students to go to France. He also took with him the younger Knights, incorporating them into his army. He closed all the churches and had their gold and silver treasures melted down for bullion and appropriated the treasury of the Knights. Captain Say, who wrote the earliest published memoir of the expedition, observed, "The possession of that island assures control of the commerce of the Levant." (The "Levant," or the "rising," refers to the southern shores of the eastern Mediterranean, the place where, from a European point of view, the sun rises.)

Bonaparte had the irons of the Turkish and Arab slaves kept by the Knights broken, and boarded them on his vessels with a view toward releasing them in

Egypt, where his magnanimity proved a public relations boon. He wrote immediately to the French consuls at Tunis, Tripoli, and Algiers to inform them that Malta was now French and that the Muslim rulers of those provinces should release their Maltese slaves or face the wrath of the French Republic. That is, it was one thing to hold Maltese in a state of captivity when they were from a small independent state, and another to hold French subjects as slaves; it was a slap in the face of the Republic. He also offered an olive branch: "I have given the order that the more than 2,000 North African and Ottoman slaves held by the Order of St. John of Jerusalem in their galleys be given their liberty."[18] Bonaparte had already begun his political wooing of Muslims. At Malta, he gained among the ex-slaves and local Maltese many Arabic speakers who would prove very useful to him as soldiers and interpreters.

Most of the French soldiers stayed at Malta only a few days, replenishing their supplies. Bonaparte left a garrison of about four thousand men there under General Vaubois and departed on 19 June. Speculation again broke out about the fleet's destination. It did not last long. Bonaparte now ordered that his second proclamation, actually written aboard the *Orient* on 12 June, be distributed to the troops. The men began thinking of Alexandria; they imagined the city of the Ptolemies and of the Roman Empire. Eighteenth-century French officers and intellectuals were immersed in Greek and Roman history, which they knew intimately, and they identified with it. Their military adventure in the east under Bonaparte evoked for them the conquests of Alexander and Augustus. Captain Moiret said that the soldiers indulged in reveries about Egyptian women, hoping they would be Cleopatras. In their memoirs of the beginnings of the expedition, French men eroticized an Orient that they imagined as resplendent.

"Soldiers," Bonaparte said, "you are about to undertake a conquest, the effects of which on the civilization and commerce of the world are immeasurable. You shall inflict on England the surest and most palpable blow, while awaiting the opportunity to administer the coup de grace." He complained of the beys or warlords who ruled Egypt, many of them former slave soldiers who rose high and won freedom and power, and who nominally served as vassals of the Ottoman sultan. He said that they had begun showing exclusive favoritism to English commerce and heaping disgrace on French merchants. Moreover, they tyrannized the unfortunate inhabitants of the Nile. He promised the troops exhausting marches, but vowed of the slave soldiers (called in Arabic *mamluk*), "A few days after we arrive, they will no longer exist." He cautioned his audience of freethinkers, deists, atheists, and Roman Catholics

to respect Islam, Muhammad, and Muslim customs, just as they had shown
tolerance to Jews and Italian Catholics in Europe, and he recalled for them
the religious toleration characteristic of Roman troops. He warned them that
Muslims treated their women differently, and he forbade pillaging. "Alexandria," he concluded, "will be the first city we shall encounter."[19]

✤

The genesis of Bonaparte's plan to invade Egypt is complex. A few French intellectuals and merchants had entertained the idea of such a project over the
previous century, given the indisputable centrality of Egypt to French commerce in the Mediterranean and points east. Bonaparte himself appears to have
begun seriously considering it in the summer of 1797 as a result of his Italian
campaign. The principalities of Italy bordering the Adriatic Sea had long had
interests in Adriatic islands and in Croatia and Ottoman Albania. Venice and
the Adriatic city of Ragusa provided the leading foreign element among merchant communities in the Egyptian port of Alexandria. And revolutionary
France, now established as an Italian power, had more interests in the Levant
than ever before—something of which Bonaparte, as the virtual viceroy of the
Italian territories, would be well aware.

A prominent politician, revolutionary, and former priest, Charles Maurice
de Talleyrand, had argued just the previous summer in a speech to the National
Institute that Republican France needed colonies in order to prosper.[20]
(Canada, Louisiana, and many of its Caribbean and Indian possessions had been
lost to it decades before.) He rooted this demand in the revolutionary ethos of
the new Republic, saying, "The necessary effect of a free Constitution is to tend
without cessation to set everything in order, within itself and without, in the interest of the human species." He related that he had been struck, during his
brief exile to the United States during the Terror, at how their postrevolution-
ary situation differed from that of France in lacking intense internal hatreds and
conflicts, and he attributed this relative social peace to the way in which settling
a vast continent drew the energies of restless former revolutionaries. Talleyrand
recalled earlier plans for a French colony in Egypt and pointed to British sugar
cultivation in Bengal, implying that such imperial commodity production
strengthened this rival and that France should also seek profits through colonial
possessions that would produce lucrative cash crops. He also suggested that the
days of slavery were numbered, and implied that colonies that generated wealth
through slave plantations should be replaced by satellite French-style republics
dominated by Paris.

Throughout the 1790s, British naval superiority had confined the expansionist French to the Continent and thwarted any attempt to overthrow the British enemy. Talleyrand argued that a renewed colonialism offered "the advantage of not in any way allowing ourselves to be forestalled by a rival nation, for which every one of our lapses, every one of our delays along these lines is a triumph." The French had lost their toehold in South India at Pondicherry to the British, but were attempting to ally with local anti-British Indian rulers in hopes of expelling the British East India Company from the subcontinent. Taking Egypt would give France control over other valuable commodities, especially sugar, and might provide a means of blocking the growth of a British empire in the East.

Talleyrand became foreign minister of France soon after broaching these thoughts. His speech marked a repudiation of the arguments of the Enlightenment philosophers—who had decried the inequalities of colonialism—and of the economic theories of Turgot, who had argued that there was no economic benefit to holding colonies, since it was apparent to him that the commodities they produced were just as inexpensive in countries without colonies.[21]

The physiocrats, economists who located value in land, had dismissed foreign trade as relatively unimportant, and they had found allies in the French landed classes before the revolution. With the rise of a revolutionary order, new interests were asserting themselves. Talleyrand also rejected the principled Jacobin argument for an end to colonialism, rooted in the Rights of Man, which they had marshaled in support for the abolition of slavery in 1794. He believed that Paris could impose the model of the middle-class Republic on tropical lands in such a way as to allow the construction of a new, postslavery colonialism. The constituencies for Talleyrand's plans included military contractors, the powerful merchant class of Marseilles, and the French network of Levantine importers and exporters in the Mediterranean. The officers of the Army of Italy, blocked for the moment from taking Vienna, newly aware from their perch in the Italian peninsula of the importance of the eastern Mediterranean, and seeking other fields of glory, comprised another. Talleyrand's speech announced a startling turn in the French left toward the revival of support for foreign expansion of a sort once championed by the most conservative courtiers of the seventeenth-century French monarchy, and so might be thought of as an eighteenth-century neoconservatism.

Victorious in Italy, Bonaparte began corresponding with Talleyrand and other leaders about the possibilities of a French Mediterranean policy as a means of hurting the British. On 16 August 1797, he wrote, "The time is not far away that we will feel that, in order truly to destroy England, we must take Egypt. The vast Ottoman Empire, which dies every day, lays an obligation on us to exercise some forethought about the means whereby we can protect our commerce with the Levant."[22] The Old Regime and the early Republic had supported the Ottoman Empire as a way of denying the eastern Mediterranean to its powerful continental rivals. Bonaparte and Talleyrand, in contrast, became convinced that the Ottoman decline was accelerating, producing a dangerous impetus for Britain and Russia to attempt to usurp former Ottoman territories. If the European powers might soon begin capturing provinces of Sultan Selim III, then Bonaparte and Talleyrand wanted the Republic of France to be first in line. Excluded by the British navy from the North Atlantic and lacking possessions near the Cape of Good Hope, they dreamed of making the Mediterranean a French lake and of opening a route to India via the Red Sea, and recovering Pondicherry and other French possessions on the Coromandel and Malabar coasts.

When Gen. Louis Desaix visited Bonaparte's headquarters near Venice in September of 1797, the two discussed the possibility of taking Egypt with five divisions. The head of the French Commission on the Sciences and Arts in Italy, Gaspar Monge, had a dossier put together for Bonaparte from the French foreign ministry archives, of reports on the chaotic governance of Egypt by putative vassals of the Ottomans and the way local French consular officials in Egypt such as Charles Magallon argued that it hurt French commerce.[23] Talleyrand convinced himself that the sultan in Istanbul was aware of British and Russian designs on Egypt, and that he would therefore welcome a preemptive strike by a strong ally to keep the province from falling into enemy hands. He was the first, but by no means the last, Western politician to overestimate the gratitude that would be generated among a Middle Eastern people by a foreign military occupation.

The French Republic from 1795 until 1799 had a two-chamber legislature: the Council of Five Hundred to propose laws and the Council of Ancients, or senators, to pass them. The latter elected a five-man joint executive called the Directory. The Directory swung back and forth politically. When it was established, in November 1795, its members repudiated the excesses of Robespierre and the radicals who had launched a Great Terror in 1793–1794, in which the extremists persecuted anyone they suspected of royalist or church sympathies and sent many to the guillotine. The new government adopted property requirements for participation in politics, strengthened constitutional protections for individual rights, and "imposed an impartial application of the law as one of the key notions of personal security."[24] All this they did, one historian has argued, because they needed to find a way out of the Terror, and then out of the

Revolution itself. The early Directory slightly loosened restrictions on Catholic worship and made attempts to have more civil politics.

The elections held in spring of 1797 brought more conservatives and a few royalists into the legislature, raising alarms on the French left that a resurgent right might undo all the achievements of the Revolution. In reaction, in early September 1797, left-of-center politicians made a sort of coup d'état, dismissing two directors and using their dominance of the Directory and of many provincial administrations to reassert republican values and dislike for aristocracy and clericalism. The coup plotters had initially wanted Bonaparte to come back to Paris from Italy to control Paris for them. He, however, wished to maintain his commanding position abroad and instead sent the antiroyalist Gen. Pierre Augereau to lend military support to the soft putsch.

Then in spring 1798 the electorate predictably swung to the left, and the Directory refused to seat dozens of elected delegates, fearing too much influence from the Jacobins. These events suggested an underlying instability in the Directory regime. It had failed to make the necessary bargains of trust between left and right that would have overcome the legacy of the Terror on both sides of the aisle, and it had undermined its legitimacy by constantly tinkering with electoral results.

Bonaparte apprehended the crucial role of the revolutionary army in shaping the outcome of political contests. Despite his public protestations of loyalty to republican ideas, he was already a critic of liberal democracy. To a visiting diplomat he remarked, "Do you think that I triumphed in Italy in order to aggrandize the lawyers on the Directory—the Carnots and the Barrases? Do you think, as well, that it was so as to found a Republic? What an idea!" He complained of the impossibility of a republic made up of thirty million persons, all with different values. (Many theorists of democracy in the eighteenth century felt the same way, and even the American James Madison had had to be convinced that sufficient checks and balances could prevent a slide into demagoguery or a tyranny of the majority in a large democratic polity.) Such a huge republic, he said, "is a chimera." He added of the French public, "They need glory and the satisfactions of vanity. But liberty? They do not understand it in the least." [25]

The continued internal cleavages in French society, the renewed militancy of the Jacobin-minded, the dangerous popularity of Bonaparte (who ruled Italy virtually as his fief), and the prospect of tens of thousands of demobilized troops returning to France after the victories in Lombardy suggested to some legislators and members of the Directory that France should undertake another major overseas campaign. Between December 1797 and February 1798, some politicians in the French government seriously considered a cross-Channel attack on

Britain. The Directory relieved Bonaparte of his Italian command and ordered him to study the feasibility of his leading the Army of England to Dover.

Bonaparte, furious at what he considered a demotion and wary of the notorious fickleness of French public opinion, wondered whether Europe was big enough for him and the petty-minded Directors. He pressed them to have the legislature install him as a director, too, but even his old friend and patron Paul Barras told him such a step would be unconstitutional, given his youth and the prescribed selection mechanisms. He intrigued for another war against Austria. Barras admitted in his memoirs that the members of the Directory began to perceive "all the dangers that the Republic ran" if Bonaparte were not sent on a mission abroad.[26]

Others in the legislature and the Directory all along favored a new French colonialism rather than a costly frontal assault on Britain. In response to the British naval blockade and to internal tensions, this war party sought to revive the commanding international position France had enjoyed before 1750. The Council of Five Hundred set up a commission to study the possibility of establishing French colonies in West Africa, given its proximity. Some members of the French parliament thought that the enterprise "seems worthy of the curiosity of a free, industrious nation whose genius is directed toward discoveries." That is, they explicitly linked colonialism to scientific exploration and knowledge. Thus did they play on a key value of Enlightenment philosophy even as they took a position that most of its philosophers disavowed. One source of this new belligerence may have been war contracting firms, who were at that time increasingly linked to French parliamentarians.[27]

In April 1798, the commission, led by legislator Joseph Eschasseriaux the Elder, reported that their deliberations had taken a surprising turn, away from Cape Verde and Sierra Leone toward the Nile Valley. The report linked modern progress in the homeland to colonies abroad and worried that the energies recently unleashed within France itself might cause instability unless a way was found to channel them elsewhere productively. Civilian politicians in the Directory era worried about popular generals becoming involved in politics, with the backing of both the people and newly mobilized citizen armies. Eschasseriaux argued that Egypt was at that time only half-civilized, was separated from France only by a little bit of water, and would be easy to conquer. He concluded, "What finer enterprise for a nation which has already given liberty to Europe [and] freed America than to regenerate in every sense a country which was the first home to civilization . . . and to carry back to their ancient cradle industry, science, and the arts, to cast into the centuries the foundations of a new Thebes or of another Memphis."

That April, the legislature commended this report to the Directory, urging it to fix upon a suitable colonial project. Another member of the Council of Ancients, J. B. Lecouteulx, pointed to the way that Venice had in the past conducted its trade with India through Egypt, using the latter as an entrepôt. Egypt lay athwart one of the routes to India, and Bonaparte had already in February suggested the dispatch of an "expedition to the Levant as a menace to the [British] trade of the Indies." Talleyrand argued to the Directory that conquering Egypt would end the predations against French merchants of the emirs that ruled the country as vassals of the Ottoman sultan, would bestow on France a wealthy new colony, and might form a springboard for expelling the British from India, the Jewel in the Crown of their empire and an additional source for the commercial wealth that they used to fight France. Bonaparte himself was pleased with this turn of events. "Great reputations," he remarked, "are only made in the Orient; Europe is too small."[28]

✦

Bonaparte's fleet sailed inexorably eastward. The 2,000 passengers aboard the *Orient* included many members of the Commission on Sciences and Arts. Bonaparte enjoyed his conversations on chemistry, mathematics, and religion with scientists he had brought along, such as the physicist and former minister of the navy Gaspar Monge, the chemist Claude-Louis Berthollet, and others. His secretary, Louis Bourrienne, thought Bonaparte much preferred Monge's penchant for wild imagination and speculations on religious subjects to the cold analytical abstractions put forth by Berthollet.

After dinner, Napoleon would arrange debates among three or four of the guests in his cabin, putting forth a proposition and asking some to argue in its support while others were to refute it. Were the planets inhabited? What was the age of the world? Could dreams be interpreted so as to tell the future? Bourrienne thought he used these debates to gauge the caliber of his men and to divine the tasks they might most usefully be assigned, and that he "gave the preference to those who had supported an absurd proposition with ability over those who had maintained the cause of reason."[29]

Bonaparte discoursed with his friends on biblical and classical history, especially subjects related to the Mediterranean islands and the lands they were passing. "The sight of the kingdom of Minos led him to reason on the laws best calculated for the government of nations," his secretary reports, "and the birthplace of Jupiter [Crete] suggested to him the necessity of a religion for the mass of mankind." These conversations contain the kernel of Bonaparte's increasingly

instrumental approach to religion, which contrasts with the way the radical partisans of the Enlightenment philosophy of reason in the French Revolution, or Jacobins, rejected it as superstition. That is, Bonaparte felt that people were
naturally religious, and using religion to manipulate them was only good statecraft, whereas the cult of Reason among many revolutionaries and intellectuals led
them to see faith as irrational and reactionary, to be wiped out before it did more
damage. The antireligious faction was influenced by the French philosopher
Voltaire, who in his letters had often used the phrase, "*Écrasez l'infame!*" ("Crush
the infamous thing!"), referring to fanatical and intolerant forms of religion.[30]

The knowledge that they were being piloted toward Egypt excited many of
the French officers. Captain Moiret, who had once studied for the priesthood,
sounded more like the intellectuals than the other officers in his musings on the
future while at Malta, and one suspects from various hints in his manuscript that
he was unusually close to them. He said that he and his friends were excited by
the prospects of this "glorious" enterprise. They would go to this antique land,
the cradle of sciences and arts, to rediscover the pharaohs' indestructible monuments, the pyramids, obelisks, temples, and cities, the valleys where the children
of Israel had wandered, "the lands glorified by the exploits of the Macedonians,
Romans and Muslims, and of the most holy of our kings." He made Bonaparte's
army a successor to the expeditions of Alexander, Octavian, 'Amr ibn al-'As, and
Louis IX himself.

It may be argued that Alexander the Great had some success in Egypt, for
his conquest led to the founding of the dynasty of Ptolemies by one of his Greek
generals and he had had its major port named after him. So, too, did Octavian
(later called Augustus), whose invasion provoked the suicide of the last Ptolemy,
Cleopatra, and who inaugurated six hundred years of Roman and Byzantine rule
on the Nile. 'Amr ibn al-'As, who in A.D. 639 spearheaded the Arab Muslim incorporation of Egypt into the new religious civilization of Islam, with its capital
in Mecca, also carried out celebrated military exploits. The same is not true,
however, of Saint Louis, the Crusader King. Louis IX took the Egyptian port
city of Damietta on 6 June 1249 and marched on Cairo, but enemies on his
flanks released the water from the Nile reservoirs and trapped his army in the
resulting inundation and easily defeated it. Moiret said that the officers flattered
themselves that they most resembled the more successful of these conquerors,
and could reestablish civilization, the sciences, and arts in Egypt. More realistically, he added, "This new colony would reimburse us for the loss of those that
the wiliness of the English had stolen from us in the New World."

Moiret mused richly on the historical and geopolitical significance of the
expedition. His allusion to the French losses in the New World concerned, of

course, the Seven Years War and the British conquest of Quebec in 1759. Winston Churchill referred to the conflicts of the 1750s and 1760s (known to Americans as the French and Indian War) as a world war that especially involved a contest of power between the French and the British, who fought not only in North America but also in the Caribbean and in South India. Both in North America and in India, the British had won, something the French military men of Bonaparte's generation had not forgotten. In the 1790s, British sea power had deprived France of most of its remaining Caribbean possessions. Egypt, Moiret implied, had been an adjunct to all the great world empires, and by taking it Republican France would be joined to them in glory.

For neither Moiret nor Bonaparte was a republican empire a contradiction in terms. Some lands conquered by France in Europe, such as Belgium, had been simply annexed and put under direct French rule. But the French Republic could also serve as an imperial center, with satellite republics. One of these, the Batavian (Dutch) Republic, had been set up in 1795 after the revolutionary army defeated the Prussians there. Ruled by a set of citizen councils, it nevertheless continued to labor under French military occupation and faced demands that it follow French policies and provide soldiers and subsidies to France. When he was preparing to invade Malta, Bonaparte treated the Dutch ambassador as though he were an agent of the French Republic, summarily relieving him of his duties and having him evacuated.[31]

Satellite republics were established in the wake of the Italian campaigns of 1796–1797, during which Bonaparte first distinguished himself as a leading general. In 1797 the French military set up what it called the Ligurian Republic at Genoa, modeled on France, and gave it a Directory. Other administrative units in French-dominated north-central Italy were merged in 1798 into the Cisalpine Republic. In late 1797 through 1798, the French subdued Switzerland and reconstituted it as the Helvetian Republic, also with a central Directory. French arms put down recalcitrant Swiss nationalists and Catholics who resisted the Republican French policy of subordinating the church to the democratic state. Thus, the French saw their Directory form of government not as a national peculiarity but as a model for other countries, which would be imposed by force if necessary.

The other Directory-ruled republics were not so much sisters as daughters. The French alleged that these satellite republics enjoyed "liberty." The inhabitants of the Italian Peninsula might be forgiven if they found it difficult to reconcile "liberty" with the massive looting by French troops and streams of wealth flowing from their country to Paris. The citizens of these new republics enjoyed an unprecedented degree of local democracy and freedom of the press, though at the price of subordination to a foreign power and of being cleaned out of treasure and objets d'art.

In contrast, the revolutionary French government had attempted to run Haiti (then Saint-Domingue) as a simple colony. Unexpectedly, the spread to this French colony of the ideals of the Revolution led to the emergence of free black former slaves and of slaves themselves as an active political force. France ended slavery there, and lost control of the territory in the 1790s to the British navy and local leaders such as the revolutionary Toussaint L'Ouverture. Moiret and others clearly wanted to see imposed on Egypt a French-enforced Directory republicanism like that of Holland or Switzerland, though aspects of a Saint-Domingue-style colony were also in their minds.

Bonaparte himself later listed among his objects in undertaking the conquest of Egypt establishing "a French colony on the Nile, which would prosper without slaves, and serve France instead of the republic of Saint Domingo, and of all the sugar islands."[32] Bonaparte's marriage to Josephine, born and bred on the West Indies island of Martinique, alerted him to Caribbean affairs. He thus represented himself, at least, as sensitive to the economic damage France had suffered in losing control of Saint-Domingue in the 1790s, and the need for a new colony to substitute for it. Both he and Talleyrand consistently mentioned sugar as a desirable commodity, and it may well be that Egypt's cane crop was its primary draw for them.

When the French arrived off Alexandria on the morning of 1 July, the ships were assailed by "impetuous winds, which mixed together all the vessels and put them in the greatest disorder."[33] Some were sure that, at dawn, they had glimpsed Nelson's sails above the horizon. Bonaparte sent a frigate to do reconnaissance, and it discovered an Egyptian vessel, which approached. The French officer induced the Egyptian captain to lead him to the Egyptian flagship, the commander of which, unable to take evasive action, came and informed the French that two days before, the English fleet had appeared in the harbor of Alexandria. The British had attempted to warn the governor, or *kashif*, Sayyid Muhammad Kurayyim, of the French intention to assault his country, but Kurayyim had haughtily refused Nelson's ships permission to remain or to take on fresh water and provisions. This intelligence produced profound consternation among the French sailors and troops, who had a healthy regard for the prowess of the British navy. Bonaparte is said to have cried out, "Fortune, do you abandon me? Only five more days!" The words implied that he could get a toehold in Egypt in less than a week, if only he could avoid Nelson for that long. Though some have denied that he spoke the words, he almost certainly felt the sentiments.

2

A SKY AFLAME

The patrician Vice Admiral François-Paul Brueys D'Aigalliers sent a frigate to pick up the French consul in Alexandria, Charles Magallon, who filled in the details of Nelson's ominous visit. He said he thought the British had headed for Alexandretta on the Syrian coast, thinking that if the French were not in Alexandria by that time, they must have gone on to that other debarkation point. If the British thought that the French intended to threaten India, then Syria and Iraq were potential gateways. The Tigris and Euphrates river valleys, despite their fast-running waters and tendency toward violent flooding, could be used for transport, and the British themselves sometimes resorted to this route to India through the Persian Gulf.

Back in Alexandria, the fierce, keening winds and turbulent seas that had prevailed for a day or two convinced Brueys that a landing should be postponed, especially since night was falling and the navy had no idea how to navigate the reefs or find the most suitable landing points in the dark. (Brueys, born an aristocrat, served the Republican navy even though he had lost family and friends to the Great Terror in the early 1790s, when radical revolutionaries executed the king and attempted to wipe out remnants of the old regime.) Bonaparte, who had command of both navy and army operations, overruled the admiral, insisting that the troops must disembark immediately. He wrote the captain of an Ottoman ship then anchored off Alexandria, "The Beys have covered our merchants with humiliation, and I have come to demand reparations. I will be in Alexandria tomorrow. You must not be anxious. You belong to our great friend, the Sultan. Comport yourself in that light. But if you commit the least hostility against the French army, I will treat you as an enemy, and you will have been the cause of it, since that is far from my intention and what is in my heart."[1] The Ottoman captain appears to have fled.

During the night the French positioned several launches equipped with cannon all along the shore, flanking Alexandria. Consul Magallon had brought along with him a local Egyptian pilot, who helped steer the French landing party through the reefs. Beginning around one o'clock in the early morning of 2 July, Bonaparte and his French troops were able to land about three miles from the city.

At 3:00 A.M., generals Bon, Kléber, and Jacques Menou each led a unit of 430 men as a combined advance guard that marched on Alexandria. It had not proved possible to land artillery or cavalry as yet. Bonaparte marched on foot with the sharpshooters of the vanguard. A mile and a half from the city, the three hundred Bedouin Arab horsemen who guarded the heights around it caught sight of the French and fired on them.

When they fully realized the size of the French force, the Bedouins hastily retired. Menou and his unit traversed the small sand dunes along the sea, to the west of the wall of the Arab quarter of Alexandria, seeking to overwhelm the Triangular Fort. Kléber took his contingent toward the great gate of that wall, which led to Pompey's Column. Bon and his troops turned to the east of the city, toward the Rosetta gate. Having taken the fort and the gates by 8:00 A.M., they halted. Bonaparte headed toward Pompey's Column and detached several officers to reconnoiter the wall of the Arab quarter, which protected Alexandria. They discovered that the wall had been well maintained, and offered them no breaches.

When Bonaparte arrived under the walls of the old city that morning, he seemed ready to begin negotiations, confident that the small city of 8,000 would capitulate in the face of an overwhelming military force. But armed townspeople, excited to combat by the cries of their leaders, women, and children, swarmed the battlements atop the wall and took up positions in its towers,. The five hundred slave-soldier cavalrymen under the command of Sayyid Muhammad Kurrayim, the governor of Buhayra Province, and the armed Alexandrian townsmen, kept up a steady gunfire against the French, which proved relatively ineffectual. Suddenly the emirs or commanders within the city unveiled their cannon and fired on their enemy.

The three or four old pieces of cannon, which were mounted on the walls and could not be swiveled, did not deter the French attackers. As for the defenders' rain of musket balls, the European infantry raised their own muskets and replied with a thunderous fusillade, cutting down some Egyptians. Then the French light artillery, which had finally arrived, weighed in with cannonballs, forcing the Ottoman-Egyptian cavalry to withdraw to a distance.

Bernoyer reported that Bonaparte sent an imperious message demanding that Kurayyim capitulate:

> I am surprised to see you take hostile measures against me. You are either extremely ignorant or extremely presumptuous, to believe you could resist me with two or three poor pieces of cannon. Moreover, my army has just vanquished one of the foremost Powers in Europe. If in ten minutes I do not see a white flag waving, you will have to be held accountable before God for the blood that you will spill needlessly, and soon, you will weep at the departure of the victims that you will have sacrificed by your blindness.[2]

A little while later the French commander in chief, having had no reply, mounted his attack. The French had still not surrounded the city, and the emirs were reassured to find that cavalry reinforcements could still reach it from the hinterland. The Ottoman-Egyptian cavalrymen prepared to engage in a second round, believing that the speed of their horses rendered them invincible against an enemy that was largely on foot. Moiret admits of the small French cavalry, "Our own, however good, could not be compared to it, because of the difference in the horses."[3]

Mounted warriors, whether pastoral nomads or professional cavalry, had generally, in medieval Middle Eastern warfare, easily triumphed over villagers, urbanites, and even a trained infantry. The great empires of the Arab Muslims, and later the Mongols, the Seljuk Turks, the Safavids, and the Ottomans, had all been founded primarily by men on horse or camel back. Advances in infantry tactics in Europe had weakened the power of cavalry, especially when combined with skilled use of artillery. In addition, the power and range of artillery during the eighteenth century in France had significantly increased through better casting of cannon and better-made powder. Bonaparte, a mathematician turned artillery specialist, had made his career by taking advantage of these breakthroughs in the organization of foot soldiers and the delivery of cannon shot. The proud mounted warriors of what we would now call the Middle East were about to meet their match, at long last, in an unlikely combination of drilled French peasants backed by cannon of unparalleled potency, all massed and thrown at a single pressure point.

French sources claimed that there were in Egypt when they arrived about 60,000 members of the ruling caste of emirs and their slave soldiers, with about 6,000 armed and outfitted. This estimate has been found plausible by subsequent historians, though it may not have included in the count all the sorts of Ottoman troops in the country. From the 1770s, the number of emirs

had declined, in part because of the toll taken by their wars with one another.[4]
The French believed that all the emirs were slave soldiers, called in Arabic
Mamluk, having been imported to serve in the Egyptian military. Since others
had never been slaves, however, this ruling group is better referred to as *emirs*
(Arabic for "commanders") or, at the higher ranks, *beys* (from a Turkish word
meaning "lord"). A government of beys is a *beylicate*, and this group ruled
Egypt as vassals of the Ottoman sultan. The Ottoman-Egyptian grandees and
their wives owned vast estates and maintained magnificent mansions. Moiret
described them, saying that the beys

> possess everything: houses, lands, and other properties, and have a consider-
> able annual income. The clothing of the rich differs from that of the poor
> only in the fineness of the material. Beneath a silk shirt, they wear a habit like
> that of former monks in France, but of an exorbitant price; trousers of such
> amplitude that they must take ten or twelve ells of cloth to make; and for
> footwear they sport slippers of Moroccan leather of enormous dimensions.
> Their turbans must, given their fineness, cost them a great deal. They shave
> their heads, except for a small tuft in the middle of their pate. It is by this,
> they say, that at their final moment Muhammad will grab hold of them and
> pull them into paradise.

The emirs and Mamluks defending Alexandria now charged for a second
time, but failed to break through the French lines, which typically had formed
into impenetrable squares of men with firearms and bayonets raised. The Ottoman Egyptians retired, then tried again, and again, never with success.
Horses, for all their spirit and maneuverability, will not charge into a disciplined
infantry square bristling with bayonets and gunfire. Fixed socket bayonets that
allowed infantrymen to fire their weapon and to use the bayonet as a pike
against cavalry had given eighteenth-century foot soldiers a powerful new advantage, as the emirs suddenly became aware. French battalions were being reinforced at every moment. Since Bonaparte still lacked heavy artillery, which the
navy had not yet been able to offload, he had no means to punch a hole in
Alexandria's walls.

Around noon, the Europeans mounted a decisive offensive. They chased
away the defenders' cavalry and then took Alexandria by scaling the walls. They
camped partly inside and partly outside the walls of Alexandria that night, while
the general staff lodged with families of wealth and position. They all suffered
from mosquitoes, the heat, and brackish water. Initially, some of the townspeople peppered the French with gunfire or pelted them with stones, even after the

defeat, but this defiance subsided in the face of French military superiority. Casualty estimates in battles such as the taking of Alexandria varied wildly from author to author. The French dead came to between 20 and 100 and wounded between 100 and 300. The wounded included generals such as Kléber and Menou. An Egyptian defender shot Kléber in the face and sent him plummeting to the ground. He nevertheless survived and recovered.

On the afternoon of the assault Bonaparte had established his headquarters in the palace of the governor. At a meeting with the city notables, he assured them that he would respect their religion and their property, and they in turn pledged to avoid any conspiracies against French rule. He kept Sayyid Muhammad Kurayyim as governor of the district and draped him in a tricolor sash.

Although Bonaparte grandiosely passed in review of his troops, Bernoyer reported that the Egyptians seemed unimpressed and defiant. Those who had not fled the city stayed inside their homes. The generality of the people still expected their lives to be forfeit and their city to be torched, given that they had actively resisted conquest. The Alexandrians seemed to Pierre Amédée Jaubert, Bonaparte's Arabic interpreter, "most astonished that we had not cut off their heads."[5] They were taking no chances, declining to come out into the streets for fear of the foreigners. Henceforth, the locals offered resistance only by pulling hapless individual French soldiers into back alleys and slitting their throats when they could do so unobserved. The French, lacking good lodging elsewhere, had initially hoped to billet some soldiers in the old city, but these attacks forced them to abandon it.[6]

Europeans had enjoyed an economic supremacy in Alexandria, and the French had now turned it into political dominance. Although Alexandria was an Ottoman port, part of the main route for seaborne trade inside the empire that connected it to Istanbul and Smyrna (now Izmir), European captains played an increasingly important role in conducting the city's commerce with the outside world. About half the merchants who chartered vessels from the city to other ports were Ottoman Turks resident in the port, but the ships themselves tended to be owned by Europeans. In the previous decade, all trade between that port and Europe went on European ships, and ninety-five percent of the trade with Tripoli, Tunis, and Algiers also was in the hands of European merchants and captains. The French predominated among the owners of European merchant vessels, and their ships accounted for half of Alexandria's trade with Europe. Earlier, in the 1790s, the ruling beys had challenged French commercial dominance of the port by favoring instead the small British mercantile community; this move provoked loud complaints among outraged French merchants back in

Marseilles, and their complaints helped impel the Directory to intervene. The spacious European mansions of the foreign merchants in Alexandria marked off the nicest part of the city, reflecting the dominance of French and Venetian capital, and that part of the city, in a way already colonized, warmly welcomed Bonaparte.

The French heavy guns were now off-loaded at Abuqir, and companies of grenadiers manned the fortifications at the lighthouse. Bernoyer, a civilian with no military experience, went to the beach to attend to his personal effects and was surprised to see the sands covered with ammunition wagons, bombs, cannonballs, and artillery pieces. More than a thousand men were scurrying about on the beach and in boats, off-loading this deadly cargo, which was intended to subdue the entire Nile Valley. He was shocked to see the Alexandrians coming to the beach and nonchalantly bathing and praying, appearing to pay no attention to the fleet's disgorgement of the weapons of large-scale terror. He took their insouciance for a strange lack of curiosity, and did not stop to think that carrying on with business as usual has often been among the secret weapons of resistance employed by vanquished populations to bolster their morale.

The Bedouins who had resisted the French advance that morning sent a delegation of thirty men to offer an alliance by breaking bread, saying they had now heard that Bonaparte was only interested in overthrowing the beylicate of Ibrahim Bey and Murad Bey, Egypt's two rulers. The commander in chief assured them that this was the case, and ate with them as a proof of the sincerity of his intentions. He reaffirmed his commitment to interfere neither with their religion nor their women, and went beyond seeking a truce, asking them to ally with him against the beys. For their part, they pledged not to harass his columns and to provide some men to fight Egypt's former masters. For his part, Bonaparte said that upon becoming master of Egypt he would return to them some lands they had formerly possessed, but which the emirs had confiscated.

For a while the Bedouins withdrew, temporarily making the roads secure. The few chieftains who made this pledge to Bonaparte were not representative, and other Bedouin, who did not feel bound by the agreement, harassed the French army relentlessly. Moiret, showing the usual disdain of urban observers, described the Bedouins as inveterate highwaymen (ignoring their valuable role as pastoralists, producers of meat and milk products from marginal land, and managers of long-distance communications and transportation). He depicted the men as well armed, typically owning a horse, a carbine, two pistols, and a saber of Damascene steel. He said that, when in camp, each was accompanied by a young female slave who took a stirrup in her hand and followed alongside the horse. Moiret, and the French generally, referred to the Bedouin as "Arabs," by which they meant pastoral nomads. The Bedouin considered themselves Arabs inasmuch as they claimed descent from tribes that had emigrated from the Arabian Peninsula. Before the rise of modern nationalism a century later, an Arabic-speaking gentleman in Cairo would generally have referred to himself as an Ottoman subject, not as an "Arab."

The French in Egypt were universally disappointed by Alexandria, having been raised on tales in the classical sources of the port's magnificence in antiquity. The merchant Grandjean lamented that the city's ancient monuments had "fallen back into nothingness" under "the domination of the Turks." He sniffed, "It offered no more than misery and half-ruined shacks on the debris of palaces and magnificent temples." He was only impressed with the foreign merchant colonies and the mansions of the consuls. Each nation had its own settlement, together forming the European quarter, "which is situated on the New Port and the great square." The rest of the city, he said, was inhabited by Muslims, Jews, and some great merchants, "who try to become as close as they can to the Europeans."[7] Alexandria's condition was in fact unreasonably bad, though only partially as a result of misrule. Lack of quarantine and frequent plague and other disease outbreaks limited its population, which had been devastated in the medieval period by the Black Death. A lack of water also afflicted it. The Nile outlet on which the city had originally been built had changed course, leaving the city high and dry. A narrow canal brought some water to the city, and even allowed shipping of goods in and out, when it was not diverted by peasant farmers for their own irrigation needs.

Bernoyer accompanied scientists such as Charles Norry, one of the 151 members of the Commission on Arts and Sciences whom Bonaparte had brought along, on their explorations of the few remaining ancient monuments in Alexandria. He lamented that some commission members strayed so far in their excitement and thirst for discovery that they fell into the hands of the Bedouin, who returned them to Bonaparte for a reward in fulfillment of their alliance with him. Norry wrote of his profound disappointment in contemporary Alexandria: "Shocked at this sight, we went to visit the remains of antiquity. We every where found columns of granite, some still standing, others promiscuously lying prostrate in the streets and squares, and even on the sea-shore, where they formed considerable piles; Egyptian monuments covered with hieroglyphics, serving for thresholds of doors, or benches used for seats." He says they found only a few ruins of the ancient port of the Ptolemies, including some fallen columns inscribed with Pharaonic characters, then still undeciphered.

The locals had incorporated some stonework with the hieroglyphs still engraved into them into the gates of the bazaars.[8]

The French officers concurred in the disappointment expressed by the scientists. Captain Moiret lamented that nothing remained in Alexandria of its ancient monuments save Pompey's Column and two obelisks of Cleopatra, one of which had already fallen to the ground. "I sat on it and walked along it," he reported. We now know that most of ancient Alexandria had fallen into the sea because of earthquakes and that the disappearance of the classical city had nothing to do with civilizational decadence. Among other beginnings visible in the French assault, we can see the birth of modern Egyptian tourism. Moiret was seeking an ancient Alexandria, and thus was dissatisfied with the bustling, Arabic-speaking, Muslim port that exported so much Egyptian grain and other goods to Anatolia and even to Europe. Talleyrand's interest in the sugar plantations of Bengal and the Antilles suggests that the French elite was primarily interested in such commodities, and that they also believed it was dangerous to allow the British to enjoy surplus profits from tropical cash crops while France was deprived of these extra sources of wealth. Cleopatra and past greatness had little to do with the reasons for which French troops now crawled all over Alexandria.

Moiret gave his impressions of the Alexandrians. He thought their "constitution" robust, and so did not find them sickly, and he remarked their "bronze color," though noting that "many are black or mulatto." He was a severe critic, however, of their fashion sense. The peasants, he maintained, often went naked. As for urban folk, "Their clothing is a few rags thrown bizarrely over their bodies, and on their heads is chiffon rolled up like a swallow's nest, which they call a turban. They wear neither hat nor shoes."[9] Moiret was most scathing about the common women and complained of the way their poverty created immodesty even as they attempted to veil their faces.

Not all French officers were as dismissive of Egyptian women as Moiret, the former seminarian, was. His allegation, that women were zealous about veiling but careless about letting slip a glimpse of their charms, concerned lower-middle-class urban women, who were presumably attempting to emulate the veiling practices of the upper-class Ottoman-Egyptians but did not have enough money to afford blouses that would guarantee their modesty. Not all social classes veiled in the premodern Middle East. Peasant and Bedouin women seldom had the luxury of worrying about full veiling and seclusion, since they performed key work outside for their social groups.

The images of Egyptian women that Moiret derived from his early experiences in Egypt take on a gritty, realistic texture very distant from woolgathering about Cleopatras. To explain the discrepancy between his reveries and the reality, Moiret resorted to a theory of degeneration. Alexandria, he lamented, was so squalid and miserable that the troops wanted immediately to turn around and repair to Europe. "We remarked," he said, "as to how the subjects and compatriots of Cleopatra had degenerated." Egypt's chief port "offered only the debris of a formerly great city, and the vices of a brutalized and enslaved people."

The theme of the degeneration of what had once been the classical world was well established by the eighteenth century, having been elaborated early in the century by French travelers to and writers about Greece.[10] Degeneration allowed the French to appropriate classical civilization for their own, displacing its splendor into the distant past and positioning its present heirs as unworthy, such that the mantle of those glories fell on the French instead. Still, it should be underlined that despite the racist overtones of the phrase, degeneration did not refer, for these Directory-era Frenchmen, to a hereditary condition of the blood. Rather, they believed that the climatic and social conditions of Egypt had produced tyranny and excess, which were amenable to being reversed. This attempt at restoring the Egyptians to greatness and curing their degeneracy through liberty and modernity was central to the rhetoric of the invasion.

On 3 July, Bonaparte issued several grand pronouncements. "The Commander in chief wants the Turks [Muslims] to fulfill their acts of worship in their mosques just as in the past. He expressly forbids all the French, military or otherwise, to enter mosques or to assemble outside their doors."[11] He demanded that within twenty-four hours all Alexandrians turn in their firearms to the site designated by the local French commander. Only Muslim clerics, jurisconsults, and prayer leaders were exempted, insofar as he envisaged them as the backbone of the new regime. He went on: "All the inhabitants of Alexandria, from whatever nation they derive, must wear the tricolor cockade. Only muftis have the right to wear a tricolor sash. The commander in chief reserves to himself the right to accord the same favor to the ordinary clerics and prayer leaders who are distinguished by their enlightenment, wisdom, and virtue."

In contrast to the Jacobin republican ideal of equality, the Directory had reinstituted certain kinds of hierarchy (e.g., between those with enough property to engage in politics and those without). Bonaparte created such hierarchies in French Egypt, between the armed and the unarmed, and the wearer of the cockade and the bearer of the sash. The sash was an honor enjoyed by city mayors under the Directory. Ironically, the first thing the heirs of Voltaire in Egypt could think to do with the Egyptian power structure was to depend on the Muslim clergy and to bestow on it the right to bear arms![12] Bonaparte attempted to coopt the Muslim clerical class as allies from the indigenous middle stratum against the beys. On the other hand, according to the contemporary Ottoman historian Izzet Hasan Darendeli, Bonaparte employed the Muslim slaves he had manumitted in Malta and brought to Alexandria as ambassadors of good will for the French when they reached Cairo, giving some Egyptians the impression that the French really had come as liberators. The French festooned the city in tricolor banners and forced the townspeople to surrender all their weapons, as they would everywhere they went in Egypt. They honored prominent citizens with cockades (knots of tricolor ribbons). Finally, they demanded a substantial tribute from the inhabitants, making rather hollow Bonaparte's boasts that he would provide a less rapacious government than that of the slave soldiers.[13] (Some of these details are from the Egyptian chronicler 'Abd al-Rahman al-Jabarti and the Ottoman historian Izzet Hasan Darendeli; the French memoirists tend, unlike the local sources, to be silent on these coercive measures.)

✤

Bonaparte, having secured Alexandria, issued a proclamation setting forth to the Egyptians the reasons for the invasion and what the French government expected from them. The French Orientalist Jean Michel de Venture de Paradis, perhaps with the help of Maltese aides, translated the document into very strange and very bad Arabic. The Maltese, Catholic Christians, speak a dialect of Arabic distantly related to that of North Africa, but they were seldom schooled in writing classical Arabic, which differs with regard to grammar, vocabulary, and idiom from the various spoken forms. Venture de Paradis, who had lived in Tunis, knew Arabic grammar and vocabulary but not how to use them idiomatically. The French thus first appeared to the small elite of literate Egyptians through the filter of a barbarous accent and writing style, making them seem rather ridiculous, despite Bonaparte's imperial pretensions. It would be rather as though they had conquered England and sent forth their first proclamation in Cockney. But ungrammaticality and awkward wording were not the worst of the statement's difficulties. Much of it simply could not be understood by most Egyptians, since it sought to express concepts for which there were no Arabic equivalents.

Eighteenth-century France had witnessed many revolutions in thought and institutions, more than any other country in the world (with the possible exception of the United States of America). New discourses had grown up, with a new vocabulary. The proclamation alleged that Bonaparte had been sent to punish the rebellious beys by the Ottoman sultan, Selim III. It denounced the beys as foreigners from the Caucasus who pitilessly overtaxed and exploited Egypt. Bonaparte insisted that the religious authorities should keep the prayers going in mosques, and that towns and villages raise the French tricolor. He warned the Arabic-speaking Egyptians not to side with their Ottoman-Egyptian overlords and said that rebellious villages would be burned.

The proclamation announces a political use of French deism and anticlericalism as proof that the French are actually "muslims" with a small "m" (which is to say, they have submitted to the one God). That is, unlike Christians, the French believe in only one God rather than in a Trinity, and have become sworn enemies of the Christian pontiff. (This mention of the pope recalled the conquest of Rome at Bonaparte's order by Gen. Louis Alexandre Berthier in 1797, and his taking Pius VI prisoner.) Bonaparte, with his cynical view of religion, was perfectly content to issue an Arabic proclamation that the French were "muslims" (as deist unitarians). This assertion is absurd, but not as absurd as the English rendering makes it appear, since in Arabic the word "muslim" could simply mean anyone who had submitted to the one God, and non-Muslims are represented in the Qur'an as calling themselves "muslim" in this sense.

Bonaparte, having no way of knowing how bad the document's Arabic style was, viewed it as a key tool of propaganda. On 7 July he issued an order for its publication. He commanded that the French, Arabic, and Greek printing presses be brought ashore: "From the instant that the Arabic press is set up, 4,000 Arabic proclamations must be printed."[14] Bonaparte was a master of what we would now call spin, and his genius for it is demonstrated by the reports in Arabic sources that several of his more outlandish allegations were actually taken seriously in the Egyptian countryside.

The Orientalist Jaubert wrote back to his brother a little while later that the few Alexandrians who had not fled the city "read with transports of joy, the proclamation which the Commander in Chief had previously printed in Arabic, and which you must long before this have seen in the public papers."[15] He related how, "the evening before, we had seized a few Turks and Arabs, and carried them on board the fleet." Desiring to "calm their apprehensions, and make them our apostles," the French determined to convey to them the proclamation, though these men appear to have been illiterate. He wrote that they pressed a Maronite priest from Damascus into service for this purpose, making fun of him for calling himself "*a Christian like ourselves.*" Many French in the age of the Revolution had become deists, that is, they believed that God, if he existed at all, was a cosmic clockmaker who had set the universe in motion but did not any longer intervene in its affairs. Most deists did not consider themselves Christians any longer and looked down on Middle Eastern Christians as priest-ridden and backward. Jaubert recalled that the priest "was ordered to read it to them, and to comment on it as he proceeded. When you consider the proclamation, you will judge how well the part he played became him!" Jaubert thought it further amusing that the poor priest had had to tell the captured Alexandrians that the French, whom he had initially greeted as fellow Catholics loyal to the pope, were actually a kind of "muslim" who had attacked the pontiff! In a later letter to another correspondent, Jaubert observed, "You will laugh outright, perhaps, you witlings of Paris, at the Mahometan proclamation of the Commander in Chief. He is proof, however, against all your raillery; and the thing itself will certainly produce a most surprising effect."

When the great Sunni Muslim clerics of the al-Azhar Seminary in Cairo received these pamphlets and they spread up the Nile, how did they react? The Cairene cleric and historian 'Abd al-Rahman al-Jabarti, among the persons Bonaparte's proclamation was supposed to impress, reacted with a combination of amusement, bewilderment, and outrage.[16] He penned a quick commentary on it, the form of which suggests an element of satire, since learned men such as al-Jabarti normally penned glosses of the Qur'an, not of French pamphlets.

Al-Jabarti began by eviscerating the broken Arabic grammar and the infelicitous style of the proclamation. He then observed that the opening phrase demonstrated that the revolutionary French in some ways agreed with the three religions (Judaism, Christianity, and Islam), but in other ways disagreed with all of them. "They agree with the Muslims in employing the phrase 'in the name of God, the Merciful, the Compassionate,' and in denying that God has any son or partner." But, he said, they also differed from the Muslims. They did not pronounce the Muslim witness to faith, which affirmed the prophethood of Muhammad, nor did they accept the very idea that messengers, whose sayings and deeds have normative and legal force in Islam, are sent by God. The French, he argued, agreed with the Christians in most of their words and deeds, but differed from them on the issue of the Trinity and, again, on the idea that God sends revelations to humankind. They rejected the church hierarchy, killed priests, and razed churches.

As for the term "republic," he explained, the pamphlet represented itself as coming from the French collective, since they did not have a grandee or sultan to whom they granted legitimacy and who spoke for them, unlike all other societies. He said that they had risen up against their king six years before and killed him, and that their collectivity had reached a consensus that there should be no single ruler, but rather that the affairs of their state, their country, their laws, and their administration should be in the hands of the wise and the leaders of opinion among them. (If al-Jabarti's description of revolutionary France sometimes makes it sound less like a democracy and more like a rule of philosophers similar to that proposed by Socrates in Plato's *Republic*, that is no accident. He was a Muslim Neoplatonist.) He described how they chose individuals to lead the army, and installed beneath them officers, men and administrators and ombudsmen to consult with them, on the condition that all would be equal and none would be exalted over the other, on the grounds that human beings are by nature equal. They made that principle, he said, the foundation of their way of life. That, he explained, is the meaning of their phrase, "which is based upon the foundation of being free and socially leveled." He did not understand the assertion that the French enjoyed "liberty," suggesting that perhaps Bonaparte meant to boast that he was not a slave like so many of Egypt's emirs.

Al-Jabarti appears to have been under the impression that the French were mostly citizen soldiers and that they ran their military in a democratic fashion. While the revolutionaries did invent the mass conscription of peasants, and while democratic consultation within military units had been attempted early in the revolution before being quickly abandoned, neither impression was correct. His description, indeed, would have been more apropos of the early 1790s, and it makes one suspect that he had been in contact with European informants, years before the invasion, who had described to him the French innovations of that time.

French men, he said, went clean-shaven. After describing their uniforms (he thought their hats especially ridiculous) and how they differed according to military rank, he concluded, "They followed that law, such that big and small, glorious and abject, men and women, are equal." He observed that they sometimes in fact disregarded this principle, out of greed or ambition. Then he turned to the subject of French women. "Their women do not veil, nor feel any shame, nor even care if they display their privates." Men and women fornicated at will, he alleged, and he went on to say that French women went to male barbers to have their pubic hair removed and paid them with favors. He remarked that the French answered the call of nature wherever they were, even in public. Coming from a culture where washing with water is de rigueur after a bowel movement, he was disturbed that the French just wiped themselves with any paper at hand, or, he said, even neglected to clean themselves at all.

Having described the French in this hostile way, he turned to the values asserted in the pamphlet, which he rejected. He brought into sharp question
Bonaparte's declaration that he respected the Prophet Muhammad and honored
the Qur'an, since, he insisted, true respect and honor could only be demonstrated by accepting their truth and converting to Islam. He pointed out that the
writer of the pamphlet, when alleging that the French were a kind of muslim,
put the word "muslims," in the wrong noun case in Arabic, and he punned that
the allegation itself made a faulty case. He also denied the pamphlet's claim that
"all the people are equal before God." He thundered, "This is a lie, and ignorance, and stupidity. How could it be, when God has chosen some above others,
and all the people of the heaven and earth have borne witness to it?"

The republican French posed a puzzle to the Muslim scholar. Theologi-
cally, they were Unitarians, like Muslims; but in their social customs they resembled other Christians, and they rejected any theory of divinely inspired
prophecy or the revelation of religious law, which for al-Jabarti was the core
of religion. Bonaparte made the typically Western error of thinking about
Islam primarily as a doctrine, whereas for a Middle Easterner such as al-
Jabarti it was a way of life. For Muslims such as the Egyptian cleric, Islam lay
in the five pillars of recognizing the uniqueness of God and the prophethood
of Muhammad, praying five times a day, fasting the month of Ramadan, giving alms to the poor, and going on pilgrimage to Mecca at least once in a life-
time. Bonaparte had nothing to say about any of these pillars except for half
of the first one (monotheism). From al-Jabarti's perspective, the concordance
of mere doctrine said little about how alike two religious systems might be
(otherwise Judaism and Islam could easily be conflated). All this is not to say
that the proclamation had no effect. Literate peasants read it differently than
the Cairene patrician, apparently, for he reported that in the countryside
Bonaparte's claim to be acting on behalf of the Ottoman sultan was believed
by some.

Al-Jabarti also drew back the curtain on the stir produced by the French occupation of Alexandria in Cairo, some 140 miles to the south.[17] Fear spread
through the populace, and many thought about taking flight. One leader,
Ibrahim Bey, rode to Qasr al-'Ayni, and was joined there by Murad Bey from
Giza and then the rest of the commanders, as well as by the chief Muslim judge
and the leading clergy. They launched into a discussion of what had to be done
about this setback to the Muslims. They decided to send a courier to the Ottoman sultan to ask for assistance, and it fell to the figurehead Ottoman viceroy
of Egypt, Ebu Bekir Pasha, to write the letter. The Ottomans occasionally sent

out a governor or viceroy, along with a chief Islamic court judge. The viceroy, who sometimes served a short term, seldom wielded much real power. In some years the insolent slave soldiers even declined to send any tribute to their liege lord in Istanbul, though this level of impudence could be dangerous, since it invited Ottoman military intervention. There were only a few thousand Ottoman troops from Turkish-speaking Anatolia in Egypt. The slave-soldier houses had increasingly marginalized them. To supplement their meager salaries, the Anatolians often worked as artisans and shopkeepers in the bazaar, especially the famed Khan al-Khalili market. Now, all of a sudden, the proud emirs needed their sultan and his Ottoman troops.

The Ottoman Egyptians decided that they would raise an army, the biggest division of which would be that of Murad Bey. The meeting of commanders having come to an end, the troops began making preparations to set out. The amassing of food, gunpowder, tents, cannon, and other necessities took five days. The rulers demanded severe exactions from the people on short notice and simply expropriated much wealth from them. In the meantime, the markets and streets of the capital were thrown into disarray as fear drove the populace to stay inside their homes. The streets were so deserted at night that thieves and burglars took control of them, to the extent that the road west was impassable. Al-Jabarti lamented that one hardly saw a pedestrian walking in the street.

The police chief, or aga, and the viceroy then intervened, insisting that the markets and coffeehouses remain open at night and ordering that candles be lit outside houses and shops. Al-Jabarti remarks that these measures were taken for two reasons, to quiet the fears entertained by the inhabitants of the city and to make it harder for enemies to sneak into it. Murad set out after Friday prayers, but made a further stop at the Black Bridge, where he waited two days, assembling his troops and cavalry. He also was joined by 'Ali Pasha of Tripoli and Nasuh Pasha. Although Murad Bey probably made this elaborate show of amassing such a force, with all its provisions and artillery, in order to reassure the populace and bolster his authority, he without any doubt committed a severe error by delaying his departure for an entire week. He then set out overland with the cavalry. A polyglot infantry consisting of provincially assigned Caucasians and Greek and North African troops followed on the Nile aboard small galleons.

The Ottoman-Egyptian elite believed themselves invincible on land and therefore mainly feared that the small French ships would come up the Nile to attack the capital. On departing the Black Bridge, Murad Bey sent orders that an enormous iron chain should be fashioned "such that it would fit across the straits at Burj Mughayzil [a tower] from one bank of the river to the other to prevent French ships from passing into the Nile."[18] Al-Jabarti reported that during Murad's absence the Muslim clergy, or ulema, held daily prayer sessions at the ancient seminary of al-Azhar and that others took up this practice, including the Sufis or mystics of the Ahmadiya and other orders. Children in the Qur'an schools (the elementary schools of the time) prayed and chanted God's name, the Kind (al-Latif). The chronicler conceded that all this prayer and chanting had no effect on the course of events. It did, he said, produce an atmosphere of greater kindness in the jittery capital.

As a precaution, the ruler Ibrahim Bey had all the Europeans in Cairo rounded up and imprisoned. He at one point ordered those kept in his palace on the island of Roda killed. Sometimes the spouses of powerful politicians have more prudence than their partners, whose authority tends to make them arrogant over time. Ibrahim Bey's chief wife, Züleyha Hanim, appears to have thought it unwise to dispatch European men of great property at a time when a force of 32,000 Europeans had landed in the country and was preparing to march on the capital. She intervened with the executioners to save their lives, arguing that a saying of the Prophet predicted that the French would seize Egypt. She then hid them in her side of the palace.[19]

♣

Back in Alexandria, Bonaparte had two reasons to make haste. He wished to deny the beys in the capital the time to make defensive preparations or to empty the storehouses of the city. But he also felt Nelson's breath on his neck. He had boots and biscuits distributed to the troops and immediately ordered the army to form three columns and to set out in pursuit of the cavalrymen, heading toward the capital, Cairo. He left 2,000 men in Alexandria with the Alsatian general Kléber, who had a head wound. During July in Egypt, a time of torrid sun and dry, hot air, the temperature often rises to 115 degrees Fahrenheit and more. Bonaparte had neglected to research the exigencies of fighting a war in such a place as the Nile Valley at such a time of the year, and appears not to have realized that water canteens were an absolute necessity. His troops had none. Perhaps he thought water would be found in village wells along the way. If so, he was mistaken. It was the season of the low Nile, and the water tables had fallen, and the Bedouin resistance to the French invasion delighted in hiding or spoiling what wells there were. Some historians have accused the general of being willing simply to use up his men, and of asking of them the impossible. No doubt he frequently did so. But the mistake with regard to water resources is most elegantly explained by simple ignorance in the beginning, combined with appalling callousness even after the problem became apparent. Bonaparte, an islander whose major military successes to date had been in Italy, did not realize the severe limitations lack of water imposed on desert warfare. In addition, he felt himself in an almost hopeless race against time, given the proximity and firepower of the British fleet.

Having landed in the northeast corner of the African continent, the French now stood at a port city in the Nile Delta, a broad alluvial plain created over the millennia by the Nile, which overflowed its banks every year, as it emptied into the Mediterranean. Most of Egypt's population huddled along the Nile and its tributaries. Although at one time the Nile put many fingers into the sea, the Delta is now mainly traversed by the Rosetta branch in the west and the Damietta branch in the east. The French would have to march to the western branch and make their way upriver toward the capital of Ottoman Egypt, Cairo, nicknamed "Misr" or "the fortified city," where the branches diverged.

On 5 July two columns prepared to set out, marching to the west along the path of the dry canal that used to bring water to the port. The next day the third column trekked east along the sea toward the wealthy port city of Rosetta and thence south, following that tributary of the Nile. Moiret was in the eastern division, commanded by Gen. Charles François Dugua, which, despite its travails, had the easier time of it. Two hours out of Alexandria they found themselves in desert sand and soon were beset by fatigue and a powerful thirst. They marched from sun to sun without encountering any habitation or source of fresh water, "roasted by a sky aflame."

They tried digging beneath the sand near the ocean, but only found a bit of dirty water that was wholly insufficient to their needs. Many soldiers died of thirst or dehydration because they could not keep down the dirty groundwater. Diarrhea and dysentery, which had spread among the troops, dehydrated them further. They only began to find fresh water when they approached Abuqir, where they spent the night. The next day the march was easier, since it was interrupted by the wait to be ferried across a small strait of the sea that separated Alexandria's territory from that of the nearby city of Rosetta.

The following morning, 8 July, they set out again at three. During that day they experienced the most horrible thirst and fatigue. The sources differ about what happened when General Dugua and his troops approached Rosetta. Al-Jabarti wrote that many of the city's inhabitants had fled before the advance of the foreign troops. A French source said the inhabitants opened the city gates and sent out a deputation draped in tricolor sashes. News of the republican

French taste in fashion accessories, it seems, had preceded them. Since Rosetta was a cosmopolitan port, it is not impossible that Christians and expatriates welcomed the conquerors, whereas many Muslims with strong ties to the beys fled. Each national historiography remembers what it pleases about the ambiguous events. No one disagrees that most of the soldiers threw themselves down in exhaustion once they arrived in the city. They ravenously devoured the refreshments that wealthy city had to offer—water, raisins, dates, and even, as Moiret observed, "some bad wine" peddled "by local Jews." The cavalryman Pierre Millet described Rosetta, then a city of 15,000 or so that had profited from the decline and neglect of Alexandria under Ibrahim and Murad: "This city is one league from the sea, on the western outlet of the Nile. It was in this city that we saw for the first time that famous river, which is so much spoken of in history. Rosetta is surrounded by gardens full of all sorts of fruit trees, such as date palms and lemon, orange, fig, and apricot trees, as well as other species."[20] The city was embellished by big square caravanserais that served as warehouses and around which shops proliferated. Its prominent guilds included fishermen, ironsmiths and bronzesmiths, water carriers, butchers, dyers, tailors, sellers of sorbets, and great import-export merchants. Its workshops produced olive oil, salted fish, textiles, and hookahs. It also had a shipyard. Moiret's division departed from the city at midnight, provisioned with hardtack, and since they were following the Nile, they had access from then on to fresh water. By 11 July the division rendezvoused at Rahmaniya with the other two columns of the army.

The quartermaster, Bernoyer, accompanied one of the western columns south and suffered much more horribly than Moiret's division, as did all the soldiers in those two columns. "We were annihilated," he wrote, "but we had to march over this immense plain of arid sand, in a climate far hotter than our own, without the benefit of a single shadow so that we might recover a bit and might be sheltered from the heat of the burning sun. In that overwhelming situation, we could not quench the thirst that was devouring us. Very quickly, our canteens were emptied, without any hope of refilling them very often." Bernoyer was lucky to have a canteen at all. The troops, lacking them, suffered appallingly. They were "crushed" by thirst and fatigue, throats parched, and sweating hot vapor. The halts at night were short, since Bonaparte, accompanying his men on horseback, wished to profit from the better marching conditions by starlight, to get out of the arid region as soon as possible, and to reach Cairo before Nelson returned. A Sergeant François recounted how on 4 July his unit discovered wells at a village on the way to

Damanhur. "In five minutes, these wells were emptied; soldiers pressed in to descend on them in such great numbers that many were smothered. Others were crushed by the mob. More than thirty soldiers died around those wells. Many, not able to get water, committed suicide." He revealed that on the march south, many of the troops felt burdened by their heavy European clothing and the provisions they had to carry. They discarded their coats and shirts and tossed away the biscuits they were given in Alexandria, confident that both clothing and food could easily be replaced later, "forgetting that we had seen the inhabitants of Alexandria clothed in an altogether different manner than Europeans."[21]

A young officer, Charles Antoine Morand, described how soldiers in search of brush to make a fire discovered in the wilderness a woman with a child in her arms. Receiving their report, Morand, curious, went out to see her. "I found a young woman of sixteen to eighteen years, covered in tatters, who was nothing more than a horrible skeleton. They had put out her eyes and the wounds were still bloody. She was laid out on the burning sand, and some inarticulate words issued with effort from her dried-out throat. Her lips were a livid black." Her newborn was at her breast. He tried to revive her with water and a biscuit. She refused the biscuit but took the water, and they took her to a cistern. She nevertheless later died there, and a mounted Bedouin used a rope to cart the carcass a hundred feet off into the wastelands. The interpreter for Gen. Louis Desaix made inquiries in the local village and discovered that she was expiating a crime of love. "Proven guilty of adultery, she had been condemned with the resulting infant to that appalling torment. They had put out her eyes nine days before, and thus abandoned, she had only lived on roots, grains and wild grasses that she found in prowling through the desert."[22]

The French soldiers were getting a quick introduction to a key value in the Middle East, where the honor of males depended on their ability to protect their women from the unwanted attentions of outsiders and keep them chaste. Women kin who dishonored the band of brothers sometimes faced such clan retribution. Such gender-based honor societies were widespread in the eastern Mediterranean, among Christian populations as well as Muslim. The Qur'an made adultery and fornication difficult to prove (requiring four witnesses!) and prescribed a punishment of whipping, though the influence on early Islamic jurisprudence of Jewish converts and halacha, or Jewish religious law, caused some authorities to favor stoning as a punishment. Putting out the woman's eyes and exposing her in the desert, much less the killing of the newborn, are not in the law books. Muslim clerics would have been as appalled as the French at the illiterate male villagers' way of avenging their honor on a wayward female relative. Morand found the punishment horrible but clearly did not view the fact of the death sentence as surprising in the circumstances. After all, French law recognized an affront to the husband's honor in the form of a wife's affair as a defense under the law for crimes of passion.

As the French troops marched to the southeast, the Bedouin began shadowing the columns, capturing anyone who fell behind. When they began following too closely, the French unveiled cannons and fired on them. Sometimes this tactic caused the Bedouin to disappear only for a short time, sometimes for an entire afternoon. But as the invaders continued to be dogged, both officers and soldiers formed a profound dislike of the pastoralists who made their lives so miserable and killed their friends and comrades. Sometimes the settled population was equally hostile. Sergeant François recounted how, entering a village on the way, the French faced concerted gunfire. "Since we never put down our arms, we riposted; the fusillade became serious. Many inhabitants were taken and executed. This severity prevented the villagers from revolting."[23] Having put down this challenge, the French were then able to buy some provisions from the peasants.

On 9 July Bernoyer marched along with the soldiers again during the day, the sun beating down on their heads, their knees trembling, thick phlegm on their lips and in their throats, their lungs barely able to draw a breath. Captain Vertray recalled, "When the sun was hot, a lake of dirty water would dry up. The deposited salt shone as though it were water. A good number of soldiers ran ahead with pitchers to draw from it, but how deceived they were when they saw that, the farther they advanced, the more the lake dried up."[24] Despite mentions of this phenomenon in classical texts the mirage had not been widely known or understood until the French invasion of Egypt. Gaspar Monge, a physicist attached to the Egyptian Institute, was to write a paper on it, long after the troops had figured out that it was an optical illusion. Once they came to this realization, however, despair gripped them even more violently. Bernoyer had to steel himself against the pitiful whimpers of those men who collapsed from dehydration and pleaded for water as they lay dying. He was surprised, not being a professional soldier, at how he could see a man fall at his feet and step over him, unmoved. But he was himself barely able to go forward and had no energy to spend on caring for anyone else. Soon thereafter they sighted the trees that signaled habitation and rejoiced "like sailors coming to shore" as they trudged into the town of Damanhur in the gloaming. Desvernois thought that 1,500 French soldiers died in the course of the four-day march from Alexandria.

Adj. Gen. Augustin-Daniel Belliard, the son of a public prosecutor, had formed a militia of patriots at the time of the Revolution, which became part of the National Guard and started him on a military career. Belliard recalled, "The gloom was thick, we were marching defiantly, when we saw by the light of torches a big group approaching us."[25] It was a deputation headed by the local mufti, or Muslim jurist. "They brought us a torch, bread, honey, and cheese." Encouraged by this attempt at propitiating them, the French asked for lodging, but the cleric flatly refused (Belliard thought it was because they were infidels and would have polluted the servants of Muhammad, but one wonders if a French town would have been eager to have German troops billeted on them.) "We were happy to be admitted to the baths, where the general staff passed the night on mats." General Desaix, who was from an aristocratic background but had thrown in with the revolutionary army, had less patience with local customs. He had the doors of a local mosque forced and established himself there. Needless to say, turning a mosque into a barracks for French soldiers made a bad impression on the Muslims of Damanhur.

Many of the 4,000 townspeople of the city, upon discovering the French advance, had fled, taking with them their provisions, their animals, even in some instances their doors (carved wood is precious in an arid land). Bernoyer exulted that the locals had been unable to carry away their water, which was what the troops mainly sought. Jean-Pierre Doguereau, a young artillery lieutenant from a modest family in Orleans, central France (his father was a wig maker), had fought in the Army of the Rhine, then been assigned to the Egyptian campaign. He described Damanhur as a "mound of huts that look a lot like dovecotes."[26] He continued, "Some mosques, the minarets of which are visible among tall palm trees, offer from afar an agreeable glimpse. The illusion ends when one approaches." Only by dint of much effort and money could the soldiers find anything to eat, and the townspeople disdained their coins. He viewed them as mischievous assassins in league with the Bedouin that surrounded them, having many relations with the latter "and much of their character." The officer memoirists often expected peasants to be subservient, but were repeatedly disappointed. Doguereau was already constructing a rationale to explain the rebelliousness of Damanhur, blaming it on the bad influence of the Bedouin.

Desvernois maintained that the other officers confronted Bonaparte at Damanhur about the unfolding disaster they were witnessing, as the desert and Bedouin harassment used up their men. General François Mireur of Montpellier, he said, condemned the Directory for sending the army to Egypt and spoke forcefully for leaving immediately for Italy, where there was unfinished business in Sardinia and Naples. He wanted to adopt a longer-term plan to dominate the eastern Mediterranean, with a return to Egypt when the time was right. Mireur's patriotism was not in question and, indeed, he had played a role in making the Marseillaise popular as the anthem of the Revolution. His impassioned speech, however, gained no support. Bonaparte, Desvernois alleged, greeted this impassioned plea for a retreat coldly. He wanted to conquer Egypt immediately. He rose and ended the session. Mireur, recognizing that his career was over, rode out to the desert and blew his brains out. Desvernois was in the party that found him. A military funeral was held for him and he was interred in the Muslim cemetery.[27]

The death of Mireur deeply affected the officers and soldiers who knew him, and many preferred to believe the rumor that he had fallen victim to the Bedouin than that he had lost his nerve. Morand wrote home in despair of how his friend Mireur had passed behind a sandy hillock and been ambushed by Bedouin hiding there. "Egypt, its campaigns, its ruins, its monuments—all of that is hideous to me. A veil of horror has enveloped me. My imagination, for so long abandoned to romantic dreams and agreeable illusions, is now filled only with ghastly images. It wanders among specters and searches for the gory shadow of Mireur. He is no more. Barbarous assassins have ripped away his life. Valiant, in the flower of his youth, good, sensible of glory and friendship, surrounded by esteem, covered with laurels, he fell to the weapons of cruel Bedouins."[28]

At Damanhur, an Arab horse kicked Bonaparte in the right leg, which an army physician said "produced so severe a contusion that one had to fear subsequent accidents. I was happy enough to prevent them, and to guide him in a very short time to healing, despite the pain when he walked and his natural activity, which kept him from resting."[29] The commander in chief set up his headquarters in the whitewashed residence of Damanhur's mayor, which, despite his wealth, was poorly furnished. Bonaparte's private secretary, Louis de Bourrienne, told the story of how the Corsican inquired of his involuntary host as to why he chose to live in such penury. The mayor replied that once he had refurbished his home, and "when this became known at Cairo, a demand was made upon me for the money, because it was said my expenses proved me rich. I refused to pay the money, and in consequence I was ill-treated, and at length, forced to pay it." Bourrienne professed himself shocked that any ruler would force people to pay crushing taxes. In fact, Bonaparte was already working on appropriation schemes of his own. The engineer Villiers du Terrage recorded in his journal for 11 July, "A commission has been charged with researching and taking possession of the goods of the Mamluks."

The prudence of the mayor in hiding and locking up his possessions was further illustrated by an anecdote told by Jacques Miot, commissary of the army, in his memoir of the invasion. He said that troops fanned out in Damanhur searching for grain, and they came upon a hidden, windowless harem containing three black slave women belonging to the elderly mayor. They were not good-looking, but "in the desert one is not choosy," he remarked, and the troops considered attempting their first Egyptian romance. They were disappointed to learn, however, that the sheikh had clapped strong iron chastity belts on all three women, which they found it impossible to remove.[30]

After they arrived in Damanhur, Bernoyer found a shady area to rest in the city and sent his servant to find food. In the meantime he slept fitfully on an empty stomach. When he awoke, he found the wife of a soldier offering him some soup, but "with a delicacy out of place in such circumstances, I declined." A few French soldiers' wives accompanied their husbands. It is unlikely many survived. Bernoyer admitted he would have gladly paid a pretty penny for the soup, but could not in good conscience accept the poor woman's hospitality. Then his servant brought him some disgusting white cheese that he could not think of eating. He sought out an officer's table, and was reprimanded and threatened with arrest for not being with the equipment detachment, as ordered. He explained that he had waited for them in Alexandria until the army was almost out of sight, and had thought it expedient to go on without them. It was then revealed to him that the Bedouin had massacred the sixty-two stragglers.

That evening the French set out again. While in town they had been able to sing some war ditties, and the Marseillaise. Now they had to fall silent again, Sergeant François remembered, for fear of the emirs. The surgeon D. J. Larrey recalled the increasingly dangerous terrain into which the French troops were venturing. "On departing Damanhur, the phalanx of the headquarters, where I was with the wounded, was assailed on all sides by a cavalry of numerous Bedouin and Mamluks. We would have no doubt succumbed without the prompt aid that we received from the division of Desaix, and without the vigilance and agile tactics of Colonel Dupas, who then commanded the army scouts. As it was, several individuals of our square were killed or wounded."[31] Bernoyer said that, next morning, he found out that nomads had captured a fine young officer and demanded a ransom. Bonaparte refused, saying that if he had to ransom everyone who fell into Bedouin hands between there and Cairo, his treasury would be bankrupted. Upon receiving this answer, the Bedouin, not wishing to feed and take care of their captive, blew out his brains in full view of the French. Bonaparte had ransomed others, so it is unclear why he declined in this instance. The price was small and the choice was fully the general's. Bernoyer, the civilian, was disgusted, and was not alone in his sentiments.

Moiret's division had barely arrived at Rahmaniya on 10 July when a few emirs appeared. Desaix's 15th Regiment of Dragoons set out after them.

3

THE FERMENT OF THE MIND

The French at Rahmaniya launched an immediate saber charge, but the speed of their enemy's Arabian steeds allowed them easily to caracole out of sword range. The dragoons, undaunted, charged again and again, but they found it difficult to achieve the kind of direct engagement that would allow them to devastate their nimble foe. The French suffered a few casualties in the ensuing skirmish, the Ottoman Egyptians about forty dead.

In the meantime, a convoy of Egyptian ships appeared from the north bearing provisions for Cairo, but the artillery of the French flotilla sent them scattering. While retreating, the Ottoman Egyptians ran into another French naval force coming from Alexandria, which attempted but failed to force them to surrender their provisions; they slipped away on the Nile. Bonaparte wrote to "Citizen General Dugua" that he had heard that General Desaix had had a brief encounter with a thousand Ottoman-Egyptian cavalrymen outside Rahmaniya, but that the latter had not acquitted themselves with much honor. He added, "I am only waiting for your arrival and that of launches with cannon to begin my grand march on Cairo."[1] It seems likely from Moiret's account that the initial encounter with the emirs at Rahmaniya was much smaller and more desultory than Bonaparte was led to believe.

As they approached Rahmaniya, the troops finally neared the sweet water of the Nile, though for strangers in unfamiliar territory its charms were attended with danger. The grenadier François Vigo-Roussillon recalled, "The entire army—men, horses and donkeys—threw themselves into that sought-after river. How delicious these healthful waters seemed to us! Nevertheless, many men were mutilated or carried away by crocodiles." He said that his unit proceeded up the left bank for about a league, then bivouacked in squares (no doubt keeping as much an eye out for the crocs as for enemy soldiers).[2]

Marmont described Rahmaniya as a village where the typical dwelling consisted of "a hut, the walls of which are made of earth or sometimes sun-baked bricks, four feet high. The size is proportional to the family. One can only enter hunched down—one cannot get in standing up straight. Typically there is a pretty structure above, gracefully constructed, serving as home to a great quantity of pigeons." He saw mounds of recently harvested lentils, beans, and onions piled outside these humble adobe homes. "Next to every village in Egypt, there is a date grove, trees of very great revenue (each date tree generates about seven francs per year). These groves are more or less extensive, depending on the population and wealth of the villages. They make for most agreeable scenery. The gracious tuft that crowns these trees gives them great elegance."[3] Marmont could not at that point appreciate the logic of these arrangements. In so hot a climate, having the foundation beneath the level of the ground helped cool the interior. And in a country where it almost never rains, it is an unnecessary expense to build from stone rather than from adobe.

Malus remembered that some town elders "came around" the French, with "Turkish banners." One does not know whether he means Ottoman flags or Islamic standards, or whether they were a sign of subtle defiance or a result of Bonaparte's propaganda that he had come on behalf of Sultan Selim III in Istanbul. Bernoyer also arrived in Rahmaniya, which lay on the west bank of the Nile, on 10 July. He had not heard about the encounter with the emirs, but recorded that the population of the city, as usual, promptly fled. The examples of Damanhur and Rahmaniya show the manner in which ordinary Egyptian women helped frustrate the French advance down the Nile by simply fleeing from the towns along the way, taking with them as much in the way of provisions as they could. They thus deprived the soldiers of food and sex. Women's willingness to desert their homes to deny the enemy any comfort showed not only a fear of the French, for that could equally well have been demonstrated by acquiescence, but a strategy of defiance. Soldiers stole flour from some deserted homes and made small biscuits of it that they devoured ravenously. Enraged French troops, faced with such empty and fairly useless towns, sometimes set destructive blazes in revenge. Bernoyer reported,

> Two hours later, on 10 July, we arrived at Rahmaniya, a city on the bank of the Nile. When the population of this town noticed us from afar, they took flight. The women uttered horrific ululations, kicking up clouds of dust in their haste, a sign of terror in that country. Despite the beauty of that city, a feeling of sadness and desolation reigned in the wake of the flight of its inhabitants. Faced

with this state of affairs, the army, finding no resources, believed they could avenge themselves by destroying it altogether by fire. What a sinister and frightful spectacle the half-consumed town offered.[4]

Dealing with recalcitrant populations in this brutal way was not something new for the French revolutionary army, nor had such violence been aimed since the early 1790s only at foreigners.

Such savage reprisals against uncooperative Egyptian peasants and townspeople recalled the way the revolutionary army dealt with the pro-monarchy, pro-Church revolt of the peasants of the Vendée in western France in the period 1793–1796. There, too, the revolutionary army had burned towns and villages and summarily executed rebels. A lower estimate for the number of persons the army killed over three years in this region of France (with a population then of 800,000) was 40,000, and some historians estimate it at many times that. Contemporary observers recognized the parallels. General Kléber's chief of staff, Adj. Gen. E. F. Damas, later wrote of the battles with the Bedouins and peasants as the French descended from Alexandria, "It is a more destructive war, on my soul! than that of La Vendée."[5] These tactics also recalled the brutal French repression of peasant revolts during the Italian campaign in 1796–1797.

A few historians on the right have argued that the Revolution was intrinsically doomed to commit the violence of the Terror and the repression of the Vendée because of its collectivist ideology, which ran roughshod over individual rights in the name of social philosopher Jean-Jacques Rousseau's conception of the general will.[6] That is, they said that the Revolution was from its inception totalitarian in inclination, because its leaders imagined the political good as unitary, rather than seeing society as pluralistic and made up of multiple, legitimate competing interests. This critique has generally been rejected as too simplistic a point of view that cannot account for the complexities of French politics in the 1790s. For one thing, the ideals of the Rights of Man and of the Citizen and the prescriptions for the working of political institutions promulgated in 1789 aimed at protecting individual rights and allowing for a pluralistic society. For another, the French state of the early to mid 1790s was not in fact centrally directed, as the totalitarian model would suggest. And how would one account for the relatively calm period between 1789 and 1792, or for the post-1794 turn toward liberalism by fervent supporters of the 1789 Revolution and its ideals, which led to the rise of the Directory? Nor were the leaders of the movements supporting a return to the Old Regime, such as the Vendée revolt, less brutal. If the violence of the French in the Vendée or in

Egypt were truly inherent in republican philosophy, then none of the committed Republicans members of the expedition would have criticized it. As we just
saw, Bernoyer was clearly already becoming uncomfortable with its extent.

The troops settled in at what was left of Rahmaniya to wait for the arrival
of two cannon-bearing launches, two half-galleys, and twenty transport ships
loaded with provisions and munitions. The 3rd Division arrived at last. In the
afternoon of 12 July Bonaparte passed in review of his troops and gave a
speech warning them that their sufferings were not at an end, that there were
more deserts to traverse and battles to fight before they arrived at Cairo,
"where we will have all the bread we want." Moiret remembered him also inspiring the men with the prospect of a quick return to France and then an assault on England. Appeals to civilizational glory had given away to the most
basic sort of motivation, the only one to which his army would have responded at that point. Bernoyer said he thought at the time that it had hardly
been necessary to come all the way to Africa to seek bread, if that was really
the goal.

Vigo-Roussillon, in his memoirs, plangently lamented the lack of foresight
displayed by the commander in chief with regard to the simplest preparations,
saying that the biscuits the army had brought down with them had spoiled.
"After having endured all the horrors of thirst, we were dying of hunger in the
midst of immense quantities of wheat."[7] Egypt had no windmills or watermills,
and the French had not brought along their small hand mills. They also lacked
wood to bake with. He lambasted Bonaparte: "How damaged the army was by
this unpardonable lack of foresight!" He said that just providing the soldiers
with canteens would have prevented immense amounts of suffering, and all the
deaths from dehydration and the suicides, on the march down. If, he said, dis-
tributing canteens at Toulon would have tipped enemies of the fleet's true destination he could have secretly loaded them on a ship and distributed them at
Alexandria.

Bonaparte boarded the scientists and some other noncombatants at Rahmaniya on his ships. The low Nile at that time of year had limited the French
river navy to smaller vessels, and they were shocked to find how shallow the fabled river was in places. The commander in chief intended to have the naval
forces he could deploy, and his troops on shore, keep within sight of one another. But strong Mediterranean winds blew the small ships toward Cairo much
faster than the troops could move, separating the two branches of the military.
The infantry now set out for Shubrakhit, on the evening of 12 July or in some
instances on the morning of the thirteenth. As they approached the town they

saw Ottoman-Egyptian cavalrymen hiding in ambush behind the dikes, preparing to attack.

One officer, Detroye, head of an engineering battalion, remembered the sight of the Ottoman-Egyptian forces. "Their troops, their banners, their baggage, covered the plain without any order. Their batteries and cannon-bearing longboats were placed advantageously in a bend. . . ."[8] The right wing of the French army at Shubrakhit was supported by the Nile, the center turned its back on it, and their left was behind the village of Shubrakhit. The commander in chief passed in front of the five divisions that composed his force and recommended that the officers give precise orders and that the soldiers attempt to keep silence until the cavalry charged in. Bonaparte ordered that the division of Desaix occupy the village of Shubrakhit. He had the division of Reynier take the right and that of Bon the left, flanking the village. The divisions of Dugua and Vial elongated the right of Reynier, stretching to the south toward the river.

A column of local cavalrymen rode out of a palm grove, intending to engage the left wing of the European army, forming a half-circle so as to envelop it. The Ottoman Egyptians called this maneuver "the circle."[9] An officer, Captain Deponthon, remembered, "Their numbers increased perceptibly, and they were ranged along a single line before the village of Shubrakhit, with their right supported by the river and their left extending toward us in the countryside. They appeared to be around 12,000 or 13,000 men, but they only had 3,000 on horse. The rest were their slaves or peasants, some of them armed with muskets, but most with staves."[10] The French maintained their formation, hoping the emirs would attack, since that would have been to their advantage, but they only detached a few cavalry units who came and pranced in front of the French until they attracted cannon fire. That went on until 8:00 A.M.

Bonaparte ordered his divisions to form infantry squares "in which they enclosed their equipment and the few cavalrymen the French possessed; they arranged themselves in stepped formation, such that each division flanked the other. The artillery occupied the center."[11] Vertray remembered, "We prepared ourselves to receive on our bayonets that superb cavalry, the valor of which was proverbial." Bonaparte ordered the cannon to fire when the emirs and their slave soldiers had gotten within range. The bouncing cannon balls terrified those at whom they were aimed, so that initially they dared not charge. The French also fired some exploding shells, to which the Ottoman Egyptians and their steeds were unaccustomed. Even when they recovered their nerve in the face of the artillery barrages of unaccustomed ferocity, the local horsemen found it impossible to penetrate the infantry squares. "The enemy," Moiret writes, "attempted several cavalry charges, but without success. They whirled on horseback and tried to find an opening in our ranks." They kept challenging the French, advancing on them and "making a movement to their left to turn us." But, Deponthon reported, "they were all astonished to meet the division of General Reynier that flanked our right, and the cannon of which dispersed their ranks pretty well. They met the same fate on our left, which was also flanked by the division of General Bon. As to the center, we took care to defend it."

The yare emirs typically overwhelmed an untrained infantry of townsmen or peasants by their fancy riding and fierce cavalry charges. The French had through drills discovered a new facility in switching from line to infantry squares, a formidable foe for any cavalry. In addition, the French had better artillery, with greater range, on their side, leaving the slave soldier horsemen unable to deploy their own cannon decisively to break up the French formations. The European troops brandished more powerful muskets, with greater range and accuracy than were at the disposal of the Ottoman Egyptians, giving them another advantage.

The local horsemen at one point thought they saw an opening between the Nile and the French army, and they poured into it. It was an ambush. They had hardly advanced before they received musket fire from hidden French troops. Many slave-soldier cavalrymen "were unhorsed and fell lifeless in the bloodied dust." The French infantry managed to seize the enemy cannons set up on the banks of the Nile and cart them off. Desperate, Murad Bey's cavalry now charged en masse, "thundering" toward the French "with the speed of lightning." The French artillerymen and musketeers let them get in range and then loosed a frightful barrage of shells and grapeshot, inflicting so much carnage that one eyewitness called it "butchery." The surviving Ottoman Egyptians now wheeled and retreated south, where they knew they could find the protection of their own gunboats. Vertray thought that this land battle lasted about four hours.

The quartermaster for uniforms, Bernoyer, had, like several other civilians, been given passage on a ship. His was commanded by Yaounsky, a Pole, and this vessel, like the rest of the flotilla, was carried willy-nilly south by the gales, unable to keep close to land or to support the army at the battle of Shubrakhit. The ship came upon an enemy encampment on the Nile. Yaounsky surveyed the shiny weaponry and opulent, silky costumes of the local soldiers with amusement and, laboring under the mistaken impression that the Egyptians were unfamiliar with artillery, remarked, "I would like to see them approach the cannon so as to enjoy their surprise when they see such an explosion." Bernoyer observed drolly that the surprise was not long in coming, but issued from other than the expected quarter. The sailors suddenly caught sight of three of Murad's cannons hidden along the Nile and realized they were in their sights. The crew panicked, with many throwing themselves in the water, rather than working together to sail the craft to the other shore and out of range. The cannons opened fire and smashed Yaounsky's ship to smithereens.

Seven Cairene gunboats appeared and engaged the French flotilla. The battle was now joined on the Nile itself. The French naval officer Jean-Baptiste Perrée, aboard the xebec *Cerf,* commanded the French flotilla. He had the ships under his command cast anchor and start blasting with their cannon. Al-Jabarti wrote that Commodore Halil Kürdlü, commander of the Nile navy, riposted with his own artillery. The victory remained in doubt for some time, but the Ottoman-Egyptian vessels appeared to have the upper hand. Perrée confessed to Bourrienne, "The Turks were doing us more harm than we were doing them." The Europeans were running out of ammunition and were still far from the army. Many of the passengers, scientists, and artists aboard ship found themselves having to take up arms to repulse the Egyptian sailors who attempted to board them. "All the French," Captain Say remarked, "were soldiers." The Ottoman Egyptians at one point seized the most powerful of the French brigs, along with several other vessels, and the sailors, Bourrienne said, "massacred the crews before our eyes, and with barbarous ferocity showed us the heads of the slaughtered men." It appeared that the French flotilla might well be destroyed, even though the main brig was recaptured in hard fighting.

Two things happened next to forestall a disaster for Bonaparte's river navy. First, al-Jabarti reported that at this point, the sail of Kürdlü's flagship caught fire. The flames spread to the hold where gunpowder was stored and caused it to explode, killing him and his sailors. Second, Perrée had managed, at considerable risk, to get word to Bonaparte of the dire straits he faced, and the commander in chief hurried the movement of his left flank along the Nile against the emirs and their slave soldiers, even though that ruined any chance for a pincer movement from the right flank that could have cut off and destroyed the cavalrymen, who therefore were enabled to flee. Bonaparte then undertook a forced march to rescue the flotilla. When the beylicate's second-in-command on the Nile saw the approach of the army, he weighed anchor and retreated toward Cairo. The French boarded the Egyptian ships that did not escape. Bourrienne confessed that the opposing navy "did us considerable injury, while on their part they suffered but little." Twenty Frenchmen were killed, and several wounded,

he says, and 1,500 cannon shots were fired during the action. He seemed unaware of the disaster aboard Commodore Kürdlü's flagship.

As for the land battle, the French estimates of Murad Bey's attacking force
of Mamluk cavalrymen range wildly, from a few hundred to four thousand. In
neither numbers could they have hoped to defeat thousands of French infantrymen backed by artillery. The 6,000 Ottoman-Egyptian cavalrymen, who had
until then proved sufficient to control some 4 million Egyptians, now had to
contend with the new dimensions of warfare introduced by the French Revolution and the advent of mass conscription. The reports of the battle of
Shubrakhit that reached Cairo cast Murad Bey and his cavalrymen in a poor
light. "It was only an hour," al-Jabarti observes, "before Murad Bey and those
with him were defeated. No proper battle occurred, only a skirmish with the
vanguard of his troops, such that few were killed on either side, though Murad
Bey's ships, with their provisions and instruments of war, were burned." He gave
more credit to naval artillery commander Halil Kürdlü, who perished in the
blaze, but who had risen like a lion to bombard the French vessels from his own
on the Nile. Al-Jabarti thought this naval disaster was key to Murad Bey's decision to withdraw to his base at Cairo and leave behind him many of his field
pieces and other heavy armaments.

Despite having defeated the emirs, many French soldiers found them
highly impressive. One wrote, "That first battle, which received the name 'the
Battle of Shubrakhit,' taught us that we would face, in Egypt, the best cavalry in
the world." Miot somewhat later attempted an assessment of his foes as fighting
men. "The Mamluks," he wrote, "taken from all the groups of the world, are ha-
bituated to the management of horses and arms from their tender infancy."[12]
They insisted that their horses be absolutely obedient and that they be able to
halt immediately; they employed for this purpose a curb bit with a long shank
and a curb chain against the animal's chin groove that came into action against
the jaw in a way that made disobedience unthinkable. They were also expert in
using their sharp stirrups as weapons in battle. "Among Europeans, who march
in order, these sorts of stirrups could not be employed, everyone would wound
his neighbor. But the Mamluks have no other line than that which indicates
courage or timidity." Their saddles allowed them to sit back, as they would on
the ground, and they could remain in them even if wounded. Their horses were
never used to carry baggage, but were rather purely warriors, like their masters,
and went to war only with battle gear. The clothing of the Cairene horsemen
was designed to blunt the slashes of a saber. They had pistols in their belts and
in their saddles carried more pistols, along with axes, sabers, a musket, and a

carbine (a short-barreled handheld firearm easier to shoot from horseback). All firearms were either attached to the man or the horse, giving him a facility with them and ensuring that he never had to put them away. Many wore coats of mail and helmets, which lacked visors but did have a bar to protect the face. Their sabers, though fine, were fragile, made for swift, direct slashing at the enemy, not for parrying sword thrusts (in the course of which they would soon break). It was the horse that evaded the opponent's blade.

Those local Egyptians who had not fled sought a modus vivendi with the newcomers. A village cleric brought Bonaparte his flag. The commander in chief told him, according to Malus, "Return to the mosque, thank God for having given victory to the most just cause." Bonaparte, elated, wrote General Menou an account of the battle. "The day before yesterday, we encountered and fought the enemy. Murad Bey and three or four thousand Mamluks on horseback, twenty artillery pieces, and some launches with cannon, desired to prevent us from getting past Shubrakhit. We took his cannons, and we killed or wounded some fifty of his men, among them many principal chiefs. A launch armed with cannon, with a Turk commander aboard, was sunk. From this day, the Mamluks have fled night and day. It is probable that we will not see them before Cairo."[13]

✤

The French had already conquered much of Buhayra province, and their columns were now daggers pointing at the capital. What was the society like over which Bonaparte aspired to rule? What exactly was he supplanting? Egypt was a largely Arabic-speaking society, but it was at that time under the nominal rule of the Ottoman Empire, with its capital in Istanbul (which had been Constantinople under the Romans and Byzantines). When the Ottomans conquered Egypt in 1517, they displaced a ruling caste of slave soldiers called Mamluks, most of them initially Christian youths from Circassia in the Caucasus, where they were taken as slaves when defeated on local battlegrounds. Medieval Muslim rulers often feared that if they depended too heavily on local tribal warriors, or on an army recruited from a pastoral population with strong clan ties, then these kinship groups would retain their own regional interests and would set the rulers aside in a coup. Rulers had often depended on imported slave soldiers, because slavery is a form of social death in which the individual is cut off from his family and place of origin. Slaves, they thought, would lack such thick networks of kinship and so would be more loyal to the sovereign. They were converted to Islam, and most lost close contact with their families abroad. Mamluks, despite starting as slaves, were often paid very handsomely and had the opportunity to rise high in the military, the bureaucracy, or the court. On reaching adulthood, they were awarded their freedom but remained loyal to their former master. Ironically, barracks full of slave soldiers often established new networks of friendship and professional contacts that allowed them in some instances to make successful revolts against their sultans. The Ayyubid dynasty in Egypt, the most famous member of which was Saladin, the nemesis of the crusaders, maintained a large number of Mamluks. In 1250, when their Ayyubid monarch died, and as Egypt faced a potential onslaught from invading Mongol hordes, the Mamluk soldiers made a military coup and took over the country and then ruled it themselves for two and a half centuries.

When, on 24 January 1517, Sultan Selim I of the Ottoman Empire swept into Cairo, he reduced it to an appendage of Istanbul.[14] The Ottomans incorporated Egypt into one of the largest empires in the history of the world, a flourishing trade emporium that linked India in the east with Istanbul via Iraq, and then Istanbul with Marseilles in the west across the Mediterranean. The empire at its height had thirty-two provinces, of which thirteen were Arabic-speaking, and Egypt, among the more populous and the most agriculturally productive, became its granary. The Ottomans subordinated the Circassian slave soldiers in Egypt to their own bureaucracy and their own system of military slavery. Istanbul famously established seven long-lasting regiments in Egypt. Five of them were cavalry regiments, and two were infantry. These regiments were staffed by a multicultural and polyglot elite, held together only by their loyalty to the sultan and Islam, their mastery of the Ottoman language (an aristocratic, Persian-inflected form of Turkish), and Ottoman military and bureaucratic techniques. They comprised Anatolian Turks, Bosnians, Albanians, converted Jews, Armenians, Georgians, and Circassians. Within the military, a strong divide existed between those soldiers originally recruited as slaves, who remained at the top of the hierarchy, and the free volunteers from the poor villages of Anatolia. Many Turkish-speaking soldiers from Anatolia could not live on their regular pay, and gradually they became artisans or shopkeepers in their spare time.

In the 1600s and 1700s Egypt emerged as the center of a vast and lucrative coffee trade.[15] Coffee trees probably came to Yemen from Ethiopia, and in the 1500s the people of Cairo first learned that brewing the beans and drinking the hot juice had become popular in Sanaa, especially among Sufi mystics seeking to stay up late for prayer and meditation. By the 1600s, the custom of coffee-drinking had spread beyond the mystics to the general public, and coffeehouses opened all over the Ottoman Empire, often to the dismay of authoritarian sultans and governors who feared them as places where sedition might brew in heated conversations as easily as a thick mocha blend. Ottoman attempts to ban coffee or coffeehouses, however, failed miserably. In the mid-to-late 1600s, a few coffeehouses began to be opened in Europe. European monarchs initially dreaded them as much as had the sultans. The first was founded in Paris in 1671. The Café Le Procope, set up in the French capital in 1689, later became a center for intellectual discussion and revolutionary ideas. Cairo was among the major entrepôts for marketing coffee in the Ottoman Empire and to Europe. It is tempting to observe in jest that, if indeed the rise of the coffeehouse had anything to do with the coming of the French Revolution, it may be that Egyptian coffee merchants inadvertently set in train the caffeinated, fevered discussions that overthrew the Old Regime and ultimately sent a French fleet on its way to Alexandria.

✦

The Ottoman Egyptians were increasingly drawn into relations with Europe. In the 1720s, one Çerkes Mehmed Bey struggled for control of Egypt with Zülfikar Bey. Çerkes lost the fight and set out for Istanbul to intrigue for imperial support. He was, however, distracted by another opportunity. He escaped via the North African coast, reaching Algeria, and then booked passage to Trieste. He attempted to intrigue with Charles VI (1711–1740) of the Austrian Empire, but the Ottoman sultan sent vehement protestations to Vienna. As a result, Çerkes Mehmed Bey was forced to return to North Africa, landing at Tripoli in Libya. He still had ambitions to build an army and invade Egypt. He gathered his forces and marched on Cairo, but met defeat at the hands of a rival, Ali Bey Qatamish. While trying to get away, he fell into the marsh over which he had sought to reign, and drowned.[16]

While the Austrians had declined to pursue the opportunity laid before them, other European powers were tempted by an Egyptian alliance. Because many of the slave soldiers were captured in Georgia in the Caucasus, some knew Russian and attempted to establish diplomatic and military ties with the government of Catherine the Great (1762–1796). For an eighteenth-century European capital to eye the Nile Valley with interest was hardly unprecedented.

During the eighteenth century, the Georgian houses of slave soldiers in Egypt grew in importance, proving able to subordinate the seven Ottoman regiments and establishing control over the lucrative coffee trade. An Ottoman-Egyptian slave soldier, Ali Bey al-Kabir, rebelled in the 1760s and 1770s, attempting to undermine the sultan's authority by asserting power in the Red Sea and opening it to European commerce, as well as by invading

Syria. His rebellion ended, but after a while the beys of Cairo again ceased paying tribute to the Ottoman sultan, provoking an Ottoman invasion in 1786 that
halted the province's slide toward autonomy. Although in earlier decades we
historians tended to write of the eighteenth century as a time of the resurgence
of Mamluk government in Egypt, as though the old state of the 1200s through
the 1400s had been revived, we now know that this way of speaking is inaccurate. The Ottomans had endowed Egypt, however independent it sometimes
became, with their own institutions, including their distinctive form of slave
soldiery. For this reason, it is more accurate to call the eighteenth-century ruling elite "Ottoman Egyptians." Arabic chronicles of the time often called them
"ghuz," a reference to the Oghuz Turkic tribe, which also implied that they
were best seen as Ottomans (a Turkic dynasty). Most gained fluency in both
Ottoman Turkish and Arabic, while retaining their knowledge of Caucasian
languages such as Georgian and Circassian. Not all of the emirs had a slave-
soldier background, and some were Arabic-speaking Egyptians.

The eighteenth century was not kind to Egypt. Between 1740 and 1798,
Egyptian society went into a tailspin, its economy generally bad; droughts were
prolonged, the Nile floods low, and outbreaks of plague and other diseases frequent. The slave-soldier houses fought fierce and constant battles with one another, and consequently raised urban taxes to levels that produced misery. Now
a new catastrophe had struck, in the form of Bonaparte's plans to bestow liberty
on Egypt.

✢

The French army resumed its progress south. From the edges of Buhayra
province to Cairo is about eighty-five miles. Vigo-Roussillon recalled, "The army
advanced, just as it had the day before, marching in deep-order squares—that is to
say, six ranks deep. The artillery was in the gaps between the battalions."[17] He said
that this formation had great advantages for fighting an enterprising enemy cavalry, but one that lacked mobile artillery. "When one wanted to form columns for
an attack, the first three ranks separated out and went ahead, and the three others
kept their formation and presented a reserve formed of squares."

Bonaparte at this point allowed his army to march near the Nile, to guarantee access to fresh water. Bread, on the other hand, was scarce, and the soldiers
had to adopt the Egyptian peasant cuisine of fava beans (*ful*). Sometimes the
French soldiers got water buffalo meat, though on occasion horse meat had to
be substituted. They marched until 16 July without encountering any more Ottoman-Egyptian soldiers, though the Bedouin dogged them mercilessly and

consistently cut off their communications with the units behind them and with Alexandria. The peasants in the villages along the way mostly disappeared, with their livestock, though they occasionally offered resistance. The soldiers, hungry and desperate, often pillaged the small villages they came upon, despite their officers' efforts to prevent it. The fastidious Captain Moiret, who had once almost become a priest, says that the officers, as gentlemen, did not feel it right to partake of stolen chickens, and that they therefore suffered more than their men, being restricted in their diet to small portions of beans. Many memoirists talked of eating nothing but watermelons. Another officer recalled, "We made war on pigeons."[18] Bonaparte himself bivouacked among his miserable troops, dining with his fellow officers on lentils. All were exhausted and perpetually hungry and thirsty as they marched up the Nile Valley in the full heat of mid-July, harassed by an alarmed and often brutalized local population.

Bonaparte in his memoirs remarked that the troops were very nearly in a mutinous mood and that "the evil was in the ferment of the mind." He said that a rumor grew up that there was no splendid capital city, Grand Cairo, only an assemblage of adobe huts such as they had seen at Damanhur, where it was "impossible to live." He remembered that in the evening the soldiers talked politics and cursed the Directory for "transporting" them. They blamed the scientists and artists who so minutely examined the Egyptian antiquities they found along the way for having thought up the harebrained scheme of coming to Egypt, and continually ribbed them, even coming to employ the word "savant" or "scientist" to refer to their donkeys.

Pelleport recalled that on 15 July, one of the divisions, suffocating in a particularly strong desert wind, went beyond merely complaining and actually refused to obey orders. Bonaparte was alerted and rode up to that division, ordering them to form an infantry square. He placed himself in the middle and addressed them, thusly: "Courage on the field of battle is insufficient to make a good soldier. It requires, as well, the courage to face fatigue and privation. Suppose I had the intention of journeying to Asia after the conquest of Egypt? To march in the traces of Alexander, I would need to have his soldiers."[19] The division, Pelleport said, resumed its march without another word.

Behind the resentments of the troops lay real misery. "One saw many soldiers," Moiret says, "fall dead of hunger and fatigue, and many others blew out their brains from despair. . . . A pair of brothers embraced one another and threw themselves into the Nile." On the seventeenth, the soldiers' precious sleep was interrupted by an Ottoman-Egyptian raid, which they easily repulsed. They then resumed the scalding march toward the capital. Each man had a ration of only three biscuits per day. An enemy ship at one point was captured and provided a supplement of biscuits "of the very worst quality, very dirty, kneaded with awful flour, mixed with old grease that even the rats avoided." Moiret observes, "One would have had to be in our position to have the courage to eat them." He divided them into four portions, making a small meal of each during the day, soaking them in water first to soften them and reduce their saltiness.

✤

At the approach of the French, who were advancing up the west bank of the Nile, Cairo's elite had met and made preparations. Ottoman Viceroy Ebu Bekir Pasha, along with local paramount leader Ibrahim Bey and a group of administrators and clerics, decided to make a stand at the riverine port of Bulaq, on the east bank. They built barricades and set up cannon pointing north in case any French troops came down on the east bank, and they mobilized Bedouins to take up positions at Shubra and elsewhere, just below Bulaq. They called all able-bodied men to the barricades and declared holy war on the advancing infidels.[20] Cairo's rulers began a search for weapons in the houses of European merchants and other residents. They also put local Christians, whether Greek Orthodox or native Copts or Syrians, under surveillance. Suspicion spread among the city's Muslim inhabitants that the Christians were disloyal to the Ottoman Empire. Al-Jabarti was convinced that rioters would have slaughtered the Christians had the authorities not restrained them.

Al-Jabarti noted that on Tuesday (17 July) the emirs ordered that the general populace begin moving to the fortifications. The crafts guilds that organized most urban workers took up a contribution so as to be able to provide tents for the guildsmen who went to Bulaq. Other Cairenes donated money so as to be able to outfit Syrian and North African troops, who therefore functioned as popularly funded militias. The Sufi mystics and dervishes raised banners in the streets, played musical instruments, and chanted love poems to God. Umar Makram, the leader of the caste of notables (*ashraf*) who claimed descent from the Prophet Muhammad, staged a sort of parade. He "went up to the Citadel and brought down from it a big banner popularly called the Prophet's Banner. He unfolded it and carried it from the Citadel to Bulaq. In front of him and around him were thousands of people with clubs and sticks, cheering and shouting, 'God is great!'"[21] The relic of the Prophet was intended to bestow his blessing, or *baraka*, on the beleaguered capital. The crowd beat on drums and played pipes and waved flags, for all the world, Darendeli wrote, as though they were hosting a traditional Egyptian wedding. Soon most of the city's able-bodied men were gathered in Bulaq as defenders of the city, and only women and children remained huddled in the city's buildings. The streets were deserted. "The markets were yellow and the roads dusty from not being swept and sprinkled."

The country's elite further advised Murad Bey to establish his fortifications at Imbaba on the west bank, north of Giza. There he had barricades constructed stretching up to a place called Bashtil, undertaking it with officers of the rank of *sanjak* and *amir*, as well as other beys such as his associates Ali Pasha and Nasuh Pasha. Al-Jabarti described the scene: "They brought the big ships and the galleons which had been constructed in Giza, anchored them at Imbaba, manned them, and equipped them with guns. The western and the eastern river banks filled with guns, soldiers, barricades, cavalry, and infantry." Murad called to himself the Bedouin tribes of Egypt, al-Khabariya, al-Qi'an, Awlad 'Ali, al-Hanadi and others to help expand his cavalry. The beys also began secreting their treasures in small, nondescript safe houses, some of them in provincial towns. This transfer of gold, jewelry, and other valuables had to be accomplished on the backs of animal trains, and could not be kept entirely secret from the Cairo public, which was gripped with panic. "The rich and those of means prepared for flight. If the *amir*s had not prevented them from this, rebuked them, and intimidated those who wanted to leave, not one would have stayed in Cairo."

In provincial towns, the Egyptian chronicler recalled, order began breaking down. Townspeople began killing and looting one another, and Bedouin began raiding into once well-defended settlements. "The whole of Egypt plunged into a state of murder, plunder, terror on the roads, rise of evil stealing, spoiling of the fields, and innumerable other kinds of corruption," lamented al-Jabarti. The disorder broke out behind French lines as well, isolating the French-dominated ports of Alexandria and Rosetta on the coast from the bulk of the army. Villiers du Terrage, in nearby Rosetta, recorded in his journal for 16 July, "We learned from the troops who arrived yesterday that there had been a small uprising at Alexandria. The inhabitants fired from the windows; an artilleryman was wounded." General Kléber, with 2,000 troops, was able to restore control in the port. But the interior was a no-man's land for the French. Bonaparte had not garrisoned the western entrepôt of Damanhur after the French passed through it. He left it to Kléber in Alexandria to have it more permanently subdued, using in part an Arabic-speaking Maltese legion that would be able to communicate with local Egyptians. The Maltese proved difficult to organize or train, however, so that Kléber gave up on sending most of them, and he dispatched a General Dumuy to secure Damanhur with some infantry companies and twenty

cavalrymen from the 3rd Demi-Brigade.²² When Dumuy approached Damanhur on the seventeenth, the people of the city launched an armed insurrection.
With the aid of allied mounted Bedouin of the area, they beat off the small
French force and killed twenty French soldiers. Dumuy and his men straggled
back to Alexandria, having grossly underestimated the size of the force that it
would take to vanquish and hold Damanhur permanently. Egyptians had already
mounted a rebellion against French rule even before the latter reached Cairo.
Kléber, faced with increased encroachments, clearly felt under siege. He wrote
to General Menou in Rosetta, "I have heard nothing of the army. . . . I am surrounded by Bedouin Arabs. The experience of Dumuy at Damanhur has made
them audacious. Yesterday we ran through 43 of them with our sabers only half
a league from the city." Behind the main French lines advancing on Cairo, the
garrisons left behind were not so much victorious as beleaguered.

❧

Meanwhile, the French army advancing up the Nile to the capital continued to
meet opposition from villagers and Bedouin. Even some peasant women offered
violence to the conquering French. Bernoyer observed, as the army neared
Cairo on 16 July, that "at the approaches to a village, an aide-de-camp was killed
when he got a bit too far ahead. A woman, her child in her arms, had the savage
cruelty to put out his eyes with her scissors. Maj. Gen. Berthier had her shot on
the spot, and returned the infant to the hands of a peasant."²³ Here the weapon
used in the assault is appropriate to the gender of the assailant, a pair of scissors
such as women used for domestic tailoring, and the baby is even still in her arms
as she strikes. Bernoyer presented a horrific image of rebellious peasant mother-
hood, monstrous and mutilating in its resistance to colonial subjugation.

The unit of Sergeant François bivouacked at the village of al-Kanqa on July
18. On the way there, he said, some officers had fallen behind to relieve themselves and were captured by Bedouin. This tribe already had one French captive, and they took their new acquisitions to the camp where they were holding
him. Busy with their new charges, however, they neglected to keep their first
prisoner properly guarded, and he escaped, making his way to Bonaparte and
revealing the location of the camp. Bonaparte, François wrote, sent Venture de
Paradis with a ransom of "500 Spanish piasters" (silver coinage) and a native
guide to the sheikh of the tribe. On their arrival, Venture held a parlay with the
chieftain and ultimately passed the money to him in full view of the other tribesmen. "The rest of the tribe came and began quarrelling." The sheikh, so as to
halt the fracas, took out his pistol and shot the officer in whom Bonaparte had

shown the greatest interest, named Desnanots. He then returned the ransom, saying he did not think he should keep it, since it had become useless. Venture left without the prisoners, whose fate remained unknown.[24] The most likely explanation of this story is there were not enough discrete coins to go around, and the sheikh knew the tribesmen would each want a share. If he could not make change, some would inevitably feel slighted and it would turn into infighting and feuds (disgruntled tribe members often split off if they felt badly treated). The anecdote says something about the way some Bedouin chieftains valued social peace within the tribe more than they did mere symbolic wealth.

Many French troops spent 18 July at the palm-grove oasis of Wardan. Bonaparte had taken the precaution of sending envoys ahead to reassure the inhabitants, who therefore did not flee in the customary numbers. From them, the troops were able to procure some provisions. They were able to mill some wheat into flour and bake their own bread, and they were refreshed by watermelon and coconut juice, available in enormous quantities. They also had a feast for the eyes. Moiret, observed, "In all the villages one commonly sees girls of from twelve to fourteen years going entirely nude. It is poverty that reduces them to this indecent state that so strongly shocks our mores and usages."[25] Moiret's Orient was clearly not the Middle East of today. Village mores in late eighteenth-century Egypt about prepubescent nudity (children of neither sex wore much clothing in June) seem not so different from those in parts of sub-Saharan Africa into the twentieth century. Even in urban literate society, prepubescent girls were not required in Islamic law to veil their faces, prompting puzzled Muslims to ask their medieval jurists why a precociously attractive thirteen-year-old need not veil but an eighty-year old woman did have to. Formal Muslim law and custom, of course, did view public nudity with horror. The remote, illiterate villagers clearly were untouched by such strictures coming out of the great mosques of the capital. It may well be that the increasing attention in subsequent times to veiling women and even girls in modern Muslim societies is intimately linked to feelings of humiliation caused by having foreign colonial administrators, troops, and other non-Muslims around in positions of local power.[26]

In Wardan, some of the troops received a boon when they rediscovered the local villagers' preference for the buttons off their uniforms instead of coins. Bernoyer, with his tailor's eye, noted that the soldiers thenceforth tore off their buttons to use for money but that many were disappointed to find that it was only the uniforms of the artillerymen that yielded acceptable currency, since these were entirely copper, while the others' buttons had wood in them. Bernoyer's observation suggests that they trusted and wanted pure copper "coins." For peasants, copper coins were in small enough denominations actually to be useful in daily shopping. Sewing coins into clothing was a common practice among rural and Bedouin women, so they probably assumed that the artillerymen were doing the same. Some have suggested that the villagers feared that accepting European coins would mark them as collaborators if the Mamluks came back. But research in eighteenth-century Egyptian court records has shown that foreign coins were already circulating in Egyptian provinces, and their possession could therefore hardly have been viewed as treasonous.[27]

The subsequently somewhat disheveled artillerymen smilingly cashed in without asking why or wherefore. During this rare day of rest, Bonaparte mixed with the ranks and spoke familiarly with the troops, allowing them to complain about their profound misery. He attempted to give them heart by promising them feasts in Cairo, once they took it, adding meat, wine, sugar, and mocha coffee to his earlier pledge of bread as inducements. Whether this move from promising an imagined bakery to evoking the fare in a fine French restaurant was persuasive is hard to know, though it speaks volumes about what Bonaparte thought would motivate his troops. Moiret wrote, "For want of anything better, we contented ourselves with his promises."[28]

Two incidents from these days speak to the realities of incipient French power in Egypt. While at Wardan the French found a cache of manuscripts closed up in a pigeon loft. Although the secular, revolutionary army did not have formal chaplains, somehow there was a Father Sicard among them (perhaps he was simply a soldier or officer who had trained for the priesthood). He insisted that these be burned on the grounds that they were books of magic. Also around this time, an army storekeeper was sent to a neighboring village to buy wheat, and while there he and his servant were attacked by Bedouin and burned at a tree. The French found their bodies still smoldering. Bonaparte was so enraged that he ordered the village burned and all its inhabitants shot or put to the sword. Like the partial torching of Rahmaniya, this collective punishment of peasants for the actions of Bedouin was irrational, a simple exercise in terror. The earlier destruction of precious manuscripts, moreover, casts further large doubts upon the claims Bonaparte had made for the contribution of his assault on Egypt to the building up of civilizational glory. That a priest should have been allowed to engage in such a superstitious auto-da-fé by the Republican army also speaks loudly to the hardy persistence of pre-Enlightenment ways of thinking among these self-proclaimed worshippers of Reason.

Sergeant François wrote of the next day, July 19, "Our generals had sent many battalions into the villages along the banks of the Nile."[29] At one of them,

Shum, 1,800 armed men had assembled to prevent the entry of the 9th and the 85th demi-brigades of the division of Reynier. François served as a scout for that expedition. He said that all the inhabitants of the village had assembled and had refused to provide supplies to the French. Then they began firing on the foreigners. General Cambise, their commander, ordered his men to charge. "We scaled the walls and entered it, all the while firing into those crowds. We killed about 900 men, not counting the women and children, who remained in their habitations, to which we set fire with our musketry and artillery. Once the village was taken, we gathered up everything we found—camels, donkeys, horses, eggs, cows, mutton. . . ." He added, "Before leaving that village, we finished burning the rest of the houses, or rather the huts, so as to provide a terrible object lesson to these half-savage and barbarous people." He maintained that that evening many village headmen came to submit to the French generals and to offer their services, "which were accepted." He said, "Our generals distributed to them the proclamation of Bonaparte to the people of Egypt." The account of François assumes a linear progression, from invasion to resistance to terror to submission and acceptance. In fact, what had begun was a cycle in which invasion, insurgency, terror, and peaceful exchange would alternate with one another. The cycle had to do with occupation and resistance rather than with a "clash of civilizations." When Egypt later occupied the Sudan or Syria, it often met resistance, as well.

After one or two days of rest, depending on when they arrived, the French columns set out from Wardan, initially refreshed, but soon they were breathing "flaming air" again and losing more men to dehydration, consequent renal failure, and suicide. "Most of the villages through which the army passed," François recounted, "had been abandoned by their inhabitants." On 21 July the French first caught sight of the awesome pyramids, then still half-buried in mounds of sand and of unknown significance, though some suspected their function as tombs of the pharaohs. The Egyptian Muslims called the nearby Sphinx Abu al-Hul, the "father of fear," regarding it as an ancient monument to some unspeakable horror. The soldiers had not gone far when they encountered the advance scouts of Murad Bey. The Europeans drove the Ottoman Egyptians before them, from village to village. Around 10 A.M., they began to discover the main body of the beylicate's army. Bonaparte addressed his troops: "Soldiers! From the heights of these pyramids, forty centuries are looking down on you."

4

GRAND CAIRO

*H*ungry, thirsty, and exhausted on the march away from Wardan, Bonaparte's army now had to fight the enemy on his terrain.[1] "The heat suffocated us and took away our breath," Moiret panted. His division had marched since the morning in a square, and there was no way a soldier might detach himself from it so as to run to the nearby Nile for a sip of fresh water. Bonaparte and his generals had imposed this discipline of marching in formation quite deliberately, since they did not want their soldiers near the Nile, which the Ottoman Egyptians controlled. Some unfortunates, unable to bear the thirst, did break ranks and run to the river. They had barely taken a few gulps when the enemy appeared, and they had hastily to rejoin their lines.

Bonaparte's grand words about forty centuries of history had gone over their heads, and Adjutant-Major Lieutenant Pierre Pelleport admitted as much, "It was Greek to most of our comrades." They did know that their bravery and ability to ignore their discomfort were about to be tested. Their army, an Enlightenment juggernaut, consisted of two huge squares, each six lines of infantrymen deep, with the artillery advancing between the squares. Captain Jean-Baptiste Vertray wrote that the few cavalry divisions were at the beginning inside the infantry squares, where they were protected from the intrepid Ottoman-Egyptian horsemen but remained available to go on the attack at the right opportunity.

The cavalry under Murad Bey had taken up a strong position in the village of Imbaba behind a formidable battery of artillery. Bonaparte knew that the cannon of his enemies were not mounted on mobile carriages, and being fixed fatally limited their utility. At the backs of the Ottoman-Egyptian horsemen was the river, across which lay Cairo proper, where Ibrahim Bey and his retainers were similarly entrenched along the banks at Shubra and Bulaq.

In the city, a panicked population either volunteered to fight alongside the emirs, or stayed home, or tried to flee on the increasingly insecure roads. Al-Jabarti lamented that the markets were abandoned and accumulating dust and that burglars and hooligans were the only ones doing any business. In the countryside, many peasants believed Bonaparte's propaganda that he had been sent by the Ottoman sultan. On the Nile itself, the big galleons of the local riverine navy, manufactured at Giza, had gathered.

The brilliance of the gold- and silver-embroidered costumes and brightly polished arms of the emirs reflected blinding arcs of sunshine into the eyes of the French. Mounted on their swift Arabians, each was armed to the teeth, with five or six ivory-handled and jewel-encrusted pistols in his belt. Their curved sabers, of Damascene steel and sharp as razors, could decapitate an enemy in a single well-executed move. Moiret thought them highly imposing as they caracoled before their camp. It seemed clear to him from their maneuvers that they intended to go on the offensive, and the French prepared to receive them.

In a memo to the Directory penned only three days later, Bonaparte wrote, "I ordered the divisions of generals Desaix and Reynier to take up a position on the right, between Giza and Imbaba, in such a manner as to cut off the enemy from communication with Upper Egypt, which was his natural retreat."[2] After 3:00 P.M., Murad Bey, the head of an elite cavalry corps, flew at the divisions of Reynier and Desaix with thousands of horsemen "as fast as lightning," Bonaparte recalled. They appear very nearly to have taken the French unawares. The rest of the Egyptian army feigned an attack on the main body of the French so as to prevent other divisions from going to their succor.

At the approach of the local horsemen, General Reynier gave the command, Vertray remembered, "and in the blink of an eye, we were arranged in a square six men deep, ready to withstand the shock. This movement was executed with a precision and coolness under fire that was truly remarkable." Then French artillerymen opened up on the attackers at long range (something the emirs and their Mamluks, unaccustomed to firearms used at anything more than medium range, did not expect). Many of the charging cavalrymen wheeled and retreated at the first shell. Across the river in the old city, the steady discharge of French muskets sounded to al-Jabarti like "a cauldron boiling on a crackling fire." Murad then attempted to come around and take the French from behind, but the divisions had already formed into squares bristling with "a rampart of bayonets" that he found impenetrable, even before the muskets began firing. As long as the French maintained their discipline and kept the infantry squares intact, they were invulnerable to the cavalry charges. If any number had broken ranks, the opposing cavalry could then have cut them down and attacked the other sides of the broken squares.

Bonaparte had the division of General Dugua advance on the bulk of the Ottoman-Egyptian army, placing his artillery between the Nile and Reynier. The commander in chief recalled, "We let them approach within 50 feet and then greeted them with a hail of balls and grapeshot that caused a large number of them to fall on the field of battle. They threw themselves into the gap between the two divisions, where they took double fire that achieved their defeat." Murad's soldiers dropped like ripe dates from a shaken palm tree, either felled by the muskets of the squares or by the artillery. Those who survived the fusillade hastily retreated. Some 1500 Ottoman Egyptians and a similar number of peasants were still resisting in Imbaba proper.

Bonaparte ordered the division of General Bon, then along the Nile, "to take itself off and attack the entrenchments" He had General Bon put his troops between the emirs coming to make a charge, and those making a stand at Imbaba. His goal, he said, was "to prevent the cavalry from entering; to cut off the retreat of those at the retrenchment; and, if necessary, to attack the village from the left." Bonaparte recalled that the first unit of each battalion "ranged themselves in attack columns, while the second and third retained the same position, continuing to form infantry squares." The latter advanced to support the attack columns. He said that the attack columns led by General Rampon "threw themselves at the retrenchments with their usual impetuousness, despite taking a great amount of artillery fire, while the Ottoman Egyptians made a charge." The valiant warriors galloped out, their satin shirts iridescent. The French abruptly halted, formed a front line, and received them with bayonets fixed to barrels that let rip a cloud of balls. The defenders watched with alarm as their routes of communication were progressively cut off and they gradually lost even the possibility of a retreat. The French offered them the opportunity to surrender. The Ottoman Egyptians refused to answer, preferring death.

The French officers had difficulty restraining their troops during the negotiations, and when the talks broke down, the enraged infantry rushed at Imbaba, first of all targeting the Ottoman-Egyptian artillerymen, bayoneting them and capturing the cannon. The local soldiers fled and found themselves cut off by the French right flank, which met them with a vicious fusillade. Those who did not fall dead now threw themselves in the Nile, seeking to swim over to join Ibrahim's forces. Many drowned or were shot in the water by the French. The Europeans captured forty artillery pieces, numerous pieces of baggage, many munitions, and four hundred camels loaded with gold and silver. For days afterward, French troops who remained on the west bank fished bodies out the Nile and went through their pockets for pieces of gold. Few French casualties were taken, perhaps 30 killed and 260 wounded. The Ottoman Egyptians suffered between 800 and 1,600 dead. Bonaparte said that many of the great beys were wounded, including Murad Bey, who was injured in the cheek. Moiret saw nothing wrong with the Ottoman Egyptians' fighting spirit or bravery; if they had been more familiar with European tactics, he admitted, they could have made the French pay dearly for their victory.

In his letter to the Directory, Bonaparte grandiosely named the contest the Battle of the Pyramids, even though these monuments were only faintly visible from Imbaba. The commander in chief wrote to the Directory of his new possession, "All the opulence of these people is in their horses and their armaments. Their houses are pitiable. It is difficult to find a land that is more fertile and a people more poverty-stricken, more ignorant, or more brutalized. They prefer the button of one of our soldiers to a six-franc coin." As others have observed, the Romantic-era painters who rendered this victory at the Battle of the Pyramids neglected to depict the artillerymen with coats buttonless and undone.

Major General Berthier boasted, "No battle had ever better proved the superiority of European tactics over those of the Orientals, of disciplined courage over chaotic bravura." One would not wish to in any way diminish the contribution of the tacticians, but it should not be forgotten that France had many advantages in the contest. In 1798, France's population was about 28 million, so that the French had a more than five-to-one manpower superiority over the Egyptians. Of course, what mattered was the number of French military men in Egypt. Even there, they were superior in the numbers that counted. The French army at Imbaba numbered some 28,000. Many of these troops had been tested by fire in the Italian campaigns. Archival documentation shows that the seven Ottoman regiments comprised a little over 18,000 troops in 1797, with about 8,000 of these being cavalry and 10,000 infantry. In addition, the slave-soldier "houses" grouped many cavalrymen who stood outside the old regimental system and so are not being counted here. But Murad and Ibrahim unwisely divided their forces, with Ibrahim keeping half for a second stand at Bulaq. At Imbaba, only a few thousand emirs and slave soldiers stood against the French in this battle. In addition, the beys summoned perhaps 3,000 allied Bedouin irregulars, along with as many as 20,000 untrained and poorly armed Egyptian peasants and townsmen, the latter little more than cannon fodder.[3] With regard to professional soldiers, the French far outnumbered the soldiers and cavalrymen gathered at Imbaba, by a factor of at least four to one.

Moreover, French artillery and muskets were indisputably far more powerful and had far greater range than those in the hands of the Egyptians. The French infantry squares, equipped with bayonets, proved virtually impenetrable to any cavalry not backed by even more powerful artillery.[4] A French intellectual later reported, "The Mamluks said of the French army, which marches in tight squares, that the French are linked with one another, and that they march like the pyramids."[5] Bonaparte's skill is not debatable, since his brilliance as an operational commander gave him victories over many organized European armies in the succeeding decade and a half as well. Finally, the emirs and the Egyptian populace generally were not at the height of their form in 1798. The eighteenth century had been a disaster for the country, with annual Nile flood waters often too low, drought, urban over-taxation, and internecine wars among the beys.

General Desaix pursued Murad Bey's retreating forces to near Giza, where the two fought a pitched battle that lasted for two hours, until nightfall. That is where Murad was wounded in the face and his cavalry was decisively defeated. He and his men decided to flee. Initially, they wanted to take a large galleon with them, but the Nile was low and it ran aground. Since it contained a big store of arms and ammunition, Murad set it afire to deny it to the French. Flames leapt high into the evening sky, further terrifying the Cairo populace. Murad and his men then escaped into the southern desert.

The French now controlled the west bank of the Nile, and prepared to cross over to Cairo. They feared they would face a determined resistance from Ibrahim Bey's contingents, ensconced on the other bank. But the capital's remaining soldiers had decided that they could not prevail against the French in conventional combat, and they set about burning merchant boats and their fine residences to deny them to the enemy and then deserted the capital. In less than a month, the French had conquered all of Lower Egypt and overthrown the Ottoman beylicate.

Al-Jabarti said that hordes of civilians, thinking that the burning vessels were the result of vindictive French vandalism, ran from Bulaq "like waves of the sea," kicking up dust and having it blown into their eyes by the strong winds that prevailed that day. Women wailed from their balconies. Ibrahim Bey abandoned his fortifications at Bulaq and sent for his wives, as did the officers in his entourage. "Whoever could do so, had his wife or daughter ride, while he walked, but most of the women exited unveiled and on foot, their children on their shoulders, crying in the black of night."[6] Al-Jabarti was probably speaking of women of the notable class, for whom being forced to walk in the street unveiled in public was a humiliation almost as bad as having to flee their homes.

Notable clerics like Abdullah al-Sharqawi and Sayyid Khalil al-Bakri also gathered up their women and effects and streamed out of the city without having any idea of their destination. Many alarmed commoners followed them. The price of carriage skyrocketed.

The panicked city folk carrying all their valuables made easy pickings for the Bedouin tribes waiting outside the gates, and one result of the French invasion was surely a vast transfer of movable wealth from the urban economy to the pastoralists. "The money and treasure that left Cairo during this night was certainly twice as much as what stayed behind. Most of the money was with the *amirs* [emirs] and the dignitaries and their women folk, and the beduins took it all." Al-Jabarti described crowds of the naked and destitute, having been picked clean, moving into the countryside. Others, remaining behind, saw an opportunity in the empty dwellings. Captain Say reported that, freed from "the despotism of the Mamluks," the "people went to the mansions of the beys, which they burned or pillaged."[7] The extent of burning and pillaging was clearly limited, since the French later moved into those mansions quite happily. The contemporary Ottoman chronicler Izzet Hasan Darendeli wrote that Cairo was emptied of the bulk of its population, becoming little more than a ghost town, making the work of the plunderers easier. The looters pillaged the mansions of Ibrahim Bey and Murad Bey in the posh Qawsun area and then set them afire.

Days later, on 24 July, a substantial contingent of the French army flowed into the subdued capital at noon, passing before the crowds. All eyes went, the junior cavalry officer Desvernois recalled, to Bonaparte, locally now referred to as "the Great Sultan." He said that the Cairenes seemed to admire the French cavalry and sappers, with their handsome beards. But, he remarked, they paid no attention to the infantrymen "because of the contempt in which they held . . . the bulk of the Ottoman infantry." The French found, as well, over time, that being clean-shaven signaled slave status. When young Mamluks were manumitted, they were allowed to grow beards, which also signaled their sexual maturity. To gain respect, the French later on had at least to maintain a mustache.

Bonaparte took for his residence the mansion of Alfi Bey at Azbakiya Square. Auguste Marmont, an aide de camp of Bonaparte, recalled that Cairo "appeared to me very beautiful for a Turkish city. The houses, built of stone, rose high, amid very narrow streets, making it appear densely populated. The great squares, around which the mansions of the principal beys had been constructed, served as embellishments. At length, the entire tableau struck us as much superior to the notion we had earlier formed."[8] The population of the capital at that time, now estimated at 267,000, was organized into around seventy-five city quarters, each with a popularly selected head approved by Ibrahim Bey.

Lieutenant Laval recalled entering Cairo on 24 July. "All the people were in great consternation."[9] The killing of so many of the Ottoman-Egyptian grandees, most of whom had contracted marriage alliances within the city, made the mourning families indisposed toward the newcomers. "The first days, we found nothing in the city. Everything was closed up." A junior officer and brilliant mathematician, Étienne Malus, said that if it were not for the cries of the women ringing out from the harems, one wouldn't have known that the city was inhabited. Slowly, Laval wrote, the French made contacts with local Egyptians and found ways of purchasing provisions. Once the local merchants discovered that the French paid well, he said, they began letting the foreigners know when there was something to buy. Al-Jabarti reported that the soldiers were offering Egyptians what were essentially European prices for products such as eggs, bread, sugar, soap, tobacco, and coffee, so that soon shopkeepers "became friendly." Communication was a difficulty, and the troops were forced to resort to sign language. Laval remembered, "It took time to learn a little Arabic. Some Jews who spoke a bit of Italian explained things, and often served as interpreters." The 1,500 cafés and public places began attracting French customers.

On arriving in the city in late July, another Bonaparte aide-de-camp, Antoine-Marie Chamans de Lavalette, was struck by how, from time to time Muslim notables mounted on mules moved through the crowds, "preceded by men with sticks, who beat above all anyone who blocked their passage, but even just those men who did not rise at their approach." Beggars, faces covered, uttered cries that sounded to him more like angry shouts than importuning. Cairo, and the Middle East generally, lacked wheeled carts and other vehicles because the pervasive dust and sand would just have bogged them down (it was hard to keep them greased, and the wheels just could not cross some terrain). Likewise, much of the Delta was a swamp in the late summer and fall because of the Nile inundation, making it inhospitable to wagons. Without wheeled vehicles, there was no reason to construct broad, straight streets, for camels and mules could navigate narrow, winding alleyways.[10] In Egypt, given that almost all habitation is along the Nile or easily within range of canals built out from it, and since water transport was far cheaper than overland, the premodern economy may not have been much disadvantaged by the lack of wheels. It did matter, however, that wheeled cannon are a great deal more maneuverable than those without, which helped the French win their victory. Lavalette sniffed that the narrow streets of Cairo were dusty and beset "by I don't know what odor of mummies." He also

witnessed how French soldiers glided through the city atop swift-footed donkeys, shouting and laughing as they jogged up and down. Their fun was interrupted late on 27 July, François said, when they were forbidden to go into the
city as a result of "a plot in which they were going to slit our throats. The principal conspirators were arrested and had their heads cut off. It was again recommended that we not go out, even inside our quarters, without arms."

Some local Coptic Christians appear to have been ecstatic about the arrival
of their French coreligionists, though the close links of many Copts to the deposed beys made their situation ambiguous. Captain Say reported that on 24
July, a high Coptic religious authority, whom incorrectly he calls a "mufti" (a
term for a Muslim legal authority), sang a hymn of praise in "the grand mosque
of Cairo" in Coptic to celebrate the entry of Bonaparte into Cairo, leading the
"warriors of the Occident." If this event actually took place in one of the capital's great mosques, it was a symbolic humiliation of the conquered Muslims on
a grand scale. It is far more likely that the sermon was given by a priest in a
Coptic cathedral in Arabic, and that a garbled account of the event reached Say.
He gave a transcript of the Copt's speech, in which the priest sighed in relief
that "God is no longer angered toward us! He has forgotten our faults, punished
sufficiently by the long oppression of the Mamluks!" He lamented the exactions
and pitilessness of the Ottoman Egyptians (and it is certainly true that the
Georgian faction had severely overtaxed the cities in particular in the last
decades of the eighteenth century).

Say described him as praising the French, saying that they "worship the
great God (Allah), they respect the laws of his prophet; they love the people and
succor the oppressed." For a Coptic priest to refer to Muhammad as God's
prophet seems a little unlikely unless the speech was scripted for him by Bonaparte, who had already used such language in his proclamations, for the purpose
of mollifying the Muslims. He continued, "And we, only a little while ago a de-
generate race; are placed today on the level of free (libres) peoples, by the arm of
the Western warriors." Say reported that the sermon was "spread through the
army."[11] Some Egyptians, Christians as well as Muslims, were in close touch
with the small French mercantile community in Egypt, and so knew something
about the revolutionary events since 1789. Unlike al-Jabarti, who initially assumed that when the French said they were "free," it meant they were not slave
soldiers, the Coptic priest was able to find meaningful ways to speak of the new
idea of political liberty to an Egyptian audience—according to Say's admittedly
garbled account (which, however, is supported also by another young officer,
Desvernois).

Bonaparte had Cairo, and, having Cairo, had Egypt. What was the human extent of his new domain? Demographers working back from later censuses estimate Egypt's population in 1800 at 4.5 million. The scientists with Bonaparte arrived at an estimate only a little over half that, but they were in no position to do a proper census. The great historian of Egypt, André Raymond, calculated that the population grew from about 3 million in 1500 (in the aftermath of the catastrophic Black Plague) to about 4.5 million in 1800, since Cairo's physical environs grew by a factor of 1.5 in the Ottoman period to 1798. If Raymond is right, Ottoman rule provided enough security and infrastructure to allow the society to flourish. The sultans of Istanbul lowered taxes, provided security and infrastructure, and eliminated many government monopolies. Most of that increase, however, probably occurred between 1500 and 1720 or so, and the horrible eighteenth century, often marred by inadequate or overly abundant Nile floods, and internecine slave-soldier wars, may have been largely stagnant with regard to population growth. Although some countries grew somewhat faster in these three centuries (Britain doubled its population from five to ten million), Egypt's growth was respectable. One limitation on demographic increase in the Nile Valley may have been continued outbreaks of epidemics, including plague, which, though tamed by increased resistance in the population, survived better in the warmer climate of the Middle East than it did in Europe.

Generations of European historians and diplomats have insisted that the Ottomans ran Egypt into the ground and depopulated it, a myth begun by the French under Bonaparte. The French cited figures from Roman sources giving highly implausible estimates of the Egyptian population under the Caesars, of 7 million or even double that. They were therefore dismayed to find so few inhabitants in the country and blamed this "decline" on Muslim misrule. European consuls propagated the myth of disappearing Egyptians all through the nineteenth century, though it can be disproved by recently discovered censuses. The slur appealed to them because it implied that European colonialism would be much better for Middle Easterners.

Bonaparte, pleasantly surprised that the capital had fallen to him so easily, set about creating yet another satellite French republic there, with its own Directory, to be drawn from the ranks of the Muslim men of religion. On 22 July (4 Thermidor of the Year 6), the general had addressed a memo to the clerics and notables of Cairo. "Yesterday the Mamluks were for the most part killed or taken prisoner, and I am in pursuit of the few who still remain. Send from that side some ships, which are on your river. Send me a deputation to let me know of your submission. Prepare bread, meat, straw, and barley for my army, and have no fear, for no one desires to contribute to your well-being more than I."[12]

The Muslim clergy of the al-Azhar Seminary was also eager to make contact with Bonaparte, even before he crossed the Nile. Those who had not fled in panic met at the seminary and decided to call on a prominent Muslim merchant from Tripoli in Libya who knew French. He wrote out a letter to the French asking for safe-conduct for civilians remaining in the capital. Bonaparte, on receiving the messengers, insisted he had already offered such safe passage and asked to meet with a clerical deputation. He gave them a proclamation that the French came in enmity only to the beys, and that "as for elders, clergy, those drawing salaries, and the common subjects, their minds should be at ease." He then explained to the messengers, "The clerics and city notables must come to us, so that I can appoint from among them a divan composed of seven wise men, who will manage affairs." He sent a delegation to them, headed by General Dupuy, bearing the letter from the commander in chief. Étienne Malus, a junior officer, went along. He recalled that at Bulaq, "we found the sheikhs of the law who, after some preliminary pleasantries, performed their prayers in front of us." The clerics received this message with some relief, and sheikhs Mustafa al-Sawi, Sulayman al-Fayyumi, and others crossed the Nile on Thursday, 27 July to meet with Bonaparte at Giza. He laughed at them for being so fearful. After that, al-Jabarti wrote, the great sheikhs began to be willing to meet with him.

The French in Egypt viewed the Arabic-speaking urban middle classes as the potential backbone of a French Republic of Egypt, just as middle-class liberals underpinned the Paris Directory, and they considered the Muslim clergy to be the natural leaders of that class. The Muslim clergymen, or ulema, congregated at seminaries such as al-Azhar. It was perhaps the world's oldest university, founded in the tenth century. Many of the 14,000 seminary students who studied there (Bonaparte's estimate) were actually destined for private business or estate management rather than for preaching in mosques. Those who completed their studies as Muslim clergymen became jurists arbitrating Islamic law, theologians, or popular preachers, and they wielded enormous moral authority. They also often owned villages and engaged in commerce and tended to be well off. It was the custom in Egypt, as in other Muslim societies, to endow property for religious (and sometimes family) purposes, and a fifth of Egypt's land was endowed. Once a farm had been designated as a pious endowment, the annual profit from the sale of its crops would go to the upkeep of a mosque or religious school, for instance. A cleric was typically appointed as overseer of the endowment, and received for his services up to ten percent of the proceeds generated by the property.

Captain Say reported of the commander in chief, "He employed these moments to organize, in this city, a government similar to that of the new republics in Europe. He named a Directory . . . and administrations were installed in various provinces."[13] At the meeting with the clerics on 27 July, al-Jabarti wrote, a deputy of Bonaparte's consulted on the appointment of ten leading Muslim men of the cloth to the divan and, in consultation with them, then made appointments to other branches of the government. The members of the divan were the cream of the country's theologians and religious jurists. They included Sheikh Abdullah al-Sharqawi, Sayyid Khalil al-Bakri, Sheikh Mustafa al-Damanhuri, Sheikh Mustafa al-Sawi, Sheikh Shams al-Din al-Sadat, and other highly respected teachers and writers, though the exact composition is controversial.

The next step was to appoint military and administrative leaders. The French initially objected to filling any such posts with persons of Georgian or Circassian ethnicity. They aimed at a "de-Mamlukization" of the Egyptian elite. The Muslim clerics, however, insisted to them that the common people of Cairo feared no one but the Ottoman Egyptians, and that no one else could control them. The French therefore relented and allowed appointments from old houses of emirs that had "not ventured tyrannical rule like the others."[14] Thus, Hasan Aga Muharrem, who had a reputation for honesty, became head of the market police (in charge of preventing price gouging and maintaining public morals in the market).

To have Egyptian, Arabic-speaking clerics appointing Circassians and Georgians to high office was a novelty, to say the least. It is something of a mystery why the French did not instead appoint great merchants to fill positions on the Divan, given their wealth and honor in the capital. Most likely, Bonaparte felt that the chief obstacle to the acceptance of French authority in Egypt would be Islam and that only a government of the clerics could plausibly lend their authority to his contention that French deists were as acceptable as Muslims when it came to rule. Of course, the prominent clerics often were themselves also great merchants or had intermarried with those families. It is ironic, in any case, that only four times in modern history have Muslim clerics come to power in the Middle East: under the republican French in Egypt, under Khomeini and his successors in Iran, under the Taliban in Afghanistan, and, it could be argued, with the victory of the United Iraqi Alliance in the Iraq elections of 30 January 2005 (the UIA was led by Shiite cleric Abdul Aziz al-Hakim). The first and fourth times both took place with Western, Enlightenment backing.

The Divan's first charge from Bonaparte when he met with them later on Thursday was to stop the widespread looting in the city. The clerics complained that they had no means of halting it. Some French troops, al-Jabarti charges, opened some of the locked mansions of the beys and took things, then left them unlocked. The little people of Cairo took away all that was in them. It took the French a few days effectively to seal the elite residences and put an end to the looting. They arrested the guild master of the street singers for his role in it and executed him and a number of others.

As part of their effort to restore order, the French "began to tear down the gates of the alleys and the connecting gates." This highly unpopular demolition work actually reduced security for ordinary Cairenes, who had the custom of closing up their quarter at night or when there was trouble.[15] Since, as the French memoirists noted to some astonishment, Egyptian homes lacked locks on their doors, the inhabitants of the quarter had depended on a kind of neighborhood watch to guard against strangers and thieves during the day, and on securing the quarter at night. The Europeans were now allowing thieves to circulate freely at night.

Many of the French took seriously Bonaparte's proclamations that he intended to bring liberty to the Egyptians through institutions such as the clerically dominated divan. The French not only interpreted Egypt in terms familiar to their eighteenth-century world, they were also capable of reinterpreting their own history in light of what they saw in Egypt. Just as the rationalist officers coded popular Islam as reactionary Catholicism, so the Republican French mapped the defeated beys as analogous to the French Old Regime and saw their overthrow and the institution of municipal elections as the advent of liberty.

"The people of Egypt were most wretched. How will they not cherish the liberty that we are bringing them?" asked Captain Say.[16] He observed that most of the land was in the hands of the Ottoman Egyptians, whereas others paid a thousand taxes and surcharges, with the peasants left only enough to keep them alive. Private property was at risk of mulcting. "A hundred spies are ready to inform on a man who has secret wealth, as are his enemies." Say described Cairo crowds as wearing rags and filthy. He said that under the slave-soldier regime, executions were common, carried out by a judge and policemen with summary justice, and life was cheap. Bernoyer concurred that tyranny and taxes produced misery among the common people. "Bonaparte," he wrote confidently back to his wife in the summer of 1798, "will without doubt end this state of affairs."[17]

The implication is that the beys had impoverished the country by grabbing the lion's share of resources for themselves. Moreover, they were seen to be only

the latest in a long line of oppressors. Bernoyer criticized the pyramids themselves as ostentatious works of tyrants seeking to immortalize themselves at
huge public expense. The French, by removing the Ottoman Egyptian elite, had
changed this age-old pattern and opened the way to a more just distribution of
wealth, he maintained. But the lot of the common folk would not be improved
just by receiving a larger portion of the existing pie. Rather, liberty itself was a
dynamic force for increasing wealth. In describing their living conditions, he
said, "Their dwellings are adobe huts, which prosperity, the daughter of liberty,
will now enable them to abandon. . . ." Liberty, in the sense of the sweeping
away of the feudal Ottoman-Egyptian ruling caste, the establishment of rights
and the rule of law, and the institution of an elected government under French
tutelage, they thought, would actively produce affluence.

Despite being the master of a new country and the architect of its liberty,
Bonaparte had fallen into a black despair and determined to return to France as
soon as possible. Josephine had long been having an affair with one of her escorts, an adjutant to General Charles Leclerc named Hippolyte Charles. Rumors had reached him of it in Italy, and he had threatened to kill her if it was
true. He also had Charles discharged from the military. (Corsica was an honor
society as much as Egypt.) On the march from Alexandria to Cairo, one suspects
that Bonaparte's sincerity and love sickness for Josephine became too much to
bear for those who cared about him, given that her brazen affair with Charles
was an open secret in Paris.

Bonaparte's promising young aide de camp, Julien, and his two old com-
rades-in-arms and fellow generals, Jean-Andoche Junot and Louis Alexandre
Berthier, staged what we would now call an intervention. Eugène de Beauharnais, Josephine's seventeen-year-old son from her first marriage and an aide-
de-camp of the commander in chief, wrote back to his mother from Giza:
"Bonaparte has seemed sad for the last five days, and that came after a conversation he had with Julien, Junot, and even Berthier. He was more affected than
I could believe by those conversations. All the words that I heard referred to
Charles having come in your carriage until three stations from Paris, that you
saw him in Paris, that you were at the theater with him in the fourth private
box, that he gave you your little dog, and that at that very moment he was with
you. This, amidst indistinct words, was what I could hear. Mama, you know
that I do not believe it, but what is sure is that the general is very affected."[18]
Eugène was careful to assure his mother that Bonaparte was not mistreating
him, as though the general was determined to show that he would not take his
marital frustrations out on his stepson. Bourrienne, who blamed Junot alone

for the indiscretion and placed the revelation months after it actually occurred, agreed that Bonaparte was grief-stricken at the revelation that he had been cuckolded. He recalled him remonstrating with his secretary for not having told him the truth and calling Junot a "true friend." He lamented, "Josephine! . . . and I am six hundred leagues away . . . you should have told me! Josephine! To have been so fooled! Curses to them! I will exterminate that race of jackanapes and dandies! . . . As for her! Divorce! Yes, divorce! A blazing, public divorce!"[19]

Crushed, Bonaparte fired off a letter to his brother Joseph. "Egypt is richer than any country in the world in corn, rice, vegetables and cattle. But the people are in a state of utter barbarism. We cannot procure money, even to pay the troops. I may be in France in two months." He was clearly deeply disappointed with his economic situation in his new conquest, and had already decided that it was not the sort of place he could make his further fortune. But his determination to retire from the field of battle in the Orient, for the sake of which he had hectored the Directory unmercifully and laid claim to the loot the Republic brought out of Switzerland, was also rooted in his personal crisis. He continued, "I recommend to you my interests. I have much domestic chagrin, since the veil is altogether lifted. You are all that is left to me on the earth; your friendship is most dear to me. It would push me to hate human beings if I lost you and saw you betray me!"

He asked Joseph to arrange a house outside Paris or in Burgundy. "I am thinking of passing the winter there and burying myself. . . . I need solitude and isolation. Grandeur bores me, my feelings are shriveled up, and glory is faded. At twenty-nine years old, I have exhausted everything."[20] Ironically, that summer Josephine was in no position to provoke Bonaparte's jealousy any further. While taking the waters at the Plombières spa and socializing with friends, she went out on a balcony that collapsed. It was a miracle that the fall did not kill her, but it left her badly bruised and laid up for months. Bonaparte's miserable wife could hardly, either, have pursued her plan of sailing to Alexandria once the general was established there. It was just as well. News came that the ship she had contemplated taking out to Egypt had been captured by the British.[21]

Exhausted or not, Bonaparte had displaced the government of a country and he had no choice but to attempt to administer it, however mundane the tasks that awaited him. The barking of ranging hounds in the streets so disturbed the French troops that the commander in chief ordered that the rebellious canines be executed en masse, an enterprise that took his sharpshooters two nights to accomplish.[22] The French memoirists were convinced that Egyptians had a superstition about the bad luck that came of mistreating a canine, and thus had let the dogs have the run of their cities. It is more likely that they were using the dogs as informal guards of neighborhoods and property, feeding them but leaving them in the streets. If so, the animals impeded the free circulation of the French. Their removal, however, left the Egyptians less secure. Since animal carcasses can be disease vectors, including for plague, the great dog massacre may have endangered public health, including that of the soldiers as well. The medieval Fatimid Caliph al-Hakim Bi Amr Allah had also had Cairo's canines killed, in A.D. 1005, and the chroniclers cited it as among their reasons for thinking him insane.

As to the humans, Bonaparte had chased away the emirs, but still worried about local militias, especially ones capable of raising a cavalry and attracting Bedouin allies. He immediately confiscated all saddled horses in Cairo, and threatened heavy fines against any owners who resisted.[23] He likewise demanded that all Cairenes who had looted elite villas turn their booty over to the French administration.

✤

The once humming, wealthy city had taken revenge on its conquerors in mid- to late-July by emptying out or declining to carry on business as usual. Bonaparte immediately suffered from a famine of cash and coin in Cairo. The warlords had hoarded most of the country's silver and gold and so Bonaparte had to look for it in their mansions. He expropriated what he could from what treasure remained in the capital and resorted to having the wives of the exiled beys support his army. Once the French had conquered Cairo and many of the Ottoman Egyptians were killed or had fled south, the Circassian, Georgian, and Armenian harem ladies continued to play their role as important nobles. The wives of the beys were wealthy in their own right and able to take full advantage of the provisions in Islamic law that gave women rights in property far beyond what was common in Europe until the later nineteenth century.[24] Unlike the case in early modern Western Europe, Muslim women did not lose control over their property to their husbands when they married (a principle the British called "couverture"). Ottoman-Egyptian women endowed important buildings for religious and charitable purposes, putting their mark on the character of the city in which they lived. Muslim noblewomen held great estates and sometimes even engaged in trade through male agents. Despite upper-class Middle Eastern norms of veiling and seclusion, which limited their ability to go out in public or confined them to ornate palanquins when they traveled, behind the scenes they were political and economic movers and shakers. In one of history's ironies, Muslim women of the ruling class were the most powerful and wealthy women in the world in the medieval and early modern period, even though many of them lived like reclusive millionaires in the inner apartments of their mansions.

The "harem" *(enderun)* was governed by clear hierarchies, with formal wives the most powerful and wealthy, while concubines had a less favored position unless they were manumitted and married. Some of the slave girls in a harem served the chief wives and seldom had anything to do with the man of the mansion, though legally he could sleep with anyone in his harem. The harem was a center of power and influence, and male anxieties about its hidden workings help account for the Orientalist stereotypes of it as a viper's nest of intrigues (as though male courtiers did not intrigue!).

The wives of the warlords now had the right to dispose of the property their husbands left behind. They acted as channels of communication with their spouses, who had fled, and were still in a position to mobilize networks of loyalty among their husbands' clients. The bodies and the property of these aristocratic women became objects of desire for the French officers. On taking Cairo, Bonaparte gave the Ottoman-Egyptian women twenty-four hours to register and to declare all their goods and jewelry which they received from their master.[25] Bonaparte allowed the wives of the beys to remain in Cairo under French "protection," and decreed that they could only remain in their mansions on payment of taxes to the French on their assessed value.[26] They also had to report the white and black slaves in the household.

Despite the guarantees given the wives of the beys, they were made to pay imposts, often repeatedly. The wives of the more prominent beys, who were still fighting the French in Upper Egypt, appear to have been specially targeted. When a squadron chief named Rapp was stabbed in the streets of Cairo, the French began to fear that warlords were still hiding out in the capital. Suspicion fell on the mansion of Murad Bey. Bonaparte sent Beauharnais, his stepson, to pay a warning visit to Nefise Hanim. "Madame Murad-Bey received me with the greatest refinement," he later recalled, "and served me coffee herself." She protested that she had met all the conditions imposed by the French and attempted to convince him that her household had not received any suspect person. She insisted that he tour the mansion with her, and he agreed, though "I was not without a sort of disquiet, fearing to see a Mamluk skilled in the art of decapitation jump up from behind the piles of cushions." The first story of the building was occupied by odalisques. On seeing him, he said, they leaped up and crowded in on him, to his embarrassment: "They manifested the most importunate curiosity; they surrounded me, pressed in on me, wanted to touch and undo my clothing, and put their hands on me to the utmost degree of indecency. In vain, Madame Murad Bey ordered them to retire; in vain, I repulsed them rudely myself. It was necessary to call the eunuchs, who came running at the sound of the voice of their mistress, struck some blows with a whip at these frenzied women, and obliged them at last to let go."[27] The slave girls, facing penury now that their master was gone, were perhaps hoping that a French officer might take them on. Their hopes were often not in vain.

In the end, Nefise Hanim returned to him with a fine shawl and some weapons of her husband's, and for the moment escaped suspicion of harboring insurgents. Initially, Bonaparte decreed that Nefise could keep her property and slaves, but had to pay 600,000 francs to the French army on pain of having the other property that her husband left her repossessed. In fact, this payment was only the beginning. "The wife of Murad Bey was made to pay imposts several times, and the last time she had to pay 8000 talaris."[28] Al-Jabarti says that the French "extorted" the other noblewomen in the same way, as they did many officers and soldiers, "using as intermediaries Syrian Christians" and "foreigners."

A young officer, Jean-Gabriel de Niello Sargy, alleged that the wife of Osman Bey was imprisoned and fined 10,000 talaris after being charged with maintaining contact with her husband's camp. The wife of Süleyman Bey was also mulcted, though her mansion in Cairo had been among the first to be pillaged by the populace after the fall of the old government. The exception here was Züleyha, the wife of Ibrahim Bey, who had played an important role in protecting the resident European merchants in Cairo from being massacred during the French invasion. Bonaparte rewarded her with a writ of safe conduct and a guard. (She nevertheless found a way to slip out of the country, joining Ibrahim in Syria.)

It was not only the jewelry and possessions of the wives of the beys that the officers coveted. Niello Sargy observed, "The common women were horrible. But the beys had left behind some pretty Armenians and Georgians, whom the generals grabbed for the so-called good of the nation." Bonaparte himself, wounded by Josephine and determined to assert his own sexuality, "relaxed at first with some women of the beys and the Mamluks. But finding with these beautiful Georgian women neither reciprocity nor any charm of society, he smelled a void in all of them, and missed all the more the lascivious Italian and friendly French women." The officers were used to flirting with a wide range of women, including others' wives.

The other group to whom the cash-starved Bonaparte turned was the great merchants and guilds of the capital.[29] Greater Cairo at the time of the invasion had nearly two hundred such guilds, though the number had declined, along with the economy, in the eighteenth century. They included wealthy gold-smiths, useful water carriers, and disreputable pimps. Bonaparte decreed that the Coptic merchants were to pay 60,000 talari, and the coffee merchants (among the richest in the country) were to pay 134,000 talari.[30] The Egyptian coffee merchants were still formidable commercial powerhouses, though they faced new competition from colonial European coffee plantations in Brazil and the Dutch East Indies. Most of his victims were in the old al-Qahira district, which housed the famed Khan al-Khalili covered bazaar and markets for gold jewelry, copper ware, carpets, cloth, spices, and leather goods. Some ninety per-cent of the money made from trade in Cairo was made in al-Qahira.[31] Al-Jabarti thought Bonaparte's assessment far too optimistic, saying that the French called the members of the merchant guilds based in the markets for a meeting, at which they imposed on them an enormous loan advance. The merchants raised "a hue and cry," and went to the al-Husayn and al-Azhar area to appeal to the Muslim clerics for help. The clerics, now the divan of Egypt, interceded for them and convinced the French to reduce the amount to half that originally de-manded and to give the merchants more time to come up with the money. The clerics and notables had long played such an intercessory role between the mer-chants and the beys, and were here instructing the French in their traditions of consultative government.[32]

Bonaparte was master of Cairo, but was not yet master of Egypt. Ibrahim Bey and Murad Bey might still rally to recover their lost province. Ibrahim and his 2,000 cavalrymen had taken control of the adjacent Sharqiya Province, with its capital at Bilbeis, and he had with him Ebu Bekir Pasha, the Ottoman gover-nor of Egypt and a symbol of legitimacy for many Egyptians. On the other side of the deserts of the Sinai Peninsula, the Ottoman governor of the province of Syria and the freebooting Ottoman vassal who ruled the region of Acre, Ahmed Cezzar Pasha, could offer Ibrahim Bey strategic depth and support. Worse, they might ride to his aid. Bonaparte determined to pursue Ibrahim Bey. Since this leader had also carried off an enormous treasure in gold and other valuables from the capital, Bonaparte wanted his resources as much as he wanted the bey himself. Detaining the Ottoman governor would also give him an important hostage and defuse a potential threat.

The Corsican began by reorganizing the army. He attached the 7th Hussars to Reynier's division and charged him with taking the province of Sharqiya.

Desvernois observed of Sharqiya that Bonaparte "wanted it cleaned out immediately." Bonaparte's military still lacked much in the way of cavalry, since they had brought few European horses and had as yet captured and retrained relatively few Arabian steeds.[33] This gap put the French at a disadvantage in catching up to and engaging Ottoman-Egyptian cavalry and Bedouin.

On 1 August, Bonaparte addressed a memo to Leclerc ordering him to head out toward Bilbeis and to establish himself in the best villages he encountered. He was to establish a relationship with the five or six Bedouin tribes in the area and to let them know that if they dared commit the least further excess, "all their camps and villages would be ravaged." Leclerc's garrison was also to gather and pass on information about the situation in the east, whether it came from the caravan, from Ibrahim Bey, or from Syria. He was also to establish flour mills in all the villages of Sharqiya so as to provision the French troops with bread.[34] Bonaparte's to-do list encapsulated the tasks of practical imperialism, centering on diplomacy, terror, spying, and food.

Leclerc, Bonaparte's brother-in-law and commander of the cavalry, departed Cairo 2 August with four squadrons, hussars and light infantry, and a battalion and two pieces of light artillery. One Captain Malus wrote a series of dispatches to General Caffarelli concerning their progress.[35] They passed al-Matariya, where they found good and abundant water and provisions, without difficulty. They then made a foray toward Abu Za'bal, having heard that it was very rich, but found it well defended by Bedouin and peasant irregulars, and so they reconsidered their detour and headed again toward al-Khanqa, a village nine miles from Bilbeis on the route to Syria. They took the town, initially with little resistance, on 4 August. On the morning of 5 August, Desvernois said, "Ibrahim Bey, leading slave soldiers and Bedouins, attacked us."[36]

5

THE FLIGHT OF IBRAHIM BEY

Leclerc's scouts initially spotted a hundred emirs leading Bedouin and peasant irregulars, but the number of Ibrahim's cavalrymen abruptly swelled to a thousand. Around 10 A.M., Captain Malus reported, the bulk of the Bedouin cavalry rode out of the Abu Za'bal date palm orchards, followed by "an immense anthill of peasants." Only about a sixth of the villagers were armed with muskets, the rest presumably having only staves. "They spread out around us and enveloped us, ambushing us in the cultivated countryside." The inhabitants of other villages now joined them. The Egyptian forces "tried to charge us at several points at once," he wrote, but the French were at first able to keep them at a healthy distance with cannon fire. A junior cavalry officer, Lt. Desvernois recalled that "as at the Battle of the Pyramids, their cadavers littered the ground."[1] The attackers kept coming, however, and forced the French guards to redeploy. "We only had six hundred infantrymen dispersed along an immense tract." Leclerc, Malus said, began to sense the consequences should he too pigheadedly attempt to defend the village.

The people of al-Khanqa themselves rose up against their new colonial masters, killing the sentinels within and assassinating the French bakers and butchers. (Peasants living close to the edge of starvation knew how to hurt the French peasant soldiers.) Leclerc decided to regroup and make a stand at an enclosure to the east of the village. Malus maintained in his report that at that very moment the enemy suddenly began to retreat. While reporting such a thing might have made his sad story slightly more palatable to General Caffarelli, it is not plausible, and Desvernois remembered no such stroke of good luck. On the contrary, he said that Leclerc's forces ran low on ammunition and had to withdraw. The French regained their camp outside the village at 4:00 P.M., the morale of the troops broken. They loudly voiced their anxieties, Malus wrote, and General Leclerc therefore decided to retire that very evening toward al-Matariya.

In recounting these battles, it would be wrong only to consider logistics, tactics, and generals' orders. The debacle at al-Khanqa draws back the veil on the centrality of the common people to these struggles. The peasant villagers of al-Khanqa, emboldened by Ibrahim Bey's stand, rose up against their new conquerors, executing not only sentinels but the food workers who provisioned these foreign troops. It was as though they had decided to try to make a difference at the level of their social class. Likewise, peasants poured onto the battlefield from surrounding villages, fifteen percent of them armed with a gun. Those who could afford firearms were probably from the families of village headmen; that is, they were rich peasants who had a claim to more land and leadership prerogatives than ordinary farmers and laborers.[2] Villages were not isolated, and their inhabitants traveled for market days and to visit saints' tombs. Many peasants had a Bedouin background and retained ties of kinship to the pastoralists, who had their own communication networks. Even the common Egyptians were not the docile, isolated population that Bonaparte had expected. And Leclerc's retreat was forced on him from below, by shaken French infantrymen (many of them conscripted peasants) who felt that they had nearly been massacred by Egyptians of their own social class.

Also central to the battle against the French were the Bedouin tribesmen. In the marginal lands too far from the Nile to be well irrigated but having some pasture some of the time, the Bedouin tribes flourished. The great, politically important tribes were those that raised camels, while smaller clans raised only sheep and goats. The French believed that the sixty tribes of such pastoral nomads could provide 20,000 armed cavalrymen to the Ottoman Egyptian government when called upon, a vast underestimate given that they were actually ten percent of the population. The Bedouin chieftains, or sheikhs, had been integrated into the political structures of Ottoman Egypt and often served as provincial governors, overseers of economic enterprises such as mines, or holders of estates where they were rewarded for providing security to the peasants so as to ensure they could bring in their crops. The sheikhs were among the wealthiest individuals in Egypt, though their tribespeople could be limited in wealth to some livestock. No Bedouin was as poor as a landless or small peasant, however.

The effectiveness of the tribesmen as fighting men provoked Bonaparte to write bitterly about them to the Directory. "We were continually harassed by clouds of Arabs, who are the biggest thieves and the biggest wretches on earth. They murder Muslims just as they do the French, all those who fall into their hands."[3] On conquering any territory, Bonaparte dealt ruthlessly with the Bedouin. He ordered them disarmed, demanded that a few heads be cut off, and took hostages. For the most part, the Bedouin successfully resisted being subdued, though a few made an alliance with the French. In the province of Cairo, there were five principal tribes: the A'id, the Bili, the Huwaytat, the Sawaliha, and the Tarrabin. The latter two remained enemies of the French, and Bonaparte ordered their villages burned and their flocks destroyed. They frequently raided the outskirts of Cairo but could be driven off by concerted cannon fire. The first three tribes eventually allied with the French. The daughters of the Sawaliha chieftain were hostages with the commissioner in Cairo. The chieftain of the Bili, along with fighters and two hundred camels, joined Bonaparte's army, as did the leader of the Tarrabin and his camel cavalry.[4] Malus wrote that Bili tribesmen, long before they allied with Bonaparte, were among those who attacked the French near Bilbeis. Without the threat of recalcitrant Bedouin, the French could have taken and held towns such as al-Khanqa much more easily and with much smaller military forces.

Leclerc and his men, having set out to conquer a province and dispatch one of Egypt's two great beys, had found themselves overmatched, and now they were surrounded by fierce tribesmen. Bonaparte, on receiving word even before the battle of the difficulties Leclerc's unit faced as it moved northeast, was constrained to do something. The commander in chief wrote the Directory that on 5 August he had decided to order General Reynier to al-Khanqa to support Leclerc's cavalry, which was battling "a cloud of Bedouin" on horse and peasant irregulars of the land of Ibrahim Bey. Bonaparte wanted more than villages. He saw the caravan then returning to this area from Mecca as a treasure trove of intelligence. "Subtly interrogate," he instructed Gen. Reynier, "all the men who came from Bilbeis or Syria and send me their report." He also instructed that the garrison to be established at al-Khanqa be hardened to withstand an attack if Ibrahim Bey decided to come back toward Cairo.[5]

Bonaparte reported that Reynier's force "killed some fifty peasants, some Bedouin, and took up a position at al-Khanqa." He ordered the divisions commanded by generals Jean Lannes (who had been an apprentice dyer in 1792 when he joined the revolutionary army) and Dugua to join the chase, and he set out himself. According to the Egyptian chronicler al-Jabarti, French troops moved toward the east from the capital wave upon wave.[6] They passed al-Khanqa, which they found deserted, with the oven destroyed. (Had the Egyptian villagers, noticing that the French rather liked their bread, deliberately sabotaged the makeshift *boulangerie?*) The army went again to Abu Za'bal, where they demanded provisions. Al-Jabarti said that the locals refused, so the French "attacked them, beat them, broke them, pillaged the town, and then burned it." The civilizational mission progressed. The Egyptian chronicler said that all the French troops, led by Bonaparte, then headed for the provincial capital, Bilbeis.

Bonaparte thought of Bilbeis as potentially a site of significant wealth, since some of the returning merchant pilgrims of the pilgrimage caravan had gone there. Al-Jabarti says, however, that most travelers had dispersed. The returning peasant pilgrims in the Mecca caravan had hired Bedouin to provide them with carriage and to deliver them and their wives and families to their hometowns in Gharbiya, Minufiya, and other provinces to the west. The caravan leader, or "amir al-hajj," Salih Bey, and some of the great merchants had initially come to Bilbeis at the invitation of Ibrahim Bey, but when he fled northeast, so did they. In earlier correspondence with them, Bonaparte had attempted to convince the merchant-pilgrims to come to Cairo and had promised them a 4,000-man escort. But at the same time, Ibrahim Bey had written to them asking that they join him at his capital. A few, willing to brave Christian rule, headed for Cairo. (Malus reported having encountered a small caravan splinter group with forty camels near al-Matariya early in the campaign.) Most went initially to Bilbeis.

With Ibrahim Bey and his supporters gone, the French found Bilbeis undefended and they took it without firing a shot. Bonaparte explained in his later dispatch to the Directory that before they arrived at the provincial capital, the French forces had rescued the caravan coming from Mecca, which the Bedouin had captured and taken to the desert. The richer merchants must have bribed some Bedouin to defect, since the French found four hundred or five hundred camels accompanied by about a hundred Bedouin guards. A commander of an engineering battalion, Detroye, said there were about 2,000 pilgrims, nearly reduced to begging, and a few poor, plain women, with some others hidden in palanquins. "At the approach of the commander in chief, the pilgrims greeted him as though he were the king of France, since he had manifested the intention of protecting them."[7] Bonaparte had this caravan escorted to Cairo in safety.

Bilbeis, Detroye reported, was a small village with little to offer save that it was an excellent site for a garrison, being a sort of amphitheater in the midst of a naked plain. The inhabitants immediately set up a market for their visitors. It was not the only commerce of the town. "The women of the country, for their part, engaged in the commerce of displaying their charms openly right in the street for a small coin, and many aficionados lined up." Along with other innovations of genius, such as liberty under foreign military occupation, the French Republic of Egypt also appears to have invented the colonial strip club. The next stop on the way to Salahiya was al-Qurayn, which also struck Detroye as desperately poor, the local fare a barely cooked flat bread. He wrote, "These villages [in Sharqiya] do not at all resemble those of the Delta. Every one of them is a vast enclosure, partitioned into many others, with uncovered habitations. One sees nothing but trees without houses, and a village really resembles a forest."

Another group of returning merchant pilgrims had fled at the French approach and found Bedouin who agreed to provide them safe passage to the village of al-Qurayn. But when they were halfway there, the Bedouin reneged on their pledge and looted the pilgrims, even to the extent of taking the clothes off their backs. Among the victims was Sayyid Ahmad al-Mahruqi, a man of very great property. When the French reached al-Qurayn, they found this remnant of the caravan.[8] Bonaparte remarked on the extensive pillaging of the Bedouin. "One merchant assured me that he had lost, in shawls and other merchandise from India, [the equivalent of] 200,000 five-franc silver pieces." The man had all his wives with him "in accordance with the customs of this land," and Bonaparte, eager for an alliance with the class of great merchants, gave the family camels for transport to Cairo. He remarked that the women were veiled, a local usage "to which the army had great difficulty becoming accustomed." Al-Jabarti implied in his account that their chaste veils had not prevented a lot of the women of the merchant pilgrims from being raped by the Bedouin: "tears were shed at their sight." The commander in chief, said the Egyptian chronicler, scolded them for having put their faith in the emirs and Bedouin. Bonaparte's sad encounter with the debris of the caravan can only have impressed on him the importance to the French imperial enterprise now underway of the trade to the east, and of providing security for it.

Al-Jabarti related that Bonaparte then had the village headman of al-Qurayn, Abu Khashaba, brought to him and demanded that he deliver up the plunder taken from the pilgrims. Abu Khashaba showed the French where some of the loot was stored, and they loaded it on their camels. Then he took them to another storehouse and went in, signaling that he would bring out more treasures. But this was a ruse, and he escaped out the back. The storehouse was empty, and the French came back to Bonaparte with only one and a half camel loads. Bonaparte is said to have exclaimed, "We must find him without fail!"

Disappointed in their quest for caravan loot and warlord treasure, Bonaparte and his units then set out in pursuit of the Ottoman Egyptians again. "We marched," Bonaparte told his political masters in Paris, "for long days toward Syria, always pushing before us Ibrahim Bey and the army he commanded." At length, on 11 August, they arrived at Salahiya, which the commander in chief called "the last inhabited place in Egypt where there is good water." It was not far from the desert frontier with the Sinai, beyond which lay Syria. They had finally caught up with Ibrahim Bey and his troops. Alerted, the latter began withdrawing in haste. The Ottoman chronicler Darendeli wrote that on their arrival in Salahiya, the Bedouin had driven a bargain with Ibrahim Bey and his men. The Bedouin chieftain is said to have pointed out, "If the French attack you here, it will be difficult for you to go out to meet them, since you have all these women and children with you. I advise you to hasten some hours to encounter them, and we will undertake to protect your women, children, and wealth in this place, and guarantee you against any misfortune befalling them."

The French were anxious. Were the emirs and slave soldiers to escape into the desert, Bonaparte's force had no supplies and no means of pursuing them. Worse, out of concern that his prey might escape, Bonaparte had set off early that day without waiting for the infantry division of Lannes. He therefore mainly had cavalry to throw at the mounted emirs and Bedouin. The latter two had acquitted themselves formidably when fighting cavalry-on-cavalry battles with the French. Night, the commander in chief recalled, was approaching and the horses were exhausted. Scouts spotted Ibrahim and his officers in a nearby coppice frantically loading their baggage and saddling their horses, said Detroye. Bonaparte ordered his cavalrymen to halt and wait for Lannes's infantry, which was marching on the double without their general, who had gotten lost. Abruptly, the Ottoman-Egyptian column exited the wood and followed, in good order, the route toward the desert, their camels richly loaded. Their rear guard waited patiently behind until the departing column was half a league from the trees.

Despite the dangers, Bonaparte had General Leclerc charge Ibrahim's rear guard. Bonaparte reported, "I pursued him with the small cavalry I had. We saw file before us his immense saddle bags." The immense saddle bags bulked larger in his memory than did the bey. Desvernois also remembered the emirs' camels weighed down with treasure and their ladies mounted in palanquins. Bonaparte said that a party of 150 Bedouin horsemen at that point deserted Ibrahim Bey's party and approached the French, proposing to fight alongside the Europeans in exchange for a share of the booty. Bedouin, always illiterate, often wore their Islam lightly and made their political alliances on practical rather than high-minded religious grounds. Al-Jabarti wrote that the Bedouin informed the

French of the location of Ibrahim Bey's hidden baggage train. Then, al-Jabarti recalled, "Ibrahim Bey learned of this as well, so he rode with Salih Bey and a number of emirs and slave soldiers. They encountered the French."

Leclerc's horsemen galloped like the wind for a good league before they came within carbine range of the Ottoman-Egyptian force. Desvernois said that the 1,500 Ottoman Egyptians had noticed that there were only at most two hundred French cavalrymen in their rear, their horses tired from riding through the desert. So the emirs and slave soldiers suddenly wheeled and came at their tormentors. Desvernois recalled, "The shock was rude and the mêlée bloody. We were one against five; the enemy approached us with a prodigious enthusiasm and horrifying cries. From the first attack, I had three killed and eight wounded in my division on the right. Five or six Mamluks, white and black, came at me relentlessly. I killed one with a pistol shot and wounded two or three with slashes of my saber." Darendeli observed that the French "cavalry was delayed, with its artillery pieces, so they fought the Mamluks with their cavalrymen alone. Although these horsemen were numerous, they did not have the capacity to confront the Mamluk braves. They attacked the French and scattered their ranks, and the courageous Mamluk *fida'is* [fighters willing to sacrifice themselves] drew their Damascene swords, plunging into the attack and inflicting a defeat on the French." Desvernois feared that his division was in danger of being destroyed. Detroye marveled of the Ottoman-Egyptian horsemen that "their agility was such that the very Frenchman who took a bullet from a carbine would receive at that very instant a saber cut from that same hand."

Luckily for Leclerc and his men, who seemed constantly to have more pluck than good sense, the 3rd and 14th Dragoons now arrived, that is, infantry and light artillery. Bonaparte related that the emirs withstood the second French charge unflinchingly and inflicted real damage on their attackers. "The squadron chief, Détrès, of the 7th Hussars, was mortally wounded. My aide-de-camp Sulkowsky took seven or eight cuts from a saber and was shot several times." The commander in chief was nevertheless able to admire the bravery of the Mamluks. "They form an excellent corps of light cavalry, richly clothed, armed with the most care and mounted on horses of the best quality." Each French soldier and officer he recalled engaged a slave soldier in personal combat. Bonaparte added, "Lasalle, chief of the 22nd Brigade, dropped his saber in the middle of the charge; he was adroit enough, and lucky enough, to be able to dismount and then to be horsed again to defend himself and carry the attack to one of the most intrepid Mamluks."

Desvernois thought that the French infantry was presented with a dilemma. If all of them just fired into the mêlée, they would hit the French amid their attackers. He said that the Dragoons therefore executed a rolling fire that sent the Mamluks fleeing. While the combination of infantry and light artillery was indeed often deadly to the slave soldiers, al-Jabarti gives another reason why they left the field at that point. Word reached Ibrahim Bey that the Bedouin, seeing the French and the Ottoman Egyptians busy with one another, had decided to plunder his treasure themselves. He and his men therefore disengaged, found the Bedouin, and chased them away from his property, killing a number of them. Then he and his party, including the Ottoman governor, Ebu Bekir Pasha, departed toward El Arish, the gateway into the Sinai.

The commander in chief concluded with evident satisfaction, "Ibrahim Bey in that moment headed out into the Syrian desert; he had been wounded in combat." Desvernois surveyed the battlefield. A hundred slave soldiers lay dead on the ground, but, he admitted, "Our losses were similar." Detroye minimized French casualties, writing that thirteen Frenchman had been killed outright and thirty-eight wounded, thirteen of them mortally. Three French officers had been cut down (Desvernois said "grievously murdered"). Detroye admitted, "Almost all of us were tagged." Bonaparte made one last attempt to turn his nemesis, sending a letter translated by the Orientalist Jean Michel Venture de Paradis to him by courier on 12 August: "The superiority of the forces that I command cannot be contested. You are on the verge of leaving Egypt and being obliged to cross the desert. You can find in my generosity fortune and well-being, of which fate is about to deprive you. Let me know, in reply, your intentions. The viceroy of the Sultan is with you. Send him to me bearing your response. I readily accept him as a mediator."[9] Gen. Augustin Belliard later wrote that Ibrahim had been in communication, through the Bedouin intelligence network, with the Egyptian coast and knew what Bonaparte had not yet learned, that the French fleet had been attacked by the British navy. Since the bey was, as a result, not sure which way the wind would blow, he declined to respond to the commander in chief's offer.[10] Bonaparte was said to be puzzled by this silence, since Murad Bey in the south had been willing to correspond, at least, with the French officers pursuing him.

Bonaparte left the division of Reynier at Salahiya to guard this approach to Egypt and ordered a fort constructed. The evolutionary biologist Geoffroy Saint-Hilaire revealed in a letter to his father a month later that, in fact, the French turned the town's main mosque into their fort. Detroye said he learned the lesson that one could not attack the Egyptian cavalry only with cavalry. The commander in chief had not managed to accomplish his four main objectives in this campaign: turning Ibrahim Bey into a client of the French, detaining the Ottoman governor, capturing the vast treasures he had taken out of the city, or bringing into Cairo unscathed the fortune of the merchant caravan.

✤

As Ibrahim Bey disappeared into the sands of the Sinai, his departure drew a curtain over nearly a quarter century of Egyptian history. He, along with his partner Murad Bey, had ruled Egypt since the mid-1770s. Now he fled east even as Murad headed south, their palatial mansions suddenly become the homes of foreign officers, their wives taxpayers to the Republic of France or mistresses to her generals, their entourages and slave soldiers scattered, killed, or suborned to new loyalties. Since the mid-eighteenth century, a small number of Mamluk beys—manumitted great slave soldiers of high office—had increasingly concentrated wealth and power in their own hands. They were not, however, a united elite, and included grandees with no background in slave-soldiery. Their vast "households," made up of slave soldiers, retainers, clients, and troops, functioned as clans that pursued vendettas with one another. Their internecine disputes had ravaged the countryside, and their crushing taxes had virtually crippled much of the urban economy. They had been forced to turn to the income from their enormous agricultural estates as the Egyptian coffee trade declined in the face of competition from European colonial plantations in the Caribbean, Brazil, and what is now Indonesia.[11] The Ottoman sultan still bothered to send out a governor every so often, but he wielded little actual power and sometimes even failed to secure an annual payment of tribute to the Sublime Porte in Istanbul.

Ibrahim Bey had been in the political wilderness before and survived to return to power. Mehmet Ebu Zahab, who had been Ibrahim's owner, died in 1775 while campaigning in Syria on behalf of the Ottoman sultan to repress a rebellious sheikh of the Galilee at Acre. In the subsequent decade, Ibrahim and Murad established themselves as the paramount beys in Egypt. The Georgian Mamluks retained ties to their homeland, which was increasingly in St. Petersburg's sphere of influence as Russia expanded into the Caucasus, and they began to explore a Russian alliance. Facing difficulties in recruiting enough Mamluks to replenish their ranks, the Mamluk leaders even brought in a brigade of five hundred Russian troops in 1786. In the early 1780s, the Ottoman government, or Sublime Porte, became concerned about the loyalty of the Qazdaghlis, and in a 1783 communiqué to the governor of Syria, it warned him that the dalliance of these "tumultuous beys" with Russia could prove injurious to the empire.[12]

The beys' external alliances were the least of the empire's problems, as it transpired. In 1784 European consuls in Alexandria were reporting back to their capitals that the beys were engaged in a virtual civil war with one another. Murad Bey had to leave Cairo, then returned with allies and forced five other beys to flee. He and Ibrahim fell out and fought a naval battle with cannonades on the Nile. They reconciled, then fell out again. The *Gazeta de Madrid* for 4 October 1784 carried a notice based on consular reports: "The reconciliation of Ibrahim Bey with Murad Bey did not last long, as one might have suspected. They are already openly at war. The former departed to Upper Egypt, where he can fortify his position. The latter is master of Lower Egypt and it is feared that the uproar will shortly move there." Murad, attempting to retain the loyalty of his troops in the Delta, was said to be tolerating much bad behavior by them toward the people, which included ordering premature harvesting of grain and its confiscation. The conditions of civil war thus interfered with the harvests.

In spring of 1785 it was reported that in order to protest the failure of the beys to send the annual tribute for three years running, the sharif of Mecca had begun refusing to allow Egyptians to come on pilgrimage or visit the tomb of the Prophet Muhammad in Medina. For 1785, al-Jabarti reported rebellious provincial governors, Bedouin factional fighting in the province of Buhayra, brawls in the streets of Alexandria, Bedouin raids on the returning pilgrimage caravan, rampant price inflation, and, to top it all off, a plague outbreak. A diplomatic row broke out when Murad Bey, strapped for cash in his struggle against the other Mamluk houses, suddenly granted the French the right to transship goods from their South Indian colony at Pondicherry through Suez. The British, believing they had an agreement with the Ottoman authorities in Istanbul that no such permission would be granted, protested loudly. The British and the French were still struggling for control of India, and Murad had abruptly given some help to Paris.

The struggle over who could transship goods looked increasingly absurd in light of the ruinous taxes and imposts the beys were imposing on the merchants. French commercial houses in Cairo were going bankrupt and their proprietors were trying to flee the country. In February and March 1786, the European consuls of Alexandria reported having received a demand from one of the beys of Cairo for an enormous sum of money and a threat that, if it were not surrendered, a Christian church that the Mamluks had refurbished for them would be destroyed. The Europeans appealed to Nefise Hanim, the wife of Murad Bey, to intercede, but to no avail. Ibrahim's men actually began demolition work at the church. Fearing for their lives, the merchants were sailing away on French ships and sending urgent messages to Istanbul. The Ottoman imperial center had for some time been disturbed by the situation in Egypt, but in that era the threats from Austria and Russia in the Balkans distracted it. This outrage against the Europeans in Alexandria forced the hand of the new grand vizier, Koca Yusuf Pasha, who took office in February of 1786.

Late that spring, a courier arrived from Istanbul with a long list of demands. The beys of Cairo were informed that they had fallen behind egregiously on the tribute that they should have been sending to the sultan in Istanbul. "The letters demanded the payment of arrears to the treasury and the expeditious dispatch of grain and money allocated to the Two Holy Cities during years past." The possession of the Islamic holy cities and pilgrimage centers of Mecca and Medina bestowed honor and authority on the Ottoman sultans. Thousands of Muslims came on pilgrimage there every year from all over the Old World. The cities, located in the Hejaz of western Arabia, had only desert or hardscrabble land as their hinterland and could not support much of a local population, much less the huge number of pilgrims, without importing food. The Ottomans had endowed enormous estates in Egypt for the purpose of feeding the Hejaz, but the beys had probably been usurping the grain and its profits for themselves, essentially stealing from the empire. Rumors flew in Cairo that warships from the imperial capital were approaching Alexandria, led by naval commodore Hasan Pasha. As it was, Ahmed Pasha, the governor of Jedda, had arrived in the major Egyptian port. Jedda was the point of disembarkation for the holy cities, and so he was in charge of seeing that the missing grain was delivered.

The Ottoman-Egyptian beys, alarmed, attempted to bargain for time. In early July, another emissary came from Sultan Abdülhamid I, repeating the earlier demands. The grandees went up to the citadel, an enormous fortress overlooking Cairo, to meet with the Ottoman viceroy, Mehmet Pasha. Murad Bey asked for a delay in the payment of the arrears and offered to have the clerics of al-Azhar Seminary write a pious petition to the sultan begging his indulgence. Sayyid Khalil al-Bakri, Sheikh Mustafa al-Sawi, and other prominent clerics later assembled to draft the petition. But Murad also issued a threat. If the sultan would not grant the respite, he would refuse to outfit the caravan from Cairo to Mecca for the pilgrimage that year, and would decline ever to pay the tribute. Ibrahim Bey, likely sensing that his partner had gone too far in the presence of the Ottoman governor, was said by al-Jabarti to have "tried to calm both of them." Meanwhile, rumors of imperial troop movements and the arrival of more ships at Alexandria inspired alarm in the populace. Ibrahim and Murad dispatched generals to the port of Rosetta in an attempt to ensure that it would be properly defended, and they made a defense pact with the Hanadi Bedouins of the region.

In July 1786, the Ottoman commodore, Hasan Pasha, arrived in Alexandria with a small contingent of troops. After his envoy conducted inconclusive negotiations with Ibrahim Bey, he marched on Rosetta. He sent couriers to the villages of the Delta announcing that the Ottoman sultan had decided to much reduce their taxes. If loyalty to their sultan and the prestige of the imperial center had not been enough to decide the issue for the peasants, this pledge of a restoration of the rule of law brought them over with enthusiasm, said the chronicler al-Jabarti.

Their backs increasingly against the wall, Ibrahim, Murad, and some other leading beys "proclaimed open rebellion and resolved to go to war." They hid their treasures in small safe houses and then went across the Nile to establish a military camp, with some other Mamluk commanders, at Imbaba. On receiving the petition now drawn up by Sheikh Mustafa al-Sawi and the other prominent clerics, Hasan Pasha pocketed it, declaring it unnecessary to pass it along to his master, given that he was the sultan's honored adviser. Likely he perceived a danger that the prestige of the al-Azhar might indeed prove persuasive at the Sublime Porte and did not want to risk a weakening of the imperial will.

Ibrahim Bey wanted to make a united stand at Imbaba but could not convince his partner. His plan was that if they could not hold Cairo, they would retreat to Upper Egypt and wait for an opportunity to come back to power. Murad Bey, said to have found this suggestion cowardly, insisted on going up to meet the sultan's army at Rahmaniya. His force was defeated, and boats brought back wounded slave soldiers and remnants of fighting units. Panic spread in Cairo. The Christian population, Spanish sources reported, feared reprisals from the beys, since it was rumored that non-Muslims had provoked the invasion by their complaints to the Sublime Porte. Ibrahim Bey set off for the Citadel with the intention of barricading himself inside it, but the Ottoman governor had succeeded in retaining the loyalty of the Azeban barracks, and he had them lock the rebellious grandees out of the fortress. The governor then demanded that the great scholars of al-Azhar join him at the Citadel as a sign of their loyalty to the empire. Sayyid Khalil al-Bakri did so immediately, but others dragged their feet and declined to condemn the beys.[13]

The Ottoman governor, Mehmet Pasha, sent word to his colleague, Commodore Hasan Pasha, that he should bring his men up to Cairo immediately, even though the bulk of the imperial troops (numbering, according to the Spanish ambassador in Istanbul, 25,000) had not yet landed. The governor assembled the lower-ranking rebels at Kara Maydan and Rumayla squares, and informed them that only Murad Bey and Ibrahim Bey were wanted men and that amnesty would be granted all who asked for it. The offer was rejected by the powerful grandees, including Süleyman Bey and Eyyub Bey the Elder, who chased the governor's messenger away, tore up his decree, and remained loyal to Ibrahim and Murad. The rebels attempted to raid the camel stables for offensive cavalry steeds, but the North African corps of the Egyptian military that guarded the camels had declared loyalty to the Ottoman governor and chased off the Mamluks. Mehmet Pasha had heard that the Janissaries had been without their daily ration for some time and that their will was sapped by resentment (and their strength sapped by hunger). He therefore had money spread around among them, and they rallied to him.

Ibrahim and Murad, who had been briefly estranged over the disastrous Rahmaniya campaign against the invading imperial troops, now made up. Their men raided the city for goods, foodstuff, beasts of burden, and ships. Cairo divided against itself in a civil war, with the area just below the Citadel loyal to the governor. Murad began constructing barricades at Bulaq, defended by his riverine navy. But the Ottoman vessels arrived before he was ready, and he and his men had to scatter. The imperial forces approached the city in great numbers now, firing cannon and gaining the loyalty of the Cairenes. Murad and Ibrahim dejectedly fired off a letter to Mehmet Pasha in the Citadel, affirming their repentance for rebelling and offering to come back into the fold. Al-Jabarti attributes these words to the cynical governor: "God be praised! How often will they repent and return?"

That evening, Hasan Pasha arrived at the Bulaq harbor to enormous popular acclaim and a cannon salute. "The people were happy and full of joy and took him for the Mahdi of the age." In folk Islam, people expected the coming at the last days of a savior figure, the Guided One, or Mahdi, who would restore justice to the world. Al-Jabarti, in invoking this belief here, was probably just engaging in rhetorical flourish, but millenarian ideas did abound in eighteenth-century Egypt. The commodore at length entered the city and went up to the Citadel to confer with the governor, Mehmet Pasha. They opened the gates of the fortress, and order was gradually established in the city. Some crowds looted Ibrahim's and Murad's mansions, but al-Jabarti maintains that when Hasan Pasha heard of it, he ordered his troops to put a halt to the pillage and to shoot the looters even if they were his own men. Al-Jabarti's fond depiction of Hasan

Pasha's brief tenure as a restoration of Ottoman order was contradicted by European consular reports, which lamented that the country remained in chaos.

One of Hasan Pasha's first moves was to abolish the irregular taxes demanded by the Ottoman Mamluks, especially of European merchants.[14] Al-Jabarti portrayed Hasan Pasha as determined to remake the administration of Ottoman Egypt. He met with the clerics of al-Azhar, who are said to have complained bitterly about the tyranny and overtaxation imposed by the beys. He then constituted a new divan, or governing council, including commanding officers of the various Janissary units and retainers of the prominent, loyal beys. He thus reversed the usurpation by "the leading Qazdaghli grandees" of the place of "the governor's council, or divan, in the citadel as loci of political power."[15] He also appointed new commanders of some of the seven Janissary barracks. He made a reactionary revolution, ordering the Janissaries to return to honoring their ancient customs and regulations. He gave the corps control once again of the spice customs and the revenues from the slaughterhouse, which had been usurped by Ibrahim Bey. The Janissaries, emboldened, began throwing their weight around with the shopkeepers and merchants, insisting on being made partners in their businesses and extorting from them. Hasan Pasha gradually reneged on his pledge of lower taxes. He demanded a huge loan immediately from the Cairo merchants. He imposed a "liberation tax" on the peasantry, making them pay for his conquest of the country.

The commodore forbade the Christians to ride horses, employ Muslim servants, or own slave girls or black slaves, to emphasize their status as second-class subjects. Christians and Jews were also forbidden to bear the names of the prophets mentioned in the Qur'an, which were for the most part the same as the biblical prophets and patriarchs (the Arabic versions of Abraham, Moses, Joseph, Isaac, and so on). This measure was intended to make it easier to distinguish between Muslims and non-Muslims by name, since religion was not always easy to discern. Making the distinctions starker allowed a demotion of non-Muslims in status. He was perhaps too successful in his aim, insofar as the Muslim crowds began to accost the Christians, and he was constrained to issue a decree guaranteeing them safety of life and property as "subjects of the Sultan." He placed restrictions on the public circulation of women as well.

Hasan Pasha summoned the wives of the rebellious Mamluks and forced them to pay a large sum of money and to forfeit jewelry. Al-Jabarti recalled, "A jeweled tiara and other objects were reclaimed from Züleyha, Ibrahim Bey's wife." Murad's wife successfully went into hiding, but Murad had given some of his treasure for safekeeping into the care of Sayyid al-Bakri, who surrendered it to the commodore. The clerics of al-Azhar attempted to intercede with Hasan Pasha for Züleyha, but with no success. Hasan Pasha then sold off the slave girls and harem favorites of the rebellious beys at an inexpensive price as a way of humiliating them. The clerics of al-Azhar, however, including Sheikh al-Sadat and Sheikh Ahmad al-Arusi, rode to see Hasan Pasha about this vindictive measure. They pointed out to him that, in Islamic law, it was illegal to sell a free person and also illicit to sell a slave woman who had borne a child to her master (the children were freeborn). The commodore is said to have angrily rebuked the clerics for daring to intervene, and to have turned against them. European diplomats circulated tales of Hasan Pasha's odious behavior toward these elite women, seeing it as a sign of barbarous tyranny.

The elevation of Ottoman-Egyptian gentlemen far above Arabic-speaking local elites such as the clerics and the great coffee merchants was a goal of Hasan Pasha's ruling style. It was no new thing, and the concentration of power through the second half of the century in the hands of the Qazdaghli beys had already contributed to such stratification.

The tumultuous events of the 1780s set the stage for the later French invasion, though they did not make it inevitable. French diplomats and merchants were alarmed at the great importance the British clearly put on their favored position at Alexandria and on Egypt as a key link in their Indian trade and communications. The interest in Egypt displayed by Russia, and the reciprocal interest of the Georgian Mamluks in the patronage, even troops, of St. Petersburg, also panicked French observers. Some French diplomats began speculating that as the Ottoman Empire declined, it seemed increasingly likely that Britain or Russia would make a play for the Egyptian province. For the next decade, these advocates of a forward policy agitated with Paris for a preemptive strike to ensure that if Egypt were to fall to any European power, it would be France.

In August 1786, Ibrahim Bey and Murad Bey had headed to Upper Egypt, where they drew to themselves a remnant of the beys and made alliances with the local Bedouin. An expedition south by the commodore, aimed at decisively defeating them, faltered in the fall when the imperial troops lost their cannon in battle with the rebels and had to retreat to the safety of Cairo. Hasan Pasha left Egypt in 1787 as the prospect of a new Ottoman war with Russia built. Before he departed, he pardoned Ibrahim Bey and Murad Bey but stipulated that they should remain in Upper Egypt. By 1791, the attention of Istanbul had turned elsewhere. In that year, an outbreak of plague in Cairo carried off members of the ruling elite as well as their supporters among the commoners and much weakened the fabric of urban society.

Plagues are urban phenomena. They are spread in conditions of urban crowding and carried by such vectors as fleas that infest rats. The clean, harsh desert and the thin population of pastoral nomads preserve them from outbreaks. One implication of this different susceptibility to epidemics in Middle Eastern societies is that the cycle of plagues weakened cities and opened them to periodic Bedouin conquest. Ibrahim Bey, Murad Bey, and their troops and Bedouin allies in Upper Egypt were left unscathed by the epidemic, while the leading pro-Ottoman bey in charge of the country was killed. They were able to march at full strength back into Cairo, reestablishing their beylicate and returning to their old ways, taxing French and other merchants into penury and defying Sultan Selim III's demand for tribute.

Only seven years after the duumvirate's restoration of 1791, Bonaparte's enormous army arrived in Alexandria in reaction to the predations they had wrought on the French merchant community and in response to the prospect that the rebellious Georgians had so detached Egypt from the Ottoman Empire that it might fall under British or Russian rule. In many ways, Bonaparte's expedition resembled that of Hasan Pasha, down to the details of the defensive camps at Imbaba and Bulaq, Murad Bey's attempt to make a stand at Rahmaniya, the appeal by both sides to the moral authority of the al-Azhar clerics, the promise of lower taxes (and its subsequent betrayal), the role of European consuls and merchants in soliciting the invasion, and the cultural revolution attempted by the new ruler. Likewise, some overthrown beys in both instances sought refuge in Upper Egypt.

The difference lay in social policy. Hasan Pasha's decrees were intended to reestablish conservative Ottoman standards and to reaffirm the social hierarchy whereby loyal, imperial appointees ranked at the top of society. Hasan Pasha clearly did not brook interference from mere Egyptians, even the clerics of al-Azhar, who theoretically were the guarantors of Islamic law. (Ottoman administrative law often took precedence over Islamic law in the empire, though Ottoman thinkers would not have said so outright.) Likewise, even the Janissaries in the barracks were to have a higher status than Arabic-speaking shopkeepers and merchants, and these Muslim Cairenes were to be superior to Christians and Jews, while women were to be controlled and kept out of the public sphere. Hasan Pasha's decrees would have been unnecessary if his vision of the good society was widely shared by Egyptians. A new, Europe-oriented sultan would soon challenge this conservative program even in Istanbul.

Bonaparte's measures turned those of Hasan Pasha on their heads. He promoted Christians as a new elite, making the Greek Bartholomew al-Rumi head of the Egyptian police and installing Copts in high provincial office. He promoted the Arabic-speaking clerics of al-Azhar as the new divan, demoting the Ottoman Turkish-speaking military elite from the top of the administration. He removed restrictions on women. The content was very different. But were the methods? We see now, in any case, why Ibrahim Bey and Murad Bey, despite their humiliating defeat, had no reason to surrender to despair. They had been this far down before, and had returned from it to pomp and opulence.

✤

As early as the twenty-seventh of July, Bonaparte first asked some associates for ideas on reforming Egypt. How best to administer civil and criminal law, for instance? Not waiting for an answer, he issued orders about provincial administration the same day. There would be in each province a divan, an Ottoman term referring to a bureau or government council, by which he apparently translated the concept of "directory." Composed of seven persons, it would prevent feuding among villages, keep bad subjects under surveillance, and punish them if necessary. It could call on French arms for this purpose and justify it to the people. Each province would likewise have a gendarmerie, headed by an aga of the Ottoman Janissaries, with a guard of sixty local men charged with keeping order. The governor of each province was an appointed French general, signaling the odd combination of military occupation with local, "democratic" steering committees that characterized republican empire.

Bonaparte's technique throughout his military career was to make the conquered pay for their conquest and to terrify them into submission. The French Republic of Egypt now became acquainted with the Corsican general's vision of liberty. The vast majority of the 4.5 million Egyptians at the time of the French invasion were peasants or *fellahin*, totaling around 3.5 million persons. They farmed their plots in small villages up and down the Nile, using sophisticated irrigation techniques and taking advantage of the annual overflow as a source of silt, which was a free natural fertilizer. Bonaparte was contemptuous of the fellahin. "In the villages, they are not even familiar with a pair of scissors. Their houses are made from a bit of mud. They have for all their furnishings only a bed of straw and two or three earthen pots. They eat and consume in general very little. They have no acquaintance with mills, to the point where we constantly bivouacked on immense piles of wheat without having flour. We nourished ourselves with vegetables and animal products. They employ stones to make a few grains into flour. In some large villages, there are mills turned by cows."[16] Bonaparte's depiction of the Egyptian peasants underestimated them. He had forgotten how the village woman blinded one of his men with her scissors.

Bonaparte now presided over a country full of peasants, and therefore had to deal with landed property and agricultural taxes. The theory and practice of land tenure in eighteenth-century Egypt is complicated, but it is better not to think of land then as a commodity with one owner. It was a resource that was "owned" by various players, each of whom extracted some profit from farming. In other words, there were overlapping layers of ownership, rather than one exclusive property holder. Theoretically, the Ottoman sultan owned all the land. The beys, his vassals, bid for tax farms, or the right to tax certain villages and to keep part of the receipts for themselves, while passing on the bulk to the government in Cairo (and supposedly to the Ottoman viceroy, though that was increasingly uncommon in the late eighteenth century). Village headmen claimed rights of tillage and profit over much village land. And the peasants claimed the plots of land they habitually farmed. Peasants bought and sold rights in fractions of plots, showing that society recognized these local rights despite the theoretical claim of the sultan and the tax-collecting prerogatives of the local elite.[17]

Each province would have a Coptic Christian chief revenue officer who would ensure the payment of taxes, such as the *miri* (assessed on peasants working crown lands) and the *feddan* (assessed on other farms in accordance with their square acreage), formerly rendered to the Ottoman-Egyptian elite, which would now be remitted instead to the Republic. He was to hire as many collectors as necessary for this task and would have a French agent to whom he would report on the administration of finances. Bonaparte had earlier promised the Egyptians liberation from the onerous imposts of the beys, but now he was claiming the same taxes for his own administration.[18] Coptic Christians were afforded rights in Islamic law of life and property and freedom to practice their religion, though they were subordinate in status to the Muslims. Approximately six percent of Egyptians were Coptic Christians. The Ottoman-Egyptian rulers had long resorted to the Christian Copts for help with keeping track of revenues. For the beys, the Copts' lack of kinship and other ties to the Muslim majority helped forestall corruption. Ethnic groups or castes often specialized in such occupations in the personalistic bureaucracies of the Middle East and India, unlike in China where the majority Han population competed for posts by examination. The rise of a centralizing, powerful military junta in the eighteenth century allowed some Coptic notables to become wealthy and powerful.

"Many of the great Mamluk households of the eighteenth century employed Coptic [notables] and gave them heavy responsibilities to run their finances, or to employ them as scribes to audit their accounts."[19] These lay notables, growing enormously wealthy, became philanthropists and benefactors of the church and emerged as the leaders of the community, shunting aside the priests. The status of Copts in Egyptian society rose with this influx of wealth, and the community leaders attended even at Muslim festivals. Bonaparte, therefore, did not innovate in depending on Copts for fiscal administration or in promoting them socially, though in placing them above Muslims in some ways, he did ruffle a lot of feathers. Bonaparte was able to take over the administration of Egypt so smoothly in part because he simply adopted the already-existing Coptic network on which the Ottoman-Egyptian rulers had also depended. Consul Magallon and other old Egypt hands would have informed Bonaparte of the importance of the Copts in this regard.

Given the French military control of the country, the installation of Copts like Mata Sirafim and Binuf Gizawi as provincial revenue chiefs looked to some Muslims like a Christian takeover of the country.[20] The Muslim cleric al-Jabarti lamented that when the French confirmed the holders of rural fiefs (iltizams) in their titles, they appointed Coptic Christian tax collectors for these estates. "They descended on the country like rulers and achieved their object with regard to the Muslims through beatings, imprisonment, and humiliation, and through coercive demands and frightening people with threats that they would call the French soldiers if the imposts they fixed were not paid immediately. All of this was through Coptic manipulation and wiles."[21]

Two weeks after taking Cairo, Bonaparte upbraided General Joseph Zajonchek, governor of al-Minufiya Province, for his poor administrative style, apparently because he had dismissed and publicly humiliated one of his Coptic revenue officers: "I did not view with pleasure the manner in which you conducted yourself toward the Copt. My intention is that one handle these people with tact and have regard for them. Let me know about a subject toward whom you have a complaint, and I will replace him. I further do not approve of your having arrested the revenue officer without investigating whether he was culpable or not, and then having released him twelve hours later. That is not the way to conciliate someone. Study the people among whom you find yourself; identify those who are most suitable to being used. Sometimes make a just and severe example of someone, but never come close to caprice or thoughtlessness."[22]

Bonaparte clearly thought that the Coptic tax collectors were one key to establishing a colonial administration of Egypt, since, as Christians with detailed knowledge of local conditions and practices, they could provide a ready-made collaborating bureaucracy to the European occupiers. He was entirely willing to dress down another officer if he felt he was endangering good relations with the Copts. By 22 August he was circularizing the generals that "it is expressly forbidden to interfere with the Coptic supply officials" charged with provisioning the army.[23]

For the moment, Bonaparte decreed that civil justice would be administered as in the past. Commercial transactions would also go on unaltered. He confirmed all the property owners in Egypt in their ownership and, at least to outward appearances, preserved pious endowments *(awqaf)* funding mosques, especially those in Mecca and Medina.[24] Endowment property was not taxable in Islamic law, and at this time an estimated one-fifth of Egyptian land had been devoted to various family, charitable, and religious purposes (supposedly forever). There were good reasons for this rhetoric. The Muslim clerics he wished to win over depended on the endowments for much of their income. Moreover, they were used by wealthy families to support public works and family monuments, and preserving them helped reassure the Arabic-speaking Muslim middle strata.

We get the flavor of this sort of thing in a letter Bonaparte wrote to General Honoré Vial, governor of Damietta Province, on 22 August: "Since it is the intention of the commander in chief that all the pious foundations be respected and conserved, you will want to be sure to accord protection and security to the villages of al-Busrat and of Kafr al-Jadid, with their dependencies, which are the pious foundations of 'Ubaydullah al-Rumi in favor of his posterity and for the support of his mausoleum, a public fountain and a reservoir, which are in Cairo. You will want to give orders that no taxes be levied on these two villages, of which the revenues are dedicated to these items of public utility."[25] In fact, al-Jabarti complains that the French made Copts and Christian Syrians overseers of many of the pious endowments, and the latter embezzled from them. He recorded that in mid-October a large crowd of Egyptian Muslims dependent on the endowments assembled at the mansion of Sheikh al-Bakri, the prominent clergyman, complaining bitterly that their pay and bread rations had been cut off. The colorful if pitiful crowd included blind men, callers to prayer, patients at the al-Mansuri hospital, children from madrasahs or Qur'an schools, and dependents of the endowment made by the great notable Abdurrahman Kethüda.[26]

Behind a façade of lawmaking and reasonableness visible in Bonaparte's correspondence crouched the grim realities of corruption, power, and terror. When

Bonaparte ordered General Menou to the key port city of Rosetta near Alexandria to organize that province, he wrote with unusual candor, "The Turks can only be led by the greatest severity. Every day I cut off five or six heads in the streets of Cairo. We had to manage them up to the present in such a way as to erase that reputation for terror that preceded us. Today, on the contrary, it is necessary to take a tone that will cause them to obey, and to obey, for them, is to fear."[27] He meant by "Turks" all Muslims, of course. The chronicle of al-Jabarti mentions executions in Cairo, though the patrician author would not have cared to mention punishments meted out to what he considered the rabble. The memoirs of French officers are full of accounts of villagers being massacred, though they speak less of the situation in Cairo itself. Bonaparte's boast should be taken at face value. If he made this rate of execution a habit, the commander in chief was massacring 150 to 180 men a month in Cairo alone under normal circumstances.

Among all Bonaparte's generals, perhaps only Menou took the commander in chief completely seriously in making these words his guide to administering the subject populations. Note the difference between Bonaparte's treatment of ordinary Muslims, some of whom were decapitated daily to keep the others in line, and his instructions that the feathers of the Coptic tax collectors never be ruffled.

6

THE MOST BEAUTIFUL NILE
THAT HAS EVER BEEN

On 1 August, the engineer and scientist Prosper Jollois, based at the port of Rosetta, went hiking with some friends to the nearby village of Abu Mandur.[1] The landmark of the village, a big square tower, impressed them despite being in a dreadful state of disrepair. Around 6 P.M. as the lambent sun sank, "suddenly, a loud sound struck my ears." He could clearly distinguish the roar of cannon. He wondered, "Where could it have come from, if not the fleet? It was being attacked." He ran to the tower and mounted it, intending at first to watch the fray. But the awful possibilities that such a confrontation might bring in its train so dispirited him that he clambered down and straggled back to his room in Rosetta. His colleagues confirmed for him that the fleet was waging battle.

Restless again, he went upstairs. "I ascended to the terrace of the house. The night was dark, permitting me to see numerous clear forms by the light of the cannon." The ships were firing broadsides at one another. "That was followed immediately by a horrifying noise, and a frightful carnage continued. Oh! Naval combat is such a terrible thought." He was lost in his apprehensions when "a steady white gleam, which grew by degrees, struck our eyes." The glaucous shimmer expanded so rapidly that it soon became indisputable that a ship was on fire. It was listing with the wind, and then the incandescent fireworks began. The fire had clearly infiltrated an ammunition magazine below decks. The ship "jumped," Jollois recalled. "Nothing is more terrifying or more beautiful." The combat appeared to have halted. He went down to try to sleep, but could not close his eyes out of anxiety.

The next morning, he sprinted to the tower at Abu Mandur. Although the combat had tapered off around 10 or 11 P.M., it had recommenced in the night, and then more fiercely at dawn. "The battle continued. The ships ran up their sails and distanced themselves." The battle lasted all day. He said that the two fleets seemed evenly matched, and at some points it appeared to him that the tricolor would wave victorious at the end of the day.

On the third of August, no longer able to discern the fleets, he awaited news impatiently. Gen. Jacques Menou bribed some Bedouin to go to Abuqir, where the French fleet had been at anchor, to bring back information. At 2 P.M. a dispatch boat arrived. Its sailors had been watching the battle from a distance, but then had had to make for the mouth of the Nile, afraid they were being pursued by the enemy. The crew, fearing that their vessel was displacing too much water for the relatively shallow river, dumped their cannon overboard. As it approached the riverbank at Rosetta, a crowd of Frenchmen gathered. The captain disembarked and reported "news too happy to allow for any doubting of his certitude."

For most of 17 Thermidor, there was no further information on the outcome of the battle. At length a letter arrived from Kléber in Alexandria for Menou. Its contents were kept secret. "They were afraid to share it. Therefore, it was bad." Persons in the circle of the general learned the truth, that "our fleet no longer existed, and that the sunken vessels were the *Orient* and the *Arthémise*." Further news was carried to Rosetta by a crowd of runaway sailors, he said. "The sadness, the despair was all the greater because the joy had been so lively." The British had captured the ship with the mailbags, and so suddenly possessed a treasure trove of intelligence on all French operations in Egypt, as well as the opportunity to amuse themselves by going through the private correspondence of the French soldiers, including that of Bonaparte. They quickly had the correspondence published.[2] Bonaparte, already depressed at the news of Josephine's infidelity, now had to stand by and watch it broadcast to the world by his worst enemies.

Adm. Horatio Nelson had come back to Alexandria with his fleet and had, spying the French sails, rushed to the attack in the late evening, risking a night battle.[3] The menace of unknown shoals and of firing blind at one's own ships usually dissuaded naval commanders from fighting in the dark, but the confident Nelson appears not to have given the matter a second thought. The two fleets were almost evenly matched, with thirteen ships of the line each, and over 900 guns actually mounted on each side (not all of the 1,026 French guns had actually been mounted). Although the French ships may have been lighter and more maneuverable, and they carried slightly heavier cannon, neither proved helpful to them. They fought at anchor, and their heavier cannon balls took the men longer to load. The French preference for firing at the rigging of the enemy vessel rather than at the hull, combined with their cannon technique, may have caused them to fire too high. They targeted the rigging for defensive purposes, to prevent the enemy from coming in for the kill. Some British memoirs speak of the French balls whizzing above them. The British captains, whether by prearranged strategy, knowledge of French charts, or sheer skill, dismasted the *Guerrier* and disabled the *Conquérant* before sunset. One British ship went aground on Alexandria's notorious shoals, but the captain was able to warn off two other vessels following him.

The ships lined up against one another by the light of their own cannon flashes, and kept up the barrage. The *Spatiate* fired shrapnel at Nelson's flagship while he was examining a chart on deck, striking him glancingly so as to split the skin of his forehead and blind him. He thought he would die, but he soon recovered his vision and had his face put back together by a surgeon. Later that evening, the British evened the score. The *Swiftsure* and the *Alexander* doubled up on the French flagship, the *Orient*. Admiral Brueys took a shot in the stomach that nearly sundered him. The *Alexander* hit the *Orient* again and again, managing to set it ablaze, rendering the ship a floating hazard to the *Alexander*, which was downwind of it. The captain of the *Alexander* had to cut anchor and run, fearing his own sails would catch fire. The French ships fled it as well. Some time before midnight the conflagration penetrated into the ammunition magazine, blowing the proud flagship to smithereens. Debris flew so far and high that it landed on some of the British decks and started a fire on one that was quickly dowsed. Most of the *Orient*'s crew was rendered red mist. Bonaparte's stateroom, with the gilded billiard table to which Bernoyer had so objected, met its end. While British sailors and officers cheered, even some of their captains felt badly about the immensity of the disaster. The British rescued fourteen survivors.

The fighting resumed later that night and continued on 2 August. Another French ship of the line ran aground and was scuttled by its crew. Two French ships of the line escaped. The British captured nine, three of which they later burned. They took 3,305 French prisoners, a thousand of them wounded, and the French may have lost as many as 1,700 dead. The British dead were 218. The British fleet also suffered substantial damage and was far from any port where repairs could easily be made. That so many British ships were dismasted or damaged made it impossible for them to think about any further assault on the French, which was perhaps the only good news for Paris and Cairo. The British, having too many captives and too few resources, were forced to return all the wounded and many healthy French sailors to Alexandria. Bedouin tribespeople along the coast came out to celebrate the British triumph, and "lit bonfires in its honour."[4]

Among the French in Egypt, the effect of the news of the loss of the fleet was electric. The mathematician Malus wrote, "We foresaw that from then on, all communication with Europe would be broken off. We began to lose hope of seeing our fatherland." He departed for Cairo from Salahiya, "tired, sick, and sad."[5] A French officer who visited the beach thereafter saw hundreds of bodies of sailors washed up on the shore and remarked that, like ancient Egyptian mummies, they seemed not to be rotting, given the extreme dryness of the climate. It did not last. Jollois revealed that the stink of death soon began rising all along the coast, remaining for weeks, and one often saw macabre arms or legs sticking up out of the sands of the beach.

The commander in chief received the news while at Salahiya around 12 August, after having chased Ibrahim Bey out of Egypt.[6] Bonaparte, on his arrival in Cairo, let his general staff know the dread news. Bourrienne, Bonaparte's private secretary, recalled that "the catastrophe of Abuqir came like a thunderbolt upon the Commander in chief." Marmont wrote a letter recounting his conversation with Bonaparte at that juncture. "We are separated from the Motherland [la Mère patrie], without sure communications. Very well, it must be known that we are self-sufficient. Egypt is full of immense resources; we must develop them. Once, it formed all by itself a powerful kingdom. . . . The important thing is to safeguard the army from a discouragement that would contain the germ of its destruction," he reported the general as saying.[7]

As he slipped into an even deeper mood of depression than the one provoked by Josephine's infidelity, Bonaparte faced the rage of his officers over being stuck in Egypt. Even before the disaster, Adj. Gen. Pierre Boyer wrote to Bonaparte to warn him of the "many generals who wish to return to France" and cautioning that "there appears to be great discontent in the army." Murat, Lannes, Berthier, and others had conveyed to Bourrienne remarks that "were so unmeasured as almost to amount to sedition." Bonaparte had hoped, having secured Egypt, to sail soon for Toulon with the fleet. Now he and his army were trapped. Disillusionment with Egypt itself, the falling away from their eyes of the scales of Orientalist fantasy, contributed to the mood of despair. As Bourrienne saw it,

> Egypt was no longer the empire of the Ptolemies, covered with populous and wealthy cities; it now presented one unvaried scene of devastation and misery. Instead of being aided by the inhabitants, whom we had ruined, for the sake of

delivering them from the yoke of the beys, we found all against us: mamelukes, Arabs and fellahs. No Frenchman was secure of his life who happened to stray half a mile from any inhabited place, or the corps to which he belonged.[8]

Desvernois remembered the thinking among the officers that, given their inability to leave Egypt, they would have to find a way to survive there and to "attach the inhabitants to the French cause." They would even have to recruit Egyptian troops, "just as the Mamluks had succeeded in doing."[9] The French readiness to accept local soldiers in their Republican army demonstrates that, whatever racist ideas they may sometimes have professed, ultimately the universalism of their revolutionary ideology convinced them that other peoples, even the most exotic, could be successfully integrated into it. Indeed, Bonaparte soon gave practical expression to this sentiment. Miot recalled, "He ordered that all the young Mamluks, those more than eight years and less than sixteen years old, and all the boys who had been slaves, whether black or white, abandoned in Cairo, should be incorporated into the demi-brigades, whether as soldiers or drummer boys."[10] Thus, unfortunately, the same universalism could lead the revolutionary French to insist on and coerce such participation in their cause. Nor were they above making invidious distinctions. Initially, their printed letterhead in Egypt carried the words "Army of the Orient" alongside the inscriptions "Liberty" and "Equality" and "The French Republic." Only a little over a year after they arrived, some letterhead was inscribed simply, "Colonies," though they retained the other elements, incongruously enough.[11]

Bonaparte had first of all to deal with the discontents in his own officer corps. The commander in chief asked Gen. Charles Joseph Dugua, who had distinguished himself at the Battle of the Pyramids, to dinner. He requested that he in turn invite a number of generals, including Murat and others whom he named, to join them. Dugua did as requested. When the meal was over, Bonaparte inquired of his colleagues how they were doing in Egypt. They all responded, "Marvelous!"

Bonaparte replied, "All the better!" He continued, "I know that many generals are fostering mutinies and preaching revolt. . . . They should take care. The distance of a general and of a drummer boy to me is the same, and if the occasion presents itself, I will have the one shot as easily as the other." The group is said to have fallen "respectfully" silent.[12]

The Cairenes' tongues began to wag. The chronicler al-Jabarti told the story of how a great soap merchant, Sayyid Ahmad al-Zarw, was gossiping about the French naval defeat at Abuqir.[13] Al-Zarw made the mistake of talking about it in the hearing of a Syrian Christian, who informed on him to the French. The French summoned him and "confronted him with this report." The soap magnate replied that he was only passing on what he had heard from a Christian he knew. That man was also brought in. The French threatened to cut out the tongues of both al-Zarw and his Christian friend unless they each paid one hundred francs, an enormous sum. Muslim clerics attempted to intercede for them, but the French rebuffed them. At length Sheikh Mustafa al-Sawi, a member of the divan, proffered two hundred francs, and his intercession was accepted. The Republican officer told him to distribute the money to the poor. Thereafter, al-Jabarti reported, the people "refrained from talking about the affair." Nevertheless, those who opposed the French took heart from the disaster that Admiral Nelson had inflicted on them. They included Murad Bey, who redoubled his resistance to the invaders from his Upper Egyptian redoubt. The anecdote suggests the ways in which the gossip that circulated in the capital, and that the Bedouin "telegraph" carried throughout the country, served as an instrument of resistance to the French, provoking them to attempt to monitor and severely punish it. The techniques for doing so would have been familiar to the agents of Louis XVI, or for that matter, to the Ottoman sultans.

✤

Among Bonaparte's chief difficulties in attempting to rule Egypt was his lack of legitimacy: he was a foreign general of European, Catholic Christian extraction. Many Egyptians feared he would constrain them to convert. The biologist Saint-Hilaire wrote that August, "The women are much more afraid. They never stop weeping and crying that we will force them to change their religion."[14] Medieval Islamic law and traditions taught Muslims that they should attempt to avoid living under the rule of non-Muslims if at all possible, even if it meant emigrating. Some jurists did allow an exception where the non-Muslim ruler was not hostile to Islam and allowed the religion freely to be practiced. This loophole was Bonaparte's one chance, and he pursued it as though he were a shyster lawyer with a make-or-break case.

In order to underscore his position as pro-Islamic ruler of a Muslim country, Bonaparte presided in August over the festivals of the Nile and of the Prophet's birth. Despite the Egyptians' having forsaken, millennia before, the pagan religion in which the swelling Nile was Hapi, a god, the great river still had a religious aura for them. They called it "the blessed Nile."[15] The quartermaster Bernoyer observed, "The Egyptians consider the Nile their father and the earth their mother, and it is all the same to them whether they are consigned at death to the one or the other." The Nile's annual inundation still served as an oracle that predicted whether life would be good or bad that year. The longest river in the world, this body of water stretched from headwaters and tributaries in Africa through Ethiopia and the Sudan, to snake through the Egyptian desert and make human habitation there possible. During winter and spring, its waters fell and stayed low. Then the summer monsoon rains began swelling the Blue Nile in the Ethiopian highlands, with water levels beginning to rise in Egypt in June. By mid-August, or early September it began inexorably overflowing its banks.

Egyptians had for millennia made their peace with this gentle, natural, annual flood, adjusting their architecture and farming to take advantage of it, living with it rather than fleeing. Half the year, Cairo was Venice and parts of the Delta were the Florida Everglades. Villagers dwelling beside the river put their huts up on stilts throughout the year, so as not to be inconvenienced by the annual rise in the waters, and they established a system of dikes that allowed them to flood their farmland and then, later, to drain it. City engineers constructed canals and urban ponds to accommodate the overflow. Every year, the receding waters left behind on farms a thick layer of silt, a natural fertilizer that made the Nile Valley the breadbasket of the Eastern Mediterranean for a succession of great empires. If the inundation in any year was too low, it would not cover enough land and the harvests would suffer. If it was too high, it would damage crops. A good deal of anxiety therefore centered every year on reading the Nilometer at Roda, which was a good predictor of how the country's economy would fare that year. The inundation had to reach at least sixteen cubits for the dikes to be broken, and Bonaparte went out to inspect it as a Muslim ruler would have done.[16]

On the morning of the Festival of the Nile, Bonaparte ordered the decoration of a river vessel, the 'Aqaba, and the few beys who had attached themselves to the French had several other galleons festooned. The commander in chief called on the people, still afraid of insecurity in the new political situation, to go out for walks along the river and on the isle of Roda as usual. Al-Jabarti recalled that many Cairenes greeted the call sullenly, given "the imposition of new taxes which were zealously collected, the looting of homes, the harassment of women and slave girls, including their abduction and imprisonment" and other such outrages. The chief deputy of the Ottoman viceroy, Mustafa Pasha, descended from his mansion and joined Bonaparte. Then the chief Sunni Muslim clerics of the divan, the aga of the Janissary Corps, and other notables arrived. They all proceeded in a parade, their horses richly outfitted, to the dam at al-Sadd Bridge. Bonaparte and the deputy viceroy, the one remaining shred of Ottoman legitimacy in Egypt, were placed beneath a magnificent pavilion. The highest-ranking

French generals were also there. The French maintained that a big crowd had assembled, on land and on water. French and Egyptian bands played.

When Bonaparte gave the signal to break the dike, Desvernois recalled, "the
waters precipitated themselves through the breech, rolling like a torrent into the
canal. The skiff, the *Vali*, crossed it slowly. Meanwhile, pell-mell, men, women,
and children plunged into the Nile and threw into it tufts of horses' mane, pieces
of cloth, and other offerings so as to obtain from Allah the fertility of their
women or the conservation of their beauty." A crowd of female dancers, Captain
Say said, "scampered along the canal, cheering the spectators with their lascivious dances." The French newspaper in Cairo, the *Courrier de L'Égypte*, reported
that Bonaparte tossed out large quantities of small coins to the people, as well as
throwing pieces of gold at the decks of passing boats. He clothed the leading
cleric in a black robe and the leader of the descendants of the Prophet in a white
one. He also distributed caftans to the leading French officers to honor them.

Workers cast into the canal a clay statuette of a woman, called the "fiancée,"
which Say identified as a survival of an ancient Pharaonic custom of sacrificing a
virgin to the river god. People, he observed, seemed drunk. Then the official
procession retired. The people escorted it, chanting praises of the Prophet and,
Desvernois maintained, "of the French army," saying that they called out to the
commander in chief, "We see very well that you are the envoy of the Prophet, for
you have for yourself a triumph and the most beautiful Nile that has ever been."

Cairo's flumes and canals filled up. The French did not allow Azbakiya
Square to become a pond for a while, because they still had military equipment
stored there. Al-Jabarti sniffed that no families went out boating on the canals
that evening as they ordinarily would have, except, he said, Christians, Syrians,
Copts, Europeans, and their wives. He wrote that, with the exception of a few
idle persons, the Muslim population essentially boycotted the evening portion of
the festival. The French remembered joyous Muslim throngs celebrating their
liberation from the beylicate during the day and acclaiming Bonaparte as a
prophet (an unlikely piece of blasphemy unless it was just an irreverent joke). Al-
Jabarti remembered a resentful populace, its wealth plundered and women raped,
forced to pretend to act normally during the day and retreating to their homes in
the evening to brood. The truth is probably that the French could not tell Copts
and Syrian Christians from Muslims, and were glad that the lower-class Muslims
were willing to come out in hopes of catching some of Bonaparte's coins. The
crowds thus seemed to them happy enough. Al-Jabarti discounted the Christian
groups and the Muslim laborers, focusing on the Muslim middle and upper
classes, which probably did more mourning than celebrating that day.

In subsequent weeks, Lake Azbakiya and the capital's canals began resuming their centrality in the lives of Cairenes as places to go boating and cool off in the evenings. Captain Say remembered fondly, "The purity of the sky, almost never veiled by fog, the gold of the stars sparkling on an azure background, the fire of so many lights reflected in the water, created enjoyment, on those charming promenades, in the clarity of the day and the delicious freshness of the night. With what intense pleasure do these people, burned for twelve hours a day by an ardent sun, come to inhale the refreshing breaths of zephyrs on these lakes."

The festival brought out the usual small time carnival acts, soothsayers, spectacles, and Sufi celebrants. Originally a festival of the pharaohs and their subjects dedicated to the river god, it had been adapted by Coptic Christians and then by Muslims but retained the pagan sense of a suspension of ordinary moral behavior, when "drunkenness, playing, entertainment, and incidents of death could occur."[17] The more rationalist French observers, as they encountered Egyptian folk Islam in public, profoundly disapproved of what they saw as the superstitious practices of the Egyptian little people.

François Bernoyer, the quartermaster in charge of designing and overseeing the production of uniforms for the soldiers in Egypt, was one such philosophically minded—one might say Jacobin—civilian. He described a ceremony conducted by mystical Sufis, which he witnessed during the celebration of the rising of the Nile. Bernoyer dismissed the Sufi leaders as charlatans who fooled the people, saying:

They were dressed like monks. The chief of this group was seated on the ground, surrounded by disciples. The first of the spectators presented himself to receive divine inspiration. He approached the venerable pontiff and prostrated himself several times before him. The chief took hold of a clump of the postulant's hair and made him rise. Then he ordered the postulant, his mien threatening, to close his eyes and open his mouth wide. He received from the chief spittle in his mouth. He then began shrieking horribly, his members stiffening. One could hear his bones making a cracking sound. It seemed as though his eyes would come out of his head. A thick foam came out of his mouth. Then he rolled naked on the sand.[18]

The sheikh (probably from the Sa'diya Sufi order) brought the ceremony to an end, he said, by bringing from his robe a sack of snakes and letting them crawl all over the postulant. Later, Bernoyer wrote that he saw an old woman of sixty or more, completely naked and mounted on a magnificent mare. She stopped at each house, receiving profound respect from its inhabitants. "They touched her buttocks with the tips of their fingers and brought them back to their lips."[19] He expressed astonishment that they should have found any blessing in the old woman's bum, but his interpreter was not along, so he could not ask the meaning of it all. In Egyptian folk Islam, blessings, or *baraka*, were thought to inhere in particular trees, shrines, or persons. The crone's reversals (nakedness, a female on a horse) endowed her with supernatural powers in the eyes of the people. The chronicler al-Jabarti also told her story, as a "God-intoxicated" female mystic of the people. He shared Bernoyer's disdain for popular religious practices.

Bonaparte was destined to disappoint both Bernoyer and al-Jabarti by his policy on religion. Despite many past statements and proclamations of an anticlerical tenor, Bonaparte had decided that he needed religion on his side. He was not overly discriminating about the forms of religion to which he was willing to appeal. His first instinct was to seek the cachet of the formally recognized great clerics in ensuring the success of his endeavor in Egypt. Failing that, or alongside it, he was entirely willing to manipulate the themes of folk Islam, of its saints and its rituals and its all-seeing charismatic holy men, if that is what would secure him the allegiance of the people. His sponsorship of the Festival of the Nile was in his view only a first step toward acquiring religious charisma in Egypt as the Great Sultan and defender of the faith.

✦

The French forced march to Cairo from Alexandria had left no time to secure the territory in Lower Egypt through which these armies had advanced. Rebellious and largely unsubdued, these populations were further emboldened to attack the French when they heard of the sinking of the fleet at Abuqir. For his part, Bonaparte, marooned in Egypt and facing concerted resistance in the south, now had to make the Delta his power base. The Mediterranean port cities blockaded by the British fleet had to be provisioned from their rural hinterland, which the French did not control. Bedouin chieftains still loyal to the deposed Ottoman-Egyptians dominated trade routes, granaries, villages, and some cities. Some emirs were hiding out in Delta towns and villages and directing the resistance. French terror tactics sometimes produced more determination than submission.

Even near the capital, unwary troops were not safe from villagers and Bedouin. Millet recounted how he and his unit were posted to the area around the Pyramids for two weeks in late July and early August.[20] There, amid the sand of the desert and the eldritch tombs of the pharaohs, they lacked basics such as bread. "One day," he wrote, "many cavalrymen and musketeers" went to a nearby village "to look for something to live on." They appear to have stolen from the villagers some local stores of wheat, and they began milling them into flour there on the spot with hand mills.

Suddenly, around forty Bedouin appeared, who, "knowing that these soldiers had no defensive weaponry with them, entered the village and cut off the heads of these unfortunate soldiers, who totaled around twenty, among whom only two escaped, who, as it happened, hid themselves—one in an oven and the other in a clay water jar." It became known at camp that the Bedouin were at that village, but the general in charge out at Giza, Millet contended, thought that the soldiers who had gone there were armed and did not send reinforcements. A fatal misunderstanding had arisen, he said, and he knew whom to blame. "Since there are always men who do more than they are commanded, a villain of an adjutant major" had forbidden "any soldier to leave camp with his arms, which was the cause of the misfortune of those ill-fated soldiers."

Even in Sharqiya, which Bonaparte had just subdued, the garrison left behind at Bilbeis faced further revolts. Sergeant François wrote that on 19 August, the headman of al-Qurayn came to warn his chief of battalion that some 1,500 to 1,800 men, both Bedouin and peasants, had gathered in his jurisdiction. "These forces were to attack us, since they knew that we were few in number (158 men)."[21] That night, "these brigands irrupted into all the points of our bivouac; but well entrenched behind earthen walls, we killed thirty-three of their men." The French continued to build their fort at Bilbeis, employing mud bricks, and were able to buy meat and poultry from the surrounding villages, as well as "puff pastry flat cakes, which are very good, and clean enough. For the Turks are generally dirty. But we did not look at them very closely; we considered that we could one day become Muslims and more miserable than they." For the servicemen and noncommissioned officers, the only prospect worse than perishing amid a hostile population was the threat that long-term survival could come only through assimilation and going native.

The provinces to the west of Bilbeis were even more dangerous to the French. Niello Sargy recalled of August 1798, "One could not even travel on the Nile without being obliged to battle Bedouin and Arabs, who were joined by the inhabitants of riverine villages. Ships descending on Rosetta and Damietta were increasingly attacked."[22] The engineer Villiers du Terrage admitted that some of the trouble derived from French rapaciousness, saying that he had to have an armed escort when traveling down from Rahmaniya to Cairo in mid-August "because we foresaw that we might take some fire, coming ordinarily from villages recently pillaged by the French or the Bedouin." On 23 August, Captain Thurman described his return by skiff from Cairo to Rahmaniya during which he and his companions constantly met with sandbars made invisible by the rising floodwater: "In these trips on the Nile, our skiffs would often run aground. The Bedouin and peasants would profit from it to fire at us, to which we responded while the sailors were occupied with getting us back afloat. We had many men killed or wounded."

At the mouth of the Nile, Niello Sargy complained, it was "almost impossible to escape British cruisers." Gen. Auguste Marmont explained why this situation was intolerable: "During this time, the army had great need of war munitions, which were stored at Alexandria. Alexandria had need of the wheat stored at Rosetta and on the Nile." The great river's distributaries in the Delta had moved over time, leaving Alexandria high and dry and without a natural source of sweet water, which had to be brought from the interior. It was necessary to discourage peasants from drawing off too much water from the canal that brought it to Alexandria, which in turn required military control of the Delta hinterland.

Niello Sargy's destination was Damanhur. There Gen. Félix Dumuy had faced a rebellion in mid-July, as a result of which he was forced to withdraw to Alexandria. In mid-August, Kléber, garrisoned at Alexandria, came up with troops to repress the Bedouin and retake Damanhur. On 18 August, Bonaparte wrote to General Marmont that if the expedition to subdue Damanhur failed, the general was to take two columns and clear all enemy troops from the province, and then punish the inhabitants of the city for the way they behaved with General Dumuy.[23] In fact, Kléber had brought the town of 4,000 back under French control, and Niello Sargy found "everything in order." Kléber had come to suspect that the old governor of Buhayra, Sayyid Muhammad Kurayyim, was implicated in the Damanhur revolt behind the scenes, and was having his staff tip hostile Bedouin to French troop movements. The upright Alsatian carefully built a case against the governor, convinced Bonaparte of it, and on 15 August had him arrested as a "traitor to the French Republic" (not a sobriquet he could have imagined earlier in life).[24]

Niello Sargy lamented that despite some encouraging news on the security front, the French at that point faced penury. The Alexandria customs on imports and exports had come to 50,000 écus (300,000 francs) a month and Bonaparte had counted on being able to appropriate that income. It had fallen to nothing since the British blockade began. They had no choice but to begin trying to realize money from the bullion they had taken from Malta, which had been moved to Rosetta for safekeeping before the British attack. They hoped to get 185,000 francs for it, about equal to two months of customs income at Alexandria in the old days. Kléber instructed Menou in Rosetta to cease even trying to send mail by water as long as the British blockade was on. The French were confined to the dry land of the Delta.

When the young officer with the wig-making father, Jean-Pierre Doguereau, came to Alexandria in August he saw the beach littered with the debris from the late French fleet. He witnessed an event that attested the insecurity faced by the French in the Delta.[25] A ship coming from France and arriving at Alexandria was spotted by the British navy between Marabout and the Tower of the Arabs, and they gave chase. The captain, feeling the enemy breathing down his neck, appeared to decide that the better part of valor was to escape by going to ground and then following the coast on foot. His sailors leapt off the vessel onto the beach with the ship's most precious cargo, but "did not take the precaution of carrying their arms off the vessel." No sooner had their feet hit the sand than a Bedouin tribe assailed them. The tribesmen "stripped them naked as a glass" and beat them, killing a few. Then the Bedouin rode off with their loot.

The French tried to depart that place, but then more Bedouin appeared and cut most of them to pieces with their sabers. Some they took captive in hopes of holding them for ransom. Of seventy men, whether passengers or sailors, only fifteen were spared. A general was among the dead. The Bedouin offered the survivors to Kléber for the right sum of money, and he ransomed them. "They arrived virtually nude, burned by the sun, and half dead."

The French hold on the Delta remained insecure. A handful of cities were lightly garrisoned, but danger lurked in the countryside. Marmont wrote that at the port of Rosetta Menou proposed an excursion into the interior, about which the French still knew little. Menou and Marmont brought with them some of the scientists, such as Alix Delile, Déodat Dolomieu, Dominique-Vivant Denon, and a landscape painter named Joly, along with an escort of sixty infantrymen armed with muskets. The officers and intellectuals, on horseback, inadvertently got slightly ahead of their escort. Outside the walls of a substantial village built atop a manmade flat hill, perhaps Kafr Shabbas Amir, they abruptly encountered two hundred angry, armed peasants shouting "'*Irga'!*' '*Irga'!*'" (Go back! Go back!) and firing some shots above the foreigners' heads. After a difficult moment, the infantry arrived and, taking in the situation, went on the attack. They scaled the crenellated walls of the village and later set fire to its wooden doors, surrounding the barricades of the village fighters within.

At length the garrison fell to the French, but the stealthy villagers kept up their attacks, hidden by the darkness, and they were able to kill or wound twenty of the soldiers. Menou had his horse shot out from under him, and one of the intellectuals, Joly, took a fatal bullet to the head. Marmont's party headed back to Rosetta. Marmont had earlier in his account contrasted the intelligence and curiosity displayed by Bedouin toward the French with what he perceived to be a lack of astonishment or perceptiveness in the peasant farmers, who passed by the French regiments "without looking at them."

It was an unfortunate piece of condescension. Marmont had not realized that in the hierarchical societies of Asia and North Africa of that time, for a social inferior to hold his head up high and look a social superior in the eye was to court death. The peasants had not been stupid or incurious, only beaten down by the old warlords and unwilling to risk casual execution at the hands of the new ones for any inadvertent impudence. But Marmont's ill-fated first foray into the Delta revealed that where they felt they had a chance, a well-armed, fortified peasant population was willing to offer determined resistance to the invaders. Jollois, at Rosetta, entered in his journal for 13 August, "Some detachments of the column sent to burn a village on the Nile have returned." [26]

General Honoré Vial was sent to the port of Damietta, east of Alexandria on the Mediterranean coast, with only about five hundred men. On his way there, on 4 August, he stationed 120 men at the regional capital of Mansura, a town of 8,000 persons some seventy-eight miles north of Cairo. [27] He organized at Mansura a local divan of notables who said they were willing to support the French. He requisitioned a hundred saddle horses and laid a large tax claim on the region's cotton when it came in, then he departed. The Syrian-Egyptian chronicler Niqula Turk observed that every Thursday in Mansura was market day, when large numbers of peasants and Bedouin came in from the countryside. The people took advantage of this gathering to launch an insurrection.

On 9 August at 8:00 A.M. an armed crowd gathered to attack the French post. The insurgents were said to number 4,000 men. The soldiers retreated to their barracks, but the crowd pursued them there. They tried to set fire to the barracks, but were driven off by French musket fire. Then the troops began running low on cartridges. They decided they would eventually be overrun if they remained in the barracks, and so they charged out, losing several men to the townsmen's musket balls. They attempted to board some boats on the Nile, but villagers on the other bank began firing at them, killing some and driving away the rest. They therefore headed south, toward Cairo, facing attrition as they weathered further sniping on the way. Reduced to a band of thirty, they had to abandon their wounded, whom the villagers immediately dispatched. Out of ammunition, they finally were set upon by their pursuers and decapitated. One survivor escaped and was given refuge in the village of Shubra, where he was later picked up by a French officer. Another, a French woman accompanying her husband, was captured and married off to an Abu Qawra Arab sheikh.

That night in Damietta, General Vial tried to send some troops southwest to Mansura on the Nile, but they found their path blocked by an armed village allied with some Bedouin, and were forced to abandon their skiffs and return by land to their Mediterranean port. They lost a man killed and six wounded, according to Capt. Pierre-François Gerbaud. Niello Sargy, who was at Rosetta, reported the Mansura rebellion as a Bedouin attack. The careful report submitted by Lieutenant Colonel Théviotte, apparently gleaned from the surviving male eyewitness, does not actually mention Bedouin, and in light of Turk's comments, it is likely that a mixture of townspeople and the Bedouin and peasants who had arrived for market day participated in the uprising.

The French tended to see sedentary Egyptians as lacking in energy and initiative and to blame the Bedouin for all concerted violence, but this was a blind spot of theirs. Mansura, a fair-sized Egyptian town, served as an entrepôt for farmers in that part of the Delta, and its population was rich enough, well armed enough, and well organized enough to stage a revolt on its own, even if peasants and Bedouin joined in. In the aftermath, Turk said, the city elders tried to put all the blame on the latter. The issue that sparked the rebellion was almost certainly resentment of the French occupation and the prospect of heavy French taxes, of which Vial appears unwisely to have forewarned them.

Vial, helpless in the face of such a large uprising, sent word of it to Bonaparte in Cairo. The commander in chief reprimanded him for having left such a small contingent behind. (Since Bonaparte hoarded thousands of troops at Cairo for his own defense and seems to have understaffed the garrisons at Rosetta and Damietta, some of the blame here actually rests with him.) The commander in chief now dispatched General Dugua to Mansura with several strong columns. They were able to disperse the surrounding Bedouin and retake the city, which was largely deserted by the time they entered it.

In symbolic retribution, Dugua sentenced to decapitation two local Egyptian Muslim men of property in Mansura, who the French believed had promoted and funded the rebellion. Turk alleged that Dugua reminded the townspeople that he was under orders to burn down rebellious settlements, but would spare them on condition that they paid a fine of 4,000 silver *kis* (an Ottoman denomination). They agreed, and followed through.[28] He also asserted that Bonaparte instructed that they fly the French tricolor from their minarets there and throughout the Delta, and any town or village that refused was to be put to the flames.

The printer A. Galland confirmed in his journal that Bonaparte ordered Nile ships large enough to have sails to fly the tricolor. "In addition, it was enjoined upon them that they hang the same flag from the highest minarets in the provincial capitals; this latter provision caused some sorrow among Muslims."[29] Nothing could have been calculated better to humiliate and outrage Muslims than to force them to fly a European, infidel flag from the minarets of their mosques.

Despite the victory at arms of the French soldiers, they faced considerable challenges to their health in the swampy, densely populated Delta. Millet was sent to Mansura briefly some time after its reconquest. "It was there that one saw a terrible disease of the eyes that was spreading among almost the entire army, and as a result of which a large number were left blind or with sight in only one eye."[30] Trachoma, which the French called "opthalmia," is a bacterial disease endemic in the Nile Valley. It causes scarring on the eyelids that turns the eyelashes inward and transforms them into lacerating weapons against the victim's own corneas, sometimes destroying them.

In al-Minufiya, generals Fugière and Zajonchek fought against "hordes of insurgent Bedouin," and they delivered many villages to the flames "in order to imprint terror on that unruly population," wrote the frank Niello Sargy. In the latter's view, the conquest of the Delta depended on subduing two major provinces, Mansura and Sharqiya. Niello Sargy wrote, "In those provinces it was impossible to seize the possessions of the Mamluks because of the resistance of those villages and the way they received our troops."[31] The cash-starved French, desperate to appropriate the treasures of the former ruling class, were stymied by local opposition. In decapitating the Ottoman-Egyptian state, the French had unwittingly unleashed a revolution from below, which they were then forced to suppress if they were to survive in the wake of the disaster at Abuqir. Had Nelson not sunk their fleet, had they been more militarily and economically secure, Bonaparte's officers might have been less rapacious, and might more easily have come to an accommodation with these provincial leaders. As it was, the signs of rebellion in the Delta were multiplying.

"*Napoleon in Egypt.*" *By Jean-Léon Gérôme. Oil on oak panel. Princeton University Art Museum. Museum purchase, John Maclean Magie, Class of 1892, and Gertrude Magie Fund. Photo credit: Bruce M. White, © Photo: Trustees of Princeton University.*

"*Alexandria.*" *By Vivant Denon,* Voyages dans la Basse et la Haute Égypte, *3 vols. (London: S. Bagster, 1807).*

"Napoleon at the Battle of the Pyramids." Engraving by Philippe Joseph Vallot, 1838, after Antoine-Jean Gros.

"Cairo." Vivant Denon.

"Denon Making a Sketch." Vivant Denon.

"Rosetta." Vivant Denon.

"The Cairo Revolt." Drawing in A. Hugo, ed., France Militaire, *vol. 2 (Paris: Delloye, 1835).*

"Bonaparte Pardons the Cairo Rebels." Drawing in A. Hugo.

"The Battle of Samanud." Vivant Denon.

"Ambulance for the Wounded." Description de l'Égypte, *24 vols. (Paris, Imprimerie de C. L. F. Panckoucke, 1820–1830).*

(left) *"Frontispiece."* Description de l'Égypte.

(below) *"River Port of Bulaq, Cairo."* Description de l'Égypte.

(above) *"Tomb of Ozymandias, Thebes."* Description de l'Égypte.

(right) *"Azbakiya Square."* Description de l'Égypte.

"Distillery." Description de l'Égypte.

"Coffee Roasting Shop." Description de l'Égypte.

"A Woman of the People."
Description de l'Égypte.

"Alimahs or Public Dancers."
Description de l'Égypte.

"Sheikh al-Sadat." Description de l'Égypte.

"Murad Bey." Description de l'Égypte.

7

ALI BONAPARTE

lthough he was being wildly optimistic, Bonaparte believed that presiding over the Festival of the Nile, with all its connotations of blessedness and prosperity in Egyptian folk Islam, had been a public relations success. He looked forward to the next such occasion, determined to turn it to advantage as well. The Great Sultan wrote to General Vial in Damietta, "I imagine that you have in mind to celebrate with yet more pomp the festival of the Prophet. . . . The festival of the Nile was very beautiful here; that of the Prophet will be even better."[1]

Al-Jabarti wrote that the Cairo Muslim elite had not intended to celebrate the birthday of the Prophet that year, and that when Bonaparte discovered their intentions, he pressed them on the matter. Sayyid Khalil al-Bakri apologized, saying that the situation was too unstable and the elite lacked the funds to act as patrons of the festival. Bonaparte therefore funded it himself, providing al-Bakri with three hundred French francs. The same initial reticence was apparent in provincial cities. The artist Dominique Vivant Denon, who had once painted a portrait of Voltaire, described with some outrage how the mufti of Rosetta had intended to let the birthday of the Prophet go uncelebrated, as a means of conveying to the people that "we oppose one of the most sacred acts of their religion."[2] Menou had discovered the importance of holding the festival at the last minute and ordered the mufti to organize it.

The festival of Muhammad's birth began on 20 August, three days before the exact anniversary.[3] Detroye recalled that Cairenes put colored lanterns atop poles at two places in Azbakiya Square, producing a beautiful effect that evening. At ten in the evening, devotees began forming processions that set out from city quarters and walked toward various mosques, led by men carrying torches or large mobile chandeliers with forty lanterns attached. Others,

Detroye complained, "chanted baroque airs accompanied by music that was even more baroque. Such is the procession that traversed the city at night, shouting, crying out, and making an infernal racket." Moiret wrote that "the principal residents circulated in the streets with the marks of their rank or function, accompanied by slaves, some of them armed and the others carrying torches." At Azbakiya they suspended in the air an illumined representation of the Prophet's tomb in Medina.

The next day, Detroye said, the festival started up again, more tumultuous than the day before. The following day saw more processions, more singing, more shouting. One can only speculate that the Egyptians took advantage of the French permission to celebrate their religious holiday to reaffirm their faith and steadfastness, at a time when both had surely been shaken by the French infidel conquest of Egypt, which had been continuously in Muslim hands since the seventh century.

The actual day of the anniversary of the Prophet Muhammad's birth, Detroye remembered, was celebrated with even more fervor than the preceding days. "The public places were crowded with small sideshows: bear or monkey trainers, singers, songstresses who performed scenes with dialogue, women who chanted poetry, magicians working with goblets who made live snakes disappear, children who performed the most indecent dances, gladiators who engaged in single combat, etc."

Despite the sacredness of the event, the street people commonly engaged in lewd dancing to celebrate it. Denon at Rosetta witnessed a similar scene, but of men, not children: "The dance that followed was of the same genre as the chant. It was not a painting of joy or of gaiety, but of a voluptuousness that turned quite rapidly toward a lasciviousness more and more disgusting, in which the actors, always masculine, expressed in the most indecent manner the scenes that even love does not permit to the two sexes save in the shadow of mystery."[4] Denon, author of the 1777 libertine short story "No Tomorrow" ("Point de Lendemain"), was no prude. He was complaining not about eroticism but about an explicit style of public performance that was common in Egypt. He may also have been especially shocked, since he mentioned the dancers' masculinity, at the homosocial character of the pornographic performance. The scout Millet observed, "They know nothing of prudishness in Egypt. A true Muslim will show the most lewd and licentious dances and recreations to his family."[5] The worldly libertines from secular Paris were continually blushing at scenes, usually involving hip action, put on by the supposedly hidebound Egyptian Muslims. At the same time, the Egyptian historian al-Jabarti took a dim view of the sexual morality of French men and women.

When evening fell, Bernoyer's least favorite people, the dervishes, or Sufi mystics, appeared, their hair long and their clothing "negligible." Malus, more frank, observed of the dervish leaders, "These are the saints of the country; their life is a continual ecstasy and everything is permitted to them; many circulate through the streets at various times of the year naked as apes. They only live on alms from the public." Villiers du Terrage said of the nude holy men that they "are a kind of madman, extremely venerated, to whom everything is permitted, whose insults are an honor, even to the women who surrender themselves to them." Devotees gathered, Detroye said, forming themselves in circles, very crowded in on one another, and taking each other by the arms. They then began "a very violent movement, of each man by himself and of the entire circle, to the left and the right. This movement was accompanied by painful efforts." They went on moving in unison until they were exhausted. "It was said that sometimes devotees died where they stood." Moving in unison and chanting religious poetry in this manner caused Sufi adepts to hyperventilate, which they believed helped them attain alternate states (hal) of consciousness and aided them in their quest to feel union with the divine.

❦

That morning, Bonaparte had ordered up an imposing parade of the troops of the garrison in honor of the great day, and a French marching band intermixed its martial strains with the chants of the Muslims. Then, Detroye recalled dryly, "The French artillery saluted Muhammad." All the high French officers were presented to a leading cleric, Sayyid Khalil al-Bakri. In the presence of the divan, Bonaparte dressed al-Bakri in an ermine coat and declared him the naqib al-ashraf, the leader of the caste of Muhammad's honored descendants, insomuch as the previous incumbent, Umar al-Makram, had fled to Syria. The festival of the Prophet's birth was especially presided over by his putative descendants, who formed an honored social stratum. Bonaparte directed that any Egyptian who had a dispute with a member of the sharif caste should bring the complaint to Sayyid al-Bakri.

In all these steps, Bonaparte was playing the role of a Muslim sultan, honoring the progeny of the Prophet, and they in turn pledged to support the status quo and employ their religious aura to mediate disputes between ruler and ruled. This attempt at gaining legitimacy through the Prophet's progeny was not entirely successful. The Christian Syrian chronicler of the occupation, Niqula Turk, remarked, "Sheikh Khalil al-Bakri loved the French Republic, and for that reason the Egyptian Muslims hated him." The ambitious and wealthy al-Bakri, cloaked in the aura of the Prophet's family and of his prominence among the clerics, weathered the disdain of the masses.

Captain Say, who disapproved of Bonaparte's dalliance with Islam, recalled that the commander in chief on the occasion of the festival of the Prophet's birth "dressed in oriental costume and declared himself protector of all the religions. The enthusiasm was universal, and he was unanimously given the name of the son-in-law of the Prophet. Everyone called him Ali Bonaparte."[6] Egyptian Sunnis considered 'Ali ibn Abi Talib, the cousin and son-in-law of the Prophet Muhammad, to be the fourth rightly-guided caliph or vicar of the Prophet. If the Egyptians bestowed this sobriquet on the Corsican, it was in sidesplitting jest. Bonaparte's secretary, Bourrienne, sensitive to the way in which the general's pandering on the subject of religion made him seem ridiculous, said that he never dressed in Egyptian robes again, finding them "uncomfortable."

That evening, the sheikh threw a great feast for Bonaparte at his mansion. A hundred prominent clerics of al-Azhar sat cross-legged on carpets around twenty low tables, while one of them recited a narrative of the Prophet's life in a voice that the French found monotonous. The French were seated at tables and offered silver cutlery and plates, with a rare bottle of wine. Afterward, roast, entrées, rice, and pastry were served, all of it spicy. Desvernois observed, "The Arabs eat with their fingers; but I must add in all justice that three times during the meal they washed their hands."

The subject of their conversations is easy to imagine. Desvernois said of Bonaparte and the al-Azhar clerics that he "conversed frequently with them, seeking to be instructed as to the needs of the country and the means of making it prosper. Sometimes, even, to flatter their religious prejudices, he let them envisage that the Republican army was not far from embracing the faith of Muhammad." Another officer observed: "Nothing was forgotten in persuading the Egyptians that the army had the greatest veneration for the Prophet. The soldiers were politic in their expressions; when they returned to their quarters, they laughed at that comedy."[7]

In a moment of unusual candor, Bonaparte at Saint Helena later recalled his straits of that August.[8] "The position of the French was uncertain. They were only tolerated by the believers, who, crushed by the rapidity with which events unfolded, had bowed before force, but were already openly deploring the triumph of the idolaters, whose presence profaned the blessed waters. They groaned at the opprobrium that had befallen the first key to the holy Kaaba. The imams made a show of reciting the verses of the Qur'an that were most opposed to the infidels." The "blessed waters" of the Nile were being coded as Muslim, he was reporting, and the non-Muslim French conquest of them rendered them ritually polluted. Likewise, the cube-shaped edifice known as the Kaaba in Mecca, around which Muslims on pilgrimage circumambulate, had been safeguarded by the Egyptian stronghold. Now, Bonaparte recalled his adversaries charging, non-Muslims held the very key to Mecca itself.

The commander in chief was fully aware that any literate Egyptian Muslim would look, in explaining the French conquest, to the medieval wars of the Crusades for a precedent. If the Egyptians decided that the French were just crusaders, and represented a specifically Christian quest for Near East dominance, they would never reconcile themselves to French rule. He recalled the words of the Count of Volney, who came to Egypt and wrote in 1788 that any conqueror of Egypt would have to fight three wars. The first would be against the British, the second against the Ottoman Empire, and the third, most difficult of all, would be against the local Muslims. Volney had urged these three as reasons not to attempt an attack on Egypt. Bonaparte took them as a challenge.

On 30 July, Bonaparte had written to General Kléber in Alexandria, asking him to establish a local divan consisting of pro-French loyalists. He had warned of the dangers if the Egyptian public panicked in terror, observing, "All these people could have thought that we came in the same spirit of Saint Louis, that they should comport themselves as though they had entered a Christian state."[9] Saint Louis's invasion had even failed on its own terms! Certainly, were Egyptians to decide that Bonaparte's was a new Crusader state, it would toll the death knell for Bonaparte's entire enterprise. He was running away from Christianity as fast as possible.

Bonaparte hoped to persuade the imams to say the Friday sermon in his name. Ordinarily in the Egypt of the time, the sermon would have been said in the name of the Ottoman Sultan, Selim III, but the commander in chief wanted the Islamically granted legitimacy that came with this privilege. It was, of course, folly to hope that the Friday prayer sermonizers would say the prayers in the name of a European Christian ruler. The commander in chief remonstrated with the clerics of the al-Azhar, whenever he met with them that summer: they were not doing enough to stop the febrile agitation stirred up by the preachers, and he wanted a fatwa or formal legal ruling from them demanding that imams advise obedience to the new state. He said that they paled and seemed seized with consternation. Sheikh Abdullah al-Sharqawi at length replied, "You want to have the protection of the Prophet. He loves you. You want the Arab Muslims to march beneath your banners. You want to restore the glory of Arabia, you are not an idolater. Become a Muslim! 100,000 Egyptians and 100,000 Arabs come from Arabia, from Mecca and Medina, will range themselves with you. Drilled and disciplined in your way, they will conquer the Orient for you, and you will reestablish in all its glory the fatherland of the Prophet."[10] Bonaparte said that at that moment, their old faces lit up and all prostrated themselves, imploring the protection of heaven.

That al-Sharqawi argued to Bonaparte that he should convert is plausible enough. That he thought in terms such as "Arab," "nation," or "fatherland" a century before such ethnic nationalism began appearing among Arabic speakers is impossible, and the Corsican was just imposing European categories on what he heard. At most, al-Sharqawi would have seen the general's conversion as a way of reinvigorating the fortunes of the Muslim world. He might have hoped that Bonaparte would convert, and then send tribute to Istanbul, asking that the sultan formally recognize him as the viceroy of Egypt. From an Egyptian point of view, such a development would not have been unusual. After all, many of the beys that ruled Egypt had been born to Christian families in the Caucasus, and the sultan routinely granted them some sort of ex post facto recognition once they became powerful.

The commander in chief, despite his later protestations to the contrary, clearly considered this option seriously, at least on a pro forma, outward basis. He wrote that he replied to the sheikh, "There are two great difficulties preventing my army and me from becoming Muslims. The first is circumcision, the second is wine. My soldiers have the habit from their infancy, and I will never be able to persuade them to renounce it." He told the story that Sheikh Muhammad al-Mahdi (who had been born a Coptic Christian and converted in order to attend al-Azhar) proposed that sixty clerics of the al-Azhar Seminary be permitted to pose the question publicly and to deliberate on the matter. He maintained that the rumor spread throughout the country that the clerics were instructing the Great Sultan in Islam. Bonaparte had an unappealing tendency to believe his own propaganda, or at least to keep repeating it long after it was completely implausible. His depiction of happy Egyptian Muslims joyous at the news that the infidel general was learning the Qur'an by heart is at odds with everything we know about the profound hostility Egyptian Muslims entertained for their new masters. Bonaparte appears to have believed that even a public debate about whether the French might become Muslims benefited his cause.

Warming to his tale, Bonaparte remembered that four Muslim jurisconsults came with a fatwa over a month later, setting aside the issue of circumcision since, they said, that was not a central Islamic duty. They also said that non-

Muslims who drank wine would be permitted to convert, but that if they continued to drink after the conversion, they would go to hell. The commander in
chief pronounced himself delighted that the first difficulty had been removed
but expressed some consternation about the second point, which would hardly
be an incentive to conversion. Sheikh al-Mahdi suggested that the first part of
the fatwa be released, in any case, which he thought would have a good effect on
the country. He maintained that the al-Azhar clerics went back to their discussions on the second matter, also corresponding with their peers in Mecca. In the
end, they agreed that the new converts might drink, but would have to pay a
penance for it. Bonaparte's story is suspect. Although the second fatwa is intended to be its denouement, he drops the subject at that point. Clearly, he
never found a way of convincing the al-Azhar clerics to allow a pro forma declaration of French "conversion" to Islam.

Although Bonaparte and his defender, Bourrienne, prefaced this account by
saying that Bonaparte never converted, never went to mosque, and never prayed
in the Muslim way, all of that is immaterial. It is quite clear that he was attempting to find a way for French deists to be declared Muslims for purposes of statecraft. This strategy is of a piece with the one used in his initial Arabic
proclamation, in which he maintained that the French army, being without any
particular religion and rejecting Trinitarianism, was already "*muslim*" with a
small "m." Islam was less important to him, of course, than legitimacy. Without
legitimacy, the French could not hope to hold Egypt in the long run, and being
declared some sort of strange Muslim was the shortcut that appealed to Bonaparte. It foundered on the orthodoxy of the al-Azhar clergy, however.

Bonaparte's admiration for the Prophet Muhammad, in contrast, was genuine. He wrote in his memoirs that "Arabia was idolatrous when Muhammad,
seven centuries after Jesus Christ, introduced to it the religion of the God of
Abraham, Ishmael, Moses, and Jesus Christ." The Corsican decried the sanguinary doctrinal wars of early Christianity, with squabbles over the nature of
the Father, the Son, and the Holy Spirit, and said admiringly, "Muhammad declared that there was only one God, who had neither father nor son and that the
Trinity imported an idea from paganism." He explained the sensual depictions
of paradise in the Qur'an by the poverty and ignorance of the Arabians of that
time, who did not have the luxury of a life of contemplation such as the Atheni-
ans could pursue. Muhammad had to promise his acolytes, with their hardscrabble lives, Bonaparte explained, "sweet-smelling groves where they would repose
in perpetual shade, in the arms of divine houris with white skin and black eyes."
Bonaparte coded the early Muslims as Bedouin who, impassioned at such a

prospect, became heroes. "Muhammad was a prince; he rallied his compatriots around him. In a few years, his Muslims conquered half the world. He rescued more souls from false gods, overturned more idols, and pulled down more pagan temples in fifteen years than the adherents of Moses and Jesus Christ had in fifteen centuries."

♣

Bonaparte did not give up his attempts to use Islamic rhetoric as part of his ruling strategy. Just a few days after the festival, on 28 August, he wrote a letter to the leading Muslim cleric of Alexandria, Sheikh al-Masiri, whom he had met on taking the city, and who later proved cooperative with Kléber as the head of the divan there. "You know the particular esteem," he wrote, "that I conceived for you at the first instant I met you." He expressed a hope of meeting soon with "all the wise and learned men of the country" to establish "a uniform regime, founded on the principles of the Qur'an, which are the only true ones, and which can alone ensure the well-being of men."[11] That is, he was offering al-Masiri a chance at national office and influence and promising to institute rule by *sharia* or Islamic canon law. At least, that is how an Egyptian man of the cloth would have taken the offer to govern in accordance with the Qur'an. Even the Ottoman Empire did not always implement sharia as it was interpreted by the clerics.

Bonaparte, isolated from France by the British blockade and faced with a hostile population and endemic Bedouin and town revolts, adopted the Qur'an as his shield and the promotion of the Muslim clerics as his program. The French Jacobins, who had taken over Notre Dame for the celebration of a cult of Reason and had invaded and subdued the Vatican, were now creating Egypt as the world's first modern Islamic Republic.

In mid-August, Bonaparte wrote to the sharif of Mecca, Ghalib ibn Musa'id al-Hashimi, announcing his arrival in Cairo "as well as the measures that I have taken to preserve for the holy mosques of Mecca and Medina the revenues that pertained to them."[12] Bonaparte had been told by the clerics of al-Azhar about the enormous endowment of farm lands in Egypt and their grain harvest that supported the holy cities. He was seeking Islamic legitimacy by supplanting the Ottoman sultan, Selim III, as guarantor of foodstuffs to the Muslim holy land. He pointed out to the sharif that he had "protected the imams, the *sharifs*, and all the men of the law." He told the Meccan potentate that he had appointed Mustafa Bey, the deputy of the (departed) Ottoman viceroy, as the leader of the pilgrimage caravan, and promised that the bey would escort the caravan with forces sufficient to prevent Bedouin predation. Bonaparte offered to send either French troops as an escort, or local Egyptian ones. Ghalib then faced a challenge from the puritan, militant Wahhabi sect based in Najd, and felt that the Ottomans had not given him much support in the struggle. He therefore was willing to consider establishing good relations with the French, especially since the economy of the Hejaz in western Arabia, where the holy cities of Mecca and Medina were located, depended profoundly on Egypt, both because of the grain endowment and because of the commerce of the pilgrimage caravan and the coffee trade. Bonaparte was drawing around himself the mantle of guarantor of the fiscal health of this region, and therefore that of key support for the Islamic pilgrimage.

On his return to Cairo from Salahiya, Bonaparte appears to have privately named as the leader *(amir al-hajj)* of the annual pilgrimage caravan one Mustafa Bey, who had been an aide to the Ottoman-appointed viceroy of Egypt. (The previous incumbent had fled to Syria with Ibrahim Bey.) On 2 September, the commander in chief held a formal investment ceremony. Bonaparte presented Mustafa Bey a superb green cloak in the presence of the divan and the clerics, along with a diamond-studded crest and a richly caparisoned horse.[13] The newly installed official set out from the Citadel with many aides, to a six-gun salute. The annual pilgrimage caravan was a major source of commercial wealth for Egypt, and Bonaparte wished to encourage this trade, which transported cloves, coffee, shawls, oils, balms, and cochineal dye between the Red Sea and North Africa. Naming the leader of the pilgrimage caravan had been a prerogative of the Ottoman viceroy, and in assuming it Bonaparte was attempting to claim the mantle of legitimate Islamic statecraft.

The Great Sultan had the al-Azhar clerics write a letter to the sharif of Mecca on that occasion. They said, "He has assured us that he recognizes the unity of God, that the French honor our Prophet, as well as the Qur'an, and that they regard the Muslim religion as the best religion. The French have proved their love for Islam in freeing the Muslim prisoners detained in Malta, in destroying churches and breaking crosses in the city of Venice, and in pursuing the pope, who commanded the Christians to kill the Muslims and who had represented that act as a religious duty." Bonaparte had a copy of the letter sent to Kléber to be printed in six hundred copies, with four hundred to be sent to the Arabian Peninsula.[14]

It is not entirely clear that the Muslim notables of Mecca would have been reassured to hear that the French had destroyed churches or broken crosses. Islamic law recognized Christians as "people of the Book," fellow monotheists with a legitimate religion. This attitude of Muslims, that it was allowed for other religions to be practiced in their midst, was somewhat unusual. Christian Europe under the Inquisition had had virtually no resident Muslims, and the hundreds of thousands who elected to remain in Spain after the Reconquista of the late 1400s were forced to convert to Catholicism. For some centuries some Christian countries forbade Jews to live there as well. In contrast, as long as they paid a poll tax and showed themselves loyal, Jews and Christians were allowed by Muslim states to dwell under their shadow and practice their faiths, though with some restrictions. There were, of course, episodes in which particularly fanatical or vicious rulers or clerics attacked these minorities, but they were not the rule, and the contrast with medieval and early modern Europe remains stark. Bonaparte's rhetoric, here put into the mouths of the clerics of al-Azhar, actually exhibited less toleration than was typical in Islamic law.

✦

Bonaparte's Islam policy provoked a lively debate among his officers and troops. Some officers were unfazed by the hypocrisy of it all. General Dupuis in Cairo wrote a merchant of Toulouse, "We celebrate here with enthusiasm the festivals of Muhammad. We fool the Egyptians with our affected attachment to their religion, in which Bonaparte and we no more believe than we do in that of Pius the Defunct."[15] The dismissive reference to the pope and Roman Catholicism betrays a lively anticlericalism and militant secularism. Incredibly, they produced in Egypt not open disdain for an alien religion but a calculated and cynical willingness to pretend respect for it as a means of deceiving the Egyptian public. "You won't believe it," he continued, "but I assure you that we are as fervent as the most fanatical pilgrims. In the end, it is the third pantomime that we will have played, since the solemn entry of the Meccan caravan that we presided over here is no small thing. You would have smiled to see me with our musicians at the head of the pilgrims." Dupuis here revealed that Bonaparte had ordered a positively pious French welcome be given the pilgrims, still covered in the dust of the holy city of Mecca.

Two months after the festival of the Prophet's birth, Captain Moiret reported that soothsayers began being paid to proclaim that Bonaparte was on a divine mission to destroy the enemies of Islam, which had been predicted "in more than twenty passages" of the Qur'an.[16] They predicted that the French sultan would soon have himself circumcised, take the turban, follow the religion of Muhammad, and bring along by his example his entire army. Moiret recalled that "the politicians" among the French forces argued that positive rhetoric about Islam and stoking the fires of such expectations among the Egyptian populace were necessary for the security of the army. They pointed to Roman practice, which they said was to avoid imposing any changes on the mores, usages, laws, or religions of the peoples they conquered. "Rather than forcing them to adopt the gods of the capital, they placed there the gods of Athens and Carthage." Moiret alleged that this view won out among the army, and was certainly that of Bonaparte himself.

Captain Moiret remarked dryly that the French troops actually would not have much minded gaining admission to the Muslim paradise. This is a joking reference to the Qur'an's promise of perpetual virgin companions, or *houris*, said to inhabit it. But, he said, they would only have wanted such a heaven if they could have obtained a dispensation to do without circumcision and to continue to drink wine. When he had first arrived in Cairo, Moiret had complained bitterly that the Egyptians had no wine, because their Legislator, the Prophet Muhammad, forbade it. He admitted that the French troops thought it unlikely that they would receive special permission to drink, were they to convert. The rationalist partisans of the Enlightenment, he reported, either satirized these predictions about Bonaparte converting or became indignant. They protested that they "had not shaken up the superstitions of Europe so as to adopt those of the Orient, and that one should never speak anything but the truth to the people."[17] He saw these militant secularists as a minority, with little support among the troops, who favored Bonaparte's pragmatic paganism on the Roman model instead.

The civilian quartermaster Bernoyer also wrote angry letters back home about Islam. At one point, he launched a diatribe against the Muslim clerics, whom he called "veritable impostors," and charged with forcing the faithful to believe absurdities such as that they were the agents or confidants of the Creator: "Nothing surprises with regard to them, but it is inconceivable that there are enough imbeciles to believe them!" Once when he saw pilgrims come back to Cairo from Mecca, a multitude in diverse dress, from different races and nations, he wrote of his desire to shout the Enlightenment truth at them that there was no deity that actively intervened in history. But, he concluded, "what would that have served?"[18]

✦

Bonaparte's Islam policy provoked lively intellectual debates, but encounters with Islam had an intimate meaning for those of the French who established close personal relations with the Egyptians around them. The most dramatic instance of wholehearted approval of the commander in chief's warming to Islam was that of Gen. Jacques Menou. Thereby hangs a tale.

The presence of French troops in the towns of the Delta profoundly upset ordinary social arrangements in Egyptian society. In Rosetta, the middle-class women had been used to being allowed to go out of their homes during the day and to gather at the communal bathhouse. Secluding females was a custom usually practiced only by the wealthiest Ottoman-Egyptian families and was rare among middle-class or lower-middle-class Egyptians. Seclusion was designed to show that the man of the house was so wealthy that he could afford servants to shop for everything the household needed and could maintain almost an entire second residence in the female quarters of his mansion. The wealthy had baths in their homes, allowing their women to dispense with the city bathhouses. Niello Sargy said that, with French soldiers patrolling the streets, Egyptian husbands in Rosetta began forbidding their wives to go out. The women organized and sent a deputation to Menou, the commander of Rosetta, asking that he take measures that would allow them to recover their liberty of movement—presumably by reining in the troop patrols around the bathhouse. They charged the two prettiest women as their spokespersons, including Zubayda, the daughter of the proprietor of the city's communal hot bath (who had an economic interest in the lifting of the informal ban on the circulation of housewives). Menou acquiesced in their request and issued a decree stating that women were an object of respect for the French and that the clan chieftains and clerics were to allow them to circulate in the town as they had ordinarily done before. Menou must have glimpsed enough of Zubayda to be smitten with her. He sought her hand, and would have been told by her father, Muhammad Ali al-Bawwab, that only by converting to Islam could he hope to marry her. Islamic law allows Muslim men to marry non-Muslim women, but Muslim women may only marry Muslim men, and the al-Bawwab family claimed descent on both sides from the Prophet Muhammad, making them members of the sharif caste and even more fastidious about such matters. Menou therefore converted to Islam, adopting the name 'Abdullah, or the "servant of God," and in the spring of 1799 he married Zubayda, the daughter of the bathhouse owner and divorced wife of Selim Aga Nimatullah.

Bonaparte tended to describe his army as unchurched, but in fact many believers served under him. For a handful, disoriented by the Revolution's anticlericalism and then by culture shock in the Middle East, adopting Islam was a way of authorizing a pious sensibility and of connecting with their new home.

Menou wrote in October to General Marmont concerning a valuable administrative suggestion he had made: "You are a man of gold, my dear general. . . . I
ask God, Muhammad, all the saints of paradise and of the Qur'an, that the
measure you proposed will be adopted."[19] Menou had been the officer in charge
of Paris security for the Republic in September 1795, at a time of royalist intrigue. Nervous politicians saw him as insufficiently forceful. They had removed
him and replaced him with Barras and Bonaparte. Three years later he was governor of Rosetta and a Muslim convert. The adoption of an almost Catholic discourse of piety in an Islamic guise by a French officer in Egypt could scarcely
have been foreseen by the Jacobins on the Directory and in the legislature who
urged the invasion.

Menou was initially rare in being willing to convert in order to make a formal marriage alliance in Egypt. Most officers simply took Egyptian women as
mistresses. Still, even some of those wrestled with the same issues as had
Menou. Captain Moiret wrote, some months later, that he conducted a clandes-
tine affair with Zulayma, the widow of a lesser grandee, who had fled to refuge
with a patron in Damietta.[20] He lived on the route to and from the mosque, and
a wealthy woman often hesitated before his door as she went to or came back
from her devotions. (Mosques sometimes had side passages where women were
allowed to pray, out of sight of the men, though this arrangement was rare.) The
tantalized Moiret could not see her face through the double veil. Once, however, he greeted her, and she put her hand to her heart. That evening, her maidservant came and arranged for him to tutor her. He was able to communicate
with her because this slave woman had originally hailed from Marseilles but had
been captured off the Barbary Coast by pirates and sold in the North Africa
slave markets. Zulayma had enough freedom and wealth left so that she could
hire him to tutor her in mathematics and French, with her slave woman as a
chaperone. He recorded her description of her life. She explained that she had
been sold from Georgia, but was sent to Cairo rather than to Istanbul because
she was not plump enough for the markets in the imperial capital. She said that
even the bey who purchased her neglected her for some time in hopes of fatten-
ing her up. He recalled that she complained of being oppressed by the more
powerful women in the harem, of being "humiliated and enslaved" and confined
to an interior apartment with no company but elderly slaves. She explained that
the wives and concubines had no society with men except their masters, who
visited their apartments occasionally, and for whom they would prepare with
perfumes and treats. They passed their days embroidering, and occasionally had
an 'alima, or Egyptian geisha girl, in to dance for them and tell them passionate

stories. In the afternoon they took tea and fruits. Sometimes they went for boat rides. The luxuries they enjoyed, however, were outweighed by the cruelties they often endured. Moiret relates from her the story of a Circassian co-wife of hers who went out to the mosque with an elderly slave. While out, she heard a strange accent and turned her head to see a European man conversing with someone nearby. The slave is said to have reported the infraction to the bey. "The furious tyrant grabbed the guilty one by the hair in the midst of us all and beheaded her with a saber."

She finally broached her feelings, presumably through her French maidservant. "Out of your grace, young lover, charming warrior, pull me out of this detestable country and lead me to France, if ever destiny calls you there." He wrote that her tears added to her beauty, and that he promised her that he would. He then pressed her, however, asking if he could hope to see his love requited in accordance with this oath he had given her. He clearly wanted, not only her gratitude for delivering her, but also an indication that she had real feelings for him. She played hard to get. How could she be sure of the sincerity of his oath, she asked, "before it had been consecrated by religion and law?" For, she said, Frenchmen were renowned for their inconstancy, being inflamed with a passion that is soon extinguished. (If Frenchmen already had that reputation, it speaks volumes about their relations with local women.)

Moiret represented himself as an exception. But he went on to press her about which ceremonies of religion, exactly, she had in mind. She should not, he said firmly, expect him to take the turban, "or to submit to the humiliating operation that is the distinctive sign of the Jew and the Muslim," or to renounce wine, "which was invented by Noah." He would not follow the example of Menou, who had converted to Islam and taken the name of 'Abdullah, setting the tongues of the entire army wagging. He refused to be an object of ridicule for his comrades. Finally, he said, "How can you believe me incapable of breaking my oaths to you if I would break my ties to the religion in which I was raised?"

She in turn protested that she could hardly leave Islam, since the man she was staying with, the merchant "Aboulferu," was deeply attached to it and would never countenance her conversion out of it.

Moiret coldly replied, "We must then bid one another an eternal farewell," though he wrote that he knew full well she would not.

Zulayma offered a compromise. He should alert her when he was to return to France, and she would accompany him, with her riches and jewelry, and once in France his God would be hers. He wrote that thereafter he continued to see her as often as possible, continuing the tutoring, until he was posted elsewhere on 19 July 1799. In the event, when the French did withdraw in 1801, Zulayma was not able to meet him in Alexandria, falling into the hands of the beys who returned with the Ottoman army.[21]

Despite the romantic touches, the veiled approach, the tears that enhanced her beauty, the pledges of eternal love, this exchange reveals a bargaining process. Moiret was offering Zulayma refuge from the Ottoman-Egyptian rulers should the French leave, and she was pledging him the riches she had obtained from her dead husband. (She specifically mentioned bringing her jewelry and wealth with her to France.) In essence, she was offering to bring her own trousseau to the marriage. Initially, he must have been attracted by the prospect of having a mate in Egypt. Finding a mate in France on his return would not have been so difficult. But the possibility of simply marrying her in Damietta was foreclosed by his unwillingness to convert to Islam and by her inability to convert to Christianity without losing her local patronage. He expressed himself unwilling to be a laughingstock or to accept alien ways, but it surely had something to do with his own religious convictions.

Unlike many of the Republican officers, he was a believing Catholic and had once gone to seminary in Lyons with the intention of becoming a Dominican priest. Moiret depicted both of them as too concerned about social conventions and personal image to accept the compromises necessary for marriage in Egypt. He was gallant enough not to even hint at what went on during her visits to him for the ostensible purpose of tutoring her.

The same barriers that stood in the way of a formal marriage alliance between the Catholic Moiret and his Zulayma also bedeviled the Jacobin unbeliever François Bernoyer.[22] Bonaparte knew that his men had arrived in torrid Egypt wearing heavy European clothing, and he ordered Bernoyer to design new uniforms better suited to local conditions and to arrange for them to be mass-produced. The quartermaster, however, faced a shortage of the necessary thick linen. He asked his Egyptian agent, Achem (presumably Ahmad), who knew a little French, to help him, and through him he contacted the local owner of a small textile manufactory that employed about three hundred workers, both male and female. The owner agreed to provide Bernoyer with four hundred yards of cloth each day.[23]

The next day he and his Egyptian agent went out to the workshop to see if production had begun on the required cloth. They found the outer gate closed, so Bernoyer dismounted and entered the premises on foot, leaving his agent to see to the horses. On crossing the threshold, he saw a beautiful young woman drawing water. She looked up at his footsteps and gasped, covering her face with her hands, and then she hurried away, leaving her jug behind. Bernoyer, "ever gallant, as you know," picked up the jug and went after her. He called out in his broken Arabic, "Look, my pretty friend, you forgot your jug!" She stopped, and he wasted not a moment in catching up to her and presenting her with the vessel. Of course, in order to accept it she had to withdraw one hand from her face, uncovering part of it. "That one portion that I saw was sufficient as a basis for concluding that this Egyptian was extremely beautiful. I fell in love at that moment, to the extent that a great confusion seized my reason and paralyzed me for a few instants." The owner of the manufactory was proud to give him a detailed tour, but Bernoyer was so distracted that he hardly heard a word the man said. He cut the tour short on a pretext. As they rode out, the agent inquired of his intentions. Bernoyer replied, "I absolutely have to come into possession of that beautiful person."

Ahmad agreed to do what he could, but raised several difficulties. First, how would he know which girl it was that Bernoyer had seen? They would all be veiled in the presence of strange men. Moreover, all the women who worked in the factory would be Egyptian Muslims, and they were forbidden to have anything to do with non-Muslim men. Muslims were so sensitive on this issue, he concluded, that they might well refuse to have anything to do with intriguing for Bernoyer. The quartermaster replied that none of these obstacles deterred him. "On the contrary, they only serve to excite my desires and increase my need to satisfy them." The forbidden status of Muslim women eroticized them for the Frenchmen. Bernoyer then threatened to cut off his agent if he would not cooperate in trying to acquire the girl, all the while ashamed that he was hurting the man's feelings and that his will was unable to rein in the "violent passion of carnal love that had so strongly subjugated" him. He wondered if it was the heat of the climate that had provoked these intense desires and swore he had never experienced anything like it. The Orient itself became the pretext for the need to subjugate the Orient.

Ahmad at length managed to locate the girl in the manufactory whom Bernoyer had described and to ascertain that her name was Fatima ("Fatmair"). She was the daughter of a destitute carpenter. Bernoyer had formulated a plan of setting up a false marriage between her and his servant 'Ali. Ahmad pointed out to him that the qadi who married the two would need to be assured that 'Ali had a sufficient source of income, his own domicile, a cooking pot, a coffee pan, and a pipe. 'Ali, in contrast, did not have shoes on his feet. Bernoyer stuffed a wad of money in Ahmad's hands and asked him to buy 'Ali the necessary accoutrements. Bernoyer then sent Ahmad to the carpenter father of the prospective bride, with "'Ali's" proposal, saying that he had caught a glimpse of her at the textile manufactory and that he was employed in a workshop belonging to the French. The carpenter was pleased at the idea of establishing an indirect link of clientelage to the masters of the country. They went to the qadi and got everything approved, though Bernoyer wrote that it was done without the girl's consent, since in Egypt "fathers exercise absolute power over their children."

The wedding was to take place 11 November. Bernoyer represents himself as now realizing that he had to find a way to avoid an "idiot like 'Ali" actually getting to spend the nuptial night with the girl. The difficulty was, he said, that the bride was typically delivered to the bedroom of the groom by her mother before he arrived, as he waited outside with his friends. She then used her finger to press her daughter's hymen enough to produce blood. She would issue from the chamber, lock the girl in, and show her sanguinary digit around proudly to the groom and his guests. They would congratulate her on having been so good a mother as to preserve the chastity of her daughter. She would relinquish the key to the bedroom to the groom and depart. His friends would accompany him to the door, give him the same wish, and then leave. Bernoyer needed a means of substituting himself for the groom at the last minute.

Desperate, he consulted with his neighbor, Madame Gontrand, the wife of one of the tailors in his employ, a man he had sent with uniforms to the soldiers at the front in Upper Egypt. He explained his straits, and she offered to solve his problem. She suggested that he switch keys, making sure that 'Ali got the key to her bedroom, which was apparently not so far from Bernoyer's on the second floor of the cavernous mansion. Thus, she could entertain 'Ali, while Bernoyer would get the key to the nuptial chamber. He hugged her for joy, but she pushed him away, saying he was about to strangle her. He remarked to himself that it was a bit odd that she was willing to take a young Egyptian like 'Ali, who was not very good-looking, to bed. "But," he concluded to himself, "he was a man, and a woman of a certain age does not look too closely." In addition, he revealed later in the letter, he had given the Gontrands large rooms at the heart of the mansion he had taken over, from which she had organized a food service for the French tailors and artillerymen on Roda Island. She thus had good reason to be grateful to him.

He locked Madame Gontrand in her room on the second floor and gave the key to Ahmad. Meanwhile the wedding was going on in the garden below, with five women around the bride on one side, all veiled, and five men with 'Ali on the other. When the ceremony was complete, save for the signatures of the witnesses, Ahmad directed the mother and the bride up the stairway that led to Bernoyer's room. Apparently, when the bride's mother came back down with bloody finger and key and proffered the latter to 'Ali, Ahmad managed to make himself a go-between, receiving the key, palming it, and giving the key to Madame Gontrand's room to 'Ali. The two men then presumably went back upstairs, and Ahmad steered 'Ali to the French woman's chambers. He then delivered Bernoyer's own key to him and gave him some Egyptian clothes to wear so as not to startle the girl.

Bernoyer represented himself as now brimming with passion and impatience. Ahmad returned below to the garden to finish scrutinizing the marriage contract before signing as a witness for the groom. Bernoyer attempted to restrain himself from bursting into his bedroom so violently as to startle the demur bride within. "Imagine my confusion when, on opening the door, I saw that Venus stretched out on a straw mat on the ground, her seductive charms directly in my view." Unable to control his passion, he united with her, expecting to find her surprised or unhappy, but instead saw that she was radiant with joy, whispering in his ear, "My friend, my sultan, my brother, my souk." They slept in late, and the next morning he showed her the clothes he intended for her and the extent of their quarters, and she was delighted. She happily tried on her new clothes, he wrote, and settled down to domestic bliss.

Bernoyer gave Madame Gontrand a small bag of diamonds and bestowed two hundred francs on Ahmad as a reward for their roles. "Moreover, I would have paid a hundred times more to find such a girl: in this country where beautiful women are very rare, I could congratulate myself on having a treasure." Bernoyer had had several prior disastrous adventures in attempting to find sexual gratification in Cairo, and he depicted only his arrangement with Fatima as a success. Paying lip service to social and religious convention had the advantage, on both sides, of keeping up appearances, and in this regard it mirrored Bonaparte's own diplomatic Islam policy perfectly. As time went on, the chronicler al-Jabarti alleged, marriage became increasingly common between the French men and Muslim women.[24] Attracted by the vast wealth the French concentrated in their hands, even good Egyptian families proved willing to make such alliances. For their part, French troops gradually lost their initial disdain for Muslim conventions and proved willing to undergo a pro forma conversion as a prerequisite to the wedding. It was not, al-Jabarti sniffed, as though they had any faith to begin with that they feared losing.

❧

The French Jacobins could not help but view Islam as a crucible of superstition. They often saw firsthand evidences of popular religious enthusiasm that involved what to them seemed like bizarre and barbarous rites. Of course, the formally trained Muslim clergy, or ulema, would have denied that such practices had anything to do with Islam. Bilingual Egyptians of the middle strata were probably the chief interpreters to the French of the meaning of popular religious practices, and they probably transmitted some of their own disgust with them to the Europeans. Far from being a sole creation of European Orientalism, this image of popular Islam was a joint production.

Arab Muslim civilization as a cultural symbol had many meanings for the French of the Enlightenment and revolutionary eras. They sometimes used Muslims and Islamic practices to stress how different the French were from Middle Easterners. The political philosopher of the mid-eighteenth century, Charles de Montesquieu had, when discussing the virtues of the separation of executive, legislative, and judicial powers, explicitly said, "Among the Ottomans, where these three powers are united in the person of the sultan, a frightful despotism reigns."[25] (Montesquieu overestimated the sultan's ability to dictate the rulings of the qadis, or Islamic court judges, and did not reckon with how powerful the grand viziers and their ministers had become vis-à-vis the sultan, so that his picture of Oriental despotism is a caricature of the Ottoman system.) Some French thinkers tried to show how close Europeans could be to Islamic practice, without knowing it, as a way of critiquing religion. Voltaire's play *Mahomet* depicted the Prophet of Islam in an unflattering light, but it was intended as a critique of institutionalized religion, not of Islam per se, and Voltaire openly admitted that he had done Muhammad an injustice. Bonaparte himself dismissed the play, saying that Voltaire had "prostituted the great character of Muhammad by the basest intrigues. He treated a great man who changed the face of the earth as though he were an abject villain, worthy of being hanged."[26] Elsewhere, Voltaire wrote that Muhammad was a great man and had formed great men, and that if he had been defeated by his pagan, Meccan enemies at the Battle of Badr in 624, world history would have been different.

The writers of the vast eighteenth-century *Encyclopédie*, the first modern attempt to encompass all knowledge in a single work, also sometimes employed Islam as a code for criticisms of the popular superstition and the dogmatism they saw in Catholicism.[27] Other writers of the articles in this encyclopedia, in contrast, saw the virtues of Arab Muslim science, and contrasted its achievements with European religious obscurantism. Bonaparte himself admired the history of Arab science.[28] He contrasted urban Middle Eastern traditions of civilization with the traditions of the pastoral nomads of the Asian steppe and deserts, who, he said, constantly overthrew settled empires. The former were "enemies of the sciences and the arts," he said, "but this reproach cannot be launched at the Arabs, or at Muhammad." He praised the Umayyad caliphs of the seventh and eighth centuries as poets and connoisseurs of fine verses, which, he said, they valued as much as they did valor on the battlefield. He lauded the Abbasid caliphs of the eighth and ninth centuries even more: "Al-Mansur, Harun al-Rashid, al-Ma'mun, cultivated arts and sciences. They loved literature, chemistry, and mathematics; they lived with scientists, and had translations made of Greek and Latin authors in Arabic. . . . Chemistry, distillation, sundials, clocks, our contemporary numerals, are all inventions of the Arabs. Nothing is more elegant than their moral tales; their poetry is full of warmth. Muhammad commended above all the erudite and men who gave themselves to a life of meditation and who cultivated belles lettres." Bonaparte had profoundly altered the arena in which these discussions were taking place. The arrival of some 32,000 French soldiers in Egypt in the summer of 1798 made the question of how to think about Islam more than a parlor game. The French were involved in the largest-scale encounter of a Western European culture with a Middle Eastern Muslim one since the Crusades.

8

THE CONSTANT TRIUMPH
OF REASON

*I*n late August Kléber wrote Bonaparte from Alexandria that the mayor of
Damanhur, Emir Ibrahim Çurbaci, had visited him and had advised him
that there would be no peace with the tribes in that area unless he took
hostages from them. Ibrahim had earlier been involved in the revolt against the
French, but had been persuaded to accept their rule, and Kléber recommended
clemency for him. He was now willing to cooperate in bringing water to
Alexandria from Rahmaniya (or rather, ensuring that it was not siphoned off
along the way) on condition that he received the same payment for these
arrangements as he had under the Ottoman Beylicate.[1]

Despite Emir Ibrahim's advice and help, however, the temptation of the
water-hungry villagers to siphon off water from the canals that should have been
delivering it to Alexandria was often too much to resist, more especially since
they saw such an act as both lucrative and a show of defiance to the European
occupier. The village of Birkat Gitas made an alliance with the Awlad Ali
Bedouin and blocked the water flow, prompting Kléber to send six hundred soldiers down on 13 September to punish them. He ordered that the heads of the
men killed in the village be cut off and mounted on poles so that passersby could
see them, and then, he said, they should burn down the village, after having
spared women, children, and the aged. When the detachment returned on 16
September, they had killed fifty Egyptians and carried away a good many livestock. Kléber sent pamphlets up and down the Nile threatening other villagers
with the same fate if they interfered with the canal.[2]

Although the revolt at Mansura had been put down in mid-August, the
province remained restive. General Dugua reported a lively insurrection at the
nearby village of Sonbat. He reported, "It is in part inhabited by three or four

hundred Bedouin of the tribe of Dirn, from the desert on the other side of Alexandria. They were summoned here four years ago by Eyyüb Bey, the patron of Sonbat, to restrain the inhabitants, who were killing one another every day." The French had a grudge with the Dirn, who had led the charge in the killing of the contingent at Mansura. Dugua wanted to mount an expedition to punish Sonbat but said he needed to be well armed, since its three hundred peasant villagers had contracted alliances with the tribesmen. He felt that the Dirn had made themselves so hated in other neighboring villages with their recent pillaging that he could count on neutrality from that quarter.[3]

Bonaparte wrote back to Dugua on 6 September, saying he was sending the cartridges that the general had requested. He added that they ought to arrive with the enclosed letter and "I hope you will have instilled some sense in the accursed Bedouin of the village of Sonbat. Burn that village! Make a terrifying example of it and do not permit these Arabs to return and inhabit the village until they have delivered to you ten hostages from among their principal men, whom you will send to me for internment in the Citadel."[4] Under the tutelage of local magnates such as Emir Ibrahim, Bonaparte and his generals were adopting Ottoman-Egyptian techniques for dealing with political forces such as the Bedouin and recalcitrant villagers, techniques terrifying in their ruthlessness.

On 12 September, Dugua dispatched Gen. Jean-Antoine Verdier up the Nile with 550 men and some artillery pieces.[5] On the fourteenth, they disembarked near Sonbat. Verdier sought out the village headman of neighboring Hanud for help in reconnoitering the area and in avoiding quagmires that had spread with the inundation of the Nile. When the French had invaded Egypt in July, the Dirn had taken advantage of the breakdown in law and order to pillage this sheikh and other village notables, starting a local feud. The sheikh of Hanud therefore "constantly marched at our head, showing us with pleasure the roads that would lead most promptly to the enemy," according to Verdier's report to Dugua. An advance party encountered a Dirn camp of six hundred outside Sonbat. About half the men came at the French, while an equal number attempted to get away with their baggage, women, and livestock.

Verdier reported, "The grenadiers, under the orders of Brigade Chief Laugier, attacking with their usual impetuosity, repulsed the three hundred Bedouin and obliged the others to abandon everything in order to come to the aid of their comrades and to attempt to jointly defend their encampment, into which Brigade Chief Laugier had entered, forcing it with his right wing." Verdier in the meantime led his own contingent of five hundred men around to come at the camp from farther to the right, disconcerting the Bedouin and provoking a mass flight in which they left everything behind. He found it difficult to pursue them, saying that Bedouin can run "like rabbits" and can swim across "every sort of river." It actually seems a little unlikely that Bedouin were such great swimmers, and one wonders if some local peasants, used to the fall marshes, were among them.

The Bedouin and villagers rallied at Sonbat, taking positions on the high ground around the village. The French again forced them back, and they fled into the surrounding swamps, throwing down their weapons so as not to be impeded. Verdier represented his troops as wading in after them, until they saw them drowned or they disappeared. One suspects that the Dirn tribesmen and Sonbat peasants mostly faded away into autumn wetlands they by then knew well.

Verdier reported with regret that many more of the enemy would have been killed had so many of the cartridges sent from Cairo not been defective, often misfiring or achieving a range of no more than twenty feet. They found hidden in the village three fine horses that servants of the emirs had secreted there when they fled the French. Some of the dead Bedouin were discovered wearing French shoes, proving their involvement in the massacre of the Mansura garrison. Verdier gloated, "You ordered me to destroy this lair. Very well, it no longer exists." He had discovered their arms cache in the mud and had broken the firearms. He assured his superior that Hanud, Shubra, and what was left of Sonbat had henceforth closed their doors to the Dirn Bedouin. "That day only cost the Republic one grenadier of the 25th Demi-Brigade, who was lightly wounded in the knee, and bestowed on it a great quantity of sheep and fifty-nine camels, large and small, which I am bringing to you." The dire straits of the Republic at that point are revealed in its need for some sheep and camels pillaged from an Egyptian village. Since Bonaparte was not able to actually pay his troops, they were often living off such looting of the local population, which they referred to in their private letters as the collection of "contributions."

❖

In Cairo, the sheer mass of French troops had initially intimidated the populace, ensuring a modicum of security. There Bonaparte was free to concentrate on institution building. In August he had convened the Egyptian Institute, modeled on the French Institute, as a scientific society that would intensively study Egypt and help with the needs of the army. Captain Say depicted Bonaparte's establishment of the Institute as a way of helping implant liberty in Egypt, consisting of "a government where equality of rights assures to all the ability to succeed without discrimination."[6] The concerns of the scientists and administrators in Egypt were made clear at the first session of the Egyptian Institute.

Bonaparte's own notes suggest the range of imperial and scientific questions raised on 23 August. "Can the furnaces providing bread to the military be improved? Is there a replacement in Egypt for hops to make beer? How can Nile water be purified? Is it better to construct water mills or windmills in Cairo? Can [gun]powder be manufactured in Egypt? What is the situation of jurisprudence, and civil and criminal law, in Egypt? How can it be improved?"[7] Bonaparte did not seem as concerned with equality before the law as he did with making the Institute a scientific adjunct to the military enterprise.

The Institute was originally intended as a cultural institution as well as a scientific one. Bonaparte shared the view that performance and theater are a "public school for morality and taste."[8] He later said of public spectacles, "What a tool, if the government knows how to use it!" Bonaparte that fall wrote the Jacobin journalist and former parliamentarian he had brought along to Egypt, Jean-Lambert Tallien, saying that, "attaching a great importance to the establishment of a theater and other festivities in Cairo," he was commanding that he and some of the other intellectuals "occupy themselves with the means of establishing in Cairo a hall for spectacles, of gathering up actors, and of presenting the repertoire of pieces that they can perform. That commission will choose a garden where once every ten-day week there will be fireworks, and twice a ten-day week there will be illuminations."

Captain Say's memoir, which was redacted by the playwright Louis Laus de Boissy (a regular at Josephine's salon and author of *The True Republican Woman*), was especially interested in the use of culture to promote civic spirit and revolutionary ideals among Egyptians. He was not alone in these interests. The Egyptian Institute, he wrote, "named a Commission composed of artists, charged with establishing at Cairo a hall of spectacles, for dance, concerts, and fireworks." These public civic performances, he hoped, "will be a new means of elevating the souls of these neophytes in liberty and of forming in this country a public spirit, the fifth element of a free people."[9]

Among the performers who he hoped would play a great role during these public spectacles were the *'alimas*, or what we would now call belly dancers. This group at that time consisted of cultured performers for the martial Ottoman-Egyptian elite. Say was perfectly aware of the sensual nature of the dancers' repertoire when he made this somewhat outlandish suggestion, and it is worth pursuing the possible reasons for it. He wrote that the professional singing girls were called *'alimas* or *savantes* (learned ones), and admitted that they "merited their name . . . because of the education they have received, much more extensive than that given other women." They were, he said, "priestesses of voluptuousness." The requirements for joining their ranks included a beautiful voice, "good control over the tongue," and an ability to compose and chant couplets on the spot that fit the social circumstances. Captain Say continued:

> No occasion can take place without these *'alimas*. After having sung, they perform small pantomime ballets in which the mysteries of love ordinarily furnish the subject. . . . At the beginning of their dance, they abandon along with their veils the modesty of their sex. A long robe of very light silk descends to their heels. A rich belt encircles them loosely. Long black hair, braided and perfumed, floats on their shoulders, and their breasts are barely veiled by a blouse more transparent than gauze, as though it were a tissue of air. When they begin to move, it is as though the contours of their bodies successively detach themselves. . . . These are bacchantes in delirium; it is then that, forgetting the crowd, they abandon themselves entirely to the disorder of their senses. At that point a people little given to delicacy, who like nothing veiled, applaud twice as loudly.[10]

The French considered recruiting the talents of the dancers as a means of promoting a republican civic culture.

Although the titillation of sex had sometimes been evoked by reformist or revolutionary authors as a way of critiquing the decadence of the Old Regime, it could also serve revolutionary purposes. The appeal to prurience as an attack on the monarchy and aristocracy can be seen in Pierre de Laclos's novel *Les liaisons dangereuses* (Dangerous Liaisons) about the way the aristocracy toyed heartlessly with feelings. It is also evident in the pornographic pamphlets that circulated among common people and critics of the monarchy in which Queen Marie Antoinette figured in shocking ways. On the other hand, the disapproval of voluptuousness by the Church also made it seem revolutionary to libertines. Whether such themes were oppressive or liberating for women has been a vexed question ever since. It is not one that preoccupied our male memoirists, since they thought of the revolution in fraternal terms and did not consider women, however much sought after for conversation and company, as public, political persons.[11]

✤

Although Say wrote that he disapproved of the more sensual aspects of the performances of the *'alimas* (he had a funny way of showing it, what with the loving descriptions of them), they did celebrate love, wine, and life. They represented a secular performance tradition that could be appropriated by Republican theatre.

Detroye saw on the streets of Cairo during the Festival of the Nile "songstresses who performed scenes with dialogue, women who chanted poetry." The social interactions of the French with local Muslim women would also have suggested that their roles could radically change. The invaders posed as liberators of Egyptian women and saw them, along with Copts and Greeks, as a potential constituency for their cultural revolution in the Nile Valley.

The French still hoped to bring even the Egyptian Muslim clergy around to republican values, and many believed in their ultimate reasonableness. Niello Sargy was clearly impressed at how interested the principal members of the divan—sheikhs al-Mahdi, al-Fayyumi, al-Sawi, al-Fasi, and al-Bakri—were in the national printing press directed by M. Marcel. The French press was far faster and more precise than the presses some of them had seen in Istanbul or at the Maronite monastery at Kisrawan. "Sheikh al-Bakri came to see the printing press. He asked if they were widespread in France and Europe generally. Then he asked about Russia." Niello Sargy told him that Russia only began to advance out of backwardness with its adoption of the printing press on a large scale (which dated from the early eighteenth century). He reported that Sheikh al-Bakri said that there were many fine Arabic works that should be printed.[12] Although Western Europe had begun printing from metal movable type around 1450, the technology was not widely used in the rest of the world until much later. Only in China, Japan, and Korea, which used wood block printing, were a few thousand books published in the early modern period. In the Middle East, Africa, India, and even much of Eastern Europe and Russia, printing was a minor, specialized activity until the 1700s at least. From about 1720, the Müta-ferrika Press in Istanbul did a good deal of printing, of which some of the Egyptian clerics were well aware. Since printing allowed the precise reproduction of scientific and technological diagrams in a way that hand copying of manuscripts did not, its widespread adoption in Western Europe gave that region an advantage in scientific progress in the early modern period. Sheikh al-Bakri and other Cairo intellectuals, prepared by earlier encounters with printing in the Ottoman Empire, were easily persuaded of its utility.

✦

Just as the French attempted to coopt the clergy into a more enlightened view of the world, grounded in modern science, so they sought to induct them into the cult of the Republic. The Republicans wore an important symbol of liberty, the tricolor cockade, or knotted ribbon.[13] It had often been worn in a hat, but could be appended elsewhere, and had become mandatory under the revolutionaries. In

1797–1798 the Directory had reaffirmed the necessity that it be worn by all French citizens and imposed short jail sentences on women who neglected it. Debates had then broken out at the Council of 500 and in the press about who should wear the cockade. The Jacobin answer had been "everybody," even visitors on French soil. But some Directory-era politicians and intellectuals argued that wearing it should be linked to military service, and so be a prerogative of male citizens. Others insisted that it signified not full military or political participation, but "Frenchness," so that it should encompass women and children, even resident foreigners.

In the summer of 1798, Bonaparte ordered all Egyptians to wear one. The engineer Prosper Jollois recorded in his journal that on 29 July in Rosetta, "We celebrated the taking of Cairo, and the new muftis or commandants named by the people were decorated with the tricolor scarf." After the festival, a civic march into the center of the city was staged, with band and drums. At the end, French dispatch boats anchored in the Nile off Rosetta discharged their cannon. Thereafter, Villiers du Terrage recorded in his journal for 30 July at Rosetta, "The inhabitants began wearing French cockades."

Rosetta, a cosmopolitan port, had a substantial Christian population, but in Cairo the Muslim divan objected. Bonaparte conducted two long meetings with the divan and in the end won the members over. "He even," Say reported, "entered into theological arguments that astonished and convinced the Muslims." The members of the divan began wearing cockades, and soon "everyone in Egypt was wearing them." The Syrian chronicler Nicola al-Turk confirmed that both Egyptian men and women wore the cockade. In Egypt, the tricolor knot of cloth was required of all Egyptians because it symbolized the incorporation of Egypt as one of "the countries of France." In essence, it was a symbol of submission.

Al-Jabarti said that on 5 September, Bonaparte summoned the clergymen of al-Azhar. When they arrived and were seated, he attempted to drape a tricolor shawl over the shoulder of Sheikh Sharqawi. The latter threw it to the ground and begged to be excused, his face flushed. The Corsican's translator addressed them, "Clerics, you have become the friends of the commander in chief, and his intention is to honor you through these shawls. If you are distinguished by them, the people and the soldiers will exalt you and you will have a place in their hearts."

The clerics, al-Jabarti said, responded, "But our place with God and our brothers the Muslims will collapse."

Bonaparte, he wrote, was angered and let loose some curses. His translators later admitted that he had brought into question Sheikh Sharqawi's suitability to be head of the divan. The other clerics attempted to butter him up, and they sought permission not to have to wear the shawls.

The commander in chief replied that in that case they would have at least to wear the cockade, a ceremonial knot of tricolor ribbon, on their breasts. They asked for twelve days to deliberate on the matter.

Bonaparte appears to have regretted his display of impatience. The next time he summoned Sheikh Sharqawi, the general greeted him warmly, took his hand in his own, smiled at him, exchanged pleasantries, and presented him with a diamond ring. He asked him to come again the next day. That day, the French guard announced that all Egyptians should wear the cockade (which al-Jabarti interpreted as a symbol of obedience and love). In his chronicle of these events, al-Jabarti wrote that "the majority of people refused, while some considered that it did not harm their religion, since they wore it only as a ruse, and more harm would come of disobeying the order. So they wore it." Later that day, the French rescinded the order with regard to the common people. (Al-Jabarti did not explain why, but given Muslim sentiments about being turned into infidels through imitating them, there was a danger of popular rage.)

The next day, Bonaparte convened the clerics again. When Sheikh Shar-qawi entered, he pinned a cockade on his chest. Then as the others entered, he did the same, and they had difficulty declining because they could see that Shar-qawi, their leader, had already acquiesced. They took the cockades off when they left the general's mansion. This way of proceeding, al-Jabarti said, briefly became standard. The French only obliged the notables and persons seeking to enter their presence with some need to sport it. They would put it on before they entered, then take it off when they left. "They only wore it for a few days, then events intervened, and they abandoned the practice."[14]

Say maintained that this incident wherein the clerics were allegedly convinced of the virtues of the cockade proved that all are open to the blandishments of reason, even the most educated (and therefore, he remarked in the tradition of Rousseau, the most susceptible to prejudices)—"especially when the arguments are put forward by someone who has in his hands force and power." He saw reason as enhanced rather than contradicted by power. He concluded, "How many have died for opinions and misunderstandings in history. May the end of the eighteenth century, so brilliant with the military exploits of a great nation, be even more fertile ground for the constant triumph of reason over prejudice!"[15]

Here again the triumph of reason over prejudice is coupled not only with Enlightenment thought processes but with the martial achievements of a "great nation." Fatherland and army are seen as key prerequisites for or helpmeets to Reason, as though Voltaire had to march with Bonaparte at his back in order to become ascendant over the city of a thousand minarets. (Say's editor and de facto coauthor, Laus de Boissy, was an admirer of Voltaire, and once received a letter from him.) In fact, as al-Jabarti's account makes clear, the al-Azhar clerics viewed wearing the cockade as a distasteful compromise of their principles, and they wore it as little as possible while still keeping on the good side of Bonaparte. Early modern Muslims had distinctive traditions of dress and fashion, and they quoted with approval a saying attributed to the Prophet Muhammad that he who imitates a people becomes one of them. They were terrified of doing anything that would rob them of their Muslim identity, and emulating French sartorial practices was high on their list of dangerous behavior in this regard. Those who wore the cockade did so as a sort of white lie. Captain Say's combination of force and reason, which he would not be the last to advocate, produced hypocrisy more often than enlightenment in modern history.

✤

The loyalty of Egyptian Muslims that Bonaparte sought to displace onto the French Republic by compelling them to wear the cockade actually belonged to the Ottoman sultan, who was determined to see that allegiance reasserted. The Sunni clerics of Egypt did not generally invest the emperor in Istanbul with any special religious status, saying that the caliphate or the Sunni equivalent of the papacy had lapsed centuries before. But they did value him as the practical defender of Sunni Muslim interests. Bonaparte had cited Volney's insight that any conquest of Egypt would require three wars, against the British, the Ottomans, and the local Muslims. At the Battle of the Nile, he had received the British response. Now he was about to discover how difficult it would be for a freebooter to overcome the vast authority and legitimacy of the sultan. Istanbul lay 679 miles due north of Alexandria across the eastern Mediterranean. There glistened the Golden Horn. On its west lay the Blue Mosque and Topkapi Palace, where the foreign ministry talked to European ambassadors. On its east lay Galata or Pera, where Europeans had made posh mercantile and diplomatic enclaves. The Ottoman Empire had suffered a century of reversals, after a seventeenth-century run of victories. It had lost several major battles to a resurgent Austrian Empire, and the rise of Russian power threatened it with further setbacks. Its hold on peripheral provinces such as Algeria was tenuous, and slave-soldier regimes had become semiautonomous in Cairo and Baghdad. Local notables and chieftains staked claims to power over parts of Syria and Anatolia, and the Balkans were newly restive. Still, the Ottoman Empire was not without resources, and the minds of its leaders had been concentrated by the sudden loss of a key province. Egypt's fate lay not only in Paris and London but also in Istanbul, amid the intrigues within the Ottoman cabinet and the conspiracies hatched against one another by the European consuls

The Ottoman chronicler Ahmad Cevdet described (based on late eighteenth century notes of Ottoman scribes) the Sublime Porte's shock at French perfidy. He pointed out that most of the crowned heads of Europe had turned against the French as a result of their revolution, but that the Ottomans had steadfastly maintained their long tradition of friendly relations with Paris. They had continued to give French merchants freedom to pursue commerce in the empire. The Ottomans took this step at some cost, Cevdet maintained, given the enormous pressure applied to them by the British ambassador and the other European powers, which were demanding that the Ottomans treat the revolutionaries as pariahs.[16]

Although some conservative Ottoman gentlemen greeted the French Revolution with hostility, it should be underlined that the Ottoman state, unlike the Austrians and British, did not respond ideologically to the Revolution. Stanford Shaw, the greatest historian of the Ottoman Empire in this period wrote, "While the ideas of the French Revolution were highly subversive to the entire Ottoman social and political structure as well as to the position of the Sultan himself, there was at no time any particular dread of them by the Sultan and his officials or a desire to join the movement to stop the contagion."[17]

Ottoman sultans had been killed by their followers, some in popular uprisings, so that from Istanbul's point of view the guillotining of the king and queen, however regrettable it might have been, was hardly unprecedented. The Ottoman elite saw the Revolution as an obscure and complicated political affair of far western Latinate Christians. Indeed, that the Europeans seemed to be caught up in such constant social turmoil was taken as a sign that it was much better to live in a stable Muslim sultanate. The geopolitical dimensions of the longstanding alliance of France and the Ottomans, based on a common fear of Russia and Austria, had not changed. Shaw added, "Selim actually went so far as to welcome the advent of the Revolution because of the very conflicts which it spawned, all serving to divert his enemies from his own empire while it lay weak and open to attack."

Although sympathetic to the French, Selim III also attempted to maintain good relations with the anti-French First Coalition, of Austria, Prussia, Britain, and Spain (1792–1797). His primary concern in the 1790s remained to reform the Ottoman military. He wanted to reorganize the Janissary Corps, and to create a "new army" (*nizam-i cedid*), with modern uniforms, drill, and equipment. He at first declined to allow a formal embassy from revolutionary France in Istanbul, to avoid enraging the other great powers. But he indulged the French by allowing his officials to meet with informal envoys. French expatriate merchants actively published stories on developments in the Republic in French-language newspapers read by many in the Ottoman diplomatic and commercial classes. The Ottomans also allowed French revolutionary societies in Istanbul to pamphleteer and to rally publicly (albeit in very small numbers), as well as to display the tricolor. The Porte greeted the vehement protests of the British and the Russians over the public display of that emblem of the Revolution with "amused toleration."

Once it became clear that the new republic would survive militarily, in 1795, Selim III allowed the appointment of a French ambassador to his capital. Ironically, Bonaparte himself almost went to the Ottoman capital in that period. In the same year, 1795, he had declined a transfer to the French infantry, which was being sent to put down the royalist Vendée peasant revolt against the revolutionary government. He viewed such internal policing duties as beneath his station and considered any transfer out of the artillery corps to be an insult. He had therefore been dismissed from the military by the Office of Public Safety and placed briefly under arrest. He was, however, soon reinstated.

In September 1795, Bonaparte was proposed for an eight-man military mission to reorganize the Ottoman artillery corps, but he had hopes for a better posting and used his relationship with Paul Barras, who was in charge of Paris security, to secure one. His friend Bourrienne represented the idea of going to Constantinople as Bonaparte's own, but the opposite appears to have been the case.[18] In the end, that October Barras drew on Bonaparte's talents in dispersing a crowd of royalists and dissidents in Paris who had threatened to overthrow the revolutionary government. The general became a hero. Barras cemented their relationship by introducing to Bonaparte his former mistress, Josephine de Beauharnais. Barras promoted the further move away from radicalism and terror that had begun with the overthrow and execution of Robespierre and his supporters in summer of 1794, and helped in the establishment of the new Directory government. He then secured for Bonaparte command of the Italian campaign, in which the Corsican distinguished himself as an innovative military thinker who put artillery to new uses. Had Bonaparte actually gone off to advise Selim III on the use of artillery, history might have been very different.

The Treaty of Campo Formio of 1797 recognized French control of part of the Italian coast along the Adriatic Sea, along with several of its islands. It therefore suddenly gave the French a presence in the Balkans and made them direct neighbors of the Ottomans. Despite the suspicions this move east inspired in Istanbul, in 1796–1797 the French ambassador in Istanbul, Gen. Jean-Baptiste Aubert-Dubayet, was popular and proved especially helpful in supplying some light artillery for Selim's military reforms. A pro-French party grew up inside the Ottoman government that advocated liberal reforms and had begun pursuing them.

Aubert-Dubayet died in office in late 1797. Talleyrand saw his passing as an opportunity to begin a new policy toward Istanbul, centered on Bonaparte's Egyptian ambitions. He proposed himself as the new ambassador but put off going.[19] He later made the *chargé d'affaires* at the Istanbul embassy, Pierre-Jean-Marie Ruffin, the acting ambassador. In secret correspondence in late spring, 1798, he alerted Ruffin to the Directory's decision to take Egypt and promised that he would be sending a high-level envoy to explain to the Ottoman government why the French occupation of Egypt was actually a sign of friendship toward the sultan.

Selim III was initially worried that the Toulon fleet would head for Crete, Cyprus, or the Morea (now southern Greece) to bolster a French presence in the eastern Mediterranean following on their establishment of a beachhead on the Adriatic.[20] When the French took Malta, the Sublime Porte called Ruffin in to explain it, and he denied any aggressive intent toward the Ottomans. In late July, the sultan communicated to Talleyrand the threat that any aggression on Ottoman territory would result in an immediate declaration of war. Talleyrand replied with a lie, suggesting that the French and Ottoman fleets might soon be in a position to cooperate against the Russians in the Adriatic and Black Seas. Ruffin wrote to Talleyrand on 1 August, emphasizing that it was essential that the negotiator from Paris arrive immediately, so that he could retain his credibility and stop keeping secrets.[21] He observed, "My experience has also taught me that this people is, at base, less exercised by our enterprise in Egypt than by the ineptitude and tyranny of the current government." Ruffin's remarks were a triumph of conviction over reality, as though saying it made it so.

Once news of the conquest of Cairo reverberated through the towns of Syria, Iraq, and Anatolia, reaching the metropolis itself, Ruffin abruptly became less sanguine. He reported on 10 August that he had had two troubling meetings with high Ottoman officials. The first was attended by the chief Sunni jurist, or mufti, who reported the mood on the street in Istanbul: "The effervescence of spirits is every day taking on a more alarming character." Ruffin recalled how Izzet Mehmet Pasha, the grand vizier, was "weighed down by the discontent of the people" and also disturbed that Bonaparte had given it out that he invaded Egypt with the permission of the sultan. Ruffin denounced the allegation as a calumny. The grand vizier assured him that he had solid evidence for it. Even empires had to take popular opinion into account, and it was clear to the chief minister that the Ottoman public would not stand for inaction.

The grand vizier called Ruffin to a second meeting on 6 August, and let him know in frank terms of the displeasure of the Sublime Porte and the public with the French. He told Paris's envoy, "You must stay inside the French palace. Citizen Dantan [the dragoman, or interpreter] is not to present himself any longer at the Porte. He will come to me at night when necessary. The French must avoid being found in public places, in promenades, and in side streets. You will remove the seal of the Republic that is placed on the exterior grill of the palace and put it inside instead." It was the considered view of the highest Ottoman authorities, in short, that Bonaparte's campaign had put all the French merchants and other residents of the sultan's realm in danger of at any moment being ripped to shreds by furious Muslim mobs.

Three days later, Sultan Selim III put the French in his realm under a sort of house arrest, forbidding them to go out. In a later letter to Paris, Ruffin gave an idea of the frustrations that were building in the Ottoman public. He said that in late August a fire had broken out in Istanbul, and, as was his custom, Izzet Mehmet Pasha had gone out to oversee its extinction. The landlady upbraided him, as she watched her building reduced to embers, saying that they were being punished for the "slowness of the government in breaking with the infidels who had stolen from them the countries neighboring Mecca."

Bonaparte, ever the optimist and confidence man, wrote Izzet Mehmet Pasha in mid-August to inform him that Talleyrand would be coming as a high-level envoy and would explain why it was necessary for the French to occupy Egypt in order to strengthen their friendship with the Ottoman Empire. The invasion was carried out so as to "procure for the Sublime Porte the support it needs against its natural enemies who, at this moment, have begun to league themselves against her."[22] Bonaparte was intimating that the Georgian Mamluks had begun a new and serious round of negotiations with the Russian Empire, a fear the Ottomans had entertained since the early 1770s.

The pro-French party in the Ottoman cabinet, including the first minister, had dragged their feet on the issue of declaring war on France. These officials received support from the ambassadors of Spain (which had a peace treaty with France by then) and of French-dominated Holland, as well as from envoys of states that feared Russia would realize an overwhelming advantage from an Ottoman alliance, such as Sweden and Austria.[23] The antiwar party lost the argument. On 31 August, the sultan made his move, having Izzet Mehmet Pasha and several other pro-French politicians at his own court arrested. He appointed Yusuf Ziya Pasha, a conservative champion of the Sunni clerics, grand vizier and made his steadfast supporter Ashir Effendi the head of the clerical corps. The

reforming, liberalizing court of Sultan Selim III, which had even greeted the tumultuous French Revolution with equanimity, had suddenly been thrown into
the arms of reaction, with a Russian alliance and a resurgent influence for revan-
chist Muslim clerics in the capital. The Istanbul conservatives had long been
alarmed at the implications of the French Revolution, but the sultan's reforming
zeal had deflected them. Now their sentiments came to dominate public discourse. Darendeli recalled that the installation of Yusuf Ziya Pasha met no opposition at all among the Ottoman officials. Selim had the right team in place for a
new, conservative foreign policy based on alliances against the French Republic.

On 2 September, Russian Tsar Paul I signaled his firm support by sending
his fleet from Sevastopol on the Black Sea to Istanbul. Selim III abruptly had
Ruffin and all the personnel in the French embassy taken into captivity and sent
to the Prison of the Seven Towers. At the same time, reprisals were ordered
against all French capital in the empire, with merchants arrested and their property confiscated. Bonaparte had, in a second, undone centuries of successful
French mercantile policy in the Ottoman Empire.

That same day, the sultan formally requested a legal ruling from the chief Islamic jurisconsult on declaring war against France. On 9 September a draft of the
declaration of war was produced, and it was formally issued on 12 September. It
complained of French perfidy after the sultan had stood with the French earlier in
the decade and underlined that "Egypt being the gate to the two holy cities, Mecca
and Medina, this affair is of the greatest importance for all Muslims."[24] In fact,
however, there had been many such *firmans*, or imperial decrees, already, beginning in late August. In a firman typical of September 1798, the sultan condemned
Bonaparte by name for having conquered Cairo "and having made war against the
Muslims of this country and having spread various lies and false reports." He
warned that the perfidious actions of the French, which were contrary to international law (*bigayr-i kaide-i düvel*), demonstrated that they intended to subjugate and
spread chaos in all the other Muslim territories as well. The firman thundered that
marching against the French infidels had become a "personal religious obligation"
(*farz-i 'ayn*)." Only thus, it said, could the Muslims hope to "accomplish the task of
purifying Cairo and its environs" from the "corrupting presence of the French"
and "to liberate the servants of God."[25] Note that the Ottoman decree accuses the
French in the first instance of violating the laws and norms of nations. Since this
was an Ottoman document directed to Ottoman authorities, it is remarkable in
showing the reformist, civil mind-set of Selim III. He did not depict the actions of
Paris as simply infidel depredations against Muslims, though they were that, but as
in the first instance an act of international criminality.

Defense of the Muslim community against attack was considered in classical Islamic law a "group obligation." That is, not every single member of the community had an individual duty to fight. When and how to fight was a decision that could not be made by vigilantes, but had to be made by the duly constituted authorities, in this case the sultan. The laws governing holy war, or jihad, required a public declaration of war, a warning to the enemy forces that they would be attacked, the provision of an opportunity for conversion to Islam by the enemy (thus obviating the need for a war), and Muslim adherence to a code of conduct that forbade the killing of noncombatants or women and children. Selim III, by declaring defensive war, said it had now become an individual duty to fight the French, and he thereby authorized guerrilla action by Egyptian subjects. Nothing could have been more dangerous to the French. He combined Islamic and international law by both invoking the duty of defensive jihad and simultaneously citing international norms of state behavior. How little the sultan viewed the conflict as a clash of civilizations is demonstrated by his immediate alliance with Russia and Britain, Christian powers, against the secular republic he had once befriended.

The Ottoman and Russian navies joined up to end the French presence in the Ionian Islands and in the Adriatic, while the British, along with an Ottoman squadron, patrolled the coasts of the Levant and Egypt. Talleyrand's attempts to intrigue with Balkan notables to overthrow the sultan were easily thwarted when Selim bestowed on them more land and privileges. They took Talleyrand's conspiratorial envoys into custody and declared for Istanbul. Thus began forming the second grand coalition against the French Republic, leaguing Paul I of Russia, the British government of William Pitt the Younger, and Selim III. At length Franz I of Austria would be drawn into this one as well. After a great deal of haggling, negotiations, and calming of jealousies, the Porte gave the province of Egypt to the governor of Sidon, Ahmed Cezzar Pasha, and promised him funds and armies with which to challenge the French there.[26]

The declaration of holy war against the French by the Ottoman sultan gradually became known in Egypt. Niello Sargy recalled that the preachers in the mosques outwardly seemed to be preaching religion, but behind the scenes they were spreading around the decree of Selim III. Al-Jabarti recorded that on 14 September, a letter had arrived from Ibrahim Bey in Syria, promising that he would return at the head of an Ottoman army. Bonaparte was informed and perused the letter with indignation, calling the beys "liars." A second missive then arrived, about which the clerics were more circumspect. Bonaparte heard rumors of it and rode out to confront Sheikh al-Sadat at his home in the al-Azhar district, but the latter had not yet received a copy. On his way out he passed the grand mosque, which was full of congregants behaving excitedly. Bonaparte inquired and was told that they were calling down blessings on him. He left. Al-Jabarti revealed that the sight of the commander in chief at that moment in that place had almost provoked a riot. One does not imagine that they were actually calling down blessings on the foreign general.

In late September, Bonaparte had two persons executed for carrying letters to and from the deposed grandees in Syria or Upper Egypt, and had their heads paraded through the streets in hopes of providing an object lesson to others. The Egyptian authorities now loyal to Bonaparte also called on the common people of Cairo to stop showing curiosity and talking about "the affairs of state" and to cease making fun of or clapping for defeated or wounded French soldiers who trailed back into the capital, "as was their habit."[27] Putting public discussion of the affairs of state off limits to ordinary subjects was an old Ottoman tactic of control, and its use by the French Republic, standard-bearer of the Rights of Man, was jarringly incongruous.

A firman calling on the Egyptians to oppose the French, under the signature of conservative Ottoman grand vizier Yusuf Ziya Pasha, began circulating in Egypt.[28] He said that the Sublime Porte had been informed of the invasion of Egypt by the French, and of their trickery and hanky-panky, spreading around counterfeit decrees of the Ottoman sultan that seemed to authorize the operation. "Their intention was disguised beneath the cloak of lies and villainy." He accused them of sowing poison among the inhabitants of the province of Egypt, declaring, "Today, they are unmasked." He said that their perfidious intentions were revealed in the letters they sent back to their country, which had been intercepted and translated. (He did not say that it was the British that intercepted them and passed them to the Porte.) Their intention, he warned, "was not solely to rule Egypt, but to conquer Syria and Iran." (Bonaparte sometimes toyed with attempting to challenge the British in India by a land campaign through Qajar Iran and Durrani Afghanistan to the Khyber Pass and thence to Delhi, in imitation of Alexander the Great.) The grand vizier warned that the French would "seize the goods of the believers; their women and children will be reduced to slavery; and your blood will be spilled (may God preserve us)!" He called on Egyptians to sacrifice everything to fight the new conquerors and promised an Ottoman expeditionary force to rescue the province from foreign rule, saying that the army was already at Damascus. (This assertion was not true, since it was taking the Ottomans some time to respond to the French attack.) He announced, "The Sublime Porte, founded on the power of the King of Kings, the sovereign of the heroes and conquerors, king of the two seas and two land masses, our master of the world, the glory of which God increases through the intercession of his Prophet and his Elect, putting his hope in God, has declared war on these enemies."

Bonaparte's hope that he could wean the al-Azhar clerics away from their loyalty to the sultan, or convince them that he was a viceroy sent from Istanbul, was entirely in vain, whatever the coerced and frightened clerics told him to his face. Sheikh Abdullah al-Sharqawi, the president of the Cairo divan, whom Bonaparte had alternately honored and humiliated, bribed and snubbed, later described the French in a book on Egyptian history, and it likely reveals what he really thought of Bonaparte's Islam policy.[29] He wrote, "The reality of the French who came to Egypt is that they were materialist, libertine philosophers." He said that outwardly they were said to be Catholic Christians following Jesus. But, he contended, in fact "they deny the Resurrection, and the afterlife, and God's dispatching of prophets of messengers." They were monotheists, asserting that God is one, but, he complained, they arrived at that belief "by means of argumentation" (i.e., rather than faith). They "make reason the ruler and make some among them managers of the regulations that they legislate by using their reason, which they call 'laws.'" That is, in Islam there is a difference between the law (sharia), which is revealed, and the mere civic regulations (al-ahkam) promulgated by sultans and governors. The French, al-Sharqawi was saying, confused the two or, rather, substituted the latter for the former. They assert, he continued, that God's envoys, such as Muhammad, Jesus, and Moses, "were a group of sages, and that the codes of religious law attributed to them are indirect expressions of civil law that they legislated by virtue of their reason, which was appropriate to their contemporaries."

For this reason, he concluded, the French established divans in Cairo and its larger villages that managed affairs in accordance with their reason, "and that was a mercy to the people of Egypt." To one of the Divans they appointed a group of clerics "and began to consult them on some matters not appropriate to the holy law." Although he seems to have rather liked the idea of municipal councils, al-Sharqawi was complaining that since the al-Azhar clerics were specialists in the revealed law derived from the Qur'an and the inspired sayings and doings of the Prophet Muhammad, they should not have had to bother themselves with civil regulations. Typically, a Muslim government would have consulted them in order to determine what the Islamic law was in a particular instance through their expert interpretation of the divine texts. The French denied that God had sent any prophets, and they interpreted the sharia, or Islamic canon law, as merely a roundabout way of convincing the common people to follow regulations that actually derived from the exercise of reason. In essence, he viewed his appointment to the divan as a demotion from dealing with sublime matters to being consulted on mundane politics by foreign unbelievers. "The reason the people of Cairo and its surrounding villages were forced to obey them to some extent," he said, "was their inability to resist them because the Mamluks had fled with the instruments of warfare."

On their arrival in Egypt, he continued, the French had written a pamphlet and spread it around. It alleged that they were not Christians because they affirmed the unity of God, whereas Christians believe in the Trinity, that they honored Muhammad and the Qur'an, and that they loved the Ottomans. They had, the pamphlets said, only come to overthrow the Mamluks, since the latter had expropriated the French merchants, and they would not disturb the ordinary subjects. Al-Sharqawi complained bitterly, "But when they came in, they did not confine themselves to pillaging the wealth of the Mamluks. Rather, they looted the subjects and killed a large number of persons."

Al-Sharqawi's description of the French deists is largely accurate, but he did see them through a nativist lens. Medieval Arab Muslim thinkers had waged culture wars over the place of reason, especially Greek reason, in Muslim learning. As Bonaparte recognized, during the Abbasid Caliphate of the eighth through thirteenth centuries, Muslim scholars had eagerly adopted scientific and philosophical works from the ancient Greek world. Philosophy was still controversial at the al-Azhar, and some of the split between clerics interested in French science and those who rejected it was rooted in their differing attitudes to the Greek tradition.[30]

✤

Later that month, the young Lieutenant Desvernois, who had fought Ibrahim's forces at Salahiya, heard the news of the 12 September 1798 Ottoman declaration of war on the French Republic with some despair. He felt Bonaparte had been betrayed by the Directory and by Talleyrand, who clearly had failed in their fantastical bid to maintain an alliance with the Porte while occupying an Ottoman province. He knew the French army was now vulnerable to attack by the Ottoman military, and perhaps by the British. From the end of September, Egypt was fermenting, he wrote, and the Bedouin were rising up, especially in the Delta.[31]

9

THE FESTIVAL OF THE REPUBLIC

*T*he northeast remained insecure, and the unstable situation threatened French control of Egypt's easternmost Mediterranean port and entrepôt for Delta rice crops, Damietta. "Daily," Niello Sargy reported, "the Arabs attacked our boats on Manzala Lake, pillaged them, and assassinated the escorts."[1] The Bedouin who formed the political power in the northeastern provinces of the Delta allied with the peasant fishermen who controlled the 700-square-mile lagoon known as Lake Manzala. The lake was important to the French as a transportation route, and only by controlling it could they secure Damietta, an important port city that it abutted. The villagers along the shores of this enormous lagoon and on the Matariya Islands, an archipelago within it, were skilled sailors and fishermen. General Andréossi, who was later charged to reconnoiter this body of water, reported that they owned some five or six hundred skiffs that had a monopoly on the right to navigate the lake or fish in it. "Along with the Bedouin, they were the tyrants of the lake and the riverine lands." They owed their allegiance to the great tax farmer *(multazim)* Hasan Tubar. The French saw Tubar, whose family had produced the paramount chieftains in that area for four or five generations, as the instigator of the revolts in the northeast.

The brackish water of the lagoon became fresh during the annual inundation of the Nile. It was between three and eight feet deep, and well stocked with fish. The Matariya villagers, owing to their relative isolation, had not had an outbreak of plague for thirty years, unlike the rest of the country, which had suffered from several debilitating epidemics. One had devastated Cairo as recently as 1791. Still, Millet reported that the swamps produced other fevers "that are quite frequent." About 1,100 men lived in the isles, not counting their wives and children. They dwelled in huts, built of adobe or sometimes kiln-hardened bricks, that covered every square inch of the islands.

The lake people of Matariya, insular and inbred, forbade their neighbors to fish in the lake, so they had little communication with them. They were almost always naked in the water, performing hard labor. Millet described them as strong and vigorous, skins bronzed by the sun, hair and beards black and rough, giving them a savage appearance. When they found themselves in the presence of their enemies, they would beat on a sort of tambourine or on the bow of their boats and "emit a thousand barbaric cries in a furious tone." Tubar ruled through four chiefs.

Sheikh Hasan Tubar's position as virtual king of the northeast Delta region arose from his riches, from the many loans he had made to clients, from his phalanx of sons, from the large number of stipends he provided, and from the support of the Bedouin tribes. He gave the latter land to cultivate, Niello Sargy explained, and plied their chieftains with opulent gifts. Niello Sargy maintained that, despite his nominal position as vassal of the Ottoman-Egyptian state, he had not paid it tribute for some years.

Captain Moiret had a contrasting view. He wrote that Tubar in fact delivered to his liege lords some 500,000 francs a year. He had been among the few, Niello Sargy alleged, to accumulate large estates under the nose of the Cairo magnates, who occasionally had attempted to mulct him, but were always beaten back by his Bedouin troops and lake-faring villagers. His terrain—of lagoon, marshland, and desert—proved an ideal barrier to penetration by the state. On Bonaparte's advent, Tubar had transferred his chief wife and her children, along with much of his treasure, to Damascus, and he vowed that, were the French to occupy his district, he would make for that destination as well. Since an Ottoman riposte to the French invasion might well come from that quarter, this boast was a threat that he would throw his resources to precisely the Ottoman forces that might eventually defeat the French. Turk maintains that Tubar was encouraged to go into revolt by Ibrahim Bey, and by the viceroy of the sultan at Sidon, Cezzar Pasha, whom Selim III had put in charge of riposting to the French invasion from Syria.

Capt. Pierre-François Gerbaud observed that there were no Western European merchants based in Damietta, because all of its commerce was with Syria, Cyprus, and what is now Turkey.[2] Its population was probably on the order of 12,000. Millet described the streets as "very narrow" but said that there was a pretty city square. "The Greek quarter surrounds . . . [that square] and renders it even more beautiful." They had constructed inns and cafes to the European taste and followed their own laws and customs even while subordinate to the Muslims. Gerbaud observed of Damietta, "There are many small boutiques and small traders, but no great merchants." The city's harbor was located on the eastern branch of the Nile, a few miles inland from the Mediterranean. One officer observed that it was only forty-eight hours from Damietta to Gaza in Ottoman Syria by sea.

Gerbaud confided in his diary on 12 September, "Fears raised by 3,000 skiffs assembled on Manzala Lake, a short distance from here." Tubar had armed the fishermen around Lake Manzala and equipped their boats as a fleet. Millet recalled that toward the middle of September he and his unit were sent up the Manzala Canal from Mansura. "After several days of traveling up the canal," he recalled, " . . . we were assaulted by Arabs and by the inhabitants of many villages who had assembled to pounce on us. The canal along which we traveled was very narrow. The boats almost touched the two banks."[3] He described his unit as arriving in front of a big village, not twenty feet away. "The last thing we were thinking was of being attacked, when all of a sudden we saw a crowd of peasants and Arabs about to throw themselves at us." The assailants prepared to jump into the French skiffs.

Unprepared and sweltering in the heat, the French had to grab up their arms. Millet characterized their attackers as being "men as well as women," armed with lances, pistols, and swords. The French only had 150 men. They began firing their muskets, scaring off the Egyptians, "who departed more quickly even than they had arrived." He said that the French now pursued the peasants, "always keeping up continual fire, which caused them great losses, both in killed and in wounded." Millet's unit suffered five dead and a dozen wounded. "The battle finished, we crossed the canal and entered the village, where we wrought a terrible carnage on all those who had withdrawn to it." After they had ransacked the hamlet, they set fire "to all four corners of it." They then went back to a village where they had left an agent and much booty ("contributions"), but found that the agent had been killed and their skiff looted. They burned that village, too. Then they returned to Mansura, having run smack into a major uprising.

Tubar loaded crowds of fierce Bedouin warriors from Daqahliya and Shar-qiya provinces into boats to support his lake people and villagers, and a squadron of 150 skiffs set out for Matariya, a town near the middle of the western coast of the lake. They then made for Damietta, toward which a swift wind carried them, allowing them to land at a village only half a league away. On 14 September, Gerbaud wrote, "Certitude of the perfidy of the headmen of Shu'ara, Manzala, etc." Around midnight, the Bedouins crowded off the skiffs, armed with muskets, lances, and picks, and managed to surprise the sleeping

General Vial and his 13th Demi-Brigade in the casernes of the port. Gerbaud said the attackers had brought straw and other flammable material into the city and laid them at the foundation of the French garrison. They captured the strongbox of his treasury, but, unable to break it open, turned to pillaging the city instead of methodically finishing their military conquest of it. Turk said that they were shouting, "Today is the day of war on these infidels and the Christians who follow them! Today we will come to the defense of our religion and kill these accursed wretches!"

The large Greek and Syrian Christian population of Damietta now allied with the French, staging a citizen resistance against the Bedouin and boat people. Turk wrote that, armed with muskets of their own, they sniped at Tubar's irregulars from the rooftops of their homes around the city square. Vial, besieged, made preparations throughout that night to depart, inspiring terror in the Christian locals that he was preparing to abandon them. Turk recorded that they told him that they had heard the attackers saying that local Christians should be killed before the French, since they were supporting the Europeans. Vial held off leaving. On 16 September the French remained in their barracks, Gerbaud said, remarking, "The enemy is not budging." They heard that Tubar was approaching from Manzala himself, joining together with the headman of Shu'ara. Vial attempted to send a small boat, escorted by two longboats armed with cannon, to General Dugua. But they were stopped en route and taken "by Bedouin" near Mit al-Khawli. The Egyptians slit the throats of twenty of the escorts. Late that night twenty French sappers made it into the city, and Vial had the hospital evacuated. On the seventeenth, Vial was dissuaded from a plan to attack Shu'ara, since he only had four hundred men and could not hope to leave behind a big enough garrison to ensure the safety of the Greek population of the city. Andréossi managed to arrive with an escort of fifty men.

On the morning of the eighteenth, French reinforcements finally arrived from Dugua in Mansura, sending morale soaring, especially among the Christians. With an extra 250 men to protect Damietta, Vial and Andréossi were freed to launch an offensive. In less than two hours, they obliged the Lake people and Bedouins to relinquish Damietta and to flee back across the lagoon. Tubar and his forces retired to the hamlet of Shu'ara, where they received reinforcements. Turk reported that the village of al-Izba heard rumors that the French had all been killed in Damietta and rose up against its own small garrison of twenty-five French troops. They killed five who were in the village outside the fort, then attacked the garrison. After hours of hard fighting, they received the news that actually the attack on Damietta had failed. The inhabitants of the village began to fear French reprisals, so they packed up their belongings and families and emigrated en masse to Syria. Vial came out to inspect the village but found it altogether deserted. The French constructed a new fort there.

Vial set out with his men to attack the Egyptians based at Shu'ara. As his troops marched overland, Andréossi supported him with a flotilla. When they reached the enemy-held town, they found the Bedouin arranged in a single line of 1,200 to 1,500 men that stretched from the lake to the Nile, with a thicket of palms behind them. The Bedouin, on spotting the French advance, discharged their carbines, but from too great a distance to hit anything. Vial dispatched a company of grenadiers with a field piece to cut them off from the palm thicket and from their boats, which were moored along the shore of the lake. The Bedouin, however, immediately saw what he was attempting to do, and he was forced to send another hundred men against them at once. As the French soldiers advanced, the Bedouin scattered, some to Shu'ara, others to the village of Minya (where, however, they found better-armed Republican troops awaiting them). Some managed to reach their skiffs on the lake. Vial's men captured two small cannon and two skiffs and killed or drowned three hundred peasants and Bedouin. They suffered a handful of killed and twenty wounded. Captain Say recalled of Shu'ara, "The village was burned down," and Turk said that the French killed the remaining inhabitants. The next day, Vial plundered the deserted village of al-Izba. On the twentieth, Gerbaud heard that General Damas, with six hundred men, had burned several villages loyal to Tubar. Bonaparte wrote Vial on 24 September: "Citizen General, the attack you launched on the village of Shu'ara does as much honor to you as to your troops."

Dugua's mobile columns patrolled the provinces of Daqahliya and Damietta. Bonaparte, who was distressed that Dugua had not managed to forestall the attack on Damietta, ordered him on 24 September to arm five hundred skiffs with cannon, so as to take control of the Manzala lagoon, "so you will be completely the master of the lake."[4] Bonaparte added, "Try to capture Hasan Tubar, and in order to do it, resort to a ruse if it is necessary." The commander in chief instructed Dugua to "make some severe examples" of the rebellious and said that since his contingents were not going to remain in Damietta and Mansura, it was important that he "profit from the moment to completely subdue them. For that, it is necessary that you disarm them, cut off some heads, and take some hostages."

The French expeditions into the northeastern Delta reveal to us important characteristics of its social geography. The lake people of Manzala, the political and military alliances of the peasants and Bedouin, the role of the swamp (especially during the Nile inundation of late summer and fall) and desert in promoting a degree of local independence, and the regularity with which both rich peasants and Bedouin resorted to handheld firearms are not reported in the Cairo-centered political chronicles that survive in Arabic as sources for eighteenth-century history. Millet's observation that female as well as male peasants joined in the attack on the French northeast of Mansura suggests a role for women in village uprisings about which male chroniclers are otherwise silent. Social alliances and disputes are also revealed. The orientation of the Mediterranean port of Damietta toward the Europeans and the significant political and even military role of the Greek, Syrian, and other Christians there suggest how fragmented Egypt's politics may have been at that time. The way in which Eyyüb Bey, a Mamluk *multazim*, or tax farmer, transplanted Bedouin from the Libyan desert to the village of Sonbat tells us about the conditions under which pastoralists and villagers could cooperate.[5] Ordinarily, there is a certain amount of conflict between Bedouin and farming villagers, because the same land can be used either for pasturage or for growing crops, but not both. Bedouin raise livestock on the hoof and wander around in search of pasture. If they encroach on farmland, they cause crop damage, and animal hooves are destructive of irrigation works. The only way the pastoralists can peacefully coexist with peasants in the same area is if they are offered fallow land and they stick to it, something that state enforcement helps ensure. In the Ottoman system, when pastoralists were used for security duty, they were given state stipends, which also helped ensure good behavior. Presumably that is what the bey who brought in the Dirn had done. He delegated to the Bedouin the task of keeping the feuding peasants in check and probably also fending off attacks by other Bedouin, and that arrangement facilitated a mutually beneficial relationship between the peasant farmers of Sonbat and the nomads. Gains in security would translate into better crop yields and more money for Eyyüb Bey. With the French invasion and the end of the beylical state (and thus of the stipends they were being paid for keeping order) the liberated Dirn had become, predictably, a nuisance to the settled villagers beyond their home base. They began raiding and looting the other hamlets, creating a social division of which the French took advantage.

Likewise, the lagoon kingdom of Hasan Tubar is unknown to the chronicler al-Jabarti. The story of Lake Manzala suggests ways in which different social formations (peasants, Bedouin, lake dwellers) were capable of forming

political alliances to keep the state out and maximize their retention of resources. The French were often not meeting new forms of resistance to foreign
rule but rather the quotidian resistance of provincials to the central government, any central government. In their rapaciousness, cruelty, and ruthlessness,
the French differed little from the beys whom they had displaced. They did
differ in being more desperate for resources and better armed in extracting
them, a hallmark of the modern state that Egyptian peasants were discovering
for the first time. Ibrahim and Murad had not found it cost-effective to devote
enormous resources to subduing Hasan Tubar. The French, starved for cash
and worried about the security of Damietta, could not afford to leave such local
potentates in power.

✦

Back in Cairo, Bonaparte pursued on a symbolic level the imposition of French
authority that his generals in the Delta sought through burning villages and lur-
ing village headmen. The first of Vendémiaire, marking the first day of the revolutionary calendar and the advent of Year 7 of the Revolution, coincided with
22 September of the Gregorian calendar. It was observed at the time, in Captain
Say's phrase, "in all the countries of France" as the Festival of the Republic. As
in France itself, the ideal of liberty was celebrated in Egypt by symbols and festivals and by the arts.[6] A historian of the period describes how, in France, liberty
and the Revolution were made the focus of "countless festivals" that were "organized all over the country for the purpose of commemoration and celebration."[7] In Egypt, the rhetoric of liberation through conquest pioneered by
Bonaparte and his officers comprised several sets of contradictions, between self
and other, civilization and barbarism, liberty and dominance, public and private,
male and female, Great Power diplomacy and local politics. The public celebrations themselves, by pulling so many motifs and elements together under the
sign of the tricolor, were one way of addressing these paradoxes.

Bonaparte ordered festivities to bring in the Year 7 "in both parts" of the
French Republic of Egypt.[8] He "wanted it to be commemorated with an un-
equaled splendor, to show the Egyptians all the opulence and all the force of our
army," wrote Bernoyer to his wife. Troops in Upper Egypt, pursuing Murad
Bey, held their commemoration at the Pharaonic ruins of Thebes (Luxor).
Smaller such festivals, of roughly the same form, were held in smaller cities such
as Rosetta as well. In Cairo, Bonaparte had a canvas pyramid erected at
Azbakiya Square and on its four faces had inscribed the names of the soldiers of
the army who died during the conquest of the country. (In the early 1790s, the

revolutionary government had erected a pyramid at the Temple of Immortality at the Convention, on which were inscribed the names of the fourteen armies of the Republic; Bonaparte had erected such commemorative pyramids in the Italian campaign, so that their use in Egypt was not a specific reference to the French being in the land of the pharaohs, though of course they took on a special meaning there.)

Ironically, the Muslim observer al-Jabarti describes the construction in a way that makes clear that he did not recognize it as a pyramid, nor did such a pagan monument have any resonance for Egyptian Muslims of that day. The pyramid was surrounded by 105 columns draped in the tricolor, bearing the names of each of the departments (i.e., provinces) of France. *Le Courrier de l'É-gypte* reported that the columns were "brought together by a double wreath, emblem of the unity and indivisibility of all the parts of republican France." One entertains a profound suspicion that Egypt was by then conceived as one of the indivisible "parts of republican France," which was the point of symbolically transporting the French departments to the middle of Cairo.

In the middle of the colonnade stood an obelisk, which rose to a height of seventy feet. On one face was inscribed in gold the phrase "To the French Republic, Year 7." On the opposite face were the words "To the Expulsion of the Mamluks, Year 6." On the two lateral faces, the phrases were translated into Arabic. An arch of triumph, on which was represented the battle of the pyramids, was raised at one of the two entrances in the colonnade. At the other entrance, a portico had been erected on which was inscribed, in Arabic, "There is no God but God and Muhammad is his Prophet." Most of the French troops would have been unaware of the significance of the Arabic, which is the profession of faith in Islam, and one of the Arabists at the Institute of Egypt must have written this notice, describing the Arabic inscription, for the official newspaper.

Bernoyer knew about the significance of this formula, and wrote, "These few words, my dear, form the sole profession of faith for Muhammadans. They are so sacred for them that, even if an infidel says them in Arabic at the moment of being massacred on the battlefield during combat, his life will be saved and he will be treated as a friend." He refrained from any of his usual Jacobin diatribes about religion here, but we know that he did not approve of this policy. Bonaparte was still attempting to associate republican virtue with an Islam coded as a sort of deism. The portico was designed to propagandize the Egyptian public and further the rumors of an impending conversion of the French. Ironically, back in France the Directory and its provincial administrations had been struggling against religion, attempting to sideline Sunday church services and

Catholic imagery and ritual in favor of civic celebrations. The revolutionary week consisted of ten days, with the tenth being a day of rest and a public festival that was increasingly poorly attended as the Directory limped along.[9]

At 6 A.M., three cannon salvos announced the beginning of the festival, and all the troops of the garrisons of Old Cairo and Bulaq were assembled "in fine form" at Azbakiya Square. Al-Jabarti remembered with evident distaste the arrival of the newly wealthy and powerful local Christians. The Copt Jirjis al-Jawhari and the Greek Philotheos wore rich, gold-embroidered coats of fur, sported "Kashmir turbans," and were mounted on "strong mules," their joy evident in their comportment, according to al-Jabarti. At 7 A.M. Bonaparte arrived with the generals, the heads of administration, the artists and scientists of the Egyptian Institute, the leader of the Meccan pilgrimage, and the members of both the Cairo and the provincial divans. One officer said it was "an almost Oriental procession." They were seated on a platform or reviewing stand. "All the musicians of the demi-brigades joined in to play warlike marches and patriotic airs, these melodies of victory so dear to all republicans." The troops then executed their maneuvers and firing exercises with "astonishing precision," after which they gathered around the obelisk.

An aide then read out Bonaparte's proclamation to the troops.[10] "We celebrate the first day of the Year 7 of the Republic. Five years ago, the independence of the French people was menaced, but you took Toulon. That presaged the ruin of our enemies." This was Bonaparte's way of reminding his men of the British and Spanish occupation of Toulon, a toehold for enemies of the Revolution on French soil, and of how his artillery techniques had defeated Admiral Nelson in 1793 and driven the foreigners from French soil. Given the recent rather dramatic victory that Nelson had gained over Bonaparte with the sinking or capture of the French fleet, it was necessary for Bonaparte to reach back in time for a victory of his own against the admiral.

The proclamation assured them of a good and honorable destiny in Egypt, like that of the men listed on the pyramids, because they were worthy of their deeds and the world's high opinion of them. There is reason to believe that that particular passage of his speech was not well received. It is clear from his officers' memoirs that Bonaparte made a misstep in those lugubrious circumstances, in bringing up the possibility that they would all die there. He then recovered: "Or you will return to our fatherland covered in laurels and the admiration of all the people. For the five months that we have been gone from Europe, we have been the object of the solicitude of our countrymen. On this day, 40 million citizens are celebrating the era of representative governments, 40 million citizens are thinking of you!" He assured them that all were saying that their blood and sacrifice would bring "general peace, repose, prosperity, commerce, and the benefits of civil liberty." Jollois remembered that the general then called out, "*Vive la République!*" (Long live the Republic!), "which was not at all repeated by the troops, so great in general was their discontent." He added, "Bonaparte, usually disposed to gaiety, all of a sudden took on a serious air. That no doubt provoked many reflections in him."

After the commander in chief emphasized to his troops that they were spreading the benefits of civil liberty and by their deeds ushering in the era of "representative governments" in Egypt and elsewhere, the music began. "The orchestra thereafter played a hymn composed by Citizen Parseval and the music of Citizen Rigel, as well as the *Marseillaise*" and other patriotic tunes. Bonaparte afterward retired with his retinue to his headquarters. Pelleporte recalled, "The army displayed only indifference toward that festival. It was the victim of melancholy that day, from which it had suffered a number of times since the loss of the fleet." Malus, worried about the news that the Ottomans were not after all grateful to the French for rescuing their province from the wayward beys, was more explicit: "It was a feeble distraction for the sorrow that had afflicted me for some time. At that epoch, that epidemic of low morale was making great progress in the army. One began to lose any illusions about the intentions of the Ottoman sultan regarding the expedition, and one could not see in the future any hope for tranquility."

Moiret described the subsequent banquet for hundreds of guests in standard language drawn from the official press report: "The divan, the principal officials of each province, and the first magistrates of each village were invited to the celebration and attended a dinner given by Bonaparte. This was the first time one saw the French colors united with Ottoman ones, the turban associated with the bonnet of liberty, the Declaration of the Rights of Man with the Koran, the circumcised and uncircumcised at the same banquet, with the difference that the former took sherbets and other beverages, while the other took [wines]." Bernoyer said that Mustafa Bey, the deputy Ottoman viceroy, was surprised to see that his portrait had been hung before him, showing him in the very clothes he had worn to the banquet. Villiers du Terrage recorded in his journal entry about the Muslim-French harmony at the banquet that the mathematician and geometer Gaspar Monge "attributed it to the improvement of humanity and the progress of Enlightenment."

Captain Say thought that the Egyptians were "astonished by the number of our troops and how well dressed they were. The precision with which the firing and artillery exercises were carried out, struck them forcefully." While the crowds may have been briefly intimidated by military spectacle, Bernoyer more realistically admitted in his letter to his wife, "It would be absurd to believe that the Egyptians invited to our festival entirely shared our overflowing joy!" He said that for all their attempts to hide their true spirits, the faces of the Egyptians betrayed to their French hosts the signs of sadness as a result of the horrible chastisements Bonaparte had visited on them for their resistance (he called it a revolt) to the French invasion. He admired their courage in putting on a pleasant and smiling countenance, despite their actual sadness. They were not alone. As we have seen, even the French army was unimpressed, and depressed about being stuck in Egypt without a fleet.

The Egyptians had all the less reason to be impressed in that the pyramid and columns were not actually as shiny as the propaganda Bonaparte ran in Cairo depicted them. Jollois, the engineer, revealed that "The execution of the project was dreadful. One had for workers only the people of the country, who did not know how to put the least thing together. One lacked wood of sufficient height. The painter Rigault committed blunders." Since Egyptian handicrafts were sophisticated, Jollois' remarks about the incompetence of the craftsmen raises suspicions that they were footdraggers and not very enthusiastic about helping the French celebrate their conquest.

At 4 P.M. the French held horse races at Azbakiya Square. That night, there were fireworks, dances, fanfares, and artillery salvos, "which offered the Egyptians a new spectacle that appeared to astonish them." In Alexandria, the French raised a tricolor flag on Pompey's Column, on which were inscribed the names of the soldiers killed before that city. They also employed multicolored lamps to illuminate the obelisk known as Cleopatra's Needle.

While Bernoyer and others had been struck by the mingling of East and West at the festival, Say stressed appropriation more than partnership: "It was a truly interesting spectacle for the French to see the tricolor flag, emblem of their liberty and of their power, floating above that antique land, from which the greater part of the nations derived their knowledge and their laws; to see that from Alexandria to Thebes and then from Thebes to the Red Sea, all recognized the dominion of their fatherland."[11] The keywords of his discourse here are knowledge, liberty, power, and dominion, and the tricolor is made to stand for all four. The irreconcilable contradictions among them appear not even to have occurred to Say. He saw no impediment to both talking of "liberating" the Nile Valley from the beys and at the same time referring to the "dominion" of the French *patrie*, or fatherland, over it. Revolutionary France was in some sense the new Egypt for the contemporary world, the present-day vanguard of science and law. He saw the French possession of the antique land of Egypt as a validation of its civilizational greatness, for it now encompassed the font of ancient knowledge and administration, as well.

These officers saw no contradiction between the demands of force and the enjoyment of liberty. After all, their political achievement had come about through revolution, which is to say through violence. Otherwise the Old Regime would never have been overthrown, or it would have managed to reassert itself. Clearly, "liberty" could not be an entirely voluntary affair in late Ottoman Egypt. It had to be imposed and bolstered by a free metropole. The intertwining of reason, nation, liberty, and terror was an important discourse in the period after the execution of the king, and despite the end of the Terror, this coupling of the Enlightenment to violence continued among some Directory-era thinkers in the context of the wars against Austria, in Italy and Germany, and the need to fight the external enemies of the Revolution. Therefore, the devotees of liberty and reason in Egypt would not have disagreed substantially with Robespierre's dictum, that terror is merely an aspect of justice, delivered swiftly and inflexibly, so that it is actually a virtue, or with his instruction to "break the enemies of liberty with terror, and you will be justified as founders of the Republic."[12] Thus, when Julien, an aide-de-camp of the general, and fifteen Frenchmen who navigated the Nile were killed in August by the inhabitants of the village of Alkam, Say remarked, "The General, severe as he was just, ordained that this village be burned. This order was executed with all possible rigor. It was necessary to prevent such crimes by the bridle of terror."[13]

Faced with continued Egyptian resistance to the occupation, Say acknowledged the necessity of accustoming "these fanatical inhabitants" to the "domination" of "those whom they call infidels." He again admitted French domination, but he hoped that Egyptians could be taught to love it. He concluded, "We must believe that a Government that guarantees to each liberty and equality, as well as the well-being that naturally follows from it, will insensibly lead to this desirable revolution." The revolution alluded to here is not a political event but the spiritual overthrow of an Old Regime of Ottoman-Egyptian dominance and religious "fanaticism." It is this revolution of ideals that so requires the arts as its propagandists, insofar as they are held to speak to the heart as well as the mind.[14]

Laus de Boisy bridled at criticisms of the Egypt project. Any man with a heart, he said, would want to rescue the Egyptians from their misery. Never-

theless, he observed, some Parisians had criticized the Directory's "noble operation." These, he complained, were mainly rich young women of the old aristocracy, representatives of a French Mamlukism who spend 20,000 francs on a
single ball and who are "born into a caste that the Mamluk Robespierre annihilated." These debutantes plead for the "poor beys whom Republican rage pur-
sues, so they say, even into the deserts of Africa." Laus de Boissy used the
Mamluks in this passage as a symbol of two separate things. First, he identified
them, as an opulent "feudal" class, with the affluent courtiers of the French
Old Regime. Second, because they stood for lawless violence, he used them as a
simile for the radical Jacobins who implemented the Terror. He painted the entire period before the turn away from extremism since the month of Thermidor in 1794 as equivalent to the internecine warfare among various sorts of
"Mamluks," comparable to the conflicts among slave-soldier houses in Ottoman Egypt. He made the Republic under the Directory the true heir to the
ideals of 1789. The Republic continued to face challenges, in his view, both
from the remnants of the Mamluks in Upper Egypt and Syria, and from their
sympathizers among the spoiled young heirs of the abolished—but still
wealthy—aristocracy in Paris. He endowed the opposition in France with a
feminine gender, making it seem not only heartless and aristocratic but also
frivolous and unmanly. He identified the class enemies of the Directory's noble
expedition as feckless young women, as heiresses and socialites. In this way, he
also made the Mamluks, the objects of the compassion of the rich young
Parisians, themselves seem effeminate.[15] The largely wealthy or middle-class
memoirists argued for a symmetry between the liberation of France from both
aristocratic tyranny and sansculotte terror and the liberation of Egypt from the
Oriental despotism and internecine squabbling of the Ottoman beylicate. In
the "family romance" of the French Egyptian colony, the 32,000 male invaders
constituted a band of brothers who saw the beys as analogous to the father-
tyrant who had been the French king, and who thus had to be destroyed.[16] Just
as in Directory France a mild form of patriarchal domesticity was reinstituted
after the excesses of the Terror, so also in Egypt the rule of French males was
configured as a form of liberty.

Some Republicans, more wedded to the liberalism that was often influential
in the Directory, explicitly condemned the methods of brutality and terror.
Bernoyer reported how disgusted he was at having to go out that fall to a poor
adobe village to demand taxes, which were extracted from the peasants only by a
threat to have the village headman bastinadoed. He complained that it was hard

for republicans to behave in this manner and blamed Bonaparte for not soften-
ing the laws so as to provide a "liberal, just, and independent government" instead of continued slavery. "What mortified us most," he remarks, "was that
Bonaparte used the same methods as the Mamluks."[17]

In the prerevolutionary period, many of the French had protested increasingly vocally against arbitrary arrests and the lettres de cachet (arbitrary royal
decrees ordering an arrest) by appealing in part to a person's natural right of
property, including the property of one's person.[18] Bonaparte's methods
seemed to liberal republicans increasingly shameful, a resurrection of the worst
abuses of the Old Regime, or a subtle metamorphosis of republicans into
Mamluks. Some French memoirists, then, used the beys not only as symbols of
Louis XVI (tyranny) and Robespierre (terror), but even of Bonaparte himself,
and by extension of all the French in Egypt. Even some French painters in the
Romantic revolutionary tradition later implicitly condemned the expedition to
Egypt by depicting French soldiers as Orientals and Bonaparte as willing to
play with lives.[19]

Bernoyer's increasing pessimism about the prospects for liberty in Egypt led
him ultimately to confess Rousseauan sentiments about the inherent harmfulness
of civilization. On the one hand, he felt that were Egyptians to be educated and
enlightened, they would never prove thereafter willing to submit to the onerous
yoke of oppression. In their present estate of ignorance, he complained, they did
not feel it, and they bore everything with patience and resignation. Both the
decadent ignorance of the peasants and the rebellious enlightenment of the educated, however, were inferior in his eyes to the happiness that could only be enjoyed by the unspoiled savage, as, he said, Jean-Jacques Rousseau maintained.[20]
Thus, the fellahin did not represent for Bernoyer the noble savage, but rather the
ignoble bearer of humiliation in a despotic civilization. In the face of the mount-
ing evidence that neither tyranny nor liberty really led to happiness, Bernoyer
took solace in resurrecting Rousseau's romanticism about the virtues of the state
of nature, a state that had the advantage for those who desired an untarnished
ideal of not actually existing. Even the ancient Egyptian monuments of civilization, in this reading, speak not of advancement but of "fanaticism and slavery"
and stand witness to an Oriental despotism. In the absence of reason and liberty,
the pyramids' tyrannical underpinnings marred their beauty.

The French employed public celebrations and spectacle both to commemo-
rate Republican values and to instill a sense of unity with regard to revolutionary victories. Such "festivals reminded participants that they were the mythic

heroes of their own revolutionary epic."[21] The universal wearing of the cockade, the flying of the tricolor, the intricate symbology of columns and banners, the impressive military parades and cannonades, all were intended to invoke fervor for the Revolution and the remaking of society as republic. That some of the French appear seriously to have expected the conquered Egyptians to join them in these festivities demonstrates how little they could conceive of their own enterprise on the Nile as a colonial venture. The greatest use of Republican ideology appears to have been precisely to hide that fact from themselves.

✦

The thousands of French soldiers in Cairo, deprived of the military action being seen by those in the Delta, depressed by the loss of their fleet, and beset by homesickness, suffered from severe tedium. The civic spectacles favored by Bonaparte appear to have left them cold. Doguereau recalled, "The life that we led bored us a great deal, even though we were so many young people together. It was so different from that which we had led in Europe that we had great difficulty in accustoming ourselves to it."[22] He complained of the considerable heat, which made them reluctant to go out during the day. And where, he asked, would one have gone for a walk in any case? "In the middle of the desert, amid the rubble, one still needed escorts; at the gates of the city we were assailed by Arabs. We had few books. We wanted desperately to return to France."

Soldiers and officers fought their boredom in the capital in various ways, devising social events, gambling like fiends, and seeking out companionship, no matter how debased. The now abandoned harems of the grandees attracted the attention of some of these young men. Doguereau recounted how, in early August, "a harem, into which two of our colleagues knew how to introduce themselves and from which they brought out Black women, provided a way of passing some moments in those first days. One quickly became bored with them."[23] He described how slave caravans, "coming from Darfur, Senar, Dongola, and Borgu," arrived in the capital several times a year or at least annually. (The physician Louis Frank asserted that only four such caravans were mounted during the French occupation and that the number of slaves imported annually had already in any case been much reduced by overtaxation, from 4,000 to 6,000 a year in earlier decades to 1,000 or less in the late 1790s.) Doguereau said that the Ethiopian slave drivers marched them on foot, as European horse merchants did their wares. "Males and females are naked, except for a loin cloth." He added, perhaps to comfort himself, "They seem indifferent to their fate."

Doguereau described the African slaves as decorated with tattoos (he called them "scars") and said the women often wore nose jewelry. They were sold for between 40 and 150 piasters, depending "on their age, beauty, and strength; the youngest are eight or nine." Other Frenchmen did not tire of their female slaves the way Doguereau had, but rather took them as mistresses for the rest of their time in Egypt. The young zoologist Saint-Hilaire revealed that at least one of his slaves was a black concubine, and he took care of another for his brother, who was stationed at Salahiya.[24] Keeping household slaves was inconvenient for those French, like Saint-Hilaire, who traveled. The biologist acknowledged that he resolved his own problem by leaving his slave in the harem of an Egyptian notable. At one point, he wrote, "I got my negress back out of the harem of the great Sheikh Sulayman al-Fayyum[i], who, because of his friendship for me, had kept her there."

As Norry admitted, Saint-Hilaire was no aberration. Many Frenchmen in Egypt purchased slaves, maintaining them for domestic service or sexual favors, or both. As we have seen, some officers took as their mistresses the former harem women of the deposed beys, many of them slave girls. Adm. Jean-Baptiste Perrée wrote back to a friend in France, "The beys have left us some pretty Armenian and Georgian wenches, whom we have confiscated to the profit of the nation."[25] Although he used the diction in jest, his phraseology underlines how the officers entertained a highly masculine conception of the French nation, and how they viewed Egyptian women as commodities to be sequestered, like so many bags of rice.

The officers at least said that they regretted the inability of local women to play a role in French social life, for lack of linguistic skills and training in French etiquette. Although they could be had for a reasonable price, Niello Sargy lamented, "They could not ornament our festivals or in any case supply the charm and amiability of our French women, who issued from the ranks of society." Although he put the blame on the Caucasian women for their lack of social skills, there is evidence that French racism helped exclude them from this role.[26] Bonaparte, having been betrayed by Josephine, had reason to revert to his bachelor habits and engage in a series of liaisons himself. It is also possible that the Ottoman-Egyptian custom of polygamy among great military leaders influenced his notions of sexual propriety, since until then he had been from all accounts exclusively dedicated to Josephine once he married her. He at first tried his luck with Georgian women of the harems. Despite their relative powerlessness, Niello Sargy hinted that they were capable of conveying to Bonaparte their true sentiments with their body language (or lack of it). The commander in chief found with these Ottoman-Egyptian women "neither reciprocity nor any charm of society." Other French officers had better luck with the abandoned wives of the beys, suggesting that the Georgians singled Bonaparte out for special opprobrium as the commander in chief of the invading army and author of their downfall.

Ironically, before he encountered Fatima, Bernoyer, that Jacobin champion of the Enlightenment and designer of uniforms, had been tempted to become a slave owner. He met a Captain Lunel, from Avignon, who proposed that the two of them go to the bazaar, where a caravan had just arrived with a large number of female slaves, "blacks for the most part."[27] They went to the slave auction, "a vast building like a monastery," and saw that in the courtyard slaves were being sold.[28] The Sudanese women were in grass skirts and "all smelled very bad." At their complaints, the auctioneer displayed for them better women, but they still were not impressed. Then, with a show of reluctance, he took them upstairs and let them inspect his two best, "marvels" that no other customer had yet seen. They were sitting on the ground. When the two Frenchmen entered, they stood and drew their veils over their faces. The auctioneer commanded them to disrobe but they refused. Bernoyer wrote,

> Then I approached one of them and, so as not to startle her, I smiled tenderly at her. Delicately, I lifted her veil. I remarked a slight resistance. I perceived, shining in her eyes, a secret joy when she saw that I was avidly following all the alluring and marvelous curves of her body. Her modesty required that I be the one who disrobed her. She covered herself from one side when I uncovered her from another. I absolutely could not stop admiring that body, so perfect—the slenderness of the arms, the harmony of the legs, the two breasts rounded and firm, the symmetrical hips, all demarcating an astonishingly flat stomach, lightly creased down the middle to the navel . . . and, lower down, that dense tuft of coiled hair, which allowed one to divine the intimate entrance to an instant of pleasure that one would never forsake.[29]

Despite his enthusiasm, Bernoyer found the price prohibitive. The auctioneer wanted 1,800 francs for each woman. Bernoyer offered 1,600. Lunel remonstrated with him that this offer was entirely too high. The auctioneer declined to bargain. So, to demonstrate their uninterest, they left, expecting him to call them back. He did not budge. They walked about the bazaar for half an hour, hoping to soften him up. When they came back, Bernoyer was dismayed to find the two women already sold.

Later he happened to pay a visit to Eugène de Beauharnais, Bonaparte's teenage stepson, and discovered that Eugène had bought the slave, now bedecked with diamonds, pearls, and finery. Bernoyer reminded Eugène of his own earlier complaints that whereas in Paris Josephine had denied him nothing, in Cairo Bonaparte left his stepson perpetually empty-handed. Eugène revealed that he had borrowed 10,000 francs from a merchant in contact with Paris, who would be reimbursed by his mother there. Bernoyer confessed that he had almost bought the woman himself, but that he was sure she could be in no better hands. Beauharnais replied, "I assure you, Monsieur Bernoyer, that I have never made such good use of my money. I have already spent 6,000 francs to make her as beautiful as a queen. I love her to madness, for her spiritual and vivacious personality has opened for me a source of inexhaustible pleasures."

Bernoyer was reduced from philosopher and admirer of Rousseau (author of the *Discourse on Inequality*), from inveterate opponent of Bonaparte's disregard for the rule of law, to a prurient voyeur willing to reduce a human being to a mere commodity. All that prevented him from doing so was the price asked for the Sudanese woman, who presumably had been of high status in her own country. His initial preference for the delights of repartee and coquettish wordplay evaporated, replaced by a gross fixation on mute body parts and pubic hair. He even repeated without qualification Beauharnais's assertions that there was something spiritual about his relationship with his new property and that it had something to do with her personality.

Some French observers justified Egyptian slavery by pointing out that slaves were much better treated than domestics and that masters were obliged, after a few years, to marry off the girls and to establish an estate for the males. Bonaparte himself argued, "In the Orient, slavery never had the same character as in the Occident. Slavery in the Orient is what one sees in the holy scriptures; the slave inherits from his master, he marries his daughter. Most of the pashas had been slaves. . . . The ideas of the Orient and the Occident are so different that it took a long time to make the Egyptians understand that the entire army was not made up of slaves belonging to the Great Sultan."[30] Doguereau wrote, "The slavery of blacks is a very happy estate in Egypt. Women are bought to keep women company or to busy themselves with housework." As for males, he said, they "are the shop boys in the boutiques and often become the adoptive children of their masters; they are only bought by wealthy persons." He concluded, "Their lot is much happier than that of poor Egyptians."[31] Saint-Hilaire concurred about the difference, writing to one correspondent, "Slavery is different here than in America. It is a veritable adoption. My two slaves never call me anything but their father and I am so satisfied with their services that I dedicate to them the same amity. In past times, only people who were bought had honor. That opinion was so dominant that the beys sent their children far away, having them sold by strangers and then buying them with a view to giving them more consideration and of being able to elevate them in honor."

These despicable sentiments demonstrate the inability of many French intellectuals to empathize with the loss of individual liberty experienced by slaves. Egypt's slavery was admittedly a different system than that of Haiti. One reason for the difference Saint-Hilaire and others perceived was that Islamic law stipulated that the children of slave women were free persons with rights of inheritance, and little or no stigma attached to them, so that they were constantly absorbed through intermarriage into the general Muslim population. No ex-slave ethnic group ever grew up. In addition, plantation slavery was rare because of the abundance of peasant labor, and the main form of the institution was household slavery. The latter may have been less harsh, but it was still a form of forced labor that denied human beings their liberty, and concubines were sexually coerced.

In contrast, Niello Sargy expressed abolitionist sentiments:

> But when one has frequented the bazaars where the traffic is pursued, when one has seen the excesses they perpetrate on these unfortunates whom they are charged with exchanging for pieces of gold; when one sees a girl barely into puberty with a baby already at her maternal breast, and knows that both will soon pass between the hands of an avid man, one cannot avoid feeling a pain that is remedied only by the hope of seeing one day philosophy and humanity obtain their triumphs along the Nile, as well.[32]

Apparently "philosophy and humanity" were not going to get much help in this regard from the officer corps of the Republic. The contradictions between liberty and coercion in the French Republic of Egypt were nowhere more evident than in attitudes toward slavery. Slavery had long been forbidden on French soil, and owners from the colonies who brought slaves back home often regretted it when the courts freed them.[33] Before the Revolution, however, it was not illegal for French citizens dwelling abroad to own slaves or maintain slave plantations. That was a result of a seventeenth-century decree promulgated by Louis XIII, for which the Catholic Church had lobbied (French slave owners in the New World had been required to convert their human chattels to Christianity).

French slave traders sent hundreds of thousands of Africans to the New World from Senegal and elsewhere in West Africa through the port of Nantes,

French slave plantations in Martinique, Guyana, and Haiti produced sugar, coffee, indigo, and other goods, while imposing the most miserable existence on the workers. Montesquieu, Rousseau, Voltaire, and the authors of the *Encyclopédie*, for all their often racist attitudes toward persons of African descent, had roundly condemned the institution of slavery as far as they could do so without falling afoul of the monarchy. The *Encyclopédie* contained articles insisting that "if a commerce of this kind can be justified by a moral principle, then there is no crime, however atrocious, that cannot become legitimate," and another asserted that "buying Negroes, to reduce them to slavery, is a trade that violates religion, morality, the natural law, and all the rights of human nature."[34] Voltaire denounced slavery in his novel *Candide* and thundered against the slave sugar plantations maintained by the French in Haiti, where, he said, people died for the luxury of others. The Revolution itself put the issue on the legislative calendar, as did the uprisings in Haiti, which provoked frantic letters from the landlord class there to Paris. The Jacobins tended to dismiss these pleas as the manipulations of effete royalist expatriates. Abolitionists pressed for antislavery legislation. After a rancorous debate in which many delegates recognized that ending slavery might well finish off French colonialism, in February, 1794 (the Year 2), the National Convention outlawed slavery in French colonies abroad, though it did not outlaw the slave trade.[35] The law forbade any compensation to the slave owners, whom the revolutionaries considered on the same level as exiled royalists, that is, thieves of the property of the people. The French planters in the Caribbean and French Guyana largely ignored the proclamation, and it is said that it never reached Martinique. The French officers and others in Egypt, despite these Enlightenment debates, often purchased household slaves and concubines, and no one seemed to invoke the 1794 law.

IO

THE OBJECT OF HIS DESIRES

*D*espite the burning of Shu'ara and other campaigns, the Delta remained unsettled. Through the first half of October, town and city
tax strikes and revolts and alliances with Bedouin cavalry in the region popped up first in one place in the Delta, then in another. If we think of
Lower Egypt as an outstretched hand, thumb on the right, all the fingers were
busy. The thumb is the Sharqiya line from Cairo through al-Khanka to Bilbeis
and Salahiya, thence east toward Suez or the Sinai. Despite the garrison at Bilbeis, this route remained parlous. The tip of the pointer finger is the villages
along Lake Manzala. The middle finger goes down the eastern branch of the
Nile through Banha, Mit Ghamr, and Zifta to the inland rice and cotton depot
city of Mansura, then out to the Mediterranean at Damietta. The ring finger
stretches between the two Nile branches through Minuf and Shibin al-Kum to
the Sufi holy center of Tanta, then over to the western Nile past Shubrakhit to
the Mediterranean port of Rosetta. This area between the two branches of the
Nile was extremely fertile and productive, and therefore valuable to French tax
collectors. One officer who traveled down the Rosetta branch of the Nile wrote,
"I can best compare the verdure of much of the countryside, crisscrossed by various canals, to brilliant emeralds in a silver setting."[1] The pinky of our imagi-
nary hand goes down the west bank of the western branch of the Nile to
Rahmaniya and then cuts northwest through Damanhur along the now-filled
canal down to Alexandria. Many of these inland urban spaces were lightly garrisoned by the French, who were nevertheless making enormous tax demands
on the livestock and still-green winter crops.

On 29 September at Bilbeis to the east, Sergeant François said, the garrison
learned from the order of the day that there was another revolt in Lower Egypt.
"We worried that night, and were obliged to double the nocturnal patrols."[2]

Their nervousness was all the greater because they were beginning to fall ill. "Many men have been stricken by opthalmia and many have gone blind; others are covered with small red pimples. More than half of the division is stricken with this malady, which devours them like the mange; a third at least have eye disease." They expected to be attacked the next day, and they designated battle positions for the blind, who were placed along the walls of the fort with muskets placed in their hands and pointed so as to hit any enemy advancing to within thirty or forty feet. They were not to fire, in case of attack, until ordered to do so by the commander. The other sick soldiers were constrained to go out and fight alongside the healthy. The next day they heard that the village of Abaka, near Bilbeis, had joined the Bedouin insurgents and taken up arms. His unit went out to confront them and received fire as they approached the hamlet. They used their two pieces of cannon to cut a breach in the village walls, then poured through, firing their muskets. "In an instant the village was invaded. The streets were covered with the dead and wounded. We returned to camp that evening, charged with divesting them of and carrying away with us their horses, camels, water buffaloes, sheep, donkeys, and grain." He remarked that Egyptian villages were typically built on slightly elevated land and surrounded by walls with two big gates. Often each gate would have a tower next to it from which village guards could fire at various angles. The fortifications, he said, were sufficient to fend off attacks by Bedouin.

Also in late September, generals Joachim Murat and François Lanusse fought Bedouin tribesmen around Mit Ghamr, a major town due north of Cairo along the eastern branch of the Nile that led to Mansura and Damietta.[3] The Europeans had to leave their cannons behind because they could not drag them across canals and through the autumn sloughs. The nomads withdrew up a hill, or *tall*, at the base of which stood water from the rising Nile. The French troops "braved the liquid element" and charged up the hill, and in the blink of an eye, Murat wrote, "there floated at its summit the flag of the Grand Nation." The Bedouin rapidly retreated to their camp in a somewhat distant meadow, putting wetlands between them and their attackers. Murat and Lanusse, despite the fatigue among their troops, decided to chase after them: "Republican ardor takes no account of perils," Murat pronounced. He added, "We marched half a league in the water and the mud." The Bedouin, taking heavy casualties, fled their camp, leaving their vast herds behind. The French pursued them relentlessly, until a broken dike and nightfall made it impossible for them to advance farther. They returned to the Bedouin camp and collected "about 5,000" animals from the herd, including sheep, camels, and donkeys, but had to shoot some of them since they could not herd so many. The troops returned to Mit Ghamr barefoot, having lost their boots in the mud.

In early October, the townspeople of the central Delta city of Tanta, site of the holy shrine of Sayyid Ahmad al-Badawi, went on a tax strike against the French. The Sufi dervishes, in their outrageous state of undress, congregated in that city and appear to have been involved in the rebellion.[4] (Al-Badawi's was a Sufi shrine, especially revered by the mystics.) General Fugière wrote Bonaparte that he wanted to restrain his men, given the veneration in which the city and its saints were held, but feared they might be provoked to fire on the dervishes. He dispatched Gen. Simon Lefebvre with some canal boats to Tanta along with Selim Çurbaci, a high officer in Bonaparte's reconstituted Janissary Corps. Çurbaci brought out as hostages four overseers of the shrine of Ahmad al-Badawi and it looked as though a crisis would be averted. But when the returning French troops neared their skiffs, the townspeople gathered, joining with 150 Bedouin, and came after them angrily. The French had to give up their hostages and flee on the canal, wreaking carnage as they fired into the infuriated crowd. Fugière wrote Bonaparte asking for artillery to punish the city.

The commander in chief must have consulted Egyptian clerical advisers such as Sheikh al-Bakri, for he wrote back sternly ordering that Tanta not be leveled. "I learned with pain, Citizen General, what happened at Tanta; I desire that this city be respected, and I would regard it as the greatest misfortune that could occur, to see ravaged this place, holy in the eyes of the entire Orient." He said that Fugière must end the matter by negotiation and that if the general wanted to subdue the Arabs, he should take hostages from them.

Several trade fairs were held every year there in conjunction with commemorations at the shrine of Sayyid Ahmad al-Badawi, attracting a crowd of merchants and customers from miles around, even as far away as Cairo.[5] A major saint's tomb made a city such as Tanta sacred ground to Muslims, and the foreign, European Catholic rule defiled it. Local tradition had it that the entombed saints formed a "spiritual government" that stood in severe judgment of the "apparent government" of this-worldly officials. In Cairo, the French had already punished a Muslim money changer who had expressed confidence that summer that Tanta's long-dead saint, "Sayyid Ahmad al-Badawi . . . will kill all the Christians that pass by."[6] Capt. Louis Thurman observed, "In Egypt there are many saints, the tombs of which one encounters at every step. It is accepted that all, each year, issue from their sepulchers and go to Medina to visit the Prophet. None dare omit the journey." He said that there was a tomb at Abu Mandur, near Rosetta, where it was said that, on the contrary, the Prophet came to visit its saint instead, since he kept the village tower from collapsing into the Nile and diverting its waters away from the port, with disastrous consequences.[7] The tombs of saints would prove more of a challenge to the French than they initially could have imagined.

As October began, General Andréossi initiated another campaign against Hasan Tubar and his men, according to Niello Sargy. The general departed for Damietta on the third and went down the Nile with a flotilla. At 7 A.M. they disembarked, and he began a march with about a hundred men, following the embankment that separated the lagoon from the Mediterranean. This tongue of land entirely lacked any wells, and they suffered from thirst. Another hundred men followed in skiffs. At three o'clock in the afternoon, the column and the flotilla arrived at Diba, a hamlet where the lake met the sea through an outlet. There, they at last found water to drink, after an eight-hour fast. The party pressed on toward Damietta, via Matariya. At the very moment when they caught a glimpse of the minarets of the village of Manzala, a hundred hostile skiffs appeared, manned by the lake people, and they maneuvered into the same canal that Andréossi's flotilla was navigating. The boatmen issued cries of fury and beat tambourines and brass instruments. Andréossi had sails lowered and consolidated his forces, ordering that a fusillade be fired. Six cannon blasts rang out. The boatmen, alarmed, fell back. Gerbaud said that the battle went on for five hours, until 10 P.M., when the boatmen withdrew.

They continued to harass the French force until they neared the Delta village of Minya, to the west of Damietta. There they again shouted war cries, approaching the shore and making as if to land. They appeared to be attempting to stampede the French off their own vessels. But the European troops stood fast, and Andréossi ordered another fusillade, both to repulse the lake people and to let General Vial know that his flotilla had arrived. At length, as the moon rose, one of Vial's lake patrols arrived, forcing Tubar's boatmen to withdraw.

A few days later, General Dugua wrote Hasan Tubar seeking an accommodation. Niello Sargy recorded the chieftain's reply as follows:

> I do not wish to see the French, either from far or from near. . . . If they give me assurances that I will be left in tranquility in my own home, at the town of Manzala, I will pay them the same tribute that I used to pay the Mamluks. But I want no communication with those infidels.

Hostilities were not at an end. On 8 October, a number of enemy skiffs appeared off the lakeside town of Minya, but fire from French ships, supported by an artillery piece, chased the boatmen away. Dugua then sent a strong column down to the town of Manzala, the residence of the recalcitrant chieftain. General Damas, tasked with this operation, dispersed a gathering of armed men and entered Manzala without encountering any opposition. Niello Sargy's division then joined his forces. The skiffs of the lake people were forced to flee. The French were able to establish military posts at Matariya and Manzala that would protect the flotilla plying the lagoon. Hasan Tubar relocated to elsewhere in the lake region, maintaining his small squadron and remaining a threat to Bonaparte's army.

✤

Bonaparte was unable to spot rising popular resentment and anger in the capital. His lack of money forced him into arbitrary policies whereby he often allowed the troops to live by looting Egyptians. On top of that he imposed stiff taxes, making the conquered population pay for its own conquest and occupation. The 20,000 French troops in the capital knew little Arabic and had no familiarity with Egyptian Muslim culture. The engineers among the officers began rearranging the city to their specifications, tearing down what they viewed as useless tombs or Sufi shrines that got in the way of straighter, broader avenues, or removing the barriers between city quarters. Turk recalled that they destroyed "the mosques and minarets at al-Azbakiya Square so as to widen the streets for the passage of their wagons."[8]

On one occasion when French engineers tore down some sacred tombs, Bonaparte said that the news spread and "excited a lively discontent."[9] In response, "a tide of people, at six o'clock in the afternoon, inundated Azbakiya Square, and performed a sort of charivari under the windows of the Great Sultan." His guards interposed themselves and took up their arms. Bonaparte says he was at dinner. "I presented myself at the window with my interpreter, Venture, who explained to me that this was a mark of confidence, that it was a manner authorized by custom of presenting a petition to a sovereign." Venture went down and asked the crowd to choose twenty spokesmen, whom he brought in to see Bonaparte, having them greeted "with the greatest distinction." Treating them like great sheikhs, he had them served coffee and sorbets and introduced them to the commander in chief, who listened to their complaints. The tombs of the saints "had been violated." The French "had behaved as infidels or idolaters would have." (The crowd leaders were reminding Bonaparte of his contention that his army was made up of neither, but were rather "muslims.") The prayer leaders and callers to prayer in the delegation were "ordinarily extremely fanatical" and "spoke rather heatedly." Bonaparte nevertheless gave them a hearing and blamed the engineers, whom he immediately ordered, he said, to stop their demolitions.

The clerics who had led the crowd went out and boasted of their success, to cries of joy. The crowd then went through the streets, chanting holy verses, and ended up at the al-Husayn Mosque. There, Bonaparte wrote, a preacher "gave a sermon, praying for the Great Sultan and imploring the Prophet to maintain him always in sentiments favorable to Islam." Either Venture really did believe that the gathering of an angry mob at a Mamluk mansion would have been met with anything but mass beheadings, or he feared that Bonaparte would overreact and turn a petitioning crowd into a violent mob. Bonaparte's conviction that he and Venture had handled the Muslim leaders and the Cairo crowd indicated a deadly overconfidence.

All unawares, Bonaparte was violating Muslim social norms of some gravity with his policies. In early September Bonaparte had Sayyid Muhammad Kurayyim, the former governor of Buhayra whom Kléber believed guilty of intriguing with the enemies of the French around Alexandria, executed for treason.[10] Kurayyim, however, was a sharif, that is, a putative descendant of the Prophet, and ordinarily would have been punished in some other way even by a Muslim ruler. For an infidel French general to kill a "grandson" of the Prophet inflamed religious passions. Kurayyim was, moreover, a man of the people. He had been a weigher at the port of Alexandria, and had gained the trust of his wealthy customers, both foreign Christians and local Muslims, because of his probity. Ultimately he had come to the attention of Murad Bey, who appointed him head of the divan and of the customs office in the city, a position that al-Jabarti maintained gradually corrupted him. Nevertheless, as an Egyptian born and bred he had many supporters. The clerics of al-Azhar, the putative government of Egypt at that point, "interceded repeatedly for" Kurayyim with the French. The Egyptian chronicler maintained that in early September, Charles Magallon, who had been the French consul in Egypt, came to Kurayyim and informed him that he could be freed for a price. It was a sum that was beyond him. Magallon is said to have given him twelve hours to raise it. Kurayyim sent pleas to the al-Azhar clerics and to Sayyid Ahmad al-Mahruqi, the great caravan merchant, asking them to raise the money: "Buy me, O Muslims!" But they did not have those sums, or were in too much uncertainty about their own futures to risk parting with what capital they had left.

At noon, time had run out. French soldiers came, swords unsheathed, for the former governor of Buhayra and master of Alexandria and escorted him through the streets, preceded by drummers. They passed al-Saliba district and arrived at Rumayla, where they bound the hands of this scion of the house of the Prophet and then dispatched him by firing squad, "as is their custom with regard to executions." Al-Jabarti recalled, "They cut off his head and raised it on a staff, parading it around Rumaylah. Their crier called out, 'This is the retribution for all who oppose the French.'" His slaves came to collect his head and buried it with his body.

Bonaparte had issued the death warrant on 5 September: "Sayyid Muhammad al-Kurayyim, convicted of treason, of having continued his intelligences with the Mamluks after having sworn fidelity to the Republic, of having served as a spy for them, shall be shot in the afternoon tomorrow. All of his assets, liquid and immovable, will be confiscated for the profit of the Republic." He apparently had not made the proclamation public, however, lending some support to al-Jabarti's account of a French attempt to extort money for his release. On 6 September the general added a postscript before publishing it: "The execution of the above judgment took place today at noon, at the square of the Citadel. The head of Kurayyim was paraded around the streets of Cairo." Turk recalled that there were several reasons for a building hatred of the French, "including the killing of Sayyid Muhammad Kurayyim, for he was a sharif."[11]

Niello Sargy watched the frustrations of the Cairenes build.[12] They resented the "overly minute" precautions the French took against the spread of plague, which included making the Egyptians spread their clothing and under things in the sun, exposing them to public view. General Dupuis, in charge of these measures, made himself particularly hated when he said in one proclamation that "the slovenliness of the houses and streets gave the inhabitants diseases unknown in Europe." Muslims disliked the sight of French troops guarding the mosques, though Bonaparte put them there to ensure that no soldiers insulted believers at prayers. The commander in chief issued a decree allowing Greeks to wear turbans of all colors, whereas they had earlier been confined to wearing white, a measure that displeased the Muslims insofar as it underlined their own reduction in status. Also, a money famine bedeviled the Cairenes, making it difficult to buy basic commodities. A "crowd of Jews, Copts, Greeks, and Europeans" had come to Egypt to offer their services to the beys in "pillaging the people," and they were employed by the French for the same purpose. "They made the French loathed," Niello Sargy remembered, "by their depredations."

The French dalliances with Egyptian women were also a source of humiliation and friction for the Cairo populace.[13] A few women attached themselves to the French and began going about unveiled. To conservative Middle Easterners, however, this discarding of the veil and growth of a public nightlife seemed more a sign of debauchery than of cultural progress. Niqula Turk recalled, "The French would bring out Muslim women and girls barefaced in the streets, and it became widely known that wine was being drunk and being sold to the troops."[14] He was implying a swelling outrage at these practices in the Cairo public, which viewed them as meretricious. Even Zaynab, the sixteen-year-old daughter of Sayyid Khalil al-Bakri, threw off her veil and began going out with French officers, though rumors that Bonaparte himself wooed her for a while are probably little more than gossip. For the daughter of the chief of the Sayyid caste, a scion of the House of the Prophet, and a member of an honored family of clerics to behave this way would have provoked an honor killing if not a formal execution under the Ottoman beylicate. The changing mores of Egyptian women also provoked fears among Egyptian men that the foreigners would change the balance of power between the sexes and that they would be emasculated. Men no longer felt in control when they saw women walking unveiled in public with European men, riding horses and laughing out loud in the streets. Al-Jabarti, who reported these outrages, said that the French men attracted Egyptian women because they were "subservient to them." A Frenchman, he said, sought to please his woman and avoided contradicting her even if she cursed or struck him. Such protected women openly walked in the street, singly or in groups of friends, preceded by guards who wielded batons to clear the crowd for them, "as though the governor were passing by." Women, he said, "order and forbid, laying down the law." It was not only a matter of the inexcusable behavior and ideas of European men. He lamented that Egyptian women themselves adopted this new, independent point of view and way of life and began attempting to convert other women to it.[15] Al-Jabarti was expressing a patriarchal backlash against what he saw as an incipient women's movement, but also a sense of emasculation under conditions of colonial subjugation.

Miot remembered the Egyptian paramours taken by the officers.[16] "Some were beautiful, and all, in giving us Arabic lessons, learned to pronounce French words: it was not ordinarily the most decent that they retained. Of this sort the most bizarre societies and exchanges were formed." He remembered lively soirées with bootleg "punch" and much laughter, where talk of Paris drowned out the present reality of exile in Egypt. "Or one brought, in order to divert the group, the dancers of the country, whose lascivious movements pandered to our imagination with gracious tableaus." He reported the universal process of acculturation, whereby one becomes accustomed to a different style of life, saying, "Muslims look with different eyes than do we. It would be a mistake to say that their gardens or their women are not pretty, for our ideas and our ways of seeing are different." Egyptians, he said, preferred their women plump, whereas Parisians wanted thin waists and small feet. "If we decry their supposed poor taste, will they not say the same of us? To love, in a foreign country, it is necessary to see with the eyes of the inhabitants." He observed that if the travel writer Claude Étienne Savary had fooled the officers with his rosy images of Egypt, "it is because he saw it as they did, or because he wrote it as a novel."

The officers could afford expensive harem women, either as slaves or mistresses. The presence of thousands of ordinary French soldiers in Cairo, most often left with little to do and baking in the capital's languid heat, fanned a rapid growth in red-light districts and prostitution. Niello Sargy wrote that he was surprised at how few brawls or duels broke out, "despite the whoring that went on. There were at that time public women in our quarters."[17] Eugène de Beauharnais recalled a disturbance not far from Bonaparte's headquarters that French soldiers provoked by entering a harem. "Already a great number of inhabitants had assembled before that mansion, expressing loudly their indignation at this desecration that they regarded as execrable. I was sent with some other officers to put a stop to it. We found in that harem soldiers of different regiments giving themselves over to all the excess and brutality that a long privation could, while not excusing it, at least allow us to understand." They broke up the debauchery, he said, by striking the soldiers with the flat of their sabers and chasing them from the harem.[18] This gang rape of the odalisques provoked a public demonstration.

Galland remarked that prostitution was widespread in Egypt, but was arranged differently from that in Paris. A pimp made the arrangements and brought the women, mounted on donkeys, to the customer, with whom they stayed as long as he desired. He alleged, "One saw girls of twelve putting themselves, completely nude, in the middle of a square for a few coins."[19] It is unlikely that the beys or the clergy would have tolerated such behavior in an urban center. Some of what shocked the French was a result of the breakdown in the Ottoman-Egyptian order that their own occupation triggered. Bernoyer regaled his cousin with the priapic story of how, that fall, before his faux marriage to Fatima, he decided to end his sexual abstinence with a public woman.[20] He was living in a confiscated Ottoman-Egyptian mansion on the Nile island of Roda. Bernoyer used go-betweens to make contact with a pimp, one Sultan Ganash, who doubled as a boatman on the Nile. After about six hours Sultan Ganash brought his boat to Bernoyer's residence with six women. All of them wore long blue tunics that descended to their heels, and a cape of the same fabric that covered their heads and obscured their faces. He said they reminded him of nothing so much as a line of penitents. He added, "I had difficulty choosing among the poor things, several of whom were barefoot; they excited my compassion more than my desires."

He wrote that his curiosity gradually got the better of his self-respect, and he began removing their veils one by one. They coquettishly made as if to resist. Then one slipped out of her clothes altogether and stood there with a big smile on her face, as if, he said, to mock his timidity and indecision. He was taken with her determined and wicked air, her large dark eyes, and above all, her fourteen years. He paid a large sum for her and dismissed Sultan Ganash and his other girls. He had his servants bathe the girl and see that she put on the clothes he had bought for her, which wrought a remarkable transformation in her appearance. He praised her "allure" and comfortable bearing, the suppleness of her waist, the "natural nobility of her gestures," and above all "her air of being a mischievous child." He wrote, "Judge, my dear cousin, if after so long a privation I could have restrained my transports!" He said she initially defended herself from his advances with a marvelous tenderness and enjoyment that would move even the hardest of hearts. At last, he delivered himself "to the delicious pleasures that this beautiful child procured for me."

After making love, they had dinner. She was amazed at the spread on the table, circling it several times. He thought her unaccustomed to chairs and she seemed to him afraid of falling off hers. She refused all the dishes offered her, however, insisting on having a plate of *ful mudammis* (mashed broad beans in butter), which he said it was easy to arrange for her. His servant must have translated for him her pronouncement on eating it with bread, that she had eaten "as well as the great empress," a reference to the senior wife of the Ottoman sultan.

Bernoyer shared the mansion with an officer, Lallemant, who also took a girl and proposed that she keep Bernoyer's company. This arrangement, logical as it might sound, led to disaster and Bernoyer's first setback in his search for romance in Egypt. Bernoyer and Lallemant heard a ruckus, and rushed up the stairs. They found that Lallemant's girl had become jealous of the nice clothes Bernoyer had provided his own, and had thrown coffee on his girl. Bernoyer decided that he had to take his girl with him to Cairo rather than leaving her there on the island. He took her to the yard below, but Lallemant's girl was in wait. She threw a stone at her rival, striking her on the cheek below the eye and leaving a gash. Bernoyer took both girls to Cairo, delivering Lallemant's to the Ottoman superintendent of police to be imprisoned for fifteen days. Instead, he learned that they intended to drown her in the Nile. So he dropped the charges and let the girl go free. His own girl was bleeding profusely and a physician worried that she might lose the eye. He delivered her to her home and gave her money to cover her medical expenses. She left, bawling. Cairo was an enormous village, with eyes everywhere. Muslim middle- and upper-class men would have seen hundreds, perhaps thousands, of such episodes that fall, which they would have viewed as severe moral corruption but even worse than that, an affront to their honor as guardians of the virtue of Muslim women.

Even French attempts to find a respectable social life often looked suspicious to the conservative Cairo middle classes, since it inevitably involved public wine bibbing and the mixing of the sexes. European and Egyptian entrepreneurs hoping to cater to the French founded cafes, restaurants, and even taverns that offered bootleg liquor made by illicit distilleries. Wine, however, was mainly imported, and the British blockade made it hard to supply. The soldiers, lacking it, learned to appreciate smoking Egyptian tobacco through the bubbles of a hookah and drinking mocha coffee in small cups. Miot said they forgot the use of chairs, lounging on pillows and divans in their apartments. Narrow cuffs and tight clothing were unsuited to the hot climate, and they switched to looser pantaloons that let the air circulate next to the skin.[21]

Doguereau recalled, "Bonaparte, who was not unaware that everyone was bored to death and that all thoughts were ceaselessly occupied with France, very much wanted the officers—many of whom desired to resign their commissions—to find some means of recreation."[22] Officers wished someone would set up a Tivoli, what we would now call an amusement park, with gardens, lights, billiards, and gaming rooms, modeled on the Tivoli Gardens of eighteenth-century Paris. Later on, a M. Dargeaud, an employee in the civil administration of Egypt, founded such an establishment, and for a while it was enormously popular. At length, Doguereau complained, it deteriorated into a dive. (The puritan al-Jabarti thought it had never been anything else.) The officers complained bitterly about the difficulty of having a proper ball, for lack of cultured women with whom to dance, flirt, and engage in witty repartee. Niello Sargy remarked of French women, "Only a few who dressed up as men got through, and they now shone in the midst of the army, being devolved on the chiefs of the administration and on the generals."[23] Almost all of the three hundred or so French women in Cairo had come belowdecks as laundresses and food preparers on some of the ships. With 20,000 Frenchmen trapped in Cairo for the duration, their stock had risen, and they were now being invited to officers' balls, and to officers' mansions, despite their rough hands and rougher language.

Wives of common soldiers who had been smuggled aboard a transport ship now often became mistresses of French officers.

Bernoyer wrote that fall that Bonaparte had given several brilliant balls, and had been imitated by the other generals, so that practically every evening in Cairo there was a big party. "The French women play a grand role in these gatherings. Although they are neither young nor pretty, one is eager to make a round with them, if only to have the pleasure of being seen with them, or to converse with the gallantry that is natural to us in France."[24] Those Frenchmen who brought Egyptian girls to such events, he said, had to suffer dreadful ribbing from their fellows. Despite a great deal of intimacy between the French and Egyptians in private, there appears to have been a color bar in public that the soldiers and officers crossed only at the risk of ridicule. For the most part, as well, they could not at that point get past the language barrier. "There is nothing more disagreeable than to be head-to-head with a woman without being able to make her understand, and to have as the only language in common that of the eyes and hands. Once these means have been utilized, it is necessary either to leave or to sit there like two blocks of wood. Accept, my dear cousin that these situations are quite sad, even though there would have been much to do!"

At the soirées being held that fall, Bonaparte's eyes fell on Pauline Fourès, the wife of a captain of the 20th cavalry regiment.[25] Although most accounts say he only noticed her on 1 December, the quartermaster Bernoyer wrote his wife a long letter about their affair on 5 December 1798, so the dalliance must have much preceded that date. Bonaparte's stepson also remembered it, painfully, as an issue that broke before mid-October. Niello Sargy recalled her: "Madame Fourès was a petite, twenty-year-old woman, kind, plump, and spiritual; she was not lacking in a certain education nor in amiability, though she had formerly been a dressmaker." He told the story of how she was much attached to her husband and had therefore braved the dangers of Egypt for him, disguising herself as a man so as to gain passage on the ship. Niello Sargy shaped his tale as one of tragic hubris, implying that Lieutenant Fourès sought, by making a brilliant impression socially with his wife, to draw the attention of senior officers to himself, hoping the contacts would advance his career.

The memoirists agree that Pauline had resisted going to the officer parties, and had been rudely ordered to do so by her vain husband, whose family had once been of higher status before the Revolution. When he saw her at one of these parties held in a grand mansion, Bonaparte could not take his eyes off her. Despite the sensational accounts of the popular historians, who rendered her as a blond, blue-eyed stunner, she was in fact a brunette, as her portrait shows, and Bernoyer, who met her, described her eyes as black. Niello Sargy remembered her as a little overweight (she did not have the thin waist preferred in French high society) and just "nice" and "spiritual," which one suspects were not synonyms for "seductive." Bernoyer said that after observing her on the French social scene for a while, Bonaparte found a way to approach her at one of the balls. He complimented her on her coiffure and asked if her fine bonnet was made in Egypt or had been brought from France. She said she had brought it with her. Then, as the dancers whirled away, Junot took Bonaparte's place and chatted her up, at length taking her to a corner and letting her know of the general's love. He told her, "You would have to be very cruel and insensitive to refuse the gift of his heart." He then, in this account, rather ruined the romance by promising her husband a big promotion. She is said to have told him firmly that she would be embarrassed to see her husband rise suddenly to such a high rank and that she would render herself contemptible in her own eyes if she accepted such an offer. Although this account depicts Bonaparte as undeterred and as having nevertheless promoted Fourès, published documents dated later that fall still refer to him as a lieutenant.

After the ball, Niello Sargy maintained, Bonaparte, "inflamed and dreaming of means to possess the object of his desires," sent his aide-de-camp Junot to invite her and her husband to a luncheon with the general. She arrived and discovered five place settings. Then trumpets announced the entry of the commander in chief, who came with Berthier. He first questioned Lieutenant Fourès about his career and made a forced attempt to seem friendly. Toward the end of the luncheon, the anecdote went, by prior arrangement Junot spilled a cup of coffee on Madame Fourès's dress. She cried out and, at Junot's suggestion, went to a neighboring chamber, either to change her dress or to try to remove the stain. Junot chatted up the husband while Bonaparte excused himself and seemed to leave with Berthier. Instead, he made his way to Madame Fourès and threw himself at her knees. "Realizing immediately what he wanted of her, she resisted the conqueror, broke out in tears, and seemed not at all interested in him." Bonaparte was said to have been touched by her innocence. She resisted his advances thereafter for some time, which included love letters and fine gifts. At length she succumbed.

Bonaparte sent Fourès down the Nile to await orders to return to France as a courier. The orders would be carried to him later by Bernoyer's housemate, "Captain Froment" (in other letters called Lallemont). The quartermaster recalled that after Fourès's departure, Pauline "played a great role at Bonaparte's." She did the honors at his mansion as his queen and moved into a house to the right of that of Alfi Bey. "She was not embarrassed before the world; to the contrary, she affected an air of taking liberty with General Bonaparte, having been persuaded to give herself more importance and to attract the praise of his courtiers."

Bernoyer wrote that in November Fourès went on the mission as far as the port, but could not bring himself to abandon his wife and went AWOL so as to return to plead with her. He arrived at night at the house Captain Froment shared with Bernoyer, so as not to be recognized. The distraught husband discovered that his wife had moved in with the commander in chief. He wanted one last chance to plead his case with his spouse. Bernoyer, touched at the man's state, offered to see Madame Mallet, an intimate friend of Pauline's, after breakfast, in hopes that she would be willing to bring Pauline over to their quarters. Bernoyer did as he was asked the next morning, but later received a letter from Madame Mallet that the mission had failed. Pauline refused to come, saying that all ties between her and her husband had been broken and that she had foreseen where his overweening ambition would take the two of them. She maintained that the end of their relationship was his fault, since he had refused to listen to her. Fourès became hysterical, and Bernoyer said he was constrained to go see Pauline himself, using his friendship with Eugène de Beauharnais to secure an entrée. She replied to his fears that Fourès would do something rash or even commit suicide by saying that her resolve was unshakable. "Calm down. I know my husband well enough to be certain that he will not cause a scandal, nor will he commit any crime. He cherishes life too much to sacrifice it so lightly. I have nothing else to say to him save that he should return to his post as soon as possible, since you know that Bonaparte wants to be obeyed, especially when his orders concern service to his army." On hearing all this from Bernoyer later that day, Fourès wanted to go to her in person, but the quartermaster dissuaded him and suggested that he simply return to France, where he could find many likable young women to replace his unfaithful wife.

Fourès appears to have become reconciled to his loss and to have recovered his ambition after a momentary lapse into sentimentality that did not fool his spouse. He no doubt realized the possibilities for career advancement that his new and personal, if awkward, relationship with Bonaparte might offer. On 17 December, Bonaparte cut orders for Fourès, who had returned to Rosetta, dispatching him first to Alexandria where he would be provided a small ship. (The date of these orders is another argument against Bonaparte having first noticed Pauline only on the first of that month.) The lieutenant would then proceed to Malta, to Italy, and ultimately to Paris. The memoirists say he was carrying dispatches to Paul Barras and the Directory. Bonaparte continued, "You will stay eight to ten days in Paris, after which you will return with all due diligence, embarking at a port in the kingdom of Naples or at Ancona. You will avoid Alexandria and come with your ship into Damietta. Before leaving, take care to see one of my brothers, a member of the legislative corps. He will give you some papers and newspapers that have appeared since Messidor."[26] The commander in chief provided him 3,000 francs to defray the cost of the mission.

Bonaparte's diction and his request that Fourès see his brother Joseph, as well as the command to return with messages from the Directory, suggest a strange bond of trust between interloper and cuckold. Other memoirists maintain that the lieutenant was captured by the British and proved unable to carry out his mission, though they also say that Commodore Sir Sydney Smith first informed Fourès of his wife's infidelity and that he came back and remonstrated with his commander in chief. It makes a good story, but Bernoyer's insider account and Bonaparte's long-published letters explode it as melodrama. If Fourès returned, he most likely simply went back to his barracks at Rosetta.

Pauline remained Bonaparte's mistress for as long as he was in Egypt. One saw her "covered with jewels and sumptuous clothing." She carried around his portrait in a locket, and he kept a lock of her hair with him. She often wore Bonaparte's clothing, and rode an Arabian horse outfitted for her, followed by the aides-de-camp. Josephine's son, Eugène de Beauharnais, one of the aides-de-camp, was forced to follow their coach when they went out for an evening ride. "Not able any longer to bear the humiliation, I went to General Berthier to ask that I be transferred to a regiment. A rather lively scene passed between my stepfather and me as a result of that action; but he ceased at that moment his rides in the coach with that lady." Eugène stayed with his stepfather, who "did not mistreat me."[27] Although Bonaparte became more circumspect, behind the scenes he remained inseparable from Pauline. Had she borne him a son, something for which they tried, he might well have divorced Josephine for her. The soldiers called her the general's Cleopatra.

This anecdote is of more than personal interest. It tells us about the system of status in the French Republic of Egypt. Bonaparte, as the Great Sultan, was stepping into the shoes of Ibrahim Bey and Murad Bey as the most powerful man in the country. Any mistress he took would have to be from the upper social echelons if he was not to lose face with both the Egyptians and the other Frenchmen. Just as the beys announced their own social standing by maintaining opulent harems, and just as the wives of high social rank were from the Caucasus, so Bonaparte in an Ottoman-Egyptian context would also be expected to have a high-status consort. I have suggested that the abandoned women of the beys' harems singled him out for the cold shoulder treatment, otherwise such a mistress might well have been politically useful to him. He clearly tried his luck in that regard. The only women in Egypt of higher social station at that point than the Georgians of the Qazdaghli households were the few hundred French women. Although most had a low standing in France itself (Pauline Fourès was the illegitimate daughter of a cook), in Egypt their rarity and their membership in the ruling ethnicity elevated them to the top of the female social ladder. Once, for whatever reason, a liaison between Bonaparte and an Ottoman-Egyptian lady had been ruled out, he was impelled by status considerations to find a French mistress. That his men were largely deprived of this possibility impelled them to form alliances with Egyptian women in various ways, whether by marrying them, taking them as mistresses, buying them as concubines, or resorting to prostitution. In a society that felt deeply about family and community honor, these thousands of public liaisons stood as a constant affront to the manhood of Egyptian Muslims and were a source of their profound hostility to the French.

♣

In early October, Bonaparte convened in Cairo a national divan or "general council." Al-Jabarti recalled that on Friday, 5 October, the delegations that Bonaparte had requested from each of thirteen provinces were called upon to convene at the house of Qayed Aqa in Azbakiya, which was where the old Ottoman-Egyptian divan had met.[28] Each delegation was made up of three clergymen, three merchants, a village headman, a peasant, and a Bedouin chief, and they received a handsome monthly stipend. The French intended these provincial caucuses, though not elective, to form a roughly representative body of 117 persons, the first Egyptian parliament. The gathering was also attended by Ottoman regimental officers who had thrown in with the French, as well as by Copts and Syrian Christians. The French officer in charge had translators read a document that blamed the Mamluks for ruining Egypt, praised the French for their good intentions of making the Nile Valley flourish through renewed trade with the Red Sea and the Mediterranean, and declared that the French "did not interfere with any of the people." Al-Jabarti had a good laugh at that one.

The French then attempted to organize the election by the delegates of a president of the assembly. Attendees began by wanting to select Sheikh Abdullah al-Sharqawi by acclamation, calling out his name. The translator exclaimed "*Non, non!*" in French, and had them instead vote on paper ballots. The result was the same, with al-Sharqawi elected. The first session went to sunset, and the divan was supposed to convene every day thereafter until the twentieth. The French insisted on the faithful attendance of the delegates (who were being paid per session). In fact, Saturday had to be skipped because Sheikh al-Sharqawi, the new president of Egypt, was accused of harboring a Libyan merchant who had partnered with a known partisan of Murad Bey. Fifty French soldiers searched the president's house, but the merchant from Tripoli had fled. When informed, Bonaparte grew angry and insisted that the man would not have left if he had not been guilty of continued collusion with Murad. The next morning the French went to his now-abandoned house and storehouse, broke the seals, and confiscated all the merchandise. Whatever shadow was cast on al-Sharqawi for the moment had passed.

On Sunday, a senate or "special council" was elected, consisting of twenty-seven members, including leading clerics as well as Ottoman-Egyptian officers, Copts, Syrians, and Muslim merchants. Apparently the two legislative bodies had a relationship similar to that of the Council of 500 and the Council of Ancients in Directory France. The lower body deliberated issues, then passed the deliberations on to the special divan for actual decision making and legislation. The French pressed the new divan to establish requirements for formal registration of property, with deeds, for assessments of its value, and for a graduated property tax. They also wished to be instructed concerning Egyptian customs with regard to dowries, saying that in France only the brides received trousseaus, but that the groom did not receive anything. Amusingly, the Egyptians misunderstood the French to be discussing inheritance practices, and so presumably believed that French men were disinherited and all property was bequeathed to their women. The Muslims insisted that inheritance be divided in accordance with the schema provided in the Qur'an, and they were supported in this by the Copts and Syrian Christians, who averred that they usually had Muslim authorities handle their own inheritances, in accordance with Muslim law. The divan also considered criminal justice, and likewise wanted Qur'anic precepts enshrined in law. Bonaparte was following through on his promise to Sheikh Masiri in Alexandria, to implement sharia or Islamic canon law in the French/Islamic Republic of Egypt. According to French sources, the village headmen pressed for an end to the practice of tax-farming, but the high clergy, themselves often tax-farmers, suppressed the motion and retained the system of venality.[29]

The French announced a new tax schedule on the morning of Saturday, 20 October, al-Jabarti said. They divided property into three categories, charging a tax of eight riyals on the more expensive, six on the middling, and three on the humbler. Properties that yielded less than a riyal a month paid nothing. But for businesses, the tax was thirty or forty riyals. It hit shops, oil presses, sesame mills, baths, and caravansaries. The French posted the tax schedule at intersections and along major thoroughfares as though it was good news. Then they started sending around appraisers to determine property and business values. The guildsmen erupted in rage. Captain Say recalled that the Muslims "in the city said that the discontent occasioned by the imposts was the sole cause" of a gathering uprising.[30]

Within Muslim Egyptian culture, the principle had long been established that non-Muslims paid a per-head poll tax to the Muslim state. Since non-Muslims did not serve in most Muslim armies, the poll tax was felt by the majority to have bought out their military service and to have helped pay for the cost of protection from marauding enemy armies. But since Christians and Jews, who paid the tax, had less status in Muslim-majority societies, the practice became tainted with that association. Egyptian Muslims read the personal property tax as a form of poll tax. From the point of view of proud Egyptian Muslim families, paying a poll tax to a European conqueror, especially via a Coptic or Syrian Christian tax collector, was a humiliation of the first order. There was, in addition, no tradition in Egypt of such a graduated urban property tax or of the state prying so closely into and measuring exact assets. Some of the more militant clerics gathered crowds at the mosque on Saturday and preached, "Muslims, holy war is a duty for you. How can you free men agree to pay the poll tax to the unbelievers? Have you no pride? Has the call not reached you?"[31] The common people formed discussion groups, not only in the al-Husayn quarter near the Great Mosque but also in surrounding districts, and worked themselves into a rage against their European masters.

✣

On the morning of Sunday, 21 October, the well-known cleric and sometime caravan merchant, Sayyid Badr al-Maqdisi, mounted on a caparisoned steed, led crowds from the al-Husayn Quarter, who were joined by the little people (al-Jabarti called them "ruffians") from outlying districts.[32] They chanted, "God give Victory to Islam!" About a thousand persons gathered that morning before the mansion of the Ottoman-appointed chief justice. Alarmed, he had his gates locked and ended up a prisoner in his home, which the demonstrators pelted with stones when they discovered he was unsympathetic. "So he pleaded with them in a polite manner, promising them the impossible. The people gathered in his courtyard demanding war and an encounter with the enemy." Merchants closed up their shops. Other huge crowds gathered in front of the al-Husayn Mosque and the nearby al-Azhar Seminary. The cleric addressed the crowds, saying "All true monotheists should come to al-Azhar Seminary, for today is the raid on the infidels, in which we shall remove this dishonor and take our revenge on them." Bernoyer, who had no use for clerics of any religion, complained bitterly about their use of Islam to whip up the emotions of the crowds: "This is the great resort of priests, which they always employ to move and lift the believers as they propose."[33]

The first responder from the French side was Gen. Dominique-Martin Dupuy, who had been born in Toulouse in 1767 and who had distinguished himself in Italy, where at one point he had been the military commander of Milan. Now officially in charge of the Citadel overlooking Cairo, he received the reports of disturbances down in the city with some skepticism and therefore took with him only a small cavalry force of twelve men. Bonaparte recalled, "Since the inhabitants of Cairo are gossips, fidgety and extremely curious about the news, General Dupuy was accustomed to such alarms." Dupuy rushed with his cavalrymen down al-Ghawriya Street and then turned toward the quarter where Sheikh Abdullah al-Sharqawi, the head of the divan, lived. Al-Sharqawi refused to see him and sent a servant out to announce that the great cleric was not at home. Dupuy then went to the mansion of the Ottoman-appointed chief justice. He entered but, noticing the extreme agitation of the crowd outside, suggested that they postpone their discussion until the following day. The chief justice, who must have been frantic to get the French off his property lest they make him even more a target than he already was, entirely agreed. "At this point a perfumer, dressed up in the guise of a cleric, with a vest and waist cloth, came forward calling out to the people, inciting them and exclaiming 'God is most great, O Muslims. The clerics have commanded you to kill the infidels. Make ready, stalwarts, and strike them everywhere.'" Guilds like that of the perfumers often overlapped with mystical Sufi orders, and this man may have been a Sufi leader—thus his claim of clerical authority. The perfumer-theologian led a mob toward al-Ashrafiya and they joined the crowds at the chief justice's mansion. Bonaparte says, "Dupuy could barely remount his steed in the midst of the crowd. The cavalrymen were being squeezed. A horse trampled a North African. This fierce man, who had arrived from Mecca, fired his pistol at the rider, killing him, and mounted his horse. The French detachment charged and dispersed the people. Dupuy, exiting the courtyard, received, as he entered the street, "a blow to the head from the lance of a man who was at a fixed post there. He fell dead."[34]

The commander in chief recounted how the rumor immediately spread among the crowd that the "Great Sultan" (i.e., Bonaparte himself) had been killed and that the French had thrown off their masks of civility and were massacring the believers. "The muezzins, from the top of their minarets, called the true believers to defend the mosques and the city." The French cavalrymen at the chief justice's home, vastly outnumbered, attempted to retreat through the city quarters of Bab al-Qasrayn and Bab al-Zuhuma, but found their passage obstructed by the dense crowds. Enraged at the sight of their occupiers, the Egyptians rushed them and killed a number of them. A handful managed to gather up wounded colleagues and to retreat with them to headquarters, where several more died of their injuries.[35]

The Muslim insurgents (as the French called them) set up citizen guards around key quarters in the vicinity of the al-Husayn district, where the revolt was centered, and out to the districts of Bab al-Zuwayla and Bab al-Sha'riya. Saint-Hilaire recalled that the crowd "occupied three enormous mosques that were rather distant from one another." Armed with swords, stakes, and some firearms, they turned the mosques into fortresses in which they sequestered themselves and from which they directed the attack or defense. The militants tried to keep the area they wanted to hold compact, al-Jabarti implies. "They did not, however, cross into any other area." They did attack the Public Treasury, located in their region of the city.

Other quarters of the city, such as the cosmopolitan riverine port of Bulaq, the posh Azbakiya district, and Old Cairo, declined to join the uprising, in part because they were better garrisoned by the French. Realistic clerical leaders also played a calming role in those parts of the city. Sayyid al-Bakri warned the inhabitants of Azbakiya not to rise up. "Sheikh al-Fayyumi did the same in the 'Abdin and Qusun quarters." A former official of the beylicate kept on by the French, the Kethüda Pasha, likewise ordered his retainers and neighbors to avoid the rebellion. The scientists and intellectuals at the Egyptian Institute were holed up in their mansion but managed to lie low. Villiers du Terrage recalled withdrawing inside to a pavilion on the far side of the garden at the Institute and hearing "the cries and threats of the women of the neighborhood."[36] The urban women of Cairo clearly played a role in the revolt, though few military memoirists brought themselves to mention it, perhaps because it challenged their masculinity. As a civilian, Villiers du Terrage perhaps had less compunction on that score. No source tells us what the Ottoman-Egyptian ladies were doing just before and during the uprising, but it is likely that at least some of them were involved behind the scenes.

Since Bulaq was quiet, the French garrison there could spare troops for a mission against the uprising. Desvernois recalled, "It was the thirtieth of Vendémiaire at 9 A.M. Our cavalrymen were quite tranquil in their quarter of Bulaq, when all of a sudden threatening howls interspersed with savage exclamations erupted. It was a horrific clamor." Within ten minutes, he says, the regiment was mounted on its horses. They galloped off to Azbakiya Square, slashing with their sabers insurgents who attempted to hold them back. Once they arrived at the general headquarters, they were dispatched to the al-Husayn quarter, where, he wrote, the little people had risen up at dawn, supported by the clerics and religious students of al-Azhar Seminary.

The militants constructed stone barricades from material like the stone benches shopkeepers had placed before their establishments, ripping them out and obstructing avenues of attack. Big crowds gathered in front of the barriers. A group of North Africans from the al-Fahhamin district manned the barricades at nearby al-Shawa'in. At one point, French cavalrymen attacked them. The North Africans "fired continuously upon the French, defeating them and driving them away." A small unit of French soldiers, lost in the thicket of unfamiliar alleyways, stumbled into insurgent territory from the direction of Nahhasin. The rebels fell upon them and "caused them to taste death" along with a Syrian Christian who had fallen in with them.[37]

Bonaparte recalled, "The merchants closed their shops. The soldiers hurried from every side, seeking to regain their barracks. The miscreants closed the gates between quarters that the French had not yet demolished. The women, from their balconies, let out terrifying shrieks." He described how the crowds now moved toward the mansion of Gen. Louis Caffarelli. The peg-legged general from Falga, down near the Spanish border, was called by the Egyptians *Abu Khashaba*, or "Woody." He had, in his commander's words, "imprudently taken up lodging next to the Grand Mosque." Caffarelli, about whose geniality the enlisted men joked that it was because he still had one leg in France, was not at home, and was, in fact, in Bonaparte's company. Bonaparte admitted that the crowds had a grudge against such officer-engineers, since they had demolished the gates between quarters, had directed the fortification works at the Citadel, and "frequently had profaned tombs in order to construct their works." Popular Islam in Cairo was centered on a cult of saints' tombs, and if Bonaparte was saying the officers casually tore these shrines down in their effort to reengineer the city, then it helps explain the hatred the people had conceived for them.

The army engineers at Caffarelli's mansion, their depot, tried to keep the crowd at bay by firing through the windows. "Suddenly," Saint-Hilaire reported, "they were surprised and pressed by a considerable crowd that arrived by the roofs, which descended on the house." The commander in chief lamented that Caffarelli's mansion was devastated "in a moment," as the crowd pillaged the books and rare scientific instruments and massacred the six or seven persons present there. It is likely that the crowd also carried away weapons and ammunition from this raid. The elderly geologist Tête-vuide, who ran out of the house trying to escape, was struck by a stone thrown from the roof, then surrounded by the crowd and crushed. The rioters paraded the heads of the French military engineers through the streets and then suspended them from the doors of the al-Husayn Mosque. "The sight of blood galvanized the fanatics," he observed, adding that the Egyptian "notables, terrified, closeted themselves at home." The people, Bonaparte recalled, ran and dragged them from their mansions and led them in triumph to the al-Azhar Seminary. Some they treated with disdain for having collaborated with the French. Another officer observed, "Sheikh El-Sarah, who had appeared to be a protégé of the French, was dressed in the uniform of an assassinated soldier; they shaved off his beard and sold him in the middle of the bazaar for thirteen piasters." The Egyptians saw being clean-shaven as the mark of a slave, and disdained many of the French soldiers on those grounds. The insurgents then created a committee, or divan, of defense, organized popular militias, dug up weapons that had earlier been buried, and took whatever measures they could to ensure the success of their rebellion. Al-Jabarti recalled that they brought out earlier-concealed "clubs, goads, truncheons, sticks, and hammers. He who had none of these, took latch-bars, axes, and hoes."[38]

Among the first victims of the rioters were French merchants established in Cairo and married to local Armenian women. Whatever was tainted with the symbols of European or Christian association became an object of rage. Rampaging mobs invaded the al-Jawaniya district, home to many Syrians and Eastern Orthodox Christians, looting their homes and raping the women and girls. Some of the crowds even attacked Muslim homes. Then they turned on the local market that specialized in women's clothing, the Khan al-Malayat, emptying its stores of goods. Some lower-class Cairene women suffered through the rest of the French occupation in fine fashion. In another incident, mobs attacked the hospital of Ibrahim Bey, apparently in order to loot it, and when two French engineers and two surgeons got in their way, they killed them. "The citizen Roussel, son of the chief surgeon of Toulon, and another officer of the first class were riddled with blows from a halberd," Saint-Hilaire lamented. Al-Jabarti observed, "They committed many disgraceful acts without thinking of the consequences." The orgy of looting and rapine went on all night.[39]

THE EGYPTIAN REVOLUTION

*B*onaparte's whereabouts on the day of the uprising are controversial. He wrote that he was absent from Cairo, having gone by the Nile to inspect the French arsenal at Giza. He may have intended to go to Giza, but eyewitnesses report that he had only gone as far as Roda Island that morning and that he was brought back to his headquarters in Azbakiya. Detroye alleged that there had been some early-morning manifestations of unrest but that Bonaparte had just ordered his troops to arm themselves and, not suspecting anything serious might arise, left to inspect the work the French engineers were doing at Old Cairo and Roda Island.[1]

This account does not exactly accord with Bonaparte's own, which raises suspicions as to why they differ. Was he stricken with depression and paralysis during the first day of the revolt, which could well have ended in the massacre of the French army had the entire city joined in? All the accounts can be reconciled if we assume that, to cover his inaction, he gave out the story of having been quite distant, at Giza, all day long. His presence that morning at Roda Island is well attested, and he was back at headquarters long before he later admitted being there.

Lt. Jean-Pierre Doguereau recalled that morning in his memoirs: "I mounted my horse with General Dommartin to go to Giza. We paid no attention to the rumors of an insurrection, which seemed vague. We met at Old Cairo with General Bonaparte, who was going to the isle of Roda. We accompanied him. While we were in the company of General Lannes, given that the general headquarters was on that island, he was brought reports that one had begun to see wounded officers in the streets. In the same instant, a runner coming from general headquarters announced that the commander of the Citadel, General Dupuy, had just been assassinated while attempting to disperse a crowd near the Grand Mosque, even though he was accompanied by a cavalry unit. Everywhere they sounded the general alarm with cannon." Detroye remembered the news as arriving at 10 A.M.

Doguereau reported that mounted guides sought out Bonaparte and were going to take him back to his quarters in Azbakiya. The lieutenant wanted to go along. "I had the disagreeable experience, in such a critical circumstance, of getting left behind. My horse, which was very spooked, did not want to descend into the boat. After many useless attempts, I abandoned it." He borrowed another mount, and went after Gen. Jean Lannes (a veteran of the Spanish and Italian campaigns), who had marched his troops off to the estate of Ibrahim Bey. "We were assailed by stones as we crossed into the Bab al-Luq quarter, then quite fortunately met up with some mounted guides who had themselves been attacked. We learned on arriving that a great number of French had had their throats cut in the streets and that the insurrection was almost universal." Bonaparte had reached his mansion in Azbakiya with difficulty, and established posts around Azbakiya Square with artillery pieces. He appointed Gen. Louis-André Bon (the son of a merchant, who had fought at Toulon, then in the Pyrenees against Spain, and in Italy) to replace the fallen Dupuy. Bon attempted to use cannon in the main thoroughfares to keep the rebels contained in al-Qahira and its environs.[2]

At some point the French gained active allies in the form of the expatriate Greek community, which had initially remained neutral but then, in the face of mob attacks on them as collaborators, declared for the French. The scientist Charles Norry exulted, "Hitherto the Greeks had taken no part in our cause; on the day of the insurrection they ranged themselves on our side and shook off the yoke of the slavery that they have long endured under the Turkish government." The Greek Bartholomew al-Rumi, whom Bonaparte had earlier made police chief, now arose to take the fight to the insurgents. Bernoyer remarked, "Those who saw him fight proclaimed his prodigious feats and compared him to one of Homer's deities at Troy."[3]

Jean-Gabriel de Niello Sargy recalled that Bonaparte was furious that the Cairo crowds were challenging him. He heard him say, "Shall we be the plaything of some hordes of vagabonds, of these Arabs whom one barely counts among the civilized peoples, and of the populace of Cairo, the most brutish and savage rogues who exist in the world?"[4]

The Sunni clergymen whom Bonaparte had installed as the leadership of the French Republic of Egypt split into three factions. The first fled and went into hiding. Al-Jabarti reported, that as for the Sunni clergymen, "there were those who

fled from their homes and sat hidden in their neighbours' houses; others feared
their enemies and bolted their gates, sitting with their womenfolk. Others left their
homes, setting out for the building of Qayitbay in the desert and living there."[5]

The second group of clerics, with residences in the al-Husayn quarter and
its vicinity, either gleefully joined in the revolt (as did Sayyid Maqdisi) or was
willy-nilly caught up in it. The insurgents, Bonaparte said, chose Sheikh Shams
al-Din al-Sadat as the leader of their revolutionary divan, composed of one hundred clerics, preachers, callers to prayer, North African notables, and "people of
the lower classes" (probably guildsmen). Even in rebellion, the Egyptians were
now governing themselves by a people's parliament, in the French way!

Sheikh al-Sadat was drafted by the rebels to be their leader, but was probably lukewarm to the rebellion, since he knew how militarily powerful the
French were. Al-Sadat, the wealthiest and most powerful of the Sunni clerics of
Egypt in that age, and a scion of one of the more prominent clerical families,
claimed direct descent from the Prophet Muhammad. From this clan came
many scholastics at al-Azhar Seminary, and their leading member headed the
Wafa'iya Sufi order, a sober mystical brotherhood, which gave them yet another
source of honor and authority among the common people. He was supervisor of
four major shrines, including that of al-Husayn, and received a portion of the
income generated by pilgrimage to them.

The French had cultivated him and let his wealth alone. They saw him as the
sort of middling "indigenous" notable, neither an Ottoman aristocrat nor a peasant, who might provide a backbone for the French Republic of Egypt. In contrast,
the militants saw him as a Muslim leader who would surely stand with them in the
holy war against the French infidel. Sayyid Khalil al-Bakri, in al-Azbakiyah with
Bonaparte, proved unable to contact his colleagues from the outside that night. It
is nevertheless possible that Sheikh al-Sadat managed to get word to Bonaparte
that he was trying to find a way to calm the rebellion. The insurgents drew up a
proclamation announcing that "the Sublime Porte [the Ottoman government] has
declared war on France; that Cezzar Pasha had arrived at Bilbeis with his army;
that the French were disposed to save themselves but that they had demolished
the internal city gates in order to pillage the city before departing."[6]

The third faction, led by Sayyid al-Bakri, actively sided with the French and
opposed the rebellion; it was helped in this stance by the lack of an uprising in
their parts of the city. The members of this faction, on the whole, tended to be
wealthier and more senior than the clerics who joined the revolt. The chronicler
al-Jabarti was among them, and his sympathies with this quietist political elite
shine through his text. Al-Bakri took two fellow clerics, sheikhs Sirsi and Mahdi,

to see Bonaparte. The commander in chief demanded to know what was happening. They assured him that "these are the deeds of the foolish among the subjects and those who do not consider the consequences of their actions."

Bonaparte wanted to know from al-Bakri why he was not accompanied by the sheikhs of the divan, "whom we have raised, chosen, and distinguished from the others."

Sheikh al-Bakri and the others replied evasively that the streets were closed and their way blocked.

Bonaparte insisted, "They must be present with the rising of the sun. If they have not arrived by that time and if they oppose us or act stubbornly, we will fire upon them with cannons and bombs, for no excuse shall save them, so you ride now and announce a safe-conduct for them in all streets and places."

The delegation of three leading sheikhs left him after sunset and wrote a letter to the clerics in the rebellious quarters. Their messenger was unable to get through the barricades, though, so it remained undelivered.

Bonaparte's own account of all this focuses on the clerics in the al-Husayn quarter and agrees remarkably closely with that of al-Jabarti. "I summoned the great clerics," he says, "but already all the routes had been cut off by insurgent guards positioned at the street corners." The militants were building defensive barricades and the city bristled with armed men. Bonaparte maintained that the prominent Muslim men of the cloth had attempted to warn the common people of the inevitable consequences of their actions, but without success. They were forced to fall silent and to go along with the irresistible course of the rebellion. Niello Sargy offered a different view. Bonaparte, he said, "ordered immediately that the principal men of the city must come to him. They replied that they were seeking a way of leading the people to submission, and their presence was necessary at the divan." On this refusal, he had weapons distributed to the troops that he had assembled and had them surround the district containing the Grand Mosque. Artillery pieces were set up during the night.[7]

Bonaparte remembered worrying. "Matters took on a most serious appearance; the reconquest of Cairo could prove extremely difficult." He could hear from four hundred minarets "the bitter voices of the muezzins" pronouncing curses on the enemies of God, infidels, and idolaters. But, he said—and this is entirely plausible—he was already attempting to think of ways of making the city submit to his authority without making permanent, fierce enemies of its residents. Bonaparte ordered Dommartin to march at midnight on Sunday with artillery and troops to assault the gate near the al-Azhar Seminary. Doguereau and the others under Dommartin spent all night dragging the big guns through unfamiliar streets, only arriving as the lilac gray dawn broke. Malus said that this attempt to deploy artillery inside the city failed, since the barricades and houses around the al-Azhar district were too effective.[8] The French position remained parlous.

By dawn on Monday morning, 22 October, the French had set up their artillery pieces more effectively at the Citadel and on the Muqattam Hills above the capital. Bonaparte was still trying to have Sayyid al-Bakri contact his colleagues in the al-Husayn quarter, in hopes of getting them to quell the revolt themselves. He put off any order to fire on the city while al-Bakri was continuing this effort at negotiation. He issued a proclamation in Arabic and Turkish: "It is not true that Cezzar has crossed the desert. The destruction of the gates between quarters was in conformity with the principles of good policing. The arming of the Citadel near the city was only the execution of a military regulation." The inhabitants were reminded of the battle of the Pyramids and the conduct of the Sultan Al Kabir with them. It ended by proposing that they put themselves under the judgment of the divan.

Bonaparte later admitted that this broadsheet worsened the situation, since it helped convince the Cairenes that the French were afraid and made them even more "insolent." The Muslim clerics advising Bonaparte, presumably including Sayyid al-Bakri, urged him to take decisive action, since, they said, the Bedouin were streaming into the city that day. The nearby tribes had already arrived at the gates, several thousand strong. Pelleport wrote, "Clouds of Bedouin, called by the chiefs of the insurrection, approached the city and cut off its communications with the outside." Bernoyer recalled, "The next morning, the rebels in the center of the city facilitated the entry of rebels from the surrounding areas." Armed with pikes and sticks, the strongest force of rebels assembled at the great cemetery, the City of the Dead, on the eastern outskirts of the city, a warren of tombs and mausoleums, some of them belonging to Mamluk sultans of the medieval period. They were reinforced by the pastoralists and by peasants coming from the villages around the capital. The commander in chief wrote, "I learned that seven or eight hundred of the Bili and the Tarrabin, were committing hostilities and interrupting the communications of Bulaq."[9] The urban insurrection was developing a Bedouin adjunct, both within and without the city walls. Indeed, the uprising quickly spread throughout the Delta, and was not merely a "Cairo revolt."

Bourrienne recalled:

Bonaparte had barely returned to headquarters (it was only 8 A.M.) when he learned, while breakfasting, that some Bedouin on horseback were threatening to enter Cairo. He was with his aides-de-camp. He ordered Sulkowski to mount up, to take with him fifteen guides, and to proceed to the point where the threat was greatest, that is, Bab al-Nasr or the Gate of Victory. His comrade, Croisier, remarked to the commander in chief that Sulkowski had barely recovered from the numerous wounds received at Salahiya. He offered to take his place. He had his reasons. Bonaparte was easily convinced. Sulkowski had already departed.[10]

Doguereau, from his perch in the hills, saw the aftermath with his own eyes. "Soon, we saw in the distance many cavalrymen—a cloud of Bedouin and peasants on horseback were upon us in the blink of an eye." He said that the French were not afraid, inasmuch as they had mounted their artillery on the hills above so as to defend the entrance to the quarter. They tried marching out against the Bedouin with the cavalry, "but their superiority in numbers forced us back. We fired our cannon, but, hidden in the tombs, the Bedouin had a refuge from our cannonballs." Then, having returned to the high ground, he saw Sulkowski and the fifteen mounted guides ride out and charge the men of the desert. "The Bedouin, seeing a small number of French, went toward them and charged. Afraid of being encircled by swirl of cavalry, the guides wanted to retreat. But, meeting on their way new troops of rebels, most of them perished. Sulkowski was cut to pieces in front of a mosque." Bonaparte, in his typical braggart way, invented a mythical death for Sulkowski, having him leave with "two hundred horsemen" and having him pursue the Bedouin "for several leagues" and "cleaning out the environs of the city" before having his horse shot out from under him and being pierced by ten lances. Bourrienne gave a better sense of the scale of events when he said that only an hour after they set out, one of the fifteen guides returned, soaked in blood, to announce that the party had been cut to pieces. He remarked, "This was speedy work, for we were still at table when the sad news arrived."[11] Desvernois suggested deliberate desecration of the French dead: "The inhabitants fed to the dogs the brave Pole Sulkowski, the aide-de-camp of the commander in chief."

The Cairo crowds could see, on that Monday morning, that the French were bringing up artillery to use against them, and they determined not to remain vulnerable to attack. The inhabitants of the rebellious Utuf quarter looked for three cannon that had been left, forgotten, in the house of the Ottoman-Egyptian notable Qayed Aga. They found them and set them up on the city wall of their quarter, facing the French. Then they fired them. "The French met this action with successive volleys of fire from muskets, rifles, and cannons." That the rebellious city folk made perhaps better use of artillery than had the emirs attests to their resolve and ingeniousness, and it must have been satisfying for them to meet the Europeans with modern weaponry rather than staves. As the morning wore on, the exchange became increasingly heated. Doguereau remembered: "We were all along being fired on by the inhabitants who were behind the wall. Soon, we suffered fire from a cannon set up a little to our right." The French replied with heavy artillery from the high ground they occupied. The quartermaster and Rousseau fan, Bernoyer, got a glimpse of ignoble savagery: "All the streets became the theater of a bloody slaughter."[12]

Al-Bakri and his two colleagues, accompanied by two French soldiers, wended their way Monday morning to the area called Bab al-Zuwayla in a further attempt to contact the great clerics in the al-Husayn quarter. They were spotted by a crowd, however, which "came upon them in a fury and prevented their entrance." They had to retreat hastily, going to the nearby Mosque of Iskandar, and sent a message to the clerics inside Muslim-held territory. At length Sheikh al-Sharqawi rode out with a group of other clerics. They attempted to clear the barricades that barred their path to the outside, but at the Kharratin quarter they encountered a band of armed militants who fired on them and forced them back. Al-Sharqawi and his group tried again to make their way to French-held territory for parleys, but were stopped at every turn.[13]

Bernoyer, the grouchy designer of uniforms, said that he then strapped on a saber and picked up a gun, despite his not being a soldier. He mounted up and joined a squadron of cavalrymen, passing through "absolutely deserted streets" until they reached the Birkat al-Fil ("Pool of the Elephant") Square, where they found a larger crowd engaged in combat with the 22nd Light. The reinforcements now set up two cannon and fired at the Egyptians. At the first volley the crowd hesitated. When the second cannonball felled several of their comrades, terror overcame them and the throng stampeded into alleyways too narrow to accommodate them. Gen. Jean Reynier, in command at that scene, gave the order to charge. "There resulted a frightful massacre. The square was emptied." Bernoyer told a story that he said convinced him that a Muslim "can resist to the death better than any other individual." A cavalryman saw a straggler attempting to flee and fired at him. The fugitive was dropped, but then got back up and threw himself into the pool after which Birkat al-Fil was named and began swimming. On his arrival at the other side, he was hit again by gunfire and fell back into the water. He crossed in a different direction, and as he was emerging was struck on the head by a French grenadier, a glancing blow with a saber. "He sank back and disappeared. I thought him dead, but not at all. He reappeared!"

He was hit by a hail of musket balls. Undaunted, he crawled out of the water and sat up. "Despite his wounds, he lived another quarter of an hour."[14]

The first battalion of the 18th Demi-Brigade attacked and routed the hundreds of rebels gathered at the City of the Dead, who were in close communication with the Bedouin.[15] With the inexorable French advance of Monday morning, which was facilitated by the use of artillery against the crowds, there was soon only one place where the insurgents remained in control: the al-Husayn quarter around its Grand Mosque near al-Azhar. To Bernoyer, they seemed determined to defend it to the last man. All entrances to this formidable position were heavily barricaded and guarded. A frontal infantry assault on it would have been extremely costly in French lives. Initial French assaults on the area did indeed go awry. The grenadiers of the 18th, commanded by Captain Bart, Pelleport recalled, went with an artillery piece toward the "most populous" quarter of Cairo. The narrowness of the streets, however, forced this small column to backtrack. When the crowd saw this retrograde motion, they moved in to attack. The French soldiers, he said, "as firm as granite, did not allow themselves to be intimidated. They killed many men and returned to headquarters."[16]

Bonaparte had the al-Azhar quarter surrounded by columns of grenadiers to ensure that none of the insurgents escaped. What with the Bedouins and peasants now flooding into the city and rallying to the revolt, there was an increasing danger of it spreading outside the capital. Vigo-Roussillon recalled that "at two P.M., General Bonaparte ordered that the quarter where the revolt was centered be shelled from the Citadel."[17]

The batteries in the Muqattam Hills began firing. Cannonballs and exploding shells struck the buildings, setting many on fire. Bernoyer wrote home, "The bombardment produced great ravages and was about to crush the mosque when the Turks, fearing that they would be entombed beneath its rubble, were obliged to implore the generosity of Bonaparte."[18] The commander in chief, he said, responded that they had refused his clemency when he offered it. "The hour of vengeance has sounded. You began it, it is for me to finish it!" The crowd, in despair, took up arms, but the grenadiers ran them through with bayonets relentlessly. "Then the principal leaders devoutly advanced unarmed toward our grenadiers, from whom they asked pity, strongly reinforcing their request with gestures and cries." He said that Bonaparte then ordered a halt to the shooting, and (temporarily) pardoned the supplicants.

A cavalryman, summoned with his unit from Bilbeis, approached the capital. "The spectacle that the unfortunate city presented caused me to tremble again. Many houses had fallen prey to blazing fires," Desvernois recalled. "The repression was terrible. We killed more than 3,000 insurgents without ourselves losing more than a hundred men." The merchant Grandjean, in contrast, estimated that the revolt took the lives of 800 Frenchmen. Detroye estimated 250 French dead, including a general, the head of a brigade, some subalterns, and several engineers and medical personnel. Bonaparte put forward for propaganda purposes the incredibly small number of 21 French soldiers killed. Grandjean felt that the uprising could have been fatal to the entire enterprise in Egypt if it had been better generaled and if the Egyptians had been better armed. Most, he said, had had no more than staves of hard wood, which were effective enough, but only at close quarters. Their muskets were "bad," and in the end they simply could not overcome the advantage that artillery bestowed on the French. The zoologist Saint-Hilaire actually boasted of how repressive French governance could be, writing back to France: "An insurrection broke out on 30 Vendémiaire and lasted until yesterday evening. The miserable inhabitants of Cairo did not know that the French are the tutors of the world in how to organize to combat insurgencies. That is what they learned to their cost."[19] In the aftermath, Desvernois was convinced, the spirit of the Egyptians was struck with a salutary terror. The chastisement inflicted on them established that the French had some sort of celestial protection and that it was futile to resist them. It might have been comforting to him to think so.

♣

Bonaparte inflicted such a horrific retribution on the insurgents that the aftermath of the revolt cost almost as much human life as the rebellion itself. Lieutenant Laval observed, "They arrested the principal leaders of the revolt, who were shot along with many of the prisoners that we had taken when they came out of the mosque. Most were Bedouin thieves."[20] They were not, of course, actually for the most part Bedouin, though some may have been mixed into the crowd making a last stand at the al-Husayn Mosque. The rallying of the Bedouin and peasants from Cairo's hinterland demonstrates that the revolt was not merely a protest by merchants and guildsmen against new taxes, but instead had a nativist dimension that appealed across social classes. Many in the Egyptian popular classes, linked across city districts and by crafts guilds and Sufi orders, simply did not accept the legitimacy of French rule. That night, Bernoyer recalled, the French made numerous further arrests. Altogether they took some 2,000 of the most active insurgents into custody.

The morning of Tuesday 23 October, Bonaparte fired off a brief, cold-blooded letter to General Berthier. "Citizen General, please give the order to the commander of the plaza to cut off the heads of all the prisoners that were taken with arms in their hands. They will be transported tonight to the bank of the Nile between Bulaq and Old Cairo; their headless cadavers will be thrown in the river."[21] Detroye recorded in his journal for 3 Brumaire (24 October), "They began to execute some of the rebels. These executions took place at the Citadel, almost secretly, with blows of bayonets."[22] This description of the executions makes French troops the executioners, and, indeed, mass murderers.

The quartermaster Bernoyer, who, as a civilian distant from the scene will only have heard lurid rumors, attempted to place the blame elsewhere, though his account is fantastic. He remarked, "Despite the ignorance and inefficiency of the Turks, they demonstrated, during this execution, a most particular intelligence and savoir-faire." Bernoyer described a procedure for the executions, which began Wednesday morning. The general in charge summoned the chief executioner of the city, who had once served the Ottoman emirs, and gave him a list of those he had to dispatch. One source identifies him as none other than Bartholomew al-Rumi, the new head of the Janissary Corps. Bernoyer observed, "His victims (I call 'victim' any person who is made to die without the determination of a court) were assembled in a great courtyard. The executioner called them one after another." They had them go out by way of a small door that led into another courtyard. There the captive was taken in hand by two guards, who grasped his arms as though to bring him before his judges. "The executioner approached him with a fistful of sand, which he threw into his eyes. The condemned, naturally, brought his hands to his eyes, lowering his head. Immediately, it was cut off with the aid of a Damascene sword that the executioner had hidden in his robe." He said that the execution hall was equipped with drains that took away the blood, that the bodies were promptly removed, and that sand was spread over the stains so that the next to arrive would not suspect what was about to befall him.

The death sentences, he wrote, began being imposed at 7 A.M. and the process ended at noon. When noon came and the soldiers informed their superiors that the task was accomplished, it seemed incredible to them. The general in charge, "who had retired to his rooms so as not to be a witness to these scenes of horror, at first believed that they wanted to fool him. He went immediately to the place, and there he was extremely surprised not to see any individual or any trace of that fairly sizable execution." Captain Joubert assured the general that all the persons on the list of condemned had been dispatched. He took him to the makeshift charnel house where the headless corpses were stacked up, the better to convince him. "At that horrific scene, [the general] could not prevent himself from a start of terror, as he cursed a hundred times the order that he had received and transmitted."

Bernoyer's depiction of Oriental efficiency in bloodletting is not plausible, however picturesque and macabre it may be. The procedure he described, with the subterfuge and the transport of the body and the cover-up with sand, might have been used in some instances. But it would have taken at least ten minutes per execution and no more than six beheadings an hour could have been carried off that way. Detroye's straightforward depiction of French troops bayoneting unarmed, presumably bound prisoners, is more plausible for most of the executions, and really could have been horrifically efficient. Niello Sargy said that 300 were executed, including five principal clerics. The others speak of 2,000 killed. If so, the carnage must have gone on for days.

That night, Bernoyer said, the corpses were dumped in the Nile, and the Cairenes were thereby kept in ignorance of the full extent of the "rigorous justice" that Bonaparte had ordered. One suspects that the crocodiles of the Delta were fat and lazy that year. To the 3,000 or so Egyptians killed during the three days of the revolt had been added at least another 300 in a single morning. The quartermaster's disgust with the arbitrary and pettily vengeful procedure, more redolent of the Sun King Louis XIV or of Robespierre's radicals during the Terror than of the careful jurisprudence of the Directory, bespoke a building suspicion among many of the French invaders that their enterprise was not, after all, about bringing liberty and the rule of law to the Nile Valley.

Bernoyer observed that Bonaparte had, for political reasons, spared several of the more important leaders of the revolt. "Although more guilty, they had a great influence on the people, either because of their occupation or because of their riches." Bernoyer was implying that some of the wealthy in the city were among the foremost organizers of the revolt, an observation that makes sense in retrospect but one which al-Jabarti largely avoided in his account. He did mention in passing that Sayyid al-Maqdisi (or al-Qudsi), one of the ringleaders, was both a minor clergyman and a caravan merchant. (Al-Maqdisi was among those sentenced to death.) The great merchants of al-Qahira, where eighty percent of the commerce in Cairo was done, were most likely Bernoyer's referent. The Egyptian chronicler, in contrast, for the most part blamed the uprising on lower-ranking clerics that lacked common sense and on rabble foolish enough to follow them. Bonaparte likewise in his memoirs suggested that the notables had been dragged into the revolt. Others, as we have seen, managed to blame the Bedouin even for this very urban display of popular resistance.

A French soldier revealed in his journal that parts of the city remained unsubdued for eight days and that there were for days afterward neighborhoods where it was dangerous for French soldiers to venture.[23] He unwisely went out from Old Cairo almost to Muski, a major commercial thoroughfare. He began noticing that "the windows were loaded with stones and earthen crocks with which to crush the French who had the misfortune to pass below." They saw not even a cat in the street, and their way was still littered with bodies drowned in their own blood. The inhabitants were standing in their doorways. "They looked out with an air of inquietude and with a doleful silence a thousand times more frightening than the tumultuous cries of a frantic population." He thought the eerie hush a harbinger of a new massacre.

Bernoyer remarked that Bonaparte employed the revolt as a pretext to further tax the population. He assessed a fine of "12 million" on the city of Cairo alone (he did not specify the currency). This sum, the quartermaster said, did not reckon all the losses suffered by the inhabitants at the hands of pillaging French military men. "In the French quarter [the quarter of Christians], several days ago a market was established among the soldiers. One can see there all the loot that they appropriated during the revolt. There one easily exchanges a watch costing three louis for a diamond, gold, or silver worth twenty." He complained that local "Greeks and Jews" followed them closely and profited by their ignorance of the real value of Egyptian goods. Meanwhile, Bonaparte was establishing a police force in each quarter that would closely watch the Muslims so as to forestall any further plots or conspiracies among them. Niello Sargy said that immediately after the revolt, all Cairenes were required to wear the tricolor cockade, and the French national flag was raised above all public establishments. Al-Jabarti hinted, in contrast, that as a result of the revolt the French authorities gradually dropped their demand that Egyptians wear the cockade.

Bonaparte ordered that extensive new fortifications be built in Cairo and environs, even if they involved tearing down mosques (al-Jabarti lamented the demise of the al-Maqs Mosque, another at Imbaba, and the al-Kazaruni Mosque at Roda Island, among others). The military engineers widened streets and chopped down date palms. Bonaparte also hunted down the suspected ringleaders.[24] His troops sought and searched the homes of the master of the blind men's guild, the secretary of the spice traders' guild, and a number of clerics. The blind, as street beggars and Qur'an reciters, were well placed to hear and share intelligence on the enemy surreptitiously. The spice traders were wealthy, and Ibrahim Effendi was accused of hiring and arming bands of ruffians for the purposes of insurgency. On 3 November, Bonaparte publicly condemned to death eleven men he considered ringleaders.[25] They included seven mostly minor and otherwise unknown clerics, such as Sheikh al-Sayyid 'Abd al-Karim, Sheikh Badr al-Qudsi (or al-Maqdisi), and Sheikh 'Abd al-Wahhab al-Shubrawi. Al-Jabarti maintained that Sheikh Badr had in fact already successfully fled. Bonaparte wished to have someone explicitly punished for the uprising, but appears to have feared he would ruin any chance of reconciliation with the city's elite if he publicly executed more than a handful of middle-ranking clergymen and merchants or guildsmen. He may have in fact executed thousands of insurgents, but did so in relative secrecy lest he make thousands of martyrs.

The North Africans from the al-Fahhamin district also had amends to make. The young men from this community agreed to join the French army, forming their own battalion. French officers trained them in drill, teaching them to present arms, fire in unison, and march. Bonaparte then deployed them in the Delta against peasant rebels. They attacked and defeated Ibn Sha'ir, headman of the village of Ashama, killing him, ransacking his mansion, and confiscating all his considerable wealth and livestock. As the story of the North African battalion demonstrates, in the aftermath of the revolt the two sides had little choice but to reconcile, at least on the surface. The Egyptians, lacking heavy artillery or a disciplined infantry, had failed to throw off the better-armed and -trained French. Bonaparte wanted a subject population, not a graveyard, and so he had to be selective about retribution. The great clerics of al-Azhar rode to his residence in Azbakiya and pleaded with him through his Arabic interpreter for safe conduct. He pressed them to turn in the leaders of the revolt. They mentioned some names. "We know every single one of them!" he replied triumphantly. They begged him to remove the troops from the al-Husayn Mosque, where they had been garrisoned and where their horses were being stabled, according to outraged Abdullah al-Sharqawi. Bonaparte acquiesced, though he kept a force of seventy men in the area.

Lieutenant Laval observed that "Bonaparte dissolved their divan (that is to say, their government)." Some members of the General Council and the Special Council were suspected of having helped plot the insurrection all the while they were planning out with the French how the new republic was to be governed. Laval said that Bonaparte, furious, "told them that the Muslims were no longer anything in Egypt, since the chiefs of the divan had wanted to slit the throats of the French. Their audience hall was closed."[26] Bonaparte "wanted to turn the people against them using the same tools that they had employed to provoke the revolt," according to Bernoyer. He decreed that if they wished to save their heads, they had to affix their names to a document he had prepared and have it published and posted at mosques in the city and throughout the provinces:

> Inhabitants of Cairo: Pray that the Almighty will preserve you from sedition and that He will protect you from those who seek to wreak evil on earth. There have just been great disorders in the city of Cairo, on the part of the populace and of wicked persons who mixed in with them. They sowed discord between the French troops and the subjects [*sic*]. This has occasioned the death of many Muslims, but the beneficent and invisible hand of God came to calm the sedition. By our intercession with the commander in chief Bonaparte, the evils that would have ensued were averted. He prevented the troops from burning the city and from pillaging, for he is full of wisdom, beneficent and merciful toward the Muslims. He is the particular protector of the poor, and without him, all the inhabitants of Cairo would no longer exist.[27]

The proclamation put into the mouths of the clerics went on to warn Cairenes against any further turbulence, having already threatened them with genocide. Later on, Bonaparte reconstituted the clerically dominated divan and attempted once more to forge a relationship with al-Azhar.

Having suffered a setback in his relations with the mainstream, literate Sunni clergy, Bonaparte turned to evoking mystical and millenarian themes in folk Islam. Later that fall, he issued a proclamation "to the inhabitants of Cairo."[28] He gloated that the "perverse men" who had led astray "a party among you" had perished. "Sharifs, clerics, sermonizers in the mosques, hear well that those who, with joyful hearts, declare themselves my enemies will have no refuge in this world or in the next." He was claiming supernatural powers to determine the fates of others even in the Muslim afterlife! "Is there a man so blind that he cannot see that Destiny itself directs all my operations?" The vast universe in turn, he reminded them, was subject to "the empire of destiny."

He continued, "Tell the people that, since the world has been the world, it was written that after having destroyed the enemies of Islam and pulled down the crosses, I would come from the depths of the Occident to fulfill the task imposed on me." He called on them to direct the people to consider "more than twenty passages" in the "holy book of the Koran" which had predicted and explained his advent. Those, he said, who called down curses on the French were simply condemning themselves. "The true believers will make vows for the prosperity of our arms." He went on to claim even greater occult powers. "I could demand an accounting of every one of you concerning the most secret feelings in his heart; for I know all, even what you have never told anyone." A day would come, he promised, when the whole world would see proof that he was guided by higher orders, "and that human efforts can do nothing against me."

It is tempting to conclude that the serial disasters Bonaparte had faced since Nelson's destruction of his fleet had slightly unbalanced him. It is possible, of course, that the smug Jacobin secularism of the revolutionary era continued to give the French a paternalistic sense of superiority over the gullible, priest-ridden, superstitious Orientals. In that case, Bonaparte was simply attempting to play on what he saw as the suggestibility and naïveté of the Egyptians when he claimed to be some sort of invincible supernatural being. And after all, if the ploy deterred even a few from further rebellion, it might be worth it, and he would have lost nothing.

It is also possible that Bonaparte was reproducing folk Muslim beliefs that had been communicated to him by the common people and by the soothsayers to whom he sometimes spoke through his interpreters. Folk Islam in Egypt contained a millenarian element, a belief in the coming of the "Guided One," or Mahdi, at the end of days. Some of Bonaparte's diction in this proclamation has resonances with those beliefs, and he may have been intimating that he was the Mahdi. He was well aware of these motifs.

In his youth, Bonaparte had written a short story about a medieval "veiled prophet" of Khurasan in eastern Iran, who challenged the just, peaceful, and "scientific" rule of the Caliph al-Mahdi in Baghdad, and who used chicanery to gather a mob, but who came to a bad end.[29] Then, he seemed to identify with the caliph, but in this proclamation he sounded more like the veiled prophet himself. The beliefs also circulated in the Egypt of the time. Saint-Hilaire had, already in August, met with prophecies of Egyptian soothsayers about the inevitability of Bonaparte's expedition: "a prophecy, they say written in a sacred book, predicted that in 1305 of the Hegira, Christians will come to save Egypt and punish the government for its impiety toward the divine. All the Turks believe that we were sent by God and respect us for that reason."[30] It is impossible to know whether Bonaparte paid for these prophecies to be put around.

Al-Jabarti copied the incredible proclamation into his journal, no doubt rendered into Arabic by Venture de Paradis, given its execrable style. He said he absolutely had to do so "because of his prevarication and boasting to weak minds, and his grandiosity in claiming to be the Mahdi or a Prophet, and the use of a 'proof by the opposite' in making that claim."[31] The severe logician and theologian, trained by a father fascinated by Aristotelian philosophy, accused

Bonaparte of the very worst sin of all: committing a logical fallacy. In actuality, the proclamation committed so many logical fallacies that it would take a while to list them all. In contrast, Moiret alleged that some of the Cairo soothsayers, whether they were fooled or perhaps bribed, got behind this image of a fey Bonaparte and helped calm the populace. Some fortune tellers predicted that the French sultan would soon convert to Islam and "bring along by his example his entire army."[32] The army generally went along with the pragmatic wisdom of appealing to Muslim superstitions if it made for less trouble, he said, but the "philosophers" were outraged at this surrender to superstition.

Bonaparte may have overestimated the place of specifically religious feelings in the opposition he faced from Egyptians. Egyptian leaders deployed the rhetoric of Islam as a way of strengthening political alliances, but both al-Jabarti and al-Sharqawi, men of the cloth, blamed the uprising specifically on secular objections to French taxation policy and on feelings of insecurity among the guildsmen and shopkeepers produced by the tearing down of the gates separating quarters. Bonaparte also tended to make excuses for the Egyptian middling and upper classes he still hoped to woo, depicting the notables as terrified of the mobs and dragged into the revolt by them. This analysis contrasts with al-Jabarti's frank admission that Sayyid Badr al-Maqdisi, both a caravan merchant and a lower-ranking cleric, led the crowd in the al-Azhar district. The North Africans from al-Fahhamin, like many other urban ethnic and occupational groups, were organized by their guild. There are no spontaneous uprisings, and the guilds of the merchant, crafts, and security guards are the most likely suspects in this one.

The impact on the morale of the French troops of the sinking of the fleet, the sultan's declaration of holy war, and the Egyptian uprising was by all accounts crushing. Moiret remembered worrying about being trapped in Egypt far from France. The officers feared the annual spring outbreaks of plague, and he could not see how the French could protect themselves from a disease that might thin their ranks as effectively as any Muslim arms. He also fretted over the Ottoman-led second coalition. "If France itself is attacked, if the peace in which we left it is violated, how could we assure to her the assistance that she will need for her own defense?" The phrase "the peace in which we left it" is an implicit critique of Bonaparte's having risked provoking another international anti-French coalition with his attack on a major Ottoman province.

The disillusionment with Bonaparte's methods was also producing some gloom. Not only did he object to extrajudicial executions, but when Bernoyer went out on a tax-collecting mission to a village and witnessed the brutality of the extortion employed, he complained that Bonaparte was using the methods of the "Mamluks."

In the aftermath of the revolt, largely led and fought by Egyptian Muslims, Bonaparte leaned more heavily on members of religious minorities. He deployed small Maltese units in the Delta and created three Greek companies of a thousand men each, at Cairo, Damietta, and Rosetta.[33] In early December he replied to a letter from the Coptic community passed on to him by Jirjis al-Jawhari, a Coptic notable who served as the financial adviser to the French Republic of Egypt. Bonaparte said of this community that when circumstances permitted, in the near future, "I will accord it the right to practice its religion publicly, as is the usage in Europe, such that everyone follows his belief. I will severely punish the villages that, in the course of various revolts, assassinated Copts. From today, you may announce to them that I permit them to carry arms, to ride donkeys and horses, to wear turbans, and to dress in whatever way they please."

Bonaparte was committing himself to lifting, over time, the marks of membership in a subordinate or "protected" community in a premodern Muslim society. Despite the protections afforded such "people of the book," Muslim rulers and jurists of the medieval and early modern periods sought to mark such non-Muslim populations as second-class subjects. They were not to dress like Muslims or enjoy the marks of Muslim high status. Bonaparte had not, however, found the Copts very satisfactory collaborators. He noted with displeasure that whereas the Muslim clergy had identified for the French many hoards of the beys' treasure kept in safe houses, the Copts, who had been their principal agents, had not turned in a single one. If, he said, he restored "to the Coptic nation a dignity and the inalienable rights of man, which they had lost, I have the undoubted right to require the individuals who comprise it to demonstrate a great deal of zeal and faithfulness in the service of the Republic." Bonaparte's minorities policy had to be actively constructed, since he found no "natural" collaborators, and he resorted to the supposedly inalienable Rights of Man only as a carrot in the quest for allies.

Some of those around Bonaparte, at least, also envisaged a similar role for the small Jewish community in Egypt and greater Syria, especially as the commander in chief more openly made plans for a military encounter with Cezzar Pasha of Sidon. There were only 3,000 to 5,000 Jews in Cairo, living in a Jewish quarter near the gold market.[34] While they had been bankers to the Ottoman Janissaries earlier in the eighteenth century, the rise of the Georgian beys had much reduced their prominence, and they played no significant role in the

French occupation. The playwright Laus de Boissy later inserted into Captain Say's memoirs his own hopes for a pro-French Jewish "colony" in "Jerusalem," which he saw as potentially useful for the French in Egypt. He first published it in the spring of 1799 in the *Decade Philosophique* (Philosophical Weekly), the magazine of a group that called themselves "The Ideologues," to which Bonaparte was close.

> The establishment of the French in Egypt and in Syria could be a joyous epoch for the Jewish nation; to receive and welcome the Jews at Jerusalem would perhaps be a means to make them more useful and happier. The Jews, dispersed in three parts of the world, could, in forming a flourishing colony there, also powerfully aid the colonization of Egypt by the French. The Jews are accused of many vices, but these vices come from the oppression under which they groan, and the Jews have virtues that we lack in our civilization and in our power. Docile sons, faithful wives, tender fathers, they profess equality, practice hospitality and fraternity toward all of their own; they are sober, hardworking, economical, disciplined, patient, industrious. There are no men on the earth who spend less or do more, who know better the miracle of savings and that of work. Born businessmen, with links to all the nations, they can serve with all and against all. Rich in capital, they can offer it to those who restore to them their original territory. One can say of the Jewish people what one says of sex: Their virtues are from them, their vices are from us. The conqueror of Egypt knows so well how to evaluate men that he will never mistake the advantage that he can draw from this people, in the execution of his vast designs.[35]

Laus de Boissy's configuring of Ottoman Jerusalem as the "original territory" of European Jews had the effect of exoticizing them, and, for all his left-handed compliments, of declaring them out of place in Paris and Rome. There were at that time only a few thousand Jews in geographical Palestine, far too few to be of any practical use to Bonaparte's colonial designs, and, as we have seen with the Copts, it cannot in any case be assumed that they would naturally give their loyalty to a European power over their own Ottoman government.

We cannot assume that Bonaparte shared Laus de Boissy's views, though since the latter was in Josephine's salon, he was almost certainly aware of them. There is no good evidence that he supported any such project himself, but it is clear that the French colonization of Egypt did provoke some in his circle to begin thinking about a modern sort of Zionist nationalism that configured European Jews as useful to imperialism, that urged their displacement to the dusty villages of Palestine, and that sought to use their supposed financial and commercial power for imperial purposes.[36]

As for his relationship with Muslims, Bonaparte clearly began to feel after the revolt in Cairo that his methods had been too harsh. On 11 November he wrote a letter to General Berthier strictly forbidding the beating of insurgents to extract information from them. "It has been recognized at all times that this manner of interrogating human beings, of putting them under torture, produces nothing good. The unfortunates say whatever comes into their heads, and everything they think you want to know."[37] As a result, he wrote, he was prohibiting further use of torture as an intelligence-gathering technique, insofar as both "reason and humanity" denounce it. He added that he did not mean to forbid the use of the bastinado (the beating of a prisoner's feet while he was held upside down), but that it should be deployed only for the purpose of punishment.

I2

THE FALL OF THE DELTA
AND THE ARABIAN JIHAD

*T*he revolt in the capital had spread rapidly into the Delta, which the French had spent the previous two months attempting to subdue. The garrison at Bilbeis heard immediately of the revolt in Cairo and began going about armed and redoubling its guard patrols.[1] On 23 October, they sent out a cavalry expedition to scout the area. At an old Roman camp in the desert, not far from Cairo itself, they discovered some 12,000 men had assembled, armed with muskets, swords, lances, and clubs. Some were mounted on horseback. The French began planning a campaign against them.

In the capital, Bonaparte ordered that artillery not be used in mopping-up operations since it could be heard for miles around. He feared giving the false impression to the rebellious countryside that the insurgency was still alive. His apprehension shows how hazardous the situation of the French still was. Sergeant François explained that a peasant–Bedouin alliance still aimed at assisting the craftsmen of Cairo. The troops at Bilbeis, originally intended as a bulwark against the return of Ibrahim Bey from Syria, now had to march toward Cairo to relieve it. Sgt. François's unit encountered attacking Bedouin cavalrymen as they moved southwest and brought up their artillery to scatter them. "We killed a few," he remarked with satisfaction. But then things turned around and they had to repair to camp, pursued "by a crowd of assailants," whom they appear to have barely fended off. They made another sortie the next evening, marching in an infantry square and supported by artillery. They encountered a large force of Bedouin and "mounted peasants," but the latter kept retreating under artillery fire, refusing to engage directly. The French returned to their makeshift fort, taking fire all night. They lost eleven dead and sixteen wounded. "Twenty-three villages recognized as the most rebellious were pillaged and burned by us; their livestock and grains were brought to camp. All the inhabitants, except for the women and children, found in these villages were killed. More than 900 were put to death." Most of the men must have fled, if that was the death toll from Reynier's destruction of twenty-three villages.

It is probably to this campaign that Bourrienne referred when he spoke of a French attack on "tribes" near Cairo who had surprised and slit the throats of "many French." The French not only killed 900 of the rural insurgents, but decapitated them. The troops who had ridden out from Cairo brought many of their severed heads back to stage a macabre public spectacle at Azbakiya Square. They gathered a crowd, and then "the sacks were opened and the heads rolled out before the assembled populace." Bourrienne was convinced that the demonstration terrified the Cairenes into submission. François was equally convinced that the sacking of the twenty-three villages had quelled their rebellion. He said that word reached the surrounding villages that Bonaparte had decisively put down the revolt in Cairo, and village headmen of Sharqiya came in delegations to General Reynier at Bilbeis to ask for mercy. They said, François reported, that they had repented and "only went to Cairo to respond to the orders of Ibrahim Bey." François' further narrative makes it clear that despite this temporary victory, the garrison at Bilbeis continued to face attacks and remained under virtual siege.

Bonaparte's aide-de-camp Lavalette recalled, "The revolt of Cairo spread down the two arms of the Nile, especially that of Damietta."[2] The key Mediterranean port fell into danger again, as did its supply lines with Cairo. The commander in chief wrote General Lanusse in alarm on 27 October that the stagecoach and wagon drivers coming from Damietta up to the capital "had had their throats slit by the villagers of Ramla and Banha al-'Asal in the province of Qalyub, and by those of Bata and Mishrif in that of Minuf. Try to seize their headmen and cut off their heads. I assure you that there will be money coming from Damietta."[3]

The commander in chief urgently wrote General Berthier on 1 November, ordering him to send General Lannes with four hundred men to the village of al-Qata, near Rosetta, "to punish the inhabitants for having confiscated this morning two skiffs bearing artillery."[4] He was to arrest the village headman, or, failing that, a dozen prominent villagers, and "do everything he could to restore to us the bayonets, cannons, firearms, etc., which were pillaged." Gerbaud heard that they also captured 4,000 muskets, and that a week later Bonaparte had dispatched General Murat with 1,300 men to join up with Lannes in recovering the guns. This account suggests that the Delta villagers were preparing for further resistance and knew where they could find the means for it. In late October, Bonaparte was also cut off from news of Alexandria by disturbances around Rahmaniya.

Lavalette wrote that he had had some insurgent villages burned, to serve as an example. It appears that the Cairo revolt had revived Bonaparte's fear that the Muslim Egyptians were construing the French as Crusaders. The officer said that "the commander in chief had a lively desire to know whether the inhabitants of Mansura had preserved any memory of their victorious resistance when the Count of Artois attacked them with such imprudence during the expedition of Saint Louis. But it appeared, after all our researches, that the Egyptians neither knew the name of Saint Louis nor the action that had made their ancestors illustrious."[5] Literate Egyptians, of course, knew all about the Crusaders, and Sheikh 'Abdullah al-Sharqawi, sometime president of the French Republic of Egypt, wrote about Saladin's defeating them in his short history of Egypt. The townspeople of Mansura had other things on their minds.

While peasants often formed alliances with Bedouin in an attempt to fend off rapacious French taxes, now that the Ottoman-Egyptian state was gone they also came into conflict with the pastoralists. Lacking stipends and tax farms from the beys, the Bedouin resorted to their stock-in-trade—animal husbandry—and sought to use land for pasturage and resisted the villagers' attempts to preserve it for farming. The resulting division sometimes allowed the French to develop new clients among the peasants. Bonaparte wrote General Leclerc at Qalyub on 14 November, sharing with him the complaint of Sayyid Khalil al-Bakri's rural agent there. He wrote that the agent "complains that the Arabs are preventing the inhabitants around the village of Mit Ghamr from sowing their land. Take the necessary measures to punish these Arabs and to ensure that they do no harm to agriculture."[6] A week later Gerbaud, stationed at Mansura, wrote in his diary, "Ravages of Arabs in the villages of the province." Bedouins and peasants often had a symbiotic relationship where they were not competing for the same land, and these conflicts likely pointed to the breakdown of social norms under the occupation. The Bedouins in the Delta were competing with the French by attempting to collect "contributions" in kind as the winter crops came in. They thus menaced French finances, since Bonaparte hoped to collect taxes on the harvest himself. The expropriation of the peasants by rival armies was nothing new: The emirs and their Mamluks, during their internecine battles, often did the same.

Bonaparte's lack of money drove the rapacious French taxation in the countryside. He needed it to govern Egypt, but even more to fund his burgeoning Syria campaign. Jollois, at Rosetta, commented in his diary late that year, "The cold continues always. The lack of money in the public treasury is so great that we are menaced with abandoning the work on the hospital of Ibrahim Bey, on the ovens of the commander in chief, and on the school." The French overtaxation of the population provoked constant turmoil. Bonaparte instructed his officers to collect the winter *miri*, an Ottoman tax on agricultural land. The rice crop was coming in. Gerbaud recalled late that fall, "The countryside appeared more beautiful than ever. Season of harvesting the rice. Rice is a plant that lives in the water. It is sown in May. It is cut when it is still very green, and one immediately husks it with the help of a machine with circular iron blades that one walks over the top of it with the aid of donkeys or cows."[7]

The commander in chief also sought to collect in kind on horses and some kinds of livestock. In late November, Gen. Louis-Nicholas Davout led three hundred French cavalrymen in an attack on a Bedouin tribe in the Delta, aimed at confiscating their large herd of camels. Bonaparte needed the camels as pack animals for further campaigns and may already have begun planning a camel corps cavalry unit. Davout was supported by ships commanded by Captain Umar, a Mamluk who had gone over to Bonaparte. The French carefully surrounded the tribesmen on land, while Umar's skiffs cut off any hope of retreat across the river. "Despite their pleas and curses, we took from them at least 1,500 camels, a large number of sheep, and thirty water buffalos. This tribe had already on numerous occasions refused to pay the *miri* tax and always had fled at the approach of infantry detachments. . . ."[8] When the Bedouin realized that the cavalry force had cut off their retreat, they submitted, giving up their livestock. "Only the women cried and pulled out their hair, cursing us with an incredible volubility." A French cavalryman praised the supporting role of the Egyptian sailors, saying that the Muslims were "very good soldiers" and "impervious to fatigue." He called Umar "extremely intelligent" and a fine leader of the unit he had raised. They were, he said, precious auxiliaries to the French army and "detest the Arabs, at whose hands they have often suffered." The adjectives employed by French officers to describe Muslim troops and officers serving the beys tended to be rather more negative. The cavalryman said that the Egyptian units that Bonaparte had created were lightening the load of the French army. Bonaparte clearly wanted more young recruits.

Gerbaud recalled in December that an order from the commander in chief had arrived "which instructs that the generals in command of the provinces grab children of from twelve to sixteen years from the villages that engage in revolt" and send them to him until he determined their destination. "If the village merits burning, one should always seize the children."[9] Bonaparte appears to have been running an orphanage–cum–military training center at the Citadel, seeking to expand the small child-Mamluk cavalry unit he had established the previous August with Egyptian peasant recruits. Egyptian peasants had not been recruited as Mamluks under Ottoman rule, though some Anatolians and Caucasians may have originally had a peasant background.

The operation reported by the cavalryman was particularly well manned and executed, but it was not typical. Many Delta villagers had a Bedouin past, and the Egyptian rural population was used to fleeing from Mamluk troops, floods and other menaces. Often peasants simply disappeared when the French tax collectors approached. Laugier described how, on 18 December, General Dugua sent him out from Mansura with 280 men against two villages, Nabiluha and Kafr Nabiluha, that had refused to pay taxes five times in a row, despite receiving repeated written French demands. "I found the village of Nabiluha absolutely deserted, the inhabitants having withdrawn to that of Kafr Nabiluha." He marched his men across the inundated Delta swamp to the latter as fast as possible. "The inhabitants fled, with the exception of some women and a very few men, among whom was found the village headman." The headman pledged that the villagers would pay up, but when the French let him go on the pledge that he would retrieve his absent compatriots, he vanished. Laugier burned the houses of the village headmen in each village and returned empty-handed.[10]

The northeast remained insecure. A fellow engineer, Fèvre, told Jollois late that fall of the dangerous situation in that part of the Delta. He had returned from an assignment under General Andréossi to map Lake Manzala.[11] The expedition downriver had, he said, been extremely costly. "The destruction of many skiffs, with twenty, thirty, or even sixty French aboard, and an attack on Andréossi himself on his way there—all these events only too well demonstrated how grievous the imprudence of the French and the fierceness of the inhabitants had been for us." On arriving again at Damietta, Fèvre informed Jollois, Andréossi had found the city in the most frightful disorder.

We do not have far to go in seeking the reason for the French despair. Captain Moiret revealed in his memoir that Hasan Tubar resumed his own assaults on the French while the troops in Cairo were tied down there. He said, "During the revolt in Cairo a local adventurer and pirate, Hasan Tubar, who was backed by a supposed firman of the Ottoman Grand Vizier, made raids by boat over the lake on Damietta."[12] That Tubar took advantage of the Cairo revolt to raid Damietta, hundreds of miles downriver, shows that the Egyptians retained the ability to communicate up and down the Nile, and strove sometimes to coordinate their resistance.

Tubar was said to derive his power in part from his many wives and concubines and the sons they bore him. Marriage in particular was a way for him to make alliances with powerful Bedouin and other clans. At length, he was defeated and Bonaparte had him arrested, stripped of property and harem, and brought to the Citadel as a hostage for the good behavior of his people. Later, the commander in chief released him from captivity, keeping his eldest son as hostage in Cairo, and returned to him his estates, provided he lived under surveillance at Damietta. Tubar, however, insisted that the French restore his women to him as well. Bonaparte had not made any stipulations in this regard, since they had been given to others and he did not want to bestow too much prestige on the newly released magnate. Later on, Kléber did return Tubar's women to him, assured of his loyalty and desiring to create him as a model for other foes of the French, such as the Ottoman-Egyptian bey Murad, whom he wished to "turn" in the same way. Niello Sargy told the story of how the oversexed Tubar would "pass the night one after another in the arms of the many women in his harem." One of them, Ziftiya, he wrote, was "excited to the highest degree of jealousy" and put a deadly poison in a cup of his coffee.[13]

Women of the notable class thus became pawns in colonial power struggles. The French officers thought nothing of "bestowing" the women of a defeated enemy on loyal compradors, as though they were inanimate spoils, and then returning them to him later when he showed loyalty to them. In this anecdote, Ziftiya's murder of her husband is configured in Orientalist terms as the result of hothouse harem passions, of an oversexed Egyptian magnate's transgression of his wives' sense of personal self-worth. Niello Sargy probably did not know enough Arabic to realize that the concubine's name ("black as pitch") indicated that she was a Sudanese slave, which might complicate the narrative further. The story that he told about Tubar's end makes no sense. Harem women in a polygamous society did not kill their husbands out of jealousy of the other women. A jealous woman would be more likely to poison a cowife or favorite slave girl, and Ziftiya's motive in killing her master must have been a response either to mistreatment or to his dishonorable capitulation to foreign, Christian rulers. The story is typical of eighteenth-century French pornography in functioning as a critique of the lasciviousness of the powerful, though in its Egyptian setting it does double duty in raising alarums about the dangers of overactive Muslim male sexuality.

Andréossi thereafter built up a flotilla of armed skiffs "to pursue the fisherman who were masters there." The engineers were assigned to survey the vast lagoon that abutted Damietta, a task they often found onerous and unpleasant; it required them to work in the water with mud up to their knees. Meanwhile, the French continued the project of building fortifications to secure the Delta.

The work went more slowly than Bonaparte would have liked, in part because November was rice harvesting season and few peasant builders were available. In particular, he wanted the fort at al-Izba finished so as to protect Damietta from any attack when he sent armies from there across the lake toward Syria. The problem of peasant revolts was by no means resolved, but late in 1798, the scout Pierre Millet recalled, "During the time we were at Damietta, we enjoyed fair tranquility. The commander in chief employed all possible means to construct forts to provide us a refuge from the insults of the populace and of the Bedouin."[14] These forts, which Bonaparte was planting throughout Egypt, were generally armed with artillery, unlike the earlier ill-fated garrisons at places such as Mansura. Bonaparte was increasingly able to expand and deploy cavalry as well.

Earlier, he had lacked horses, and anyway they could not be used in the Delta when the water was high and the earth was inundated or turned to marsh. By December, as the water level was falling rapidly, Bonaparte had "requisitioned" large numbers of horses, and mounted cavalrymen could again be sent against rebellious peasants. The French could not forestall a steady drumbeat of attacks and occasional revolts in the Delta, but with Nile skiffs mounted with cannon, with a growing cavalry, and with newly built forts provided with at least a few cannon, they were less open to simply being massacred. The lack of wood in Egypt was increasingly, however, a limitation on further French building of fortifications and ships, which suggested to some officers that a forest would have to be found. As the Bible mentioned in ancient times, the nearest woodlands were the cedars of Lebanon, in Bonaparte's time a part of Ottoman Syria.

✤

The introduction of the French Republic into the midst of the Muslim world created several distinct responses. Sultan Selim III declared conventional war on the French, in concert with his Christian allies, the British and the Russians. But the sultan also called for an Islamic holy war against the Army of the Orient, charging Ahmed Cezzar Pasha of Sidon with gathering a vassal army loyal to the sultan that would attack the French and drive them from Egypt.[15] The sultan declared fighting the French to be an individual duty for Muslims. In Arabia and Yemen, Muslim scholars and activists called for volunteers to go to the aid of Murad Bey and to fight the forces of Gen. Louis Desaix in Upper Egypt. All of these challenges from the Muslim world—that of Cezzar, that of the Arabian devotees of holy war, and that of Egyptian Muslim irregulars in Egypt—were making themselves felt that winter.

Bonaparte held that the best defense is a good offense, and he began preparing to take the battle to the enemy. First, he needed to finish securing Egypt. The French, despite garrisoning Sharqiya province, had not yet taken the key Red Sea port of Suez, which was important to the coffee trade and also formed a weak point in French defenses, since enemy troops could be landed there. Suez was one of two great Red Sea ports for Egypt, the other being Qusayr in the south, but Bonaparte was finding it difficult to prevail in Upper Egypt because of Murad Bey's continued challenge there. In contrast, Suez lay relatively nearby and he could grasp it. A move into the Red Sea would challenge Ottoman control over it as well as block an important British maritime route. The Ottomans allowed the British to bring some commodities from India across the Indian Ocean, through the Arabian Sea, and up the Red Sea to Suez, then to transport them by caravan to Alexandria. At the least, he could deprive the British of that shortcut, which was particularly suited to lightweight luxury goods and to emergency dispatches. Bonaparte dispatched General Bon to establish control of Suez in early November. Capt. Eugène de Beauharnais, made commander of the vanguard, remembered the expedition as risky, involving a relatively small force that had to march, thirsty, due east across the desert.[16] On hearing of Bon's approach, the Suez city elders sent out a delegation to declare their submission to the French. On the morning of 9 November, Beauharnais entered Suez at the head of a vanguard unit without having to fire a shot. They found there four disarmed naval vessels, six skiffs, and nine merchant ships to whom he offered protection. The French troops settled into the sturdier mansions in an attempt to protect themselves from enemies within the city and without, though the port itself had become a ghost town. Al-Jabarti remarked that the principal inhabitants of Suez had fled, taking with them their women and maritime workers, and that the French then plundered the town.

In mid-December, the day before he left to tour Suez, Bonaparte had Bourrienne write out a long letter giving detailed and precise orders for the supplying of Qatiya, a forward staging ground in the middle of shifting sand dunes for his planned invasion of Syria. He instructed that Qatiya be provisioned from Damietta.[17] Bonaparte had urgently desired his army to secure the northeastern Delta and the port of Damietta in part because he had already decided to attack Syria and needed this eastern region for logistical support.

The next day, on 24 December, Bonaparte himself set out with an expeditionary force to Suez. He followed the route the pilgrimage caravans plied on their way to the Muslim holy land, taking with him not only French soldiers and troops but an Egyptian entourage as well. His Egyptian companions included the great caravan merchant Ahmad al-Mahruqi, whom Bonaparte had rescued from the Bedouin near Bilbeis the previous summer, and Ibrahim Effendi, secretary of the spice trade, who narrowly escaped being executed for sedition after the Cairo revolt. The Coptic financier Jirjis al-Jawhari went along as well.[18] Given that he brought the Egyptian commercial and financial elite along with him, his trip to Suez in part aimed at preparing for the assertion of dominance over the trade of the Red Sea by the French Republic of Egypt, and for the expansion of that commerce. He would also want it fortified against an Ottoman or British counterattack during his planned campaign in Syria. Suez was an important link in Egyptian commerce with the Arabian Peninsula. From Suez, the Egyptians dispatched wheat to Jidda and Hudayba, and to it those merchants sent back valuable commodities such as coffee.

The opportunity to get out of Cairo no doubt also attracted the restless Corsican. On exiting the capital, Doguereau remembered, "The general in chief broke into a gallop, and we all rode hell for leather, our horses arriving winded."[19] The next day they entered the desert and camped that night in a desolate spot, shivering as the winter desert quickly radiated the heat it had borrowed from the daytime sun. They made a fire the Bedouin way by rubbing camel bones together. The chieftains of the Tarrabin and Bili tribes accompanied them and taught them how to mix into their grub some dry herbs they knew how to spot in the environs. What the French called the desert was most often not the completely desolate yellow sand dunes characteristic of, say, the deep Sahara. It was a brown and chartreuse land dotted with hardy shrubs. They arrived at Suez, horses exhausted, the night of 26 December, having outrun their baggage. Al-Jabarti complained that before the commander in chief arrived, French troops plundered coffee and other merchandise from the port.

On the twenty-seventh, Bonaparte toured Suez and ordered it fortified, lest the British prove able to land troops there from India. The few remaining local merchants complained to him about having been pillaged, and he promised to make restitution to them, asking for a list of what had been taken. One of the two larger vessels anchored at the port and bearing coffee from Yemen had sunk. Bonaparte had French divers bring the coffee up, according to al-Jabarti. The French conquest of Suez alarmed the merchants of the Red Sea ports, and Amir Ghalib of Mecca abruptly forbade ships to go there from Jidda. Bonaparte pursued a correspondence from Suez with notables of the Hejaz in nearby Arabia, urging them to resume trade ties with Egypt, and he wrote the sharif of Mecca personally. Despite his having received Sultan Selim III's declaration of war against the French, Amir Ghalib, on receiving Bonaparte's letter, showed an inclination to trade with Suez.[20]

On the twenty-eighth, Doguereau recalled, Bonaparte and some of his troops took advantage of a low tide to cross the Gulf of Suez at the head of the Red Sea, the water up to their horses' bellies, and easily reached the shore of the Sinai Peninsula on the other side. They drank the slightly brackish water of the springs called the "fountains of Moses." Bonaparte had the scientists look around, and they found the ruins of a square building and "a canal bringing water just to the shore of the sea. Our scientists supposed that that was the place where the Venetian ships came to take on water when that nation used to conduct commerce with India by the Red Sea." The commander in chief was also interested in the ancient shallow canal that classical sources alleged once linked the Red Sea to the Mediterranean. Such a canal would shave thousands of miles off the journey from Marseilles to India, and if the French could ever rebuild their fleet and more effectively challenge British naval superiority, it might allow them at last to challenge their rival in Asia. General Belliard spoke to one of the sheikhs of Tur who inquired about their interest in Sinai geography, telling him, "If this route is found practicable . . . the commerce of India will once again take its ancient course. Coffee, gums, all the products of Arabia, will flow on the Nile, and Egypt, become the entrepôt of the world, will recover its antique splendor."[21] India lurked in the background of this little expedition as both threat and promise in the long term.

At Bonaparte's insistence, they stayed in the peninsula longer than was wise, and darkness began falling. Their Bedouin guides, fearing an attempt to ford the water at night, had disappeared. The water, normally three to five feet deep, could surge in high winds and rough weather to double that. It submerged a mixture of harder soil, soft mud, and sandy patches that functioned as quicksand. During the day, riders could distinguish these three through the limpid water. At night, the passage turned treacherous, with horses sinking into mud or quicksand, and the tide rapidly rising. Not wanting to be marooned away from camp all night, the force of sixty men cautiously attempted the return, taking bridles in hand.

On the way back, Doguereau's horse, facing water almost as high as his back, tumbled into an underwater trough, and both rider and steed had to swim to the other shore. It is controversial whether Bonaparte had a similar mishap, and some say he had to be hauled along by his epaulettes at one point. The news reached Suez of the misadventure and caused a little panic, but no men were lost. It became a cliché among the memoirists that Bonaparte almost met the pharaoh's fate, of being drowned when the Red Sea closed up. The officers and troops likely drew the parallel because they felt themselves mired in Egypt like the ancient Hebrews and oppressed by a commander who was just as single-minded as Moses' royal nemesis.

The conquest of Egypt had all along been conceived by the French consul Charles Magallon, and probably by Bonaparte himself, as the first step toward a French attack on British India and the French recovery of its Indian possessions. Deprive Britain of India, the thinking went, and you reduce it from a maritime empire to a small island off the coast of Europe, ripe for the plucking. It made no sense to take 32,000 soldiers to Egypt (4,000 had been left in Malta), since conquering and holding that country simply did not need so huge a force. The initial plan had been for Bonaparte to intrigue with Indian potentates such as Tipu Sultan of Mysore, who was still resisting a British onslaught in the south, and to transport 20,000 men to India from the Red Sea. Late that fall an ambassador from Mysore arrived at Suez and came to Cairo to see Bonaparte. He said he had been robbed of his papers at Jidda, but he "assured him that Tipu Sahib was making great preparations and that he was counting a great deal on the arrival of the French. He wanted relations with Bonaparte."[22]

The conviction, often met with in officers' memoirs, that the Indian leg of the expedition had become impossible reflected the commander in chief's determination not to risk a mutiny by openly and prematurely broaching yet another arduous Oriental campaign. Lavalette maintained, "The political goal of the expedition had encountered a great obstacle in the loss of the fleet. It was no longer possible to think, even in the future, of taking the army to India, since the superiority of the British on all the seas had become incontestable."[23] Bonaparte had not entirely given up on an attack on India. Desvernois recalled how the Corsican, on his return from the exploratory expedition to the Red Sea, noticed the speed and agility of camels.[24] His aides-de-camp had learned to ride camels at a gallop. Bonaparte raced them on his horse but could not catch them. Desvernois said that Bonaparte became convinced that an army mounted on swift camels, a beast that could be acquired in large numbers in Egypt, could easily reach India. The invasion force would have probably gone to Syria and along the Tigris to Baghdad, turned east and gone up to Kermanshah in Iran, transited the Iranian plateau, entered Afghanistan, and then crossed through the Khyber pass down into North India.

This route resembled that of Alexander the Great in antiquity and had been followed more recently by the Iranian Nadir Shah in the 1730s and 1740s. He briefly put together a nomad-driven world empire that stretched from Baghdad to Delhi. Bonaparte's was a desperate and unlikely plan but not an impossible

one. The technique of Alexander and of Nadir had been to take territory in
lightning campaigns, to overtax the newly conquered to pay for their own conquest and to stake the commander to launch the next one. In each new territory,
new recruits signed up, eager to seek booty in the next fallen metropolis. The
successive triumphs and looting left behind wastelands rather than a flourishing
empire, and the conqueror's domain fragmented immediately on his death.
Bonaparte contemplated it not as a fixed plan but as one option among many.
Any such campaign in West and South Asia would in any case require that he
first break out of his Egyptian cage and bring Syria under his control.

In late January, Bonaparte wrote to Tipu Sultan, "You are of course already
informed of my arrival on the banks of the Red Sea, with a numerous and invincible army. Eager to deliver you from the iron yoke of England, I hasten to request that you will send me, by the way of Muscat or Mocha, an account of the
political situation in which you find yourself."[25]

Lavalette thought Bonaparte's best chance for improving on his catastrophic isolation was rather to regain the confidence of Selim III and break up
the Ottoman alliance with the British and the Russians. The commander in
chief now chose for a special mission the astronomer and Orientalist Joseph
Beauchamp. The latter had spent a decade in Ottoman Baghdad, where his
uncle was French consul, and had been commissioned by the French Academy
to fix the latitude and longitude of the Caspian Sea, a task prevented by the political turbulence of Iran at that time.[26] He had happened to be in Egypt when
the French troops landed. He had the linguistic abilities and experience in the
region to conduct delicate diplomacy. Venture de Paradis, Bonaparte's Arabic
interpreter, deeply distrusted local translators or dragomans and wanted French
diplomats to be able to negotiate in the local language.[27]

An Ottoman caravel rode at anchor off Alexandria, its captain taken prisoner by the French. The man, a notable in Istanbul, had his two children with
him. Bonaparte insisted that he leave them in Alexandria as hostages and then
proposed to him that he secretly transport Beauchamp to the Ottoman capital.
The captain, eager to be released and apparently confident that the British
would let him through, agreed to the plan. Beauchamp was to go first to Cyprus
and gather information about the military and political situation in the eastern
Mediterranean and to send back an espionage report. He was then to go on to
Istanbul and negotiate the release of French merchants and military personnel
who had been taken prisoner in Syria and to see to it that they were allowed to
return to France or to come to Egypt. He was also to conduct negotiations with
the grand vizier, intimating that the French would abandon Egypt under two

conditions. First, the British and Russians had to pledge not to attempt to take any of the Ottoman possessions in the Balkans. Second, the Ottomans had to renew their friendship with France and break off relations with the British and Russians. Beauchamp was to warn the Sublime Porte that a refusal to treat with France would trigger an invasion of Syria. In the event, the British captured Beauchamp and delivered him to the Ottomans, who imprisoned him with the other French diplomats in the Seven Towers. Bonaparte had given the Ottomans an ultimatum: negotiate with Beauchamp, or face an invasion of Syria. The invasion was on.

❧

Lavalette recalled that when he escorted Beauchamp to the port in late December, he met General Marmont, who was in charge of its security.[28] "You have arrived," he told him, "at a very bad time. . . . The plague was declared yesterday among our troops." He said that the order given when the French first arrived in Alexandria, that the clothing of anyone who came down with the plague should be burned, had not been fully implemented. The clothing of the stricken had been put back into circulation among the healthy Egyptians. "And since our troops have intimate relations with a section among them, the contact had caused the plague to develop among the French." That is, the French soldiers and officers were sleeping with local women. Marmont said that four had died the day before, and eight had been stricken.

Soon thirty persons were dying each day in Alexandria, counting both troops and civilian Egyptians. The general then ordered that the French troops stay in cantonments and away from the local population. Lavalette was skeptical about the idea of keeping the troops away from Egyptian women, since, he said, they were convinced that the plague was just something they would have to risk, "and relations of the soldiers with them continued despite the most severe discipline." As time went on, the French became so alarmed that they occasionally made war on prostitutes. "All the public women who are surprised having relations with the French are closed up in a sack and tossed in the water," the printer Galland remarked some time later.[29] Such measures were more an occasional hysteria than a systematic policy and hardly made a dent in the sex trade. Lavalette remembered being charged with ordering a military administrator, Michaud, and ten men to come from Rosetta to Alexandria. They lodged with Marmont. Two days later, Michaud was alone—all the others, he said, had died. One of them, Renaud, had gone to town to sign papers to receive his rations. The next morning his eyes were wild, his tongue thick, his sweat cold and abundant, and pain racked all his joints. The physician who came to see him examined him with a baton, at arm's length, and prescribed cold water. Toward the end Renaud asked for pen and paper to write his family.

French soldiers attempted to minimize the spread of the disease with quarantines and even body language. "We don't encounter one another except with suspicion, and carefully avoid touching one another or even being downwind of one another," Captain Thurman wrote in nearby Abuqir in late January. "When we assemble, something that only happens in an emergency, we arrange ourselves in a circle, keeping several feet away from one another. Promissory notes, orders, and letters are treated with vinegar and are picked up with a wooden pincer."[30] Millet, in Rosetta, recalled, "This disease begins with a high fever, and afterward a huge headache, with a bubo or gland that rises in the groin or some other juncture of one's members, which is as big as an egg. When it has come out, the stricken can hardly any longer be counted among the living. If four days, pass, there is much hope; but that happens only rarely. It is to that illness that we lost the greatest number in our army."[31]

Soon the progress of the plague in Alexandria and the port cities took on "a terrifying character." The French physicians began dying one after another. One officer joked darkly that as the news spread, the soldiers pursuing Murad Bey in Upper Egypt "are more afraid of us than of the Mamluks." It quickly became impossible to enter the small French military hospitals, and the stricken who could afford it hired expensive Muslim *hakims*, or traditional doctors trained in the Islamic version of ancient Greek medicine, to care for them. The *Canon*, the medical textbook in the Greek tradition produced by the medieval Muslim physician and philosopher Avicenna, had been widely taught in European medical schools in the late medieval and even early modern periods. Some Muslim medical thinkers had concluded that epidemics were spread by contagion, going beyond the ancient Greek emphasis on climate or astrology. The gap between Western and Middle Eastern medicine was not as great in the 1790s as we might now imagine, and the *hakims* had the advantage of practical experience with the disease.

We cannot assume that the French were always contracting what we would now call the plague, nor that they correctly perceived the sources of the outbreak. It is likely that the soldiers suffered from a range of diseases, including tuberculosis, scrofula, and anthrax. As for plague, there are three sorts: of the lymph nodes, of the lungs, and of the blood. For the most part, plague is transmitted by fleas infesting an animal such as a rat. French troops alleged that they caught bubonic plague, which takes several days to incubate. If so, they were contracting it from fleas, to which they were exposed in bordellos or in filthy, crowded, rat-infested apartments. Plague bacteria can also live in the soil. The onset of pneumonic plague, an infection of the lungs, can come quickly, even in a matter of hours, and the disease can also be spread by aerosol transmission, that is, through inhaling droplets of moisture in the breath of an infected person. Since Lavalette in his account of Renaud's illness did not mention the buboes or inflammatory swelling of the lymph gland characteristic of bubonic plague, the symptoms he reported would be most consistent with the pneumonic form of the disease, caught by the French from their Egyptian paramours or from the coughing of infected fellow soldiers. The French troops, not having been exposed to Egypt's endemic illnesses, had no antibodies to protect them from these exotic maladies.

The news that French troops were falling ill in Alexandria, Lavalette lamented, had encouraged the Bedouin outside the city to renew their attacks. The pastoralists had the advantage of being relatively impervious to epidemics, because they lived isolated from dense human habitation and away from disease vectors such as rats. They typically had good intelligence on epidemic outbreaks in cities and took advantage of weakened populations to loot them. Kléber, then at Damietta making preparations for the Syria campaign, received from Bonaparte a note that revealed the ways in which the onset of the disease affected those plans. He forwarded Bonaparte's comments to the divisional chief physician: "The letters sent to me from Mansura cause me to fear that the 2nd Light Infantry may be so infected with the contagious disease that it may be dangerous to put it in line with the other demi-brigades. Compose a detailed report of the situation of that demi-brigade and if you judge that it can transmit the contagious malady that torments it to other corps, you can send it back to Mansura."[32]

♣

The increasing reluctance of the physicians to expose themselves to stricken soldiers further demoralized them. Physicians who treated the stricken were at that time immured with them, and those who thought the disease contagious viewed this procedure as a death sentence. Alarmed, the commander in chief intervened forcefully. "Bonaparte learned that at Alexandria the chief of pharmacy, Boyer, had refused to care for those stricken by plague. He immediately issued an order: 'Boyer will be dressed as a woman and promenaded on an ass in the city with a sign saying, "He does not deserve to be a French citizen, he fears death." He will then be imprisoned and sent back to France.'"[33]

Marmont acted quickly, moving the French troops away from the interior of Alexandria, establishing an observation hospital in a large mosque, opening a special hospital for those already showing obvious symptoms, such as buboes, and establishing an active surveillance of the city, the two ports, and the hospital.[34] Even the commander in chief's fabled severity terrified his men less than did the fevers and buboes of the plague. When he could not prevail by strictness, he resorted, as usual, to propaganda, going so far into unreality as to deny the outbreak altogether. He wrote Dugua on 2 February, "The malady of which I informed you still exists, but its progress is less disquieting. . . . I gathered a commission of two physicians of this country, with one from the hospital; they examined all those fallen ill with fever and buboes. They declared that these had nothing in common with plague, and the cold, poor nourishment, and above all too much date juice were the principal causes."[35] It is difficult to believe that Dugua or anyone else paid much attention to these "findings," and they are contradicted by his own refusal to let the stricken troops at Mansura mingle with his other demi-brigades. Only the assertion that the outbreak had for the moment been contained was true. The significance of the outbreak lay in how it pointed toward a health threat that would dog the French military in succeeding months and years.

♣

The clerics in the Arabian Peninsula viewed Egypt as a near neighbor and as the strategic key to controlling the Red Sea littoral and the Islamic holy cities of Mecca and Medina. Although merchants and notables dependent on commerce with Egypt often cooperated with the new order, risking the wrath of the weak Ottoman government and that of the British navy, some of the more religiously committed in this region viewed the French conquest with outrage. The Yemeni historian Lutf Allah Jahhaf recounted the story of the Arabian response to the French invasion and the exploits of the volunteers who went off to fight a jihad against it in Upper Egypt.[36] He described Bonaparte's arrival, saying that "the hand of unbelief stretched out" to Egypt and conquered its Muslims, causing great corruption. In Yemen, a garbled account of the invasion had reached observers through the gossip network among Red Sea sailors and pilgrims. Jahhaf ascribed the expedition to the machinations of a great French merchant whom the Ottoman-Egyptian beys mistreated, a reference to Charles Magallon. But he made the consul the "son of their king." Magallon is said to have been imprisoned, then released, so that he returned to France and complained to "the sultan of their realm, Bonaparte." On hearing of the wealth of Egypt, he dropped everything else and prepared "his horses and camels," setting out in ships.

Jahhaf told a sort of fairy tale about Bonaparte first going to Istanbul to get permission from Selim III to transit Egypt on the way to India, and being initially refused, until finally the Ottoman sultan's chief wife relented and permitted it. Bonaparte then, however, conquered Malta out of his enmity with the British, which the Qur'an had predicted. And then he subdued Alexandria. Selim III became alarmed at these developments and prepared armies that would take the Syrian route in order to oppose this attack on his realm. Despite the inaccuracies and the *Thousand and One Nights* folktale elements, such as the softhearted empress, the narrative captured the dynamics of the conflict well enough. Some of the inaccuracy derived from Bonaparte's own tall tale that Selim III had sent him to Egypt.

Al-Jabarti related how news arrived in the Hejaz that the French "had conquered the lands around Cairo," and the people of Mecca went to the holy sanctuary, crying out, and they took down from the sacred Kaaba the drapery with which it had been adorned.[37] That drapery *(kiswa)* was typically made in Egypt and brought to Mecca with the annual pilgrimage caravan. The crowd announced by this action that the cosmic balance had been upset, that Islam itself had been denuded of one of its most resplendent embellishments. Jahhaf explained that one Sheikh Muhammad al-Jilani of North Africa began agitating for a jihad against the French. He preached to the people who gathered around him. Women came to listen to his speeches about the need for holy war and donated their jewelry, valuables, and even clothing to help fund the effort. He was helped in his preaching by Muhammad Ba Islah al-Hadrami, from southern Yemen, and then by numerous other helpers, who provided weapons, including muskets. Men from prominent clerical teaching families dedicated themselves to the cause, such as Muhammad al-Sindhi, grandson of Muhammad Hayat al-Sindhi, the great teacher of the sayings of the Prophet who contributed to the rise of eighteenth-century reformist movements in Islam.[38] The sharif of Mecca, Amir Ghalib, whom Bonaparte was then cultivating, and who had begun some forms of trade cooperation with the French, played both sides by also donating to al-Jilani.

News reached Mecca in December that in Upper Egypt the French were fighting Murad Bey's forces, just across the Red Sea from the Hejaz, defeating them and forcing them to retreat. The army of Desaix had been pursuing the former ruler of Egypt for months after having inflicted a severe setback on him at Sediman in October.[39] But Murad Bey had not been completely defeated, and conducted a fighting retreat up the Nile. Desaix had initially only commanded about 1,500 fighting troops, and had lacked cavalry. The emirs and their Mamluks, the Bedouin, and the peasants he faced therefore tended to melt away when he won an engagement. Bonaparte's relentless requisition of horses from the Delta had allowed him to assemble a cavalry unit of three hundred men, which he sent south with more infantry under General Davout in December.

Murad Bey himself and the sharif caste or putative descendants of the Prophet Muhammad in Upper Egypt are said by the memoirists to have been in touch with the Meccans and to have called for volunteers. Al-Jabarti wrote that some six hundred mujahidin, or holy warriors, gathered in Arabia and took a ship across the Red Sea to the Egyptian port of Qusayr, which the French had not yet proved able to capture. They were joined by further volunteers from the north Arabian port of Yanbu, above Jidda, so that the number of volunteers swelled to 2,000. These mujahidin caught up with Murad Bey's Mamluks, which were also joined by Hasan Bey Cuddavi and his Mamluks from Esna, and by reinforcements from Nubia. Their arrival much improved the morale of the Muslims in Upper Egypt. After his early January victory at Tahta, Desaix waited at Girga for the supply-laden French flotilla to catch up with him, since he had left it far behind as it struggled against northerly winds.

Belliard in his journal expressed the severest skepticism about rumors of the coming of an Arabian volunteer force. He wrote on 10 January, "The inhabitants continue to believe in the reinforcement that Murad Bey has received from Qusayr. It is no doubt a rumor that he surely spreads so as to encourage them to insurrection. For it is not at all credible that troops should arrive from Mecca. What interest would they have in making such a long voyage? And who would they be coming to aid? Men who are enemies of the Turks, and with whom they are almost always at war."[40] Belliard and other French officers, who expressed similar doubts, had so imbibed Bonaparte's propaganda about the beys as rebels against the sultan that they could not even imagine that Muslim solidarity and fury at infidel depredations might create an anti-French jihadi movement in the Hejaz. With the advantage of hindsight, Captain Desvernois recalled, "Murad profited from the French delay to engage in negotiations with the Arabs of Jidda and Yanbu, encouraging them to cross the sea to Qusayr and join up with him to exterminate the infidels come to destroy the religion of Muhammad."

A battle brewed at the small Upper Egyptian town of Samhud.[41] Murad Bey still had 1,500 emirs and Mamluks, and Hasan Bey had brought him another 400 troops. Another Hasan, of Yanbu, commanded between 1,000 and 2,000 jihadis from Arabia. Some 7,000 Bedouin cavalrymen rode with Murad, accompanied by 3,000 Egyptian infantry irregulars. On 18 January, just in the nick of time, the flotilla caught a favorable wind and arrived at Girga with supplies. On 20 January Desaix and his forces departed Girga. On the twenty-first, as he advanced, Desvernois saw fleeing toward him a crowd of Copts who had been sent as tax collectors by Desaix. They informed him that Murad Bey and his supporters had taken up a strong position at the village of Samhud. Copts, especially numerous in Upper Egypt, sometimes gave key support to the French there.

Desaix later wrote to Bonaparte, "Our advance guard, composed of the 7th Hussars, had two platoons in front, commanded by Captain [Desvernois]. They were suddenly assailed by the troops from Mecca, supported by some Mamluks." The implication is that the volunteers, armed mainly with lances, were on foot, facing French light cavalry. The French pushed them back. "Finding themselves hard pressed, they made an about-face, and running through twenty of them with sabers was the affair of a moment." The jihadis managed to put a bullet through one French cavalryman.

Desaix then had his infantry form two big squares, with artillery on their wings and the cavalry enclosed in one of them, and they marched on Samhud. He detailed two companies of musketeers, supported by a light cavalry Hussar platoon led by Desvernois, to attack the village defended by "the sharifs of Mecca." He recalled, "The enemy was on the bank of a canal. They put up a vigorous resistance." The holy warriors killed a musketeer and wounded Desaix's aide-de-camp, Rapp, while Desvernois suffered a dagger cut to the tendons of his forearm, forcing him to wield his saber left-handed as he struggled to escape the battlefield. He managed to ride into the center of an infantry square, bloody and covered with dozens of cuts.

It was now the turn of the French, Desaix gloated. As the enemy closed in too near for shooting, the musketeers made a bayonet charge and wielded the butts of their weapons with deadly effect, killing thirty. "And the village was ours." The rest of the battle was predictable, with the infantry squares and artillery impenetrable to their opponents' cavalry. With reinforcements, Desaix had 2,500 men, including light cavalry, and was better placed to win than he had been earlier. The Ottoman Egyptians charged, firing at will and uttering fearsome war cries, then met the wall of muskets and bayonets and cascading cannonballs that had pushed them inexorably toward the African interior. Desaix and Davout glimpsed Murad at the head of his cavalrymen and exposed, and Davout took out after him with the French Hussars, but the beys and their Mamluks vanished.

The Meccan volunteers had not made the difference in the battle, though as untrained civilians they had brought no dishonor on themselves, either. They did, however, greatly improve morale for Murad and his allies who continued to fight against the French occupation in Upper Egypt. Nor was this the last contingent of such volunteers to arrive in Egypt from the Hejaz. The significance of the mujahidin lay elsewhere than in the likelihood that seminarians and townspeople could by dint of sheer enthusiasm bring down a modern European army. The jihadis were a harbinger that the Muslim world was gathering against the French. The Muslim world was not led politically by Mecca but by Istanbul. Sultan Selim III was in a better position than al-Jilani to raise trained and well-equipped holy warriors who could make a stand against the Republican army. He was also willing to ally with powerful Christian empires in a way that would not have occurred to al-Jilani, but which increased the effectiveness of his riposte by several orders of magnitude. Not mere religious enthusiasm but steadfast, cultured, and pragmatic faith had the better chance of success.

Bonaparte marshaled 10,000 troops in early February to begin the assault on Cezzar Pasha's forces in Syria, preparing to face the sultan's holy war in earnest. The other challenges that he faced that winter in Egypt, whether recalcitrant Bedouin and villagers unwilling to submit to crushing taxes and expropriation or the spread of plague and other infectious diseases among his troops, were omens of things to come rather than obstacles surmounted. It was clear that the Egyptian public alone could not throw off the French yoke, however hard it tried, though it likely had already killed a few thousand soldiers altogether and over time could inflict substantial attrition. Six months into the occupation, the French had likely killed at least 12,000 Egyptians. The French had a marginal advantage over the Egyptians in organization, tactics, and quality of weaponry. It was small enough, but it was sufficient in the medium term.

Bonaparte thought of himself as having remade Egypt, but his impact was so far superficial. He was deeply in debt, and his troops' pay months in arrears. The Islamic legitimacy he had quixotically sought still escaped him whenever he was not physically present among the clergy. The Delta was still unsettled, especially in the west. The parliament of saints was restless, and millenarian noises were bruited abroad. As long as Murad Bey eluded Desaix, Upper Egypt and the Red Sea remained the soft underbelly of the French Republic of Egypt. Bonaparte's army was marooned without a fleet and facing steady attrition from battle, disease, and sabotage. His one chance to rescue triumph from the maw of failure lay not in further securing Egypt but in breaking out of it and finding a way to neutralize the deadliest menace to his enterprise, the second Grand Coalition.

♣

Bonaparte led his force of 10,000 men against Cezzar Pasha, who was making preparations to invade French Egypt, in early February. His army took the Mediterranean city of El Arish, the gateway to the Sinai Peninsula and to Ottoman Syria, on 20 February, after a weeklong siege. Five days later he had Gaza. In early March the French besieged Jaffa, and brought dishonor on French arms by the massacre they conducted there when it fell to them on the 8 March. Even worse was the execution, ordered by Bonaparte, of several thousand unarmed Ottoman prisoners of war. By 18 March the French were before the fortress of Acre.

Bonaparte had not been able to bring heavy artillery overland. He attempted to ship some big field pieces from Damietta, but his transport vessels were captured by the British and they never arrived. With only light artillery, Bonaparte was never able to punch a hole in the walls of the Crusader fortress where Cezzar and his troops were ensconced. Bonaparte struck again and again. Stubborn, inattentive to the cost in the lives of his troops, desperate because he knew that the success of his entire campaign in the Orient hung in the balance, the commander in chief threw his men at the fortress no less than thirteen times, and they were beaten back every time by the newly reformed, Western-drilled army of Cezzar, who enjoyed naval backing from the British. Several of the officers we met above, including the engineer, Captain Horace Say, and the peg-legged General Caffarelli, died fighting in Syria.

By late May, Bonaparte had reluctantly accepted defeat at Acre. His forces simply could not take the fortress, and without it could not hope to take Syria. He returned to Cairo, his troop strength much depleted by battles and plague, but he put out propaganda about the campaign having been a glorious success. He and his bedraggled soldiers did a victory lap around the Egyptian capital, and he issued another of his Muslim decrees as the great Sultan, promising to build a huge mosque in honor of his triumph.

In late July, the British navy landed an Ottoman expeditionary force of 15,000 men at Abuqir, near Alexandria. General Murat's cavalry fought it off, but at the cost of several hundred French lives. The Abuqir campaign clearly pointed toward the future, in which the French, boxed up in Egypt, would face repeated attempts to dislodge them by joint British and Ottoman forces, and would suffer from steady attrition. The Army of the Orient had already lost nearly 6,000 fighting men since the campaign began. In France that summer, however, the victory at Abuqir played as another token of military glory.

Bonaparte knew a dead end when he saw one. He secretly slipped out of the country in August, leaving behind a note for the surprised General Kléber informing him that he was henceforth in charge of Egypt. Equally surprised to be left behind was Pauline Fourès, his paramour. The Corsican arrived in France on October 9 and went straight to Paris, where he began to intrigue. In November of 1799 he came to power as First Consul through a coup. He reconciled with Josephine.

Back in Egypt, Kléber finally convinced Murad Bey to ally with the French, but soon thereafter the old Georgian died of plague. Kléber was assassinated by a disgruntled Egyptian in the summer of 1800, and succeeded by the inept and brutal Abdullah Menou. The Ottoman and British military alliance forced the Army of the Orient out of Egypt in 1801, and the remaining French troops were given safe passage back to France on British vessels. Many of our memoirists came back home in that humiliating way, including Captain Moiret (who thereby lost his Zulayma), Captain Desvernois, and the Jacobin designer of uniforms, François Bernoyer. Pauline Fourès had slipped out of Egypt in 1800 after an earlier attempt failed, and after an alleged dalliance with General Kléber. She remarried, divorced again in 1816, and then went off to Brazil to start a lumber business. Returning to France in 1837, she lived to an advanced age.

Ibrahim Bey lived to see the old beylicate in Egypt replaced by the rule of an Albanian Ottoman officer and later the sultan's viceroy, Mehmet Ali Pasha. Mehmet Ali wiped out most of the remaining Mamluks in an 1811 massacre at the Citadel and embarked on new policies of modern authoritarian rule, some of which imitated Bonaparte's. Ibrahim died in irrelevancy in 1818.

Bonaparte's Egyptian experience shaped his own subsequent policies more than European historians generally admit. In 1804, he crowned himself emperor, an office more customary in the Middle East than in revolutionary France. The habits of sexual prerogative for the great Sultan, which he first acquired in Egypt, continued to roil his marriage with Josephine, though she became his empress (until he divorced her in 1810). Through the Concordat, Napoleon sought the same sort of accord with the Catholic Church as he had had with the Muslim clerics of al-Azhar, for the sake of social peace. In creating Bonaparte as the Great Sultan, the grand emperor, over the Nile Valley, the Directory had accustomed him to a station in life that he proved unwilling to relinquish. France itself, and much of Europe, met the fate that the Directors and Talleyrand had intended for Egypt.

EPILOGUE

*T*he French invasion and occupation of Egypt in 1798–1801 have served as a litmus test for sentiments about the enterprise of empire among historians and their publics. Bonaparte, having become Emperor Napoleon I, was among the first to recognize that the fiasco along the Nile had the potential for undermining his reputation, and he ordered many of the state papers for the French Republic of Egypt burned. Some military records and dispatches have survived, and a great many have been published (notably at the turn of the twentieth century by the invaluable Clément de la Jonquière), but it seems clear that Napoleon intended his own memoir of the invasion and occupation to substitute for the suppressed archive. His hope proved forlorn, inasmuch as scholars have strangely neglected Bonaparte as Orientalist. As it happened, his account has had to compete with the narratives of a cloud of other witnesses, Egyptian and French, which often have the virtue of contradicting Bonaparte's propaganda.[1]

In the first half of the twentieth century, French historians such as François Charles-Roux read the occupation as a prologue to what they saw as the glories of French Algeria.[2] They depicted Egyptian peasants as overjoyed at the French invasion and they downplayed its brutality and cupidity. Early twentieth-century Egyptian nationalists often, ironically enough, also viewed Bonaparte's expedition as the irruption into a traditional society of dynamic modernity, bringing with it printing, the press, modern commerce, hospitals, and science, including the archeology that eventually allowed the recovery of Egypt's Pharaonic past through the decipherment of the Rosetta Stone.

Subsequent historians pointed out that Egypt had been in intense economic and diplomatic interaction with Europe and the Greater Mediterranean in the eighteenth century and was hardly virgin wilderness to be "discovered" or introduced to modernity by Bonaparte. They argued that, moreover, most of the specific innovations imported by the Army of the Orient did not survive the French departure in 1801, and that on the ground there was little long-term impact, save perhaps for the killing of tens of thousands and the disruption of Ottoman-Egyptian society.[3] Decolonization in the 1950s and 1960s caused historians to view the incursion with greater skepticism. The earlier Egyptian romantic nationalist view of the French period gave way after the officers' coup of 1952 to a depiction of it as a mere colonial occupation.

Bonaparte would have found it more humiliating for his project to be ignored than to be critiqued. With the end of the colonial era in the 1960s, French imperial history declined as a preoccupation of scholars. Historians anachronistically began to project the postcolonial metropole back into time, so that they write the history of France, and Britain likewise, within their present borders, as though these two did not between them rule two-fifths of the world in the nineteenth century.[4] In most contemporary synthetic treatments of modern France, Egypt, Algeria, and Vietnam barely make cameo appearances. François Furet typified this syndrome when he wrote, "I will omit the Egyptian expedition from this account, because it forms a special history of its own, independent of French events, but essential to an understanding of the Eastern question in the nineteenth century."[5] The modern history of countries such as Egypt, for their part, is increasingly written from their own archives in an internalist manner that downplays crucial colonial and neocolonial interventions. The social historians of the 1970s and after pronounced the French interlude in Egypt trivial in its impact on the secular rhythms of the Egyptian economy and the distribution of wealth in society, and therefore as unworthy of having words wasted on it.[6]

Literary critic Edward Said, in his seminal *Orientalism*, put Bonaparte's Egypt back at the center of a scholarly debate about imperialism and postcolonial ways of knowing the world. He depicted the invasion as the European pursuit of total knowledge of and total control over an Oriental society, as the original sin in the modern nexus of hegemonic Western power and knowledge.[7] Said's critique was widely influential. When French and Egyptian authorities planned a joint bicentennial commemoration that would focus on the positive legacy of the invasion, popular outcry forced the Egyptian minister of culture to cancel Cairo's part in it.[8] In Paris, the French National Assembly responded to such severe critiques of colonial policy by attempting, in 2005, to pass a law that would have compelled teachers to stress the positive accomplishments of the French Empire. President Jacques Chirac found this measure excessive and vetoed it.

Bonaparte's was the first modern attempt to incorporate a major Near Eastern society into a European empire. It was not the last. What we now call the Middle East is not only a congeries of nation-states with internal histories, but a set of thick interactions with dominant global powers. But so, too, has the international order been crafted by Middle Eastern politicians and publics, as when the Algerian FLN (National Liberation Front) expelled the French from that country in 1962 and established a new relationship with the former metropole. European colonialism did not end because that was what then French President Charles DeGaulle wanted. It ended because Middle Eastern politicians and publics ceased being willing to cooperate with it, and because they had gained the tools to stand up to it (through urbanization, industrialization, better education, better communications, more organizational capacity through political parties, and more advanced technology, including military technology). The end of large-scale direct colonialism in the 1950s and 1960s ushered in an era of North Atlantic neoimperialism, with economic penetration now the major expression of domination, along with occasional, targeted military interventions. It also initiated a wave of unprecedented Middle Eastern immigration into Western Europe that has had a profound impact on European politics and even foreign policy. As a result, the meaning of Frenchness itself is being renegotiated.

Bonaparte's expedition was not, as many historians have seen it, an aberration in an otherwise Eurocentric career. He was pioneering a form of imperialism that deployed Liberal rhetoric and institutions for the extraction of resources and geopolitical advantage. As emperor, he continued to take a keen interest in Levantine trade. His vision of an imperial France with valuable overseas possessions was realized by later French governments. Even his premonition of the end of the Ottoman Empire, and the way European powers would carve it up, was vindicated during and after World War I. In his often cruel and cynical way, Bonaparte was inventing what we now call "the modern Middle East," an arena of North Atlantic military and economic hegemony with a hybrid culture and political institutions. The similarities of the Corsican general's rhetoric and tactics to those of later North Atlantic incursions into the region tell us about the persistent pathologies of Enlightenment republics. As Edward Said wrote, the enterprise was "To restore a region from its present barbarism to its former classical greatness; to instruct (for its own benefit) the Orient in the ways of the modern West; to subordinate or underplay military power in order to aggrandize the project of glorious knowledge acquired in the process of political domination of the Orient . . . with full recognition of its place in memory, its importance to imperial strategy, and its 'natural' role as an appendage to Europe."[9] A binary opposition of Western hegemony and Middle

Eastern resistance, however, cannot capture the full complexity of these rela-tionships. Successful imperialists are by definition dominant, but the discourse of the conquered subject is not without its own cultural power.[10] How to make sense of Bonaparte's defense of the Prophet Muhammad from Voltaire, or Sheikh 'Abdullah al-Sharqawi's approval of the French introduction of govern-ing councils in the Egyptian provinces? The contradictory detail of the mem-oirs, recounted in this book, suggests that in order to understand colonialism we must appreciate the mutual appropriation of cultural forms by colonized and colonizer.

Still, the major conflicts between the French and the Egyptians were not driven by culture but by contests over power and resources, cleverly reworked by Bonaparte into a rhetorical battle between liberty and fanaticism. Which side championed which with more fervor became murkier and murkier as time went on.

FURTHER READING

Recent good biographies of Napoléon Bonaparte include those of Alex Schom and Robert B. Asprey. Readers seeking a better understanding of eighteenth-century France should look at the works of Robert Darnton, Lynn Hunt, Roger Chartier, D. M. G. Sutherland, and Howard Brown, among many others. French attitudes toward the Middle East in this period are discussed by the late Edward Said in his *Orientalism* (New York: Vintage Books, 1978, 2003 [with a new introduction]).

English-language readers desiring more background on modern Egypt should consult Afaf Lutfi al-Sayyid Marsot's *Short History of Modern Egypt* (Cambridge: Cambridge University Press, 1985) and her *Egypt in the Reign of Muhammad Ali* (Cambridge: Cambridge University Press, 1984). Also invaluable is M. W. Daly, ed., *The Cambridge History of Egypt*, vol. 2: *Modern Egypt, from 1517 to the End of the Twentieth Century* (Cambridge: Cambridge University Press, 1998). The houses of the beys and their Mamluks are analyzed in Jane Hathaway, *The Politics of Households in Ottoman Egypt: The Rise of the Qazdaglis* (Cambridge: Cambridge University Press, 2002). For our period, a primary source is available in paperback: 'Abd al-Rahman al-Jabarti, *Napoleon in Egypt: Al-Jabarti's Chronicle of the French Occupation, 1798*, trans. Shmuel Moreh (Princeton and New York: Markus Wiener Publishing, 1995). J. Christopher Herold, *Bonaparte in Egypt* (New York: Harper & Row, 1962) republished by Pen and Sword in 2005, remains valuable despite the author's dismissive attitude toward and relative lack of knowledge of Arab culture, and has the advantage of covering the entire three years of the French occupation. For the military history side, see David G. Chandler, *The Campaigns of Napoleon* (New York: Macmillan, 1966).

Several of the French memoirs have been translated, including Jean-Pierre Doguereau, *Guns in the Desert: General Jean-Pierre Doguereau's Journal of Napoleon's Egyptian Expedition*, trans. Rosemary Brindle (Westport, Conn.: Praeger, 2002), and Joseph-Marie Moiret, *Memoirs of Napoleon's Egyptian Expedition, 1798–1801*, trans. Rosemary Brindle (London: Greenhill Books, 2001).

NOTES

CHAPTER 1

1. John R. Elting, *Swords Around a Throne: Napoleon's Grande Armée* (New York: Da Capo Press, 1997), p. 33. Joseph-Marie Moiret, *Mémoires sur l'expédition d'Égypt* (Paris: Pierre Belfond, 1984), p. 33; quotes in following paragraphs are from this same source, pp. 23, 25–26. The English translation appeared after I had written most of the passages where it is quoted, and so the translations of it below are my own, and citations are to the French text.

2. Auguste Frédéric Louis Viesse de Marmont, *Mémoires du duc de Raguse de 1792 à 1832* (Paris: Parrotin, 1857), p. 350.

3. Jean-Honoré Horace Say with Louis Laus de Boissy, *Bonaparte au Caire* (Paris: Prault, 7 R. [1799]), p. 3. This book was published anonymously, but Gabriel Guémard convincingly showed from internal evidence collated with Bonaparte's correspondence that it must have been written by Say, a captain in the engineering corps who died in the Palestine campaign in 1799. See Gabriel Guémard, *Histoire et bibliographie critique de la commission des sciences et arts et de l'Institut d'Égypte* (Cairo: Chez l'Auteur, 1936), pp. 94–95. Say had managed to spirit this manuscript back to France in 1799 with Louis Bonaparte, and it came into the hands of the minor playwright Louis Laus de Boissy (who was in the salon of Josephine Bonaparte), who admits to having extensively reworked it. I see the book as coauthored. For Say, see J.-M. Quérard, *La France littéraire ou dictionnaire bibliographique*, 12 vols. (Paris: Firmin Didot Frères, 1827–1864), 8:500. For Laus de Boissy, see ibid., 4:625–626, and Nicolas Toussaint Lemoyne Desessarts, *Les siècles littéraires de la France*, 7 vols. (Paris: Chez l'auteur, Imprimeur-Libraire, 1800–1803), 7:302–303 via Google Books at http://books.google.com/books?id=TsJ6W15Fj7wC&vid=OCLC05719202&dq=Louis+de+Laus+de+Boissy&jtp=302.

4. Charles Coulston Gillispie, "Scientific Aspects of the French Egyptian Expedition, 1798–1801," *Proceedings of the American Philosophical Society* 133, no. 4 (Dec. 1989), pp. 447–474; Patrice Bret, ed. *L'Expédition d'Égypte, une enterprise des Lumières, 1798–1801* (Paris: Technique & Documentation, 1999).

5. Napoléon Bonaparte, *Lettres d'amour à Joséphine*, ed. Chantal de Tourtier Bonazzi (Paris: Fayard, 1981), pp. 46–47; the letter from Bologna cited below is from pp. 137–138.

6. J. Christopher Herold, *Bonaparte in Egypt* (New York: Harper & Row, 1962), p. 4.

7. Jean-Gabriel de Niello Sargy, *D'Égypte*, vol. 1 of M. Alph. de Beauchamp, ed., *Mémoires secrets et inédits pour servir à l'histoire contemporaine*, 2 vols. (Paris: Vernarel et Tenon, 1825); Christopher Hibbert, *Waterloo: Napoleon's Last Campaign* (London: Wordsworth, 2005), p. 43.

8. Lynn Hunt, *Politics, Culture and Class in the French Revolution* (Berkeley: University of California Press, 1984), p. 21.

9. Say/Boissy, pp. 14–15.

10. Quotations in this paragraph are from Napoléon Bonaparte, *Correspondence de Napoléon Ier*, 34 vols. (Paris: H. Plon, J. Dumaine, 1858–1870), 4:109, 4:113.

11. F. E. Sanglée-Ferrière et al., *L'Expédition d'Égypte: Souvenirs, mémoires, et correspondence* (Paris: Librairie Historique F. Teissèdre, 1998), pp. 23–24; Louis Joseph Bricard, *Journal du canonnier Bricard, 1792–1802* (Paris: C. Delagrave, 1891), p. 299.

12. François Bernoyer, *Avec Bonaparte en Égypte et en Syrie, 1798–1800: Dix-neuf lettres inédits,* ed. Christian Tortel (Abbeville: Les Presses Françaises, 1976), p. 20. Quotation cited below is also from p. 20.

13. Malcolm Crook, *Toulon in War and Revolution* (Manchester: Manchester University Press, 1991).

14. Jean-Joël Brégeon, *L'Égypte française au jour le jour, 1798–1801* (Paris: Perrin, 1991), p. 97.

15. Samuel Taylor Coleridge, *Confessions of an Inquiring Spirit* (New York: Cassell & Co., 1892), < http://ibiblio.org/gutenberg/etext01/cfinq10.txt>.

16. Désiré Lacroix, *Bonaparte en Egypte (1798–1799),* (Paris: Garnier, 1899), pp. 43–44; Roderick Cavaliero, *The Last of the Crusaders: the Knights of St. John and Malta in the Eighteenth Century* (London: Hollis & Carter, 1960), pp. 216–220.

17. Napoléon I, *Napoleon's Memoirs,* ed. Somerset de Chair (New York: Howard Fertig, 1988), p. 279.

18. Napoléon, *Corr.* 4:155, no. 2665.

19. The bibliography for the French expedition to Egypt is vast. Most of it is covered in Darrell Dykstra, "The French Occupation of Egypt, 1798–1801," in M. W. Daly, ed., *The Cambridge History of Egypt,* vol. 2: *Modern Egypt, from 1517 to the End of the Twentieth Century* (Cambridge: Cambridge University Press, 1998), pp. 113–138. The major synthetic account in English remains J. Christopher Herold, *Bonaparte in Egypt* (New York: Harper & Row, 1962). Bonaparte's Egypt campaign is told as military history in David G. Chandler, *The Campaigns of Napoleon* (New York: Macmillan, 1966), pp. 212–245. In addition to the works listed by Dykstra, recent monographs include Henry Laurens et al., *L'Expédition d'Égypte: 1798–1801* (Paris: A. Colin, 1989), André Raymond, *Égyptiens et Français au Caire, 1798–1801* (Cairo: Institut Français d'Archéologie Orientale, 1998); Patrice Bret, *L'Égypte, au temps de l'expédition de Bonaparte: 1798–1801* (Paris: Hachette littératures, 1998); Yves Laissus, *L'Egypte, une aventure savante: avec Bonaparte, Kléber, Menou 1798–1801* (Paris: Fayard, 1998); and Jean-Jacques Luthi, *Regard sur l'Égypte au temps de Bonaparte* (Paris: Harmattan, 1999).

20. Charles Maurice de Talleyrand, *Essai sur les avantages à retirer de colonies nouvelles dans les circonstances présentes* (Paris: Chez Baudouin, Imprimeur de l'Institut National, R. 5 [1797]); Carl Ludwig Lokke, "French Dreams of Colonial Empire Under Directory and Consulate," *Journal of Modern History* 2, no. 2 (Jun. 1930), pp. 237–250; subsequent quotations of Talleyrand, Eschasseriaux, etc., are from this article unless otherwise noted. For a long view of the background to the invasion, see Henry Laurens, *Les Origines intellectuelles de l'expédition d'Égypte: L'Orientalisme Islamisant en France (1698–1798)* (Istanbul and Paris: Editions Isis, 1987).

21. Vincent Confer, "French Colonial Ideas Before 1789," *French Historical Studies* 3, no. 3 (Spring, 1964), pp. 338–359; Michel Poniatowski, *Talleyrand et le Directoire, 1796–1800* (Paris: Librairie Académique Perrin, 1982), pp. 66–74.

22. Bonaparte/Directory, 16 August 1797, in François Charles-Roux, *Les Origines de l'expédition d'Égypte* (Paris: Librairie Plon, 1910), chap. 10; this quotation appears on p. 298. Subsequent paragraphs here are also based on Charles-Roux.

23. Elements of this dossier survive in the papers of the man who became Bonaparte's Arabic interpreter: Jean Michel Venture de Paradis, *Papiers,* Bibliothèque Nationale, Département des Manuscrits, 9135.

24. Howard G. Brown, "Mythes et Massacres: Reconsidérer la 'Terreur Directoriale,'" *Annales Historiques de la Révolution française,* no. 325 (2001), pp. 23–52; this quotation appears on p. 27. This and the next paragraph are indebted to Brown. For France in this period see Isser Woloch, *Jacobin Legacy: The Democratic Movement Under the Directory* (Princeton: Princeton University Press, 1970); Martyn Lyons, *France Under the Directory* (Cambridge: Cambridge University Press, 1975); Jean Tulard, *La France de la Révolution et de l'Empire* (Paris: Presses Universitaires de France, 1995); D. M. G. Sutherland, *The French Revolution and Empire: The Quest for a Civic Order* (London: Blackwell, 2003).

25. André François Miot de Melito, *Mémoires du comte Miot de Melito, ancien ministre, ambassadeur, conseiller d'état et membre de l'Institut,* 3 vols. (Paris, Michel Lévy Frères, 1858), 1: 163; cited in Alan Schom, *Napoleon Bonaparte* (New York: Harper Perennial, 1998), pp. 64–67.

26. Paul François Barras, *Mémoires de Barras, membre du Directoire*, ed. Georges Duruy (Paris: Hachette, 1895), pp. 184, 205–215.
27. Howard G. Brown, *War, Revolution and the Bureaucratic State: Politics and Army Administration in France, 1791–1799* (Oxford: Clarendon Press, 1995), pp. 216–219.
28. Elie Krettly, *Souvenirs Historiques*, 2nd ed. (Paris: Nouveau Monde Editions, 2003), p. 42.
29. Louis Antoine Fauvelet de Bourrienne, *Memoirs of Napoleon Bonaparte*, ed. R.W. Phipps, 4 vols. (New York: Charles Scribner's Sons, 1892), p. 131.
30. See Roger Chartier, "Dechristianization and secularization," in *The Cultural Origins of the French Revolution*, trans. Lydia G. Cochrane (Durham, N.C.: Duke University Press, 1991), chap. 5.; Charles Gliozzo, "The Philosophes and Religion: Intellectual Origins of the Dechristianization Movement in the French Revolution," *Church History* vol. 40, no. 3 (Sep. 1971), pp. 273–283.
31. Napoléon, *Corr.*, 4:135, no. 2633.
32. Napoléon I, *Napoleon's Memoirs*, p. 350.
33. F. E. Sanglée-Ferrière et al., *L'Expédition d'Égypte*, p. 36.

CHAPTER 2

1. Napoléon Bonaparte, *Correspondence de Napoléon Ier*, 34 vols. (Paris: H. Plon, J. Dumaine, 1858–1870), 4:190, no. 2721.
2. François Bernoyer, *Avec Bonaparte en Égypte et en Syrie, 1798–1800: dix-neuf lettres inédits*, ed. Christian Tortel (Abbeville: Les Presses françaises, 1976), p. 41. Subsequent Bernoyer quotations in this section are from this same source. Bonaparte's Egypt campaign is told as military history in David G. Chandler, *The Campaigns of Napoleon* (New York: Macmillan, 1966), pp. 212–245.
3. Joseph-Marie Moiret, *Mémoires sur l'expédition d'Égypt* (Paris: Pierre Belfond, 1984), p. 33; The English translation of this source appeared after I had written most of the passages where it is quoted, and so the translations of it below are my own, and citations are to the French text. See *Memoirs of Napoleon's Egyptian Expedition, 1798–1801*, trans. Rosemary Brindle (London: Greenhill Books, 2001).
4. Daniel Crecelius, "The Mamluk Beylicate of Egypt," in Thomas Philipp and Ulrich Haarman, eds., *The Mamluks in Egyptian Politics and Society* (Cambridge: Cambridge University Press, 1998), pp. 128–149; Jane Hathaway, *The Politics of Households in Ottoman Egypt: The Rise of the Qazdaglis* (Cambridge: Cambridge University Press, 1997).
5. *Correspondance intime de l'armée d'Égypte, interceptée par la croisière anglaise* (Paris: R. Pincebourde, 1866), p. 11.
6. Grandjean, "Journal," in Gaston Wiet, ed., *Journaux sur l'expédition d'Égypte* (Paris: Librairie Historique F. Teissedre, 2000), p. 63. This is a reprint of the 1943 Cairo edition, published by the *Revue du Caire*, which mysteriously omits Wiet's name as editor and gives none of the previous publication history.
7. Grandjean, ibid., p. 66.
8. Charles Norry, *An Account of the French Expedition to Egypt: Comprehending a View of the Country of Lower Egypt, its Cities, Monuments, and Inhabitants, at the Time of the Arrival of the French; . . .* Translated from the French (London, 1800), pp. 26–27 (source: Eighteenth Century Collections Online. Gale Group, <http://galenet.galegroup.com.proxy.lib.umich.edu/servlet/ECCO>).
9. Moiret, p. 36. Moiret quotations in ensuing paragraphs: pp. 36, 37.
10. Julia V. Douthwaite, *Exotic Women: Literary Heroines and Cultural Strategies in Ancien Régime France* (Philadelphia: University of Pennsylvania Press, 1992).
11. Napoléon, *Corr.*, 4:198–199, no. 2733.
12. For inequality in the Directory era, see Martin Lyons, *France Under the Directory* (Cambridge: Cambridge University Press, 1975), chapter 5.
13. Izzet Hasan Efendi Darendeli, *Al-Hamlah al-Firansiyyah 'ala Misr fi Daw' Makhtut 'Uthmani*, trans. Jamal Sa'id 'Abd al-Ghani (Cairo: al-Hay'ah al-Misriyyah al-'Ammah li'l-Kitab, 1999), p. 138.

14. Napoléon, *Corr.*, 4:228, no. 2784.
15. Pierre Amedée Jaubert/brother, 20 Messidor 6 (8 July 8, 1798), in *Copies of Original Letters from the Army of General Bonaparte in Egypt, Intercepted by the Fleet under the Command of Admiral Lord Nelson.* Part the first. With an English translation. (London, 1798, 9th ed.), p. 19 (in Eighteenth Century Collections Online. Gale Group, <http://galenet.galegroup.com.proxy.lib.umich.edu/servlet/ECCO>). The second letter discussed in this paragraph is from the same source, p. 31.
16. 'Abd al-Rahman Al-Jabarti, *Ta'rikh, Muddat al-faransis bi misr,* ed. Abd al-Rahim A. Abd al-Rahim (Cairo: Dar al-Kitab al-Jami'i, 2000), pp. 33–41; idem, *Napoleon in Egypt: Al-Jabarti's Chronicle of the French Occupation, 1798,* trans. Shmuel Moreh (Princeton and New York: Markus Wiener Publishing, 1995), pp. 27–33.
17. Al-Jabarti, *Mudda,* pp. 41–46; idem, *Napoleon,* pp. 33–35; 'Abd al-Rahman al-Jabarti, *Muzhir al-taqdis bi dhihab dawlat al-faransis* (Cairo: Matba'at al-Risalah, 1969), pp. 36–39; 'Abd al-Rahman al-Jabarti, *'Aja'ib al-athar fi al-tarajim wa al-akhbar,* 4 vols. (Bulaq: al-Matba'ah al-Amiriya, 1322/1904, 2nd ed.), 3:4; *'Abd al-Rahman al-Jabarti's History of Egypt ('Ajaib al-athar fi 'l-tarajim wa-'l-akhbar: text),* trans. and ed. Thomas Philipp & Moshe Perlmann (Stuttgart: Franz Steiner Verlag, 1994). This English translation is keyed to the Bulaq text, so only the original page numbers will be given here, but I warmly acknowledge the great value of the translation to my own book, and often quote it below. For the panic in Cairo, see also André Raymond, *Égyptiens et Français au Caire, 1798–1801* (Cairo: Institut Français d'Archéologie Orientale, 1998), pp. 91–93.
18. Al-Jabarti, *'Aja'ib,* 3:3–4.
19. Moiret, p. 55.
20. Pierre Millet, *Souvenirs de la campagne d'Égypte (1798–1801),* ed. Stanislas Millet (Paris: Emile-Paul, 1903), p. 48; Nivin Mustafa Hasan, *Rashid fi al-'Asr al-'Uthmani: Dirasah Tarikhiya wa Watha'iqiya* (Cairo: Dar al-Thaqafa al-'Ilmiya, 1999).
21. Charles François, *Journal du capitaine François, dit le dromadaire d' Egypte 1792–1830,* ed. Charles Grolleau, 2 vols. (Paris: Carrington, 1903–1904), 1:195–197.
22. Charles Antoine Morand, *Lettres sur l'expédition d'Égypte (De l'Italie à la prise du Caire)* (Paris: La Vouivre, 1998), pp. 43–44.
23. François, p. 196.
24. M. Vertray, *Journal d'un officier de l'armée d'Egypte,* ed. H. Galli (Paris: Charpentier, 1883), p. 36; for Desvernois's estimate of dead on this march, see Nicolas-Philibert Desvernois, *Mémoires du Général Baron Desvernois,* ed. Albert Dufourcq (Paris: Plon, 1898), p. 109.
25. Lt. Gen. Augustin-Daniel Belliard, *Mémoires du Comte Belliard,* ed. M. Vinet (Paris: Berquet et Pétion, 1842), pp. 107–108.
26. Gen. Jean-Pierre Doguereau, *Journal de l'expédition d'Egypte,* ed. C. de La Jonquière (Paris: Perrin et Cie., 1904), p. 58; an English translation is Jean-Pierre Doguereau, *Guns in the Desert: General Jean-Pierre Doguereau's Journal of Napoleon's Egyptian Expedition,* trans. Rosemary Brindle (Westport, Conn.: Praeger, 2002). It appeared after I had taken my notes on and written many passages using this work, so citations here are from the French and translations are my own.
27. Desvernois, pp. 109–111.
28. Morand, p. 53.
29. Cites for this paragraph are: D. J. Larrey, *Mémoires de chirurgie militaire, et campagnes,* vol. 1 (Paris: J. Smith, 1812), pp. 194–95; Louis Antoine Fauvelet de Bourrienne, *Mémoires de M. de Bourrienne,* 10 vols. (Paris: Ladvocat, 1829), 2:101–102; Édouard de Villiers du Terrage, *Journal et souvenirs de l'expédition de l'Égypte (1798–1801)* (Paris: Librairie Plon, 1799), p. 49.
30. J. Miot, *Mémoires pour servir à l'histoire des expéditions en Égypte et en Syrie* (Paris: Le Normant, 1814), pp. 37–38.
31. Larrey, 1:205; François, 1:198–199.

CHAPTER 3

1. Napoléon Bonaparte, *Correspondence de Napoléon Ier,* 34 vols. (Paris: H. Plon, J. Dumaine, 1858–1870), 4:232, no. 2793.

2. François Vigo-Roussillon, *Journal de campagne (1793–1837)* (Paris: Éditions France-Empire, 1981), p. 63.
3. Auguste Frédéric Louis Viesse de Marmont, *Mémoires du duc de Raguse de 1792 à 1832* (Paris: Parrotin, 1857), pp. 372–373.
4. François Bernoyer, *Avec Bonaparte en Égypte et en Syrie, 1798–1800: Dix-neuf lettres inédits*, ed. Christian Tortel (Abbeville: Les Presses Françaises, 1976), p. 53; Étienne-Louis Malus, *L'Agenda de Malus: Souvenirs de l'expédition d'Égypte, 1798–1801*, ed. Gen. Thoumas (Paris: Honoré Champion, 1892), p. 52.
5. Damas/Kléber, July 27 1798, in *Copies of Original Letters from the Army of General Bonaparte in Egypt, Intercepted by the Fleet Under the Command of Admiral Lord Nelson. Part the first.* With an English translation (London, 1798, 9th ed.), p. 77 (in Eighteenth Century Collections Online. Gale Group. <http://galenet.galegroup.com.proxy.lib.umich.edu/servlet/ECCO>).
6. Hugh Gough, "Genocide and the Bicentenary: The French Revolution and the Revenge of the Vendée," *Historical Journal* 30, no. 4 (Dec., 1987), pp. 977–988; Michael Scott Christofferson, "An Antitotalitarian History of the French Revolution: François Furet's 'Penser la Revolution française' in the Intellectual Politics of the Late 1970s," *French Historical Studies* 22, no. 4 (Autumn, 1999), pp. 557–611; D. M. G. Sutherland, *The French Revolution and Empire: A Quest for Civic Order* (Oxford: Blackwell, 2003), pp. 13–74. Howard Brown has argued that debates on French constitutional ideals should be separated out from assessments of the state's use of violence, which he argues had a Hobbesian character and was a response to insecurity, communal disturbances, and rebellions: See his *Ending the French Revolution* (Charlottesville: University of Virginia Press, 2006).
7. Vigo-Roussillon, p. 64.
8. Detroye in Clément de la Jonquière, *L'Expédition d'Égypte 1798–1801*, 5 vols. (Paris: H. Charles-Lavauzelle, 1899–1906), 2:159–160. The following account is based on 'Abd al-Rahman al-Jabarti, *Muzhir al-taqdis bi dhihab dawlat al-faransis* (Cairo: Matba'at al-Risalah, 1969), pp. 5–6; Louis Antoine Fauvelet de Bourrienne, *Memoirs of Napoleon Bonaparte*, ed. R.W. Phipps, 4 vols. (New York: Charles Scribner's Sons, 1892), pp. 155–157; Bernoyer, pp. 55–57; and sources cited below.
9. Sulkowski in la Jonquière, 2:156–158
10. Captain Deponthon in la Jonquière, 2:158–159.
11. Jean-Honoré Horace Say with Louis Laus de Boissy, *Bonaparte au Caire* (Paris: Prault, 7 R. [1799]), p. 73.
12. Vigo-Roussillon, p. 65; J. Miot, *Mémoires pour servir à l'histoire des expéditions en Égypte et en Syrie* (Paris: Le Normant, 1814), pp. 62–66.
13. Napoléon, *Corr.*, 4:236–237, no. 2803; Étienne-Louis Malus, *L'Agenda de Malus: Souvenirs de l'expédition d'Égypte, 1798–1801*, ed. Gen. Thoumas (Paris: Honoré Champion, 1892), p. 56.
14. Michael Winter, *Egyptian Society Under Ottoman Rule, 1517–1798* (London: Routledge, 1992).
15. Michel Tuchscherer, ed., *Le commerce du café avant l'ère des plantations coloniales* (Cairo: Institut Français d'Archéologie Orientale, 2001); Nelly Hanna, *Making Big Money in 1600: The Life and Times of Isma'il Abu Taqiyya, Egyptian Merchant* (Syracuse, N.Y.: Syracuse University Press, 1998); Ralph S. Hattox, *Coffee and Coffeehouses: The Origins of a Social Beverage in the Medieval Near East* (Seattle: University of Washington Press, 1985).
16. Jane Hathaway, "Ottoman Responses to Çerkes Mehmed Bey's Rebellion," in Jane Hathaway, ed., *Mutiny and Rebellion in the Ottoman Empire*, pp. 108–109; see also Daniel Crecelius, "The Mamluk Beylicate," in Thomas Philipp and Ulrich Haarman, eds., *The Mamluks in Egyptian Politics and Society* (Cambridge: Cambridge University Press, 1998), 138–147; Daniel Crecelius and Gotcha Djaparidze, "Relations of the Georgian Mamluks of Egypt with Their Homeland in the Last Decades of the Eighteenth Century," *Journal of the Economic and Social History of the Orient* 45, no. 3 (September 2002), pp. 320–341.
17. Vigo-Roussillon, p. 65.
18. Joseph-Marie Moiret, *Mémoires sur l'expédition d'Égypt* (Paris: Pierre Belfond, 1984), p. 42–43; Pierre de Pelleport, *Souvenirs militaires et intimes* (Paris: Didier & Co., 1857), p. 120; Louis Alexandre Berthier, *Mémoires de Maréchal Berthier . . . 1ʳ Partie: Campagne D'Égypte* (Paris: Baudouin Frères, 1827), pp. 16–17.

19. Pelleport, pp. 120–121; Moiret, pp. 43 and 43n.
20. Izzet Hasan Efendi Darendeli, *al-Hamlah al-Firansiyyah 'ala Misr fi Daw' Makhtut 'Uthmani*, trans. Jamal Sa'id 'Abd al-Ghani (Cairo: al-Hay'ah al-Misriyyah al-'Ammah li'l-Kitab, 1999), p. 148.
21. This and the subsequent quotations are from 'Abd al-Rahman al-Jabarti, *'Aja'ib al-athar fi al-tarajim wa al-akhbar,* 4 vols. (Bulaq: al-Matba'ah al-Amiriya, 1322/1904, 2nd ed.), 3:7, as translated by the team under Philipp and Perlmann.
22. Édouard de Villiers du Terrage, *Journal et souvenirs de l'expédition de l'Égypte (1798–1801)* (Paris: Librairie Plon, 1799), p. 50; Kléber/Dumuy, 17 July 1798; Kléber/Bonaparte, 21 July 1798; Kléber/Menou, 24 July 1798, in Henry Laurens, *Kléber en Égypte, 1798–1800,* 2 vols. (Cairo: Institut Français de l'Archéologie Orientale, 1988), 1:134–135, 1:145–152, 1:155; Henry Laurens et al., *L'Expédition d'Égypte: 1798–1801* (Paris: A. Colin, 1989), p. 99.
23. Bernoyer, p. 57.
24. Charles François, *Journal du capitaine François, dit le dromadaire d' Egypte 1792–1830,* ed. Charles Grolleau, 2 vols. (Paris: Carrington, 1903–1904), 1:202–203.
25. Moiret, p. 34; for another mention of naked village youngsters, see Bernoyer, p. 84.
26. Nada Tomiche, "The Situation of Egyptian Women in the First Half of the Nineteenth Century," in P. M. Holt, ed., *The Beginnings of Modernization in the Middle East* (Chicago: University of Chicago Press, 1968), pp. 171–184, esp. p. 175.
27. Kenneth M. Cuno, *The Pasha's Peasants: Land, Society and Economy in Lower Egypt, 1780–1858* (Cambridge: Cambridge University Press, 1992), chapter 3.
28. This and subsequent paragraph based on Moiret, pp. 45–46; for the burned village see Bernoyer, p. 58
29. François, 1:203–204.

CHAPTER 4

1. The following account of the Battle of the Pyramids·is drawn from M. Vertray, *Journal d'un officier de l'armée d'Egypte,* ed. H. Galli (Paris: Charpentier, 1883), pp. 56–59; Alfred de Besancenet, *Le Général Dommartin en Italie, et en Égypte* (Paris: Téqui, 1887), p. 410; Pierre de Pelleport, *Souvenirs militaires et intimes* (Paris: Didier & Co., 1857), pp. 121–124; Nicolas-Philibert Desvernois, *Mémoires du Général Baron Desvernois,* ed. Albert Dufourcq (Paris: Plon, 1898), pp. 121–128; Joseph-Marie Moiret, *Mémoires sur l'expédition d'Égypte,* (Paris: P. Belfond, 1984), pp. 46–51; Louis Alexandre Berthier, *Mémoires de Maréchal Berthier . . . 1ᵉʳ Partie: Campagne D'Égypte* (Paris: Baudouin Frères, 1827), pp. 17–22; David G. Chandler, *The Campaigns of Napoleon* (New York: Macmillan, 1966), pp. 219–227; John Dellinger, "Napoleonic Wars: Battle of the Pyramids," HistoryNet.com at <http://www.historynet.com/wars_conflicts/napoleonic_wars/3459076.html?page=1&c=y>; James W. Shosenberg, "The Battle of the Pyramids: Futile Victory," in Aryeh Shmuelevitz, ed., *Napoleon and the French in Egypt and the Holy Land, 1798–1801* (Istanbul: Isis Press, 2002), pp. 235–251; and 'Abd al-Rahman al-Jabarti, *Muzhir al-taqdis bi dhihab dawlat al-faransis* (Cairo: Matba'at al-Risalah, 1969), pp. 39–43.
2. Napoléon Bonaparte, *Correspondence de Napoléon Ier,* 34 vols. (Paris: H. Plon, J. Dumaine, 1858–1870), 4:251, no. 2834. Subsequent quotations from Bonaparte on the Battle of the Pyramids are from this source.
3. For the French forces, see Pierre Dominique Martin, *Histoire de l'expédition française en Égypte,* 2 vols. (Paris: J.-M. Eberhart, 1815), 1:203–204; some of these figures on the slave-soldier forces come from Besancenet, ibid.; others from Leila 'Abd al-Latif Ahmad as cited in Daniel Crecelius, *The Roots of Modern Egypt* (Minneapolis: Bibliotheca Islamica, 1981), p. 21.
4. John Keegan, *The Face of Battle* (New York: Viking Press, 1976); I am also grateful to my colleague John Shy for his observations on eighteenth-century warfare, though I want to be careful to say any mistakes are my own.
5. Etienne Geoffroy Saint-Hilaire, *Lettres d'Égypte, 1798–1801* (Paris: Paleo, 2000), p. 43.
6. 'Abd al-Rahman al-Jabarti, *'Aja'ib al-athar fi al-tarajim wa al-akhbar,* 4 vols. (Bulaq: al-Matba'ah al-Amiriya, 1322/ 1904, 2nd ed.), 3:10.

EAD

7. Jean-Honoré Horace Say with Louis Laus de Boissy, *Bonaparte au Caire* (Paris: Prault, 7 R. [1799]), p. 79.
8. Auguste Frédéric Louis Viesse de Marmont, *Mémoires du duc de Raguse de 1792 à 1832* (Paris: Parrotin, 1857), p. 385.
9. This and subsequent quotations from Laval, "Journal," in Gaston Wiet, ed., *Journaux sur l'-expédition d'Égypte* (Paris: Librairie Historique F. Teissedre, 2000), pp. 176–178; Étienne-Louis Malus, *L'Agenda de Malus: Souvenirs de l'expédition d'Égypte, 1798–1801*, ed. Gen. Thoumas (Paris: Honoré Champion, 1892), p. 66; Édouard de Villiers du Terrage, *Journal et souvenirs de l'expédition de l'Égypte (1798–1801)* (Paris: Librairie Plon, 1799), p. 71; Charles François, *Journal du Capitaine François (dit le Dromedaire d'Egypte), 1792–1830*, ed. Charles Grolleau, 2 vols. (Paris: Charles Carrington, 1903–1904), 1: 216; on mustaches see Saint-Hilaire, p. 50; on blindness see Say/de Boissy, p. 98.
10. Richard Bulliet, *The Camel and the Wheel* (Cambridge, Mass.: Harvard University Press, 1975); quotations from Lavalette are Comte de Lavalette, *Mémoires et souvenirs du Comte de Lavalette* (Paris: Mercure de France, 1994), pp. 188–189.
11. Say/de Boissy, pp. 136–38; Desvernois, p. 128.
12. Napoléon, *Corr.*, 4:240, no. 2817.
13. Say/de Boissy, p. 126; Malus, *L'Agenda*, pp. 64–65.
14. Al-Jabarti, *'Aja'ib*, 3:11.
15. Ibid., 3:11–13.
16. Say/de Boissy, p. 104.
17. François Bernoyer, *Avec Bonaparte en Égypte et en Syrie, 1798–1800: Dix-neuf lettres inédits*, ed. Christian Tortel (Abbeville: Les Presses françaises, 1976), p. 75.
18. Eugène de Beauharnais/Josephine, Giza, 6 Thermidor 6 (24 July 1798), in Frédéric Masson, "Les Préliminaires de la divorce impériale," *Revue de Paris* 6 (Nov.-Dec. 1900): 227–243; this quotation on p. 236.
19. Louis Antoine Fauvelet de Bourrienne, *Mémoires de M. de Bourrienne*, 10 vols. (Paris: Ladvocat, 1829), 2: 212.
20. Napoléon Bonaparte/Joseph Bonaparte, 7 Thermidor 6 (25 July 1798), no. 36, portfolio 13, *Lettres*, "Le site Tascher de La Pagerie," at <http://www.tascher-de-la-pagerie.org/>; this letter at <http://www.tascher-de-la-pagerie.org/fr/index.php?menu=lettres&ID=36>.
21. Louis Constant, *Mémoires de Constant, premier valet de chambre de l'empereur, sur la vie privée de Napoléon, sa famille et sa cour*, 6 vols. (Paris: Ladvocat, 1830), 1:36–38.
22. Bernoyer, p. 68.
23. Napoléon, *Corr.*, 4:260, no. 2846.
24. Afaf Lutfi al-Sayyid Marsot, *Women and Men in Late Eighteenth-Century Egypt* (Austin: University of Texas Press, 1995); Jane Hathaway, *The Politics of Households in Ottoman Egypt: The Rise of the Qazdaglis* (Cambridge: Cambridge University Press, 1997), chap. 6; Leslie Peirce, *The Imperial Harem: Women and Sovereignty in the Ottoman Empire* (New York: Oxford University Press, 1993). For the history of the women in the medieval Mamluk period see Ahmad Abd ar-Raziq, *La femme au temps des mamlouks en Égypte* (Cairo: Institut Français d'Archéologie Orientale, 1973).
25. This and subsequent points from Jean-Gabriel de Niello Sargy, *D'Égypte*, vol. 1 of M. Alph. de Beauchamp, ed., *Mémoires secrets et inédits pour servir à l'histoire contemporaine*, 2 vols. (Paris: Vernarel et Tenon, 1825), 1:72, 182, 194, 199; al-Jabarti, *'Aja'ib*, 3:19.
26. Napoléon, *Corr.*, 4:267, no. 2860.
27. Eugène de Beauharnais, *Mémoires et correspondance politique et militaire du prince Eugène*, ed. Albert du Casse (Paris: Michel Lévy frères, 1858), pp. 43–44. For Nefise see Agnieszka Dobrowolska, "Lady Nafisa and her sabil," *Al-Ahram Weekly Online*, no. 757 (25–31 August 2005) at <http://weekly.ahram.org.eg/2005/757/heritage.htm>.
28. Niello Sargy, 1:182. Niello Sargy quotations in later paragraphs are also from this source.
29. André Raymond, *Artisans et commerçants au Caire au XVIIIe siècle* (Cairo: Institut Français d'Archéologie Orientale, 1999); idem, *Arab Cities in the Ottoman Period* (London: Ashgate, 2002), chapter 15; Gabriel Baer, *Egyptian Guilds in Modern Times* (Jerusalem: Israel Oriental Society, 1964); Pascale Ghazaleh, *Masters of the Trade: Crafts and Craftspeople in Cairo, 1750–1850* (Cairo: American University in Cairo Press, 1999).

30. Napoléon, *Corr.*, 4:294, no. 2920.
31. André Raymond, *Le Caire des Janissaires: L'apogée de la ville ottomane sous 'Abd al-Rahman Katkhuda* (Paris: CRNS Editions, 1995), p. 68; for coffee in the eighteenth century, see Raymond, *Artisans et commerçants*; idem, "A Divided Sea: The Cairo Coffee Trade in the Red Sea Area During the Seventeenth and Eighteenth Centuries," in C. Bayly and L. Fawaz with R. Ilbert, eds., *Modernity and Culture from the Mediterranean to the Indian Ocean* (New York: Columbia University Press, 2002), pp. 46–57; "Kahwa," *Encyclopedia of Islam Online*, and the articles in Michel Tuchscherer, ed., *Le commerce du café avant l'ère des plantations coloniales* (Cairo: Institut Français d'Archéologie Orientale, 2001), by Idris Bostan, André Raymond, and Julien Berthaud.
32. Napoléon, *Corr.*, 4:307, nos. 2949 and 2950; Al-Jabarti, *'Aja'ib*, 3:13.
33. Anon., *Journal d'un dragon d'Égypte (14e Dragons)* (Paris: E. Dubois, 1899).
34. Napoléon, *Corr.*, 4:288–289, no. 2911.
35. Malus/Cafarelli, 17 Thermidor (4 August 1798), Malus/Cafarelli, 19 Thermidor (6 August 1798), in Clément de la Jonquière, *L'Expédition d'Égypte 1798–1801*, 5 vols. (Paris: H. Charles-Lavauzelle, 1899–1906), 2:349–350.
36. Desvernois, p. 129.

CHAPTER 5

1. This and subsequent references to Desvernois's account of the Sharqiya campaign are from his *Mémoires du Général Baron Desvernois*, ed. Albert Dufourcq (Paris: Plon, 1898), pp. 130–133. This and subsequent references to Captain Malus's contemporary reports come from Malus/Cafarelli, 17 Thermidor (4 August 1798), Malus/Cafarelli, 19 Thermidor (6 August 1798), in Clément de la Jonquière, *L'Expédition d'Égypte 1798–1801*, 5 vols. (Paris: H. Charles-Lavauzelle, 1899–1906), 2:349–350.
2. Cf. Kenneth M. Cuno, *The Pasha's Peasants: Land, Society and Economy in Lower Egypt, 1780–1858* (Cambridge: Cambridge University Press, 1992).
3. Napoléon Bonaparte, *Correspondence de Napoléon Ier*, 34 vols. (Paris: H. Plon, J. Dumaine, 1858–1870), no. 2834.
4. Napoléon, *Corr.*, 5:307, no. 3950; Jean-Gabriel de Niello Sargy, *D'Égypte*, vol. 1 of M. Alph. de Beauchamp, ed., *Mémoires secrets et inédits pour servir à l'histoire contemporaine*, 2 vols. (Paris: Vernarel et Tenon, 1825), 1:77–79, 87; Étienne-Louis Malus, *L'Agenda de Malus: Souvenirs de l'expédition d'Égypte, 1798–1801*, ed. Gen. Thoumas (Paris: Honoré Champion, 1892), p. 75. The spelling of the names of the tribes is nonstandard and often garbled among these sources.
5. Napoléon, *Corr.*, 4:319–320, no. 2975.
6. 'Abd al-Rahman al-Jabarti, *Muzhir al-taqdis bi dhihab dawlat al-faransis* (Cairo: Matba'at al-Risalah, 1969), pp. 51–53; idem, *Aja'ib al-athar fi al-tarajim wa al-akhbar*, 4 vols. (Bulaq: al-Matba'ah al-Amiriya, 1322/ 1904, 2nd ed.), 3:14–15.
7. Detroye in Clément de la Jonquière, *L'Expédition d'Égypte 1798–1801*, 5 vols. (Paris: H. Charles-Lavauzelle, 1899–1906), 2:371. Subsequent quotations from Detroye are from this same source.
8. The following account of the battle of Salahiyah is based on: Bonaparte, *Corr.*, 4:357–361, no. 3045; al-Jabarti, *'Aja'ib*, 3:14–15; Izzet Hasan Efendi Darendeli, *al-Hamlah al-Firansiyyah 'ala Misr fi Daw' Makhtut 'Uthmani*, trans. Jamal Sa'id 'Abd al-Ghani (Cairo: al-Hay'ah al-Misriyyah al-'Ammah li'l-Kitab, 1999), pp. 161–164; Desvernois, pp. 132–133; Lt. General Augustin-Daniel Belliard, *Mémoires du Comte Belliard*, ed. M. Vinet (Paris: Berquet et Pétion, 1842), pp. 11–115; Malus, *L'Agenda*, pp. 81–84; Detroye in la Jonquière, 2:375–376; Charles François, *Journal du capitaine François, dit le dromadaire d' Egypte 1792–1830*, ed. Charles Grolleau, 2 vols. (Paris: Carrington, 1903–1904), 1: 217–221; and, for the aftermath, Étienne Geoffroy Saint-Hilaire, *Lettres d'Égypte, 1798–1801* (Paris: Paleo, 2000), pp. 59–60.
9. Napoléon, *Corr.*, 4:334, no. 3005.
10. Belliard, p. 114.

11. Jane Hathaway, "The Military Household in Ottoman Egypt," *International Journal of Middle East Studies* 27, no. 1 (Feb. 1995), pp. 39–52.

12. The account here of Murad and Ibrahim's falling out in the 1780s and Ghazi Hasan Pasha's invasion is based on al-Jabarti, *'Aja'ib*, 2:79–124; M. Arribas Palau, "Sobre la expedición del capitán bajá Gazi Hasan a Egipto (1786–1787)," *Revista del Instituto Egipcio de Estudios Islámicos en Madrid* 22 (1984): 207–257; Daniel Crecelius, "Orders of Ghazi Hasan Pasha to the Egyptians," *al-Majallah al-Ta'rikhiyah al-'Arabiyah li al-Dirasat al-'Uthmaniyyah* nos. 17–18, (1998): 23–33; François Charles-Roux, *Les Origines de l'expédition d'Égypte* (Paris: Librairie Plon, 1910), chap. 6; and Daniel Crecelius and Gotcha Djaparidze, "Relations of the Georgian Mamluks of Egypt with Their Homeland," *Journal of the Economic and Social History of the Orient*, 45, no. 3 (2002), pp. 320–341.

13. André Raymond, *Égyptiens et Français au Caire, 1798–1801* (Cairo: Institut Français d'Archéologie Orientale, 1998), pp. 68–69.

14. Crecelius, "Orders of Ghazi Hasan Pasha," p. 28.

15. Hathaway, "Military Household," p. 47.

16. Napoléon, *Corr.*, 4:252, no. 2834.

17. Cuno, *The Pasha's Peasants*.

18. Napoléon, *Corr.*, 4:266, no. 2858; cf. Patrice Bret, *L'Égypte, au temps de l'expédition de Bonaparte: 1798–1801* (Paris: Hachette littératures, 1998), pp. 113–118.

19. Magdi Guirguis, "The Organization of the Coptic Community in the Ottoman Period," Nelly Hanna and Raouf Abbas, eds., *Society and Economy in Egypt and the Eastern Mediterranean 1600–1900: Essays in Honor of André Raymond* (Cairo and New York: American University in Cairo Press, 2005), pp. 201–216, this quotation on p. 209; see also Muhammad 'Afifi, *al-Aqbat fi Misr fi al-'Asr al-'Uthmani* (Cairo: al-Hay'ah al-Misriya al-'Amma li al-Kitab, 1992).

20. Napoléon, *Corr.*, 4:270, no. 2868.

21. Al-Jabarti, *Muzhir*, p. 57; idem, *Mudda al-faransis bi misr*, ed. Abd al-Rahim A. Abd al-Rahim (Cairo: Dar al-Kitab al-Jami'i, 2000), p. 83; idem, *Napoleon in Egypt: Al-Jabarti's Chronicle of the French Occupation, 1798*, trans. Shmuel Moreh (Princeton and New York: Markus Wiener Publishing, 1995), p. 54.

22. Napoléon, *Corr.*, 4:348, no. 3030.

23. Ibid., 4:382–383, no. 3080.

24. Ibid., 4:285, no. 2902.

25. Ibid., 4:378, no. 3074.

26. Al-Jabarti, *'Aja'ib*, 3:24.

27. Napoléon, *Corr.*, 4:286–287, no. 2907.

CHAPTER 6

1. Prosper Jollois, *Journal d'un ingénieur attaché a l'expédition d'Égypte, 1798–1802* (Paris: Ernest Leroux, 1904), pp. 51–53. Jollois quotations in ensuing paragraphs are from this same source.

2. *Copies of Original Letters from the Army of General Bonaparte in Egypt, Intercepted by the Fleet under the Command of Admiral Lord Nelson. Part the first.* With an English translation (London, 1798, 9th ed.), in Eighteenth Century Collections Online. Gale Group. <http://galenet.galegroup.com.proxy.lib.umich.edu/servlet/ECCO>.

3. This account is a paraphrase of Brian Lavery, *Nelson and the Nile: The Naval War Against Bonaparte 1798* (London: Chatham Publishing, 1998), with reference also to Michèle Battesti, *La Bataille d'Aboukir 1798: Nelson contrarie la stratégie de Bonaparte* (Paris: Economica, 1998).

4. Lavery, p. 221.

5. For this and subsequent quotations and points see Étienne-Louis Malus, *L'Agenda de Malus: Souvenirs de l'expédition d'Égypte, 1798–1801*, ed. Gen. Thoumas (Paris: Honoré Champion, 1892), pp. 88–89; Auguste Frédéric Louis Viesse de Marmont, *Mémoires du duc de Raguse de 1792 à 1832* (Paris: Parrotin, 1857), p. 392; Jollois, p. 54, Boyer/Bonaparte, 10 Thermidor 6

(27 July 1798), *Correspondance intime de l'armée d'Égypte, interceptée par la croisière anglaise* (Paris: R. Pincebourde, 1866), pp. 39–42.

6. Comte de Lavalette, *Mémoires et Souvenirs du Comte de Lavalette* (Paris: Mercure de France, 1994), p. 191.

7. Marmont in Émile Brouwet, ed., *Napoléon et son Temps: Catalogue de lettres autographes, de documents et de souvenirs napoléoniens faisant partie de la collection de M. Émile Brouwet; troisième partie* (London: Sotheby, 1936), p. 28; Louis Antoine Fauvelet de Bourrienne, *Memoirs of Napoleon Bonaparte*, ed. R.W. Phipps, 4 vols. (New York: Charles Scribner's Sons, 1892), p. 163.

8. Bourrienne, *Memoirs*, ed. Phipps, p. 165.

9. Nicolas-Philibert Devernois, *Mémoires du Général Baron Desvernois*, ed. Albert Dufourcq (Paris: Plon, 1898), p. 134.

10. André François Miot de Melito, *Mémoires du comte Miot de Melito, ancien ministre, ambassadeur, conseiller d'état et membre de l'Institut*, 3 vols. (Paris, Michel Lévy frères, 1858), p. 80.

11. LeRoy/Jacotin, 6 Prairial 8, in Jacotin, *Papiers*, BN 11275.

12. Auguste Napoléon Joseph Colbert-Chabanais, *Traditions et souvenirs; ou, Mémoires touchant le temps et la vie du général Auguste Colbert (1793–1809)*, 5 vols. (Paris: F. Didto frères, 1863–73), 2:89; this author saw the unpublished memoirs of Pierre-David Edouard Colbert-Chabanais, a young officer of aristocratic background who barely avoided being purged in 1796, had joined the Army of the Orient, and later was wounded in Upper Egypt. According to this book, he therein relayed the story from Bonaparte's old comrade-in-arms in Italy, Gen. Joachim Murat (an eyewitness).

13. 'Abd al-Rahman al-Jabarti, *'Aja'ib al-athar fi al-tarajim wa al-akhbar*, 4 vols. (Bulaq: al-Matba'ah al-Amiriya, 1322/1904, 2nd ed.), 3:15.

14. Étienne Geoffroy Saint-Hilaire, *Lettres d'Égypte, 1798–1801* (Paris: Paleo, 2000), p. 43.

15. The following account of the Festival of the Nile is based on al-Jabarti,'Abd al-Rahman al-Jabarti, *Muzhir al-taqdis bi dhihab dawlat al-faransis* (Cairo: Matba'at al-Risalah, 1969), pp. 53–54; idem, *'Aja'ib*, 3:14–15; Jean-Honoré Horace Say with Louis Laus de Boissy, *Bonaparte au Caire* (Paris: Prault, 7 R. [1799]), pp. 129–135; Desvernois, *Mémoires*, pp. 135–137; *Le Courrier de L'Égypte* in Clément de la Jonquière, *L'Expédition d'Égypte 1798–1801*, 5 vols. (Paris: H. Charles-Lavauzelle, 1899–1906), 2:480; and Henry Laurens et al., *L'Expédition d'Égypte: 1798–1801* (Paris: A. Colin, 1989), pp. 110–111. For the Nile as father of the Egyptians, see François Bernoyer, *Avec Bonaparte en Égypte et en Syrie, 1798–1800: Dix-neuf lettres inédits*, ed. Christian Tortel (Abbeville: Les Presses françaises, 1976), p. 127.

16. Kenneth Cuno, *The Pasha's Peasants* (Cambridge: Cambridge University Press, 1992), pp. 17–19.

17. Huda Lutfi, "Coptic Festivals of the Nile," in Thomas Philipp and Ulrich Haarman, eds., *The Mamluks in Egyptian Politics and Society* (Cambridge: Cambridge University Press, 1998), pp. 254–282; this quotation appears on p. 265.

18. Bernoyer, p. 72; cf. Edward William Lane, *An Account of the Manners and Customs of the Modern Egyptians*, 5th edn., ed. Edward Stanley Poole (London: John Murray, 1860), p. 454.

19. Ibid., p. 76; al-Jabarti, *'Aja'ib*, 2:106–107; for the nudity of dervishes see Victor Cousin, *Fragments Philosophiques*, vol. 2 (Paris: Ladrange, 1838, 2nd ed.), p. 391, citing a letter of the divan to Menou.

20. Pierre Millet, *Souvenirs de la campagne d'Égypte (1798–1801)*, ed. Stanislas Millet (Paris: Emile-Paul, 1903), pp. 54–55.

21. Charles François, *Journal du Capitaine François (dit le Dromadaire d'Egypte), 1792–1830*, ed. Charles Grolleau, 2 vols. (Paris Charles Carrington, 1903–1904), 1: 222–223.

22. Jean-Gabriel de Niello Sargy, *D'Égypte*, vol. 1 of M. Alph. de Beauchamp, ed., *Mémoires secrets et inédits pour servir à l'histoire contemporaine*, 2 vols. (Paris: Vernarel et Tenon, 1825), 1:142; the following pages depend on this source, pp. 142–175, and upon Édouard de Villiers du Terrage, *Journal et souvenirs de l'expédition de l'Égypte (1798–1801)* (Paris: Librairie Plon, 1799), p. 69.

23. Napoléon Bonaparte, *Correspondence de Napoléon Ier*, 34 vols. (Paris: H. Plon, J. Dumaine, 1858–1870), 4:352–53, no. 3040.

24. Kléber in Henry Laurens, *Kléber en Égypte, 1798–1800*, 2 vols. (Cairo: Institut Français de l'Archéologie Orientale, 1988), 1:209–211, 213.
25. Gen. Jean-Pierre Doguereau, *Journal de l'expédition d'Egypte*, ed. C. de La Jonquière (Paris: Perrin, 1904), pp. 83–84.
26. Auguste Frédéric Louis Viesse de Marmont, *Mémoires du duc de Raguse de 1792 à 1832* (Paris: Parrotin, 1857), pp. 371, 393–395, 398; see also the account of Menou in La Jonquière, 2:113–116; Villiers du Terrage, pp. 65–66; Jollois, p. 53. There is a discrepancy in the sources about when this event occurred, whether in mid-August, as Villiers du Terrage wrote in his journal, or in early September. The journal is more trustworthy than later memoirs with regard to the dating, and it is also possible that there were two such disastrous outings, which were later conflated in the minds of memoirists.
27. Report of Lt. Col. Théviotte in Paul Guitry, *L'Armée de Bonaparte en Égypte* (Paris: Ernest Flammarion, 1898), pp. 144–147; Pierre-François Gerbaud, *Le Capitaine Gerbaud, 1773–1799*, ed. Maxime Mangerel (Paris: Plon, 1910), pp. 237–239; Niqula al-Turk, *Dhikr Tamalluk Jumhur al-Firansawiyyah al-Aqtar al-Misriyyah wa al-Bilad al-Shamiyyah*, ed. Yasin Suwayd (Beirut: al-Farabi, 1990), pp. 51–52; Millet, p. 57; J. Christopher Herold, *Bonaparte in Egypt* (New York: Harper and Row, 1962), pp. 139–140; Cuno, p. 93.
28. Laurens, *L'expédition*, pp. 122–123.
29. A. Galland, *Tableau de l'Égypte pendant le séjour de l'armée française*, 2 vols. (Paris: Cerioux et Galland, R. 11 [1804]), 1:50–51.
30. Millet, 57.
31. Niello Sargy, 148.

CHAPTER 7

1. Napoléon Bonaparte, *Correspondence de Napoléon Ier*, 34 vols. (Paris: H. Plon, J. Dumaine, 1858–1870), 4:363, no. 3050.
2. Dominique Vivant Denon, *Voyage dans la Basse et la Haute Égypte* (Paris: Editions Gallimard, 1998 [first published 1802]), pp. 95–96.
3. The following account is based on al-Jabarti, *Mudda al-faransis bi misr*, ed. Abd al-Rahim A. Abd al-Rahim (Cairo: Dar al-Kitab al-Jami'i, 2000), pp. 77–78; idem, *Napoleon in Egypt: Al-Jabarti's Chronicle of the French Occupation, 1798*, trans. Shmuel Moreh (Princeton and New York: Markus Wiener Publishing, 1995), p. 51; Niqula al-Turk, *Dhikr Tamalluk Jumhur al-Firansawiyyah al-Aqtar al-Misriyyah wa al-Bilad al-Shamiyyah*, ed. Yasin Suwayd (Beirut, al-Farabi, 1990), p. 46; Nicolas-Philibert Desvernois, *Mémoires du Général Baron Desvernois*, ed. Albert Dufourcq (Paris: Plon, 1898), p. 137; Jean-Gabriel de Niello Sargy, *d'Égypte*, vol. 1 of M. Alph. de Beauchamp, ed., *Mémoires secrets et inédits pour servir à l'histoire contemporaine*, 2 vols. (Paris: Vernarel et Tenon, 1825), 1:176–177; Étienne-Louis Malus, *L'Agenda de Malus: Souvenirs de l'expédition d'Égypte, 1798–1801*, ed. Gen. Thoumas (Paris: Honoré Champion, 1892), pp. 89–90; Joseph-Marie Moiret, *Mémoires sur l'expédition d'Égypt* (Paris: Pierre Belfond, 1984), p. 58; Detroye in Clément de la Jonquière, *L'Expédition d'Égypte 1798–1801*, 5 vols. (Paris: H. Charles-Lavauzelle, 1899–1906), 2:481–82; Édouard de Villiers du Terrage, *Journal et souvenirs de l'expédition de l'Égypte (1798–1801)* (Paris: Librairie Plon, 1799), pp. 71–72. See also Georges Spillman, *Napoléon et l'Islam* (Paris: Librairie Académique, 1969); Henry Laurens, *Orientales I: Autour de l'expédition d'Égypte* (Paris: CNRS Editions, 2004), pp. 147–164; John W. Livingston, "Shaykh Bakri and Bonaparte," *Studia Islamica* 80 (1994), pp. 125–143; and Mary Kathryn Cooney, "Egypt Was Worth a Turban: Bonaparte's Flirtation with Islam," in Aryeh Shmuelevitz, ed., *Napoleon and the French in Egypt and the Holy Land, 1798–1801* (Istanbul: The Isis Press, 2002), pp. 87–100.
4. Denon, *Voyage*, p. 97.
5. Pierre Millet, *Souvenirs de la campagne d'Égypte (1798–1801)*, ed. Stanislas Millet (Paris: Emile-Paul, 1903), p. 63.
6. Jean-Honoré Horace Say with Louis Laus de Boissy, *Bonaparte au Caire* (Paris: Prault, 7 R. [1799]), p. 126.
7. Pierre de Pelleport, *Souvenirs militaires et intimes* (Paris: Didier & Co., 1857), p. 429.

8. Napoléon Bonaparte, *Campagnes d'Égypte et de Syrie*, ed. Henry Laurens (Paris: Imprimerie Nationale, 1998), pp. 142–147; Louis Antoine Fauvelet de Bourrienne, *Memoirs of Napoleon Bonaparte*, ed. R. W. Phipps, 4 vols. (New York: Charles Scribner's Sons, 1892), 1:170n.
9. Bonaparte/Kléber, 12 Thermidor 6 (30 July 1798), no. 2880, in Christian Cherfils, *Bonaparte et l'Islam d'après les documents français et arabes* (Paris: A. Pedone, 1914), pp. 19–20.
10. Napoléon, *Campagnes*, pp. 140–141; Mustapha al-Ahnaf, "Cheikh al-Mahdi (1737–1815): uléma, médiateur et businessman," *Monde arabe*, n. 1, 2ème série (1er semestre 1999), pp. 115–149. Quotations in ensuing paragraphs are from this same source.
11. Napoléon, *Corr.*, 4:420, no. 3148.
12. Napoléon, *Corr.*, 4:413, no. 3136; M. Abir, "The 'Arab Rebellion' of Amir Ghalib of Mecca (1788–1813)," *Middle Eastern Studies* 3 (1971), 185–200.
13. Desvernois, *Mémoires*, pp. 135–137; Étienne Geoffroy Saint-Hilaire, *Lettres d'Égypte, 1798–1801* (Paris: Paleo, 2000), p. 57.
14. La Jonquière, 2:8–9.
15. Gen. Dupuis/Deville, 19 August 1798, in Paul Guitry, *L'Armée de Bonaparte en Égypte* (Paris: Ernest Flammarion, 1898), p. 152.
16. Moiret, p. 79.
17. Moiret, p. 80; for condemnation of Muhammad over the prohibition on wine, see p. 100.
18. François Bernoyer, *Avec Bonaparte en Égypte et en Syrie, 1798–1800: Dix-neuf lettres inédits*, ed. Christian Tortel (Abbeville: Les Presses françaises, 1976), pp. 126–127.
19. Auguste Frédéric Louis Viesse de Marmont, *Mémoires du duc de Raguse de 1792 à 1832* (Paris: Parrotin, 1857), p. 422.
20. Moiret, pp. 104–113.
21. Ibid., p. 180.
22. This adventure is covered in Bernoyer, pp. 108–116.
23. The text has two hundred fathoms (*brasse*); a fathom is six feet.
24. 'Abd al-Rahman al-Jabarti, *'Aja'ib al-athar fi al-tarajim wa al-akhbar*, 4 vols. (Bulaq: al-Matba'ah al-Amiriya, 1322/1904, 2nd ed.), 3:162.
25. Charles de Secondat de Montesquieu, *L'Esprit des lois*, ed. Laurent Versini (Paris: Gallimard, 1995), p. 113; on the web at <http://www.ecole-alsacienne.org/CDI/pdf/1400/14055_MONT.pdf>
26. G.-H. Bousquet, "Voltaire et l'Islam," *Studia Islamica* 28 (1968): 109–126; this quotation p.110n.
27. Rebecca Joubin, "Islam and Arabs through the Eyes of the *Encyclopédie:* The 'Other' as a Case of French Cultural Self-Criticism," *International Journal of Middle East Studies* 32, no. 2 (May 2000): 197–217.
28. Napoléon, *Campagnes*, pp. 152–153.

CHAPTER 8

1. Kléber/Bonaparte, 28 August 1798, in Clément de la Jonquière, *L'Expédition d'Égypte 1798–1801*, 5 vols. (Paris: H. Charles-Lavauzelle, 1899–1906), 2:75–78.
2. Kléber, "Journal," in la Jonquière, 2:104; Henry Laurens et al., *L'Expédition d'Égypte: 1798–1801* (Paris: A. Colin, 1989), p. 107.
3. Dugua/Bonaparte, 18 Fructidor 6 (4 September 1798), in la Jonquière, 2:130–131.
4. Napoléon Bonaparte, *Correspondence de Napoléon Ier*, 34 vols. (Paris: H. Plon, J. Dumaine, 1858–1870), 4:471–72, no. 3252.
5. Verdier/Dugua, 15 September 1798; and Laugier, "Journal," in la Jonquière, 2:134–137, 136n.
6. Jean-Honoré Horace Say with Louis Laus de Boissy, *Bonaparte au Caire* (Paris: Prault, 7 R. [1799]), pp. 153–154.
7. Napoléon, *Corr.*, 4:390, no. 3091; Henry Laurens et al., *L'Expédition d'Égypte: 1798–1801* (Paris: A. Colin, 1989), pp. 111–112.
8. Sarah C. Maza, *Private Lives and Public Affairs: The Causes Célèbres of Prerevolutionary France* (Berkeley: University of California Press, 1993), pp. 60–62; Sarah Maza, "Luxury, Morality,

and Social Change: Why There Was No Middle-Class Consciousness in Prerevolutionary France," *Journal of Modern History* 69, no. 2. (June 1997), pp. 199–229, esp. 224–228; Susan Maslan, *Revolutionary Acts: Theater, Democracy, and the French Revolution* (Baltimore: Johns Hopkins University Press, 2005); Cyrole Triolaire, "Contrôle Social et arts du spectacle en province pendant le consulat et l'empire: L'exemple du Puy-de-Dôme," *Annales historiques de la Révolution française* 333 (2003), pp. 45–66, quotation on p. 47; Bonaparte/Tallien, 16 Vendémiaire 7 (7 October 1798), in Émile Brouwet, ed., *Napoléon et son Temps: Catalogue de lettres autographes, de documents et de souvenirs napoléoniens faisant partie de la collection de m. Émile Brouwet; troisième partie* (London: Sotheby, 1936), p. 3; François Bernoyer, *Avec Bonaparte en Égypte et en Syrie, 1798–1800: Dix-neuf lettres inédits*, ed. Christian Tortel (Abbeville: Les Presses françaises, 1976), p. 93; Etienne Geoffroy Saint-Hilaire, *Lettres d'Égypte, 1798–1801* (Paris: Paleo, 2000), p. 103.

9. Say/de Boissy, p. 161; see also Edmond et Jules de Goncourt, *La Femme au dix-huitième siècle* (Paris: G. Charpentier, 1877), pp. 74–75, at <http://freresgoncourt.free.fr/texfemmeau/8e/texte.htm>; Louis Laus de Boissy, *La Vraie Republicaine* (Paris: De l'Imprimerie de Cailleau, 1794); Eugène Jauffret, *Le Théâtre revolutionnaire (1788–1799)* (Paris: Furne, Jouvet et Cie., 1869), pp. 296–297.

10. Say/de Boissy, pp. 118–120; cf. for women's use of Arabic poetry in self-expression, Lila Abu-Lughod, *Veiled Sentiments: Honor and Poetry in a Bedouin Society* (Berkeley: University of California Press, 1986).

11. Robert Darnton, *The Forbidden Bestsellers of Prerevolutionary France* (New York: Norton, 1996); Lynn Hunt, ed., *The Invention of Pornography: Obscenity and the Origins of Pornography, 1500–1800* (New York: Zone Books, 1993); Christie McDonald, "Changing Stakes: Pornography, Privacy, and the Perils of Democracy," *Yale French Studies* 100 (2001), pp. 88–115.

12. Jean-Gabriel de Niello Sargy, *d'Égypte*, vol. 1 of M. Alph. de Beauchamp, ed., *Mémoires secrets et inédits pour servir à l'histoire contemporaine*, 2 vols. (Paris: Vernarel et Tenon, 1825), 1:335–338.

13. Prosper Jollois, *Journal d'un ingénieur attaché a l'expédition d'Égypte, 1798–1802* (Paris: Ernest Leroux, 1904), p. 49; Édouard de Villiers du Terrage, *Journal et souvenirs de l'expédition de l'Égypte (1798–1801)* (Paris: Librairie Plon, 1799), p. 58; Say/de Boissy, p. 147; Niqula al-Turk, *Dhikr Tamalluk Jumhur al-Firansawiyyah al-Aqtar al-Misriyyah wa al-Bilad al-Shamiyyah*, ed. Yasin Suwayd (Beirut, al-Farabi, 1990), p. 27; Henry Laurens et al., *L'Expédition d'Égypte: 1798–1801* (Paris: A. Colin, 1989), p. 114; for French debates on the cockade during the Directory, see Jennifer Heuer, "Hats On for the Nation! Women, Servants, Soldiers and the 'Sign of the French,'" *French History* 16, no. 1 (2002) pp. 28–52.

14. 'Abd al-Rahman al-Jabarti, *Muzhir al-taqdis bi dhihab dawlat al-faransis* (Cairo: Matba'at al-Risalah, 1969), pp. 59–60; 'Abd al-Rahman Al-Jabarti, *Ta'rikh Muddat al-faransis bi misr*, ed. Abd al-Rahim A. Abd al-Rahim (Cairo: Dar al-Kitab al-Jami'i, 2000), pp. 91–92; idem, *Napoleon in Egypt: Al-Jabarti's Chronicle of the French Occupation, 1798*, trans. Shmuel Moreh (Princeton and New York: Markus Wiener Publishing, 1995), pp. 59–60; idem.,*'Aja'ib al-athar fi al-tarajim wa al-akhbar*, 4 vols. (Bulaq: al-Matba'ah al-Amiriya, 1322/1904, 2nd ed.), 3:16–17.

15. Say/de Boissy, p. 148.

16. Wajda Sendesni, *Regard de l'historiographie Ottomane sur la révolution française et l'expédition d'Égypte: Tarih-i Cevdet* (Istanbul: Les Editions Isis, 2003), pp. 79–117, this point on p. 85. For Ottoman-French diplomatic relations in this period, see Ismail Soysal, *Fransiz ihtilali ve Türk-Fransiz Diplomasi Münasebetleri (1789–1802)* (Ankara: Türk Tarih Kurumu Basimevi, 1987), esp. chapters 14–15 for the period of this book. For the background, see Fatma Müge Göçek, *East Encounters West: France and the Ottoman Empire in the Eighteenth Century* (Oxford: Oxford University Press, 1987); Henry Laurens et al., *L'Expédition d'Égypte: 1798–1801* (Paris: A. Colin, 1989), p. 132–141.

17. Stanford J. Shaw, *Between Old and New: The Ottoman Empire Under Sultan Selim III, 1789–1807* (Cambridge, Mass.: Harvard University Press, 1971), p. 147; subsequent quotation on p. 148.

18. Alan Schom, *Napoleon Bonaparte* (New York: Harper Perennial, 1998), pp. 26–27; cf. Louis Antoine Fauvelet de Bourrienne, *Memoirs of Napoleon Bonaparte*, ed. R. W. Phipps, 4 vols. (New York: Charles Scribner's Sons, 1892), pp. 28 – 37.

19. Michel Poniatowski, *Talleyrand et le Directoire, 1796–1800* (Paris: Librairie Académique Perrin, 1982), pp. 432–434, 454–456.

20. Shaw, *Between Old and New*, pp. 255–257; Soysal, *Fransiz ihtilali*, pp. 208–254.

21. Correspondence of Ruffin cited in this and following paragraphs is Ruffin/Talleyrand, 14 Thermidor 6 (1 August 1798); and Ruffin/Talleyrand, 23 Thermidor 6 (10 August 1798), in La Jonquière, 2:600–609; see also Soysal, *Fransiz Ihtilali*, p. 241.

22. Bonaparte/Grand Vizir, 5 Fructidor 6 (22 August 1798), in Napoléon, *Corr.* 4:379, no. 3076.

23. Shaw, *Between Old and New*, pp. 263–265; Soysal, *Fransiz Ihtilali*, pp. 243–44; Izzet Hasan Efendi Darendeli, *al-Hamlah al-Firansiyyah 'ala Misr fi Daw' Makhtut 'Uthmani*, trans. Jamal Sa'id 'Abd al-Ghani (Cairo: al-Hay'ah al-Misriyyah al-'Ammah li'l-Kitab, 1999), pp. 182–183, 188–195.

24. Soysal, *Fransiz Ihtilali*, p. 244; La Jonquière, 2:233–235

25. Imperial Firman, ca. 1 September 1798, in Joseph Kabrda, *Quelques firmans concernant les relations Franco-Turques lors de l'expédition de Bonaparte en Égypte (1798–1799)* (Paris: Imprimerie Nationale, 1947), Ottoman text, p. 6; Kabrda's translation on pp. 74–78; Rudolph Peters, *Islam and Colonialism: The Doctrine of Jihad in Modern History* (The Hague; New York: Mouton, 1979).

26. Darendeli, *al-Hamlah*, pp. 177–182; Kevin McCranie, "The Operations and Effectiveness of the Ottoman Navy During Napoleon's Invasion of Egypt, 1798–1801," in Aryeh Shmulevitz, ed., *Napoleon and the French in Egypt and the Holy Land, 1798–1801* (Istanbul: Isis Press, 2002), pp. 155–164; this period, pp. 155–158.

27. Al-Jabarti, *'Aja'ib*, 3:18–21; Niello Sargy, 1:184.

28. "Firman du Grand Vizir," in Joseph-Marie Moiret, *Mémoires sur l'expédition d'Égypt* (Paris: Pierre Belfond, 1984), pp. 74–76.

29. Abdullah al-Sharqawi, *Tuhfat al-Nazirin fiman waliya Misr min al-Muluk wa al-Salatin*, ed. Rihab Abd al-Hamid al-Qari (Cairo: Madbuli, 1996), pp. 122–123.

30. For ulema culture and sciences in the eighteenth century, see Peter Gran, *The Islamic Roots of Capitalism: Egypt, 1760–1840* (Austin: University of Texas Press, 1979).

31. Nicolas-Philibert Desvernois, *Mémoires du Général Baron Desvernois*, ed. Albert Dufourcq (Paris: Plon, 1898), p. 142.

CHAPTER 9

1. Jean-Gabriel de Niello Sargy's detailed account of the fighting in the Manzala district is in *D'Égypte*, vol. 1 of M. Alph. de Beauchamp, ed., *Mémoires secrets et inédits pour servir à l'histoire contemporaine*, 2 vols. (Paris: Vernarel et Tenon, 1825), 1:148–174; see also Niqula al-Turk, *Dhikr Tamalluk Jumhur al-Firansawiyyah al-Aqtar al-Misriyyah wa al-Bilad al-Shamiyyah*, ed. Yasin Suwayd (Beirut: al-Farabi, 1990), 52–54; Pierre-François Gerbaud, *Le Capitaine Gerbaud, 1773–1799*, ed. Maxime Mangerel (Paris: Plon, 1910), pp. 250–252; Jean-Honoré Horace Say with Louis Laus de Boissy, *Bonaparte au Caire* (Paris: Prault, 7 R. [1799]), pp. 140–141; Joseph-Marie Moiret, *Mémoires sur l'expédition d'Égypt* (Paris: Pierre Belfond, 1984), pp. 73–74; Pierre Millet, *Souvenirs de la campagne d'Égypte (1798–1801)*, ed. Stanislas Millet (Paris: Emile-Paul, 1903), pp. 57–60; Clément de la Jonquière, *L'Expédition d'Égypte 1798–1801*, 5 vols. (Paris: H. Charles-Lavauzelle, 1899–1906), 2: 129–191; Henry Laurens et al., *L'Expédition d'Égypte: 1798–1801* (Paris: A. Colin, 1989), pp. 125–126.

2. Gerbaud, p. 246; Millet, p. 61.

3. Millet, pp. 57–59; Gerbaud, p. 250.

4. Napoléon Bonaparte, *Correspondence de Napoléon Ier*, 34 vols. (Paris: H. Plon, J. Dumaine, 1858–1870), 5:5–6, no. 3374.

5. Daniel Bates, "The Role of the State in Peasant-Nomad Mutualism," *Anthropological Quarterly* 44, no. 3 (July 1971): 109–131.

❖ NOTES ❖ 265

6. See Mona Ozouf, *La fête révolutionnaire, 1789–1799* (Paris: Gallimard, 1976); tr. Alan Sheridan, *Festivals and the French Revolution* (Cambridge, Mass.: Harvard University Press, 1988).

7. Lynn Hunt, *Politics, Culture and Class in the French Revolution* (Berkeley: University of California Press, 1984), pp. 19–20.

8. Sources for Festival of the Republic: La Jonquière, 2:22–29; Say/de Boissy, pp. 141–149; Nicolas-Philibert Desvernois, *Mémoires du Général Baron Desvernois*, ed. Albert Dufourcq (Paris: Plon, 1898), pp. 138–140; Moiret, pp. 64–65; Charles Norry, *An Account of the French Expedition to Egypt: Comprehending a View of the Country of Lower Egypt, Its Cities, Monuments, and Inhabitants, at the Time of the Arrival of the French; . . .* Translated from the French (London, 1800), pp. 26–27, Eighteenth Century Collections Online. Gale Group. <http://galenet.galegroup.com.proxy.lib.umich.edu/servlet/ECCO>, p. 19; François Bernoyer, *Avec Bonaparte en Égypte et en Syrie, 1798–1800: Dix-neuf lettres inédits*, ed. Christian Tortel (Abbeville: Les Presses françaises, 1976), pp. 79–80; Étienne-Louis Malus, *L'Agenda de Malus: Souvenirs de l'expédition d'Égypte, 1798–1801*, ed. Gen. Thoumas (Paris: Honoré Champion, 1892), pp. 92–93; Niello Sargy, 1:176–177; Prosper Jollois, *Journal d'un ingénieur attaché a l'expédition d'Égypte, 1798–1802* (Paris: Ernest Leroux, 1904), pp. 61–62; Pierre de Pelleport, *Souvenirs militaires et intimes* (Paris: Didier & Co., 1857), pp. 130–131; Édouard de Villiers du Terrage, *Journal et souvenirs de l'expédition de l'Égypte (1798–1801)* (Paris: Librairie Plon, 1799), p. 76; Henry Laurens et al., *L'Expédition d'Égypte: 1798–1801* (Paris: A. Colin, 1989), pp. 120–121, J. Christopher Herold, *Bonaparte in Egypt* (New York: Harper and Row, 1962), pp. 153–155; for commemorative pyramids in revolutionary France, see Arthur Maxime Chuquet, *L'École de Mars, 1794* (Paris: E. Plon, Nourrit, 1899), p. 195.

9. Joseph F. Byrnes, "Celebration of the Revolutionary Festivals Under the Directory: A Failure of Sacrality," *Church History* 63, no. 2 (June 1994): 201–220.

10. Bonaparte, *Corr.*, 5:1, no. 3365.

11. Say/de Boissy, p. 142.

12. Robespierre in Hunt, *Politics*, p. 46.

13. Say/de Boissy, p. 139.

14. Ibid., pp. 166–167.

15. Ibid., p. 107. I see this passage as an addition by Laus de Boissy because it displays knowledge of debates in France after the expedition landed in Egypt, something which Horace Say would have had difficulty knowing.

16. Lynn Hunt, *The Family Romance of the French Revolution* (Berkeley and Los Angeles: University of California Press, 1992).

17. Bernoyer, pp. 85–86.

18. Sarah C. Maza, *Private Lives and Public Affairs: The Causes Célèbres of Prerevolutionary France* (Berkeley: University of California Press, 1993), pp. 279–280.

19. Darcy Grimaldo Grigsby, "Rumor, Contagion, and Colonization in Gros's Plague-Stricken of Jaffa (1804)," *Representations* no. 51 (Summer, 1995), pp. 1–46.

20. Bernoyer, p. 86.

21. Hunt, *Politics*, p. 28.

22. Gen. Jean-Pierre Doguereau, *Journal de l'expédition d'Egypte*, ed. C. de la Jonquière (Paris: Perrin et Cie., 1904), pp. 69–70.

23. Ibid., pp. 70–77; see also, Louis Frank, "Mémoire sur le commerce des nègres au Kaire, et sur les maladies auxquelles ils son sujets en arrivant," trans. Michel Le Gall, in Shaun E. Marmon, ed., *Slavery in the Islamic Middle East* (Princeton, N.J.: Markus Wiener, 1999), pp. 69–88; and Patrice Bret, *L'Égypte au temps de l'expédition de Bonaparte, 1798–1801* (Paris: Hachette Littératures, 1998), pp. 132–138.

24. Etienne Geoffroy Saint-Hilaire, *Lettres d'Égypte, 1798–1801* (Paris: Paleo, 2000), p. 81; the remark below about the harem of Sheikh al-Fayyumi is on p. 117.

25. Admiral Perée/La Jolle, July 28, 1798 in *Copies of Original Letters from the Army of General Bonaparte in Egypt, Intercepted by the Fleet under the Command of Admiral Lord Nelson. Part the first. With an English translation.* (London, 1798, 9th ed.), p. 121. Eighteenth Century

Collections Online. Gale Group. <http://galenet.galegroup.com.proxy.lib.umich.edu/servlet/ECCO>.
26. Niello Sargy, 1:193–195.
27. This escapade is covered in Bernoyer, pp. 98–101.
28. For the Sudan-Egypt slave trade in this period see Terence Walz, *Trade Between Egypt and Bilad as-Sudan, 1700–1820* (Cairo: Institut Français d'Archéologie Orientale du Caire, 1978); for the medieval background, see Ahmad Abd ar-Raziq, *La femme au temps des mamlouks en Égypte* (Cairo: Institut Français d'Archéologie Orientale, 1973), pp. 49–57.
29. Bernoyer, p. 99.
30. Napoléon Bonaparte, *Campagnes d'Égypte et de Syrie*, ed. Henry Laurens (Paris: Imprimerie Nationale, 1998), p. 153.
31. Doguereau, pp. 70–77
32. Niello Sargy, 1:218–19.
33. Sue Peabody, *There Are No Slaves in France* (Oxford: Oxford University Press, 1996).
34. Claudine Hunting, "The Philosophes and Black Slavery: 1748–1765," *Journal of the History of Ideas* 39, no. 3 (Jul.-Sep., 1978), pp. 405–418; the quotations are on p. 411.
35. Yves Benot, *Les Lumières, l'esclavage, la colonisation* (Paris: Éditions de la Découverte, 2005), pp. 252–263; Jean-Daniel Piquet, "Robespierre et la liberté des noirs en l'an II," *Annales historiques de la Révolution français* 323 (2001): 69–91; Arthur L. Stinchcombe, *Sugar Island Slavery in the Age of Enlightenment: The Political Economy of the Caribbean World* (Princeton, N.J.: Princeton University Press, 1995); Laurent Dubois, *Avengers of the New World: The Story of the Haitian Revolution* (Cambridge, Mass.: Harvard University Press, 2004).

CHAPTER 10

1. Pierre-Louis Cailleux in Antoine Bonnefons et al., *Souvenirs et cahiers sur la campagne d'Egypte* (Paris: Librairie Historique F. Teissedre, 1997), p. 100.
2. Charles François, *Journal du Capitaine François (dit le Dromadaire d'Egypte), 1792–1830*, ed. Charles Grolleau, 2 vols. (Paris: Charles Carrington, 1903–1904), 1: 228–229.
3. Murat/Bonaparte, 10 Vendémiaire 7 (October 1, 1798), in Jean-François Massie, *François Lanusse, General de Division, 1772–1801* (Pau: Imprimerie graphique Marrimpouey successeurs, 1986), pp. 124–125.
4. Fugière/Bonaparte, 6 Oct. 1798 and 10 Oct. 1798, in Clément de la Jonquière, *L'Expédition d'Égypte 1798–1801*, 5 vols. (Paris: H. Charles-Lavauzelle, 1899–1906), 2:291–293; Napoléon Bonaparte, *Correspondence de Napoléon Ier*, 34 vols. (Paris: H. Plon, J. Dumaine, 1858–1870), 5:66–67, no. 3484.
5. Edward B. Reeves, "Power, Resistance and the Cult of Muslim Saints in a Northern Egyptian Town," *American Ethnologist* 22, no. 2 (1995): 306–323.
6. Abd al-Rahman al-Jabarti, *'Aja'ib al-athar fi al-tarajim wa al-akhbar*, 4 vols. (Bulaq: al-Matba'ah al-Amiriya, 1322/1904, 2nd ed.), 3:21.
7. Louis Thurman, *Bonaparte en Égypte: Souvenirs Publiés* (Paris: Émile Paul, 1902), pp. 52–53.
8. Niqula al-Turk, *Dhikr Tamalluk Jumhur al-Firansawiyyah al-Aqtar al-Misriyyah wa al-Bilad al-Shamiyyah*, ed. Yasin Suwayd (Beirut, al-Farabi, 1990), p. 59; cf. André Raymond, *Égyptiens et Français au Caire, 1798–1801* (Cairo: Institut Français d'Archéologie Orientale, 1998), pp. 110–113.
9. Napoléon Bonaparte, *Campagnes d'Égypte et de Syrie*, ed. Henry Laurens (Paris: Imprimerie Nationale, 1998), p. 151.
10. 'Abd al-Rahman al-Jabarti, *Muzhir al-taqdis bi dhihab dawlat al-faransis* (Cairo: Matba'at al-Risalah, 1969), pp. 57–59; idem, *Ta'rikh Muddat al-faransis bi misr*, ed. Abd al-Rahim A. Abd al-Rahim (Cairo: Dar al-Kitab al-Jami'i, 2000), pp. 83–89; idem, *Napoleon in Egypt: Al-Jabarti's Chronicle of the French Occupation, 1798*, trans. Shmuel Moreh (Princeton and New York: Markus Wiener Publishing, 1995), 54–59.
11. Napoléon, *Corr.*, 4:470–471, no. 3248; Turk, p. 59.

12. Jean-Gabriel de Niello Sargy, *d'Égypte*, vol. 1 of M. Alph. de Beauchamp, ed., *Mémoires secrets et inédits pour servir à l'histoire contemporaine*, 2 vols. (Paris: Vernarel et Tenon, 1825), 1:181–184.
13. Raymond, pp. 303–306.
14. Turk, p. 59; Victor Cousin, *Fragments Philosophiques*, vol. 2 (Paris: Ladrange, 1838, 2nd ed.), p. 447; Afaf Lutfi al-Sayyid Marsot, "Social and Political Changes After the French Occupation," in Irene Bierman, ed., *Napoleon in Egypt* (Reading, U.K.: Ithaca Press, 2003), p. 104.
15. Al-Jabarti, *'Aja'ib*, 3:162.
16. J. Miot, *Mémoires pour servir à l'histoire des expéditions en Égypte et en Syrie* (Paris: Le Normant, 1814), pp. 97, 239–240.
17. Niello Sargy, 1:392.
18. Eugéne de Beauharnais, *Mémoires et correspondance politique et militaire du prince Eugène*, ed. Albert du Casse (Paris: Michel Lévy frères, 1858), p. 44.
19. A. Galland, *Tableau de l'Égypte pendant le séjour de l'armée française*, 2 vols. (Paris: Cerioux et Galland, R. 11 [1804]), 1:171–172.
20. François Bernoyer, *Avec Bonaparte en Égypte et en Syrie, 1798–1800: dix-neuf lettres inédits*, ed. Christian Tortel (Abbeville: Les Presses françaises, 1976), pp. 94–98.
21. Miot, pp. 81, 99–100.
22. Gen. Jean-Pierre Doguereau, *Journal de l'expédition d'Egypte*, ed. C. de la Jonquière (Paris: Perrin et Cie., 1904), p. 101.
23. Niello Sargy, 1:193–195; cf. Patrice Bret, *L'Égypte, au temps de l'expédition de Bonaparte: 1798–1801* (Paris: Hachette littératures, 1998), pp. 132–138. For Niello on Pauline, see Niello Sargy, 1:199–206.
24. Bernoyer, pp. 93–95.
25. Ibid., pp. 116–125.
26. Napoléon, *Corr.*, 5:216, nos. 3774 and 3775.
27. Beauharnais, p. 46.
28. Al-Jabarti, *'Aja'ib*, 3:24–25; Stanford J. Shaw, *Between Old and New: The Ottoman Empire Under Sultan Selim III, 1789–1807* (Cambridge, Mass.: Harvard University Press, 1971), pp. 260–261; Henry Laurens et al., *L'Expédition d'Égypte: 1798–1801* (Paris: A. Colin, 1989), pp. 144–148.
29. Raymond, pp. 122–123.
30. Al-Jabarti, *'Aja'ib*, 3:25; Jean-Honoré Horace Say with Louis Laus de Boissy, *Bonaparte au Caire* (Paris: Prault, 7 R. [1799]), p. 162.
31. Al-Jabarti, *Tarikh Mudda*, p. 125; idem, *Napoléon in Egypt*, p. 83.
32. The following account of the Cairo revolt is based on: Étienne Geoffroy Saint-Hilaire, *Lettres d'Égypte, 1798–1801* (Paris: Paleo, 2000), pp. 69–73; François Vigo-Roussillon, *Journal de campagne (1793–1837)* (Paris: Éditions France-Empire, 1981), p. 76; Niello Sargy, 1:186–193; Nicolas-Philibert Desvernois, *Mémoires du Général Baron Desvernois*, ed. Albert Dufourcq (Paris: Plon, 1898), pp. 144–145; Anon., *Journal d'un dragon d'Égypte (14e Dragons)* (Paris: E. Dubois, 1899), p. 40; al-Jabarti, *'Aja'ib*, 3:24–27; al-Jabarti, *Mudda*, pp. 123–140; idem, *Napoléon in Egypt*, pp. 84–95; Turk, pp. 59 ff; and sources cited below. Recent accounts by contemporary historians include Henry Laurens et al., *L'Expédition d'Égypte: 1798–1801* (Paris: A. Colin, 1989), pp. 148–153 and Raymond, pp. 124–138.
33. Al-Jabarti, *'Aja'ib*, 3:24–25; al-Jabarti, *Mudda*, pp. 124–125; idem, *Napoléon in Egypt*, pp. 84–85; Turk, p. 59; Bernoyer, p. 88.
34. Say/de Boissy, p. 162; al-Jabarti, *Mudda*, pp. 124–125; idem, *Napoléon in Egypt*, p. 85.
35. Al-Jabarti, *'Aja'ib*, 3:25–30 (trans. Philipp and Perlmann); Say/de Boissy, p. 162.
36. Al-Jabarti, *Mudda*, p. 130; idem, *Napoléon in Egypt*, p. 86; Say/de Boissy, p. 163; Niello Sargy, 1:185; Édouard de Villiers du Terrage, *Journal et souvenirs de l'expédition de l'Égypte (1798–1801)* (Paris: Librairie Plon, 1799), p. 83.
37. Al-Jabarti, *'Aja'ib*, 3:25–26; al-Jabarti, *Mudda*, p. 131; idem, *Napoléon in Egypt*, p. 87; Say/de Boissy, p. 163; Niello Sargy, 1:185.

38. Napoléon Bonaparte, *Campagnes d'Égypte et de Syrie*, ed. Henry Laurens (Paris: Imprimerie Nationale, 1998), p. 162; Niello Sargy, 1:185; al-Jabarti, *Mudda*, p. 126; idem, *Napoléon in Egypt*, p. 84.
39. Al-Jabarti, *Aja'ib*, 3:25–26; Niello Sargy, 1:185; Desvernois, pp. 144–145.

CHAPTER 11

1. Jean-François Detroye in Clément de la Jonquière, *L'Expédition d'Égypte 1798–1801*, 5 vols. (Paris: H. Charles-Lavauzelle, 1899–1906), 2: 279.
2. Jean-Pierre Doguereau, *Journal de l'expédition d'Egypte*, ed. C. de la Jonquière (Paris: Perrin et Cie., 1904), pp. 90–91; François Bernoyer, *Avec Bonaparte en Égypte et en Syrie, 1798–1800: dix-neuf lettres inédits*, ed. Christian Tortel (Abbeville: Les Presses françaises, 1976), pp. 88–89.
3. Bernoyer, p. 88; Charles Norry, *An account of the French expedition to Egypt: comprehending a view of the country of Lower Egypt, its cities, monuments, and inhabitants, at the time of the arrival of the French;* ... Translated from the French (London, 1800), Eighteenth Century Collections On-line. Gale Group. <http://galenet.galegroup.com.proxy.lib.umich.edu/servlet/ECCO>, pp. 22–23.
4. Jean-Gabriel de Niello Sargy, *D'Égypte*, vol. 1 of M. Alph. de Beauchamp, ed., *Mémoires secrets et inédits pour servir à l'histoire contemporaine*, 2 vols. (Paris: Vernarel et Tenon, 1825), 1:187.
5. 'Abd al-Rahman Al-Jabarti, *Ta'rikh Muddat al-faransis bi misr*, ed. Abd al-Rahim A. Abd al-Rahim (Cairo: Dar al-Kitab al-Jami'i, 2000), pp. 131–132; idem, *Napoleon in Egypt: Al-Jabarti's Chronicle of the French Occupation, 1798*, trans. Shmuel Moreh (Princeton and New York: Markus Wiener Publishing, 1995), p. 87
6. Napoléon Bonaparte, *Campagnes d'Égypte et de Syrie*, ed. Henry Laurens (Paris: Imprimerie Nationale, 1998), p. 163.
7. Bonaparte, *Campagnes*, p. 163; Niello Sargy, 1:186.
8. Bonaparte, *Campagnes*, p. 163–64; Doguereau, pp. 90–91; Étienne-Louis Malus, *L'Agenda de Malus: Souvenirs de l'expédition d'Égypte, 1798–1801*, ed. Gen. Thoumas (Paris: Honoré Champion, 1892), p. 95.
9. Pierre de Pelleport, *Souvenirs militaires et intimes* (Paris: Didier & Co., 1857), p. 131; Bonaparte, *Campagnes*, p. 163.
10. Louis Antoine Fauvelet de Bourrienne, *Mémoires de M. de Bourrienne*, 10 vols. (Paris: Ladvocat, 1829), 2:182.
11. Doguereau, pp. 92–93; Louis Antoine Fauvelet de Bourrienne, *Memoirs of Napoleon Bonaparte*, ed. R.W. Phipps, 4 vols. (New York: Charles Scribner's Sons, 1892), p. 176; Nicolas-Philibert Devernois, *Mémoires du Général Baron Desvernois*, ed. Albert Dufourcq (Paris: Plon, 1898), p. 145.
12. Al-Jabarti, *Mudda*, pp. 133–134; idem, *Napoleon in Egypt*, p. 89; Doguereau, p. 93; Bernoyer, p. 89.
13. Al-Jabarti, *Mudda*, pp. 134–135; idem, *Napoleon in Egypt*, p. 90.
14. Bernoyer, pp. 89–90.
15. Pelleport, pp. 131–132.
16. Ibid., p. 132.
17. François Vigo-Roussillon, *Journal de campagne (1793–1837)* (Paris: Éditions France-Empire, 1981), p. 76.
18. Bernoyer, pp. 90–92. The following paragraphs are also largely based on this source.
19. Grandjean, "Journal," in Gaston Wiet, ed., *Journaux sur l'expédition d'Égypte* (Paris: Librairie Historique F. Teissedre, 2000), pp. 98–100; Detroye in La Jonquière, 2:282; Étienne Geoffroy Saint-Hilaire, *Lettres d'Égypte, 1798–1801* (Paris: Paleo, 2000), p. 75.
20. Laval, "Journal," in Wiet, ed., *Journaux*, pp. 181–182.
21. Napoléon Bonaparte, *Correspondence de Napoléon Ier*, 34 vols. (Paris: H. Plon, J. Dumaine, 1858–1870), 5:89–90, no. 3527.
22. Detroye in la Jonquière, 2:283.

23. Alex. Lacorre, "Journal d'un commis aux vivres," in Paul Guitry, *L'Armée de Bonaparte en Égypte* (Paris: Ernest Flammarion, 1898), p. 168.
24. 'Abd al-Rahman al-Jabarti, *'Aja'ib al-athar fi al-tarajim wa al-akhbar*, 4 vols. (Bulaq: al-Matba'ah al-Amiriya, 1322/1904, 2nd ed.), 3:27–33.
25. Napoléon, *Corr.*, 5:112, no. 3571.
26. Laval, "Journal," in Wiet, ed., *Journaux*, pp. 181–182.
27. Bernoyer, p. 92.
28. Bonaparte in Joseph-Marie Moiret, *Mémoires sur l'expédition d'Égypte*, (Paris: P. Belfond, 1984), p. 79.
29. Andrew Martin, "The Mask of the Prophet: Napoleon, Borges, Verne," *Comparative Literature* 40, no. 4 (Autumn, 1988), pp. 318–334.
30. Saint-Hilaire, p. 42.
31. Al-Jabarti, *Mudda*, pp. 168–169; idem, *Napoléon in Egypt*, pp. 113–114.
32. Moiret, p. 80. Quote below, p. 76.
33. Napoléon, *Corr.*, 5:98, no. 3542, and la Jonquière, 2:290; for the Copts see Napoléon, *Corr.*, 5:184–185, no. 3717.
34. André Raymond, *Égyptiens et Français au Caire, 1798–1801* (Cairo: Institut Français d'Archéologie Orientale, 1998), pp. 63–64.
35. Jean-Honoré Horace Say with Louis Laus de Boissy, *Bonaparte au Caire* (Paris: Prault, 7 R. [1799]), p. 99n. I believe I am the first historian to identify correctly the author of this passage, which some have attributed to Lucien Bonaparte (it was signed "L.B.," for Laus de Boissy).
36. Henry Laurens, *Orientales I: Autour de l'expédition d'Égypte* (Paris: CNRS Editions, 2004), pp. 121–142.
37. Napoléon, *Corr.*, 5:128; no. 3605.

CHAPTER 12

1. Charles François, *Journal du Capitaine François (dit le Dromadaire d'Egypte), 1792–1830*, ed. Charles Grolleau, 2 vols. (Paris: Charles Carrington, 1903–1904), 1: 232–144; Louis Antoine Fauvelet de Bourrienne, *Mémoires de M. de Bourrienne*, 10 vols. (Paris: Ladvocat, 1829), 2:185; idem, *Memoirs of Napoleon Bonaparte*, ed. R. W. Phipps, 4 vols. (New York: Charles Scribner's Sons, 1892), 1:177.
2. Comte de Lavalette, *Mémoires et Souvenirs du Comte de Lavalette*, (Paris: Mercure de France, 1994), pp. 193–194.
3. Napoléon Bonaparte, *Campagnes d'Égypte et de Syrie*, ed. Henry Laurens (Paris: Imprimerie Nationale, 1998), 5:97, no. 3540.
4. Napoléon Bonaparte, *Correspondence de Napoléon Ier*, 34 vols. (Paris: H. Plon, J. Dumaine, 1858–1870), 5:107, no. 3565; Pierre-François Gerbaud, *Le Capitaine Gerbaud, 1773–1799*, ed. Maxime Mangerel (Paris: Plon, 1910), pp. 264–265.
5. Lavalette, pp. 193–194.
6. Napoléon, *Corr.*, 5:133, no. 3616; Gerbaud, pp. 259, 267.
7. Prosper Jollois, *Journal d'un ingénieur attaché a l'expédition d'Égypte, 1798–1802* (Paris: Ernest Leroux, 1904), p. 77; Gerbaud, 259.
8. Anon., *Journal d'un dragon d'Égypte (14e Dragons)* (Paris: E. Dubois, 1899), p. 49; for Captain Umar, see Napoléon, *Corr.*, 5:97, no. 3541.
9. Gerbaud, p. 273.
10. Laugier in Clément de la Jonquière, *L'Expédition d'Égypte 1798–1801*, 5 vols. (Paris: H. Charles-Lavauzelle, 1899–1906), 2:461–2. The French text gives "Tabiluhah," but this is likely a mistake from misreading the Arabic (one dot, not two). Nabiluhah is a village in Buhayrah west of Mansura.
11. Jollois, p. 75.
12. Joseph-Marie Moiret, *Mémoires sur l'expédition d'Égypt* (Paris: Pierre Belfond, 1984), pp. 72–73.
13. Jean-Gabriel de Niello Sargy, *D'Égypte*, vol. 1 of M. Alph. de Beauchamp, ed., *Mémoires secrets et inédits pour servir à l'histoire contemporaine*, 2 vols. (Paris: Vernarel et Tenon, 1825), 1:172–174.

14. Pierre Millet, *Souvenirs de la campagne d'Égypte (1798–1801)*, ed. Stanislas Millet (Paris: Emile-Paul, 1903), p. 66; La Jonquière, 2:457.

15. Letters from Sultan Selim III to the Muslims and to Cezzar Pasha in Haydar Ahmad Shihab, *Ta'rikh Ahmad Jazzar Basha* (Beirut: Librairie Antoine, 1955), pp. 123–130.

16. Eugène de Beauharnais, *Mémoires et correspondance politique et militaire du prince Eugène*, ed. Albert du Casse (Paris: Michel Lévy frères, 1858), pp. 47–48; François, p. 245; La Jonquière, 2:443–502; al-Jabarti's description below from 'Abd al-Rahman al-Jabarti, *Muzhir al-taqdis bi dhihab dawlat al-faransis* (Cairo: Matba'at al-Risalah, 1969), p. 100.

17. Bonaparte/Daure, 3 Nivose R. 7 (23 December 1798), in Émile Brouwet, ed., *Napoléon et son Temps: Catalogue de lettres autographes, de documents et de souvenirs napoléoniens faisant partie de la collection de M. Émile Brouwet; troisième partie* (London: Sotheby, 1936), p. 7; Bonaparte/Caffarelli, 22 Dec. 1798, in la Jonquière, 2:476.

18. Abd al-Rahman al-Jabarti, *'Aja'ib al-athar fi al-tarajim wa al-akhbar*, 4 vols. (Bulaq: al-Matba'ah al-Amiriya, 1322/1904, 2nd ed.), 3:36–37.

19. General Jean-Pierre Doguereau, *Journal de l'expédition d'Egypte*, ed. C. de La Jonquière (Paris: Perrin et Cie., 1904), pp. 103–113; Bourrienne, *Mémoires*, 2:190–197; idem, *Memoirs*, 1:181–182.

20. M. Abir, "The 'Arab Rebellion' of Amir Ghalib of Mecca (1788–1813)," *Middle Eastern Studies*, 3 (1971), pp. 192–193; Lutf Allah Jahhaf, *Nusus Yamaniya 'an al-hamla al-Faransiya 'ala Misr*, ed. Sayyid Mustafa Salim (Cairo: Markaz al-Dirasat al-Yamaniyah, 1975), pp. 128–129.

21. Lt. Gen. Augustin-Daniel Belliard, *Mémoires du Comte Belliard*, ed. M. Vinet (Paris: Berquet et Pétion, 1842), p. 176.

22. Doguereau, pp. 132–133.

23. Lavalette, p. 194. Subsequent points also from this source.

24. Nicolas-Philibert Desvernois, *Mémoires du Général Baron Desvernois*, ed. Albert Dufourcq (Paris: Plon, 1898), pp. 146–148.

25. Bourrienne, *Mémoires*, 2:188–189; idem, *Memoirs*, 1:179.

26. Joseph Beauchamp's account of his astronomical and geographical researches in Iraq and Iran are in Bibliothèque Nationale (BN), Ms. 10157; for Bonaparte's description of his mission, see *Corr.* 5:199, 201, nos. 3742 and 3746; Henry Laurens et al., *L'Expédition d'Égypte: 1798–1801* (Paris: A. Colin, 1989), pp. 160–170.

27. Jean Michel de Venture de Paradis, "Mémoire sur la nécessité d'encourager en France l'étude des langues Orientales," *Papiers*, Bibliothèque Nationale, Département des Manuscrits, 9137, foll. 2b–8b.

28. Lavalette, pp. 195–198.

29. A. Galland, *Tableau de l'Égypte pendant le séjour de l'armée française*, 2 vols. (Paris: Cerioux et Galland, R. 11 [1804]), 1:171.

30. Louis Thurman, *Bonaparte en Égypte: Souvenirs Publiés* (Paris: Émile Paul, 1902), p. 76.

31. Millet, pp. 61–62.

32. Kléber in Henry Laurens, *Kléber en Égypte, 1798–1800*, 2 vols. (Cairo: Institut Français de l'Archéologie Orientale, 1988), p. 366.

33. Édouard de Villiers du Terrage, *Journal et souvenirs de l'expédition de l'Égypte (1798–1801)* (Paris: Librairie Plon, 1799), p. 93; Napoléon, *Corr.*, 5:239, no. 3818.

34. Paul Triaire, *Dominique Larrey et les Campagnes de la Révolution et de l'Empire* (Tours: Maison Alfred Mame et Fils, 1902), p. 210.

35. Bonaparte/Dugua, 14 Nivose R. 7 (2 February 1799), in Brouwet, ed., *Napoléon et son Temps*, p. 11.

36. Jahhaf; Henry Laurens et al., *L'Expédition d'Égypte: 1798–1801* (Paris: A. Colin, 1989), p. 160.

37. Al-Jabarti, *'Aja'ib*, 3:44.

38. John Voll, "Muhammad Hayya al-Sindi and Muhammad ibn 'Abd al-Wahhab: An Analysis of an Intellectual Group in Eighteenth-Century Madina," *Bulletin of the School of Oriental and African Studies* 38, no. 1 (1975), pp. 32–39.

39. Philippe Bourdin, "Le sultan dévoilé," in *Annales historiques de la Révolution française* 324, [En ligne], mis en ligne le 22 mai 2006. <http://ahrf.revues.org/document365.html>. Consulté le 15 novembre 2006; Jean-Joël Brégeon, *L'Égypte française au jour le jour, 1798–1801* (Paris: Perrin, 1991), pp. 132–143; J. Christopher Herold, *Bonaparte in Egypt* (New York: Harper and Row, 1962), chapter 8.

40. Belliard in la Jonquière, 2:518; cf. Donzelot/Berthier, 18 January 1799, in ibid., 2:525; Desvernois, p. 157.

41. Desaix/Bonaparte, 9 Pluviose R. 7 (28 January 1799), in la Jonquière, 2:531–532; Desvernois, pp. 160–163.

EPILOGUE

1. Philippe de Meulenaere, *Bibliographie raisonnée des témoignages oculaires imprimés de l'expédition d'Egypte (1798–1801)* (Paris: F. et R. Chamonal, 1993).

2. François Charles-Roux, *Bonaparte, gouverneur d'Égypte* (Paris: Plon, 1936); idem, *Bonaparte: Governor of Egypt*, translated from the French by E. W. Dickes (London, Methuen & Co., Ltd., 1937).

3. James L. Gelvin, "Napoleon in Egypt as History and Polemic," in Irene Bierman, ed., *Napoleon in Egypt* (Reading, UK: Ithaca Press, 2003), pp. 139–160.

4. Edward W. Said, *Culture and Imperialism* (New York: Knopf, 1993).

5. François Furet, *Revolutionary France, 1770–1880*, trans. Antonia Nevill (London: Blackwell, 1995), p. 199.

6. Peter Gran, *Islamic Roots of Capitalism: Egypt, 1760–1840* (Austin: University of Texas Press, 1979).

7. Edward W. Said, *Orientalism* (New York: Vintage Books, 1978).

8. Thomas Koszinowski, "Die Kontorverse um die Feiern zum Ägypten-Feldzug Napoleons," *Nahost-Jahrbuch* (1998), pp. 191–196; Elliott Colla, "'Non, non! Si, si!': Commemorating the French Occupation of Egypt (1798–1801)," *MLN*, 118.4 (2003) 1043–1069.

9. Said, *Orientalism*, p. 86.

10. Homi K. Bhabha, *The Location of Culture* (London: Routledge, 2004).

INDEX

CPSIA information can be obtained at www.ICGtesting.com
Printed in the USA
BVOW070907240112

281218BV00002B/5/P